F

International Library of Psychology
Philosophy and Scientific Method

Plato's Theory of Art

International Library of Psychology Philosophy and Scientific Method

GENERAL EDITOR—C. K. OGDEN, M.A. (*Magdalene College, Cambridge*)

* *Asterisks denote that other books by the same author are included in the series.*

PLATO'S
THEORY OF ART

by

RUPERT C. LODGE

M.A. (OXON), F.R.S. (CANADA)

ROUTLEDGE & KEGAN PAUL LTD
Broadway House, 68–74 Carter Lane
London

First published in 1953
by Routledge & Kegan Paul Ltd
Broadway House, 68–74 Carter Lane
London E.C.4
Printed in Great Britain
by J. W. Arrowsmith Ltd
Bristol

Contents

v

Acknowledgements

I T will be obvious, that my chief obligation is to Plato himself, as edited by John Burnet; and it is probable that a phrase here and there is due to the influence of Jowett's *Translation of the Dialogues*—although I have not deliberately quoted directly from Jowett. For my use, however, of both these sources, I owe a debt of gratitude to the Clarendon Press, Oxford.

I also owe a good deal to all well-known commentators and writers on Plato, both past and present, especially those to whom my notes refer. And I desire to make further acknowledgement to the following: To Messrs. Chapman and Hall, of London, for permission to quote from F. C. Tilney, *The Lure of the Fine Arts* (1931); to the Clarendon Press, Oxford, for permission to quote from R. G. Collingwood, *The Principles of Art* (1938); to the Harvard University Press, for permission to quote from J. Wild, *Plato's Theory of Man* (1946); to Macmillan and Company, of London and New York, for permission to quote from (1) B. Croce (tr. Ainslee), *Aesthetic as Science of Expression* . . . (1922), (2) Grove's *Dictionary oj Music and Musicians* (ed. Colles, 1948), and (3) R. L. Nettleship, *Lectures on the Republic of Plato* (ed. Benson, 1901); to Minton, Balch and Company (*via* G. P. Putnam's Sons), of New York, for permission to quote from J. Dewey, *Art as Experience* (1934); to *Philosophical Library, Inc.*, of New York, for permission to quote from M. Schoen, *The Enjoyment of the Fine Arts* (1944); to Messrs. Routledge and Kegan Paul, of London, for permission to quote from R. C. Lodge, *Plato's Theory of Education* (1947); and to the University of Chicago Press, for permission to quote from J. Dewey, *School and Society* (1916).

I desire also to express a debt of gratitude to the Art Galleries, Museums, and Libraries which have made available to me many of

vii

viii   *Acknowledgements*

the great paintings (or reproductions), and to the Publishers and Libraries which have made available for my use the scores or other reproductions of the great musical compositions of the world.

Mamaroneck, N.Y.   RUPERT C. LODGE

Introduction

READERS of *The Dialogues of Plato* fall, I think, into three groups: groups which differ considerably in background and outlook. The *first group* consists of what we may call 'general readers'. These read Plato much as they would read Shakespeare: from an interest in great literature, in culture, in human achievement. Plato is one of the great minds of all time. Such readers understand that his *Republic* is one of the great books of world-literature. It is the most famous of all Utopias. It is widely read and studied; and the ideas it expresses, however quaint and fantastic some of them may seem at a first reading, have been, and still are, influential in relation to present-day behaviour and thought. There is even a certain magic, an uncanny persuasiveness, about many of the Dialogues in which 'Socrates' is the chief speaker. They do more than awaken curiosity and wonder. They make the reader 'think', and they suggest somehow that thinking to some purpose is still a hopeful enterprise.

In the first group I would place also many of the students who read Plato for the first time in connexion with college assignments. Their interest is primarily in securing for themselves a 'general education'. But, by attending lectures and class discussions, and by preparing themselves for examination, they acquire a good deal of information, and a certain degree of insight: as they shine (at first) by the reflected light of their professors' wisdom.

Members of this first group realize that Plato (like Shakespeare) is a 'dramatic' writer. He has, they feel at once, no 'system', no cut-and-dried doctrinal propaganda. He is a sort of dramatic reporter of the currents of thought which were in the air in his time: currents not very different, many of them, from the ideas floating about in our own time. At least we recognize, as we read, the well-known gospel of pleasure, wealth, and power or success. We recognize in Plato a tendency to spring to the refutation of 'sophistry', wherever found: a tendency which amounts (we fancy) almost to a prejudice.

We also recognize, perhaps a little more hesitantly, tendencies which we should call 'idealistic', a little unpractical: such as Socrates's attitude toward his own country, right or wrong, perhaps especially when wrong. Again, there is his expressed intention of in some sense founding a more ideal community of Utopian enthusiasts. There is an exaggerated faith in conceptual logic-chopping, or in 'dialectic', as opposed to trust in ordinary, sensuously verified experience. In some of the Dialogues there are constructive, speculative attitudes toward biological and physical science, toward psychology and epistemology; and in nearly all of them there is an almost over-powering interest in philosophy itself, the 'love of wisdom'. On the other hand, there is a rather baffling claim of 'ignorance' in the face of speculative theories, a claim to be interested not so much in artistic or executive brilliance, as in a rather simple, almost banal thing called 'truth'. If we look closely at what we are reading, we even begin to wonder whether there is not, after all, an underlying faith in 'realism', in some sort of factuality.

There is in all this a great deal of stimulation for the general reader. He easily realizes that dramatic presentations (as with Bernard Shaw) may have systematic implications; and he can see that it might be possible, in following through the implications of this or that current of thought, to develop a rather complete and far-reaching system. But, as long as he remains a member of the first group of readers, whose interest is and remains 'general', such a reader does not let himself go in any of these possibly fascinating directions. He feels that Plato is, after all, a dramatic, rather than a systematic, writer; and he confines himself to enjoying, as dramatic literature, 'what Plato says'.[1]

The *second group* consists of scholars and students of philosophy who endeavour to understand and interpret Plato's Dialogues as a complete series of publications. Such students realize, even more clearly than members of the first group, that dramatic presentations may have highly systematic implications; but they are conscious of the dangers involved in going beyond the legitimate expansion of individual contexts; and they are even more conscious of the differences which underlie the implicational fringes attaching to this and that specific context.

Thus, they tend to distinguish sharply the alleged 'hedonism' of the *Protagoras* from the modern hedonism associated with the name of Bentham; and they refuse to allow any slipshod identification of the idea of beauty (in the *Symposium*) with the idea of good (in the *Republic*): not to mention the (widespread) identification of the position of Callicles (in the *Gorgias*) with the position of Thrasymachus (in the *Republic*). Any light-hearted readiness to apprehend analogies between the 'humanism' of Protagoras and the humanism 'founded by' the late F. C. S. Schiller or the 'instrumentalism' associated with the name of John Dewey, is met by a supercilious smile or a crushing frown. More serious-minded attempts to interpret Plato by reference to Aristotle, Plotinus, or St. Thomas Aquinas—not to mention the late Professor A. N. Whitehead—are simply refuted by drawing attention to the important differences of background and outlook (personal, social, and spiritual), which distinguish these later thinkers from Plato.

In fact, scholars in this (second) group rather easily go further. They tend to break up a Dialogue like the *Republic* into some three or four parts: separating an 'introductory portion' and an 'appendix' rather sharply from 'the main body of the work'. Some of them even treat the traditional 'Book I' as a separate Dialogue (the *Thrasymachus*), and draw a very sharp line between 'Book VI' (as 'Socratic') and 'Book VII' (as 'Academic—i.e. Platonic').

Be that as it may, it is usual for representatives of this group of scholars to break up the series of Dialogues into three divisions, labelled (1) Early Platonism, (2) Middle Platonism, and (3) Later Platonism. Under the first head are included the so-called 'Socratic Dialogues of Search', such as the *Laches, Lysis, Charmides, Meno*, and *Protagoras*. Under the second head are included the so-called 'Constructive Dialogues', such as the *Phaedo, Symposium, Republic*, and *Phaedrus*. Under the third head are included the so-called 'Dialectical Dialogues', such as the *Parmenides, Theaetetus, Sophistes*, and *Politicus*, with the *Philebus* and *Laws* tacked on as a sort of appendix.

Such interpreters use 'the genetic method', and profess to give an account, not so much of 'Plato's Philosophy' (if any), as of his 'philosophical development'. This can be, and frequently is, accompanied by an account of Plato's literary development, the evolution of his techniques as a writer of philosophical dramas and sermons. It is sometimes stated that Plato's 'own' philosophy is revealed, not at all in the Dialogues, but only in oral teaching given to his students in the Academy. But this view, while maintained by some scholars of the very highest reputation for scholarship, is simply not believed by the vast majority of interpreters.

In this second group I would include many professors of Greek literature, and almost all professors of philosophy. Professional teachers of philosophy have all studied Plato much as they have studied Kant. And so thorough has been their study that, for the rest of their lives, they seldom hesitate to sit in judgement upon the work of all scholars who specialize in this field: with complete confidence that, to all questions which can reasonably be asked, they are in assured possession of the answers; and that if questions are asked to which they do *not* know the answers, these are clearly questions which ought not to have been raised.

If well-trained minds can be authoritative anywhere, they are authoritative in this field; and if it were not for the (well-established) fact that their interpretations differ enormously, their authoritativeness would indeed be overwhelming.[2] Actually, the evolution of scholarly publications in this field has been, and continues to be, so rapid, that the books become labelled and dated, almost as soon as they appear in print—if not indeed earlier.

Thus, as a simple matter of the historical record: a Grote sees in Plato—Victorian democracy and a liberal utilitarianism indistinguishable from the position of John Stuart Mill. A Natorp, with a dialectical insight of the most painstaking thoroughness, discovers in Plato's Dialogues—an introduction to Neokantian idealism of the Marburg School. A Wilamowitz sees in his author—a distinguished Professor (*nur noch Lehrer*), disillusioned by the failure of his Vaterland's great war of aggression, and dedicating himself to stimulating his academic students to appreciate the inner life of the spirit. A recent writer of great distinction sees in Plato's account of man—the systematic philosophy of Neoscholasticism: in assured possession of 'the truth', and with all others relegated to their proper places as 'theorists' and 'sophists'.

Such evidence (and it could be extended indefinitely) indicates that what scholars, however erudite and however well equipped with the techniques of objective scholarship, regard as '*Plato's* Philosophy', is usually a full-length self-portrait. What Plato in his lifetime did for his own students: turning them, not into little replicas of Plato, but each into himself—i.e. a self approximating, in each case, to the student's own Platonic Idea—Plato's Dialogues still do for the modern reader. They constitute a kind of philosopher's mirror: in which the student, sincerely bent upon discovering Plato, eventually emerges with the outlines of an image which *others* can readily see is a somewhat idealized projection of what is at the back of the student's own mind. It is doubtless in this that the vitality of Platonism largely consists. At any rate, there is as yet no sign that the stream of scholarly interpretations of 'Plato's Philosophy' is either losing contact with its source and drying up, or is becoming so broad as to be in danger of losing its individuality in the vast ocean of general culture.

The *third group* of readers consists of those who study the Dialogues with some specific question in mind. They are looking for applications of Platonic insight to their own fields of interest, whatever these may be. With an initial faith that by putting together the evidence contained in Plato's writings, they may be able to discover something of genuine value for themselves and for others with like interests, one researcher after another investigates 'Plato's Theory of Government', 'Plato's Theory of Science', 'Plato's Theory of Ethics', 'Plato's Theory of Education', 'Plato's Social Philosophy', 'Plato's Theory of Man', and the like. The present investigation of 'Plato's Theory of Art' falls within this third group.

On a subject of such importance as Plato's Theory of Art, it is to be expected that a good deal is already known. And it might well be supposed that nothing new remains to be gleaned by a latter-day writer. Thus Eduard Zeller, when graduate students approached him with the suggestion that they might, possibly, venture to investigate this or that phase of the subject, drew their attention, somewhat sharply, to the pages in which his own publications had already 'dealt with' the topic. It was implied that the Master's treatment was (of course) final. And yet, who now refers to Zeller, except *honoris causa*—and for no other reason? So also the late Professor Paul Shorey used to maintain that all recent books on Plato should be reduced to 'papers', magazine-contributions containing the one or two points in respect of which the writers had anything to say which was *new*. He added that almost all papers should similarly be reduced to footnotes. And yet, who ever really believed that all questions which could reasonably be asked about Plato were finally settled by a thesis on the unity of Plato's thought, or by establishing, without further interpretation, what Plato said?

It is well known, for instance, in the history of art, that this or that great painter adopted (as he supposed) from Plato, the technique of grouping subjects in geometric patterns, especially in the pattern of the equilateral triangle.[3] So also in the history of music, we are assured that, for three centuries or so after Plato's death, practising musicians endeavoured to compose their melodies in accordance with the 'perfect system of the scales' attributed to the philosopher;[4] and it is pretty generally believed among poets to this day, as well as among artists of other types, that the artist, as such, is able somehow to penetrate beneath the surface of phenomena to some Platonic Idea, some secret source of creative inspiration revealed intuitively to the artistic sensitivity of the born poet.[5]

There are also a few learned papers, dissertations, and other special studies which assemble and discuss the material in the Dialogues, so as to establish what Plato actually does say. And nearly all works of a broader character, which profess to deal with Plato's 'philosophy' as a whole, or with the philosophy of art in general, have something either interpretative or critical to say about Plato's *aperçus* on the origin, nature, extent, functions, and limitations of art: and especially of the arts of poetry and rhetoric.

It is true, however, that many of these publications, however authoritative their findings, are narrow and one-sided; and however flawless the scholarship of this treatise or that, the possibility of further interpretation is by no means excluded. The reason for this is that so much, so very much, depends upon the point of view adopted by the interpreter. If you decide that what is fundamental in the philosophy of Plato is his theory of the State (as well you may), you take one good look at Book X of the *Republic*, and you draw your own conclusions about his theory of art. You associate this source with the philosopher's rather cold attitude toward poetry as an educational medium (not only in the *Republic* and *Laws*, but in other Dialogues as well); and with his even colder attitude toward rhetoric. You discover, further, that he does not appear to be highly enthusiastic about music and about many kinds of dancing; and with that, you are well away. You find yourself immediately relegating human art to a very humble position in Plato's estimation, if indeed you do not exclude it altogether from the higher reaches of the life of reflective citizenship.

Or if (as so many do) you regard as focal in Plato's thought the theory of knowledge, whether you understand by this the theory of science (both empirical and *a priori*) or the theory of 'ideas' (methodological or metaphysical?): you find yourself treating art, or at least the non-mathematical arts, as almost infra-cognitive. They sink so low on the epistemological scale of values (which you accept as Platonic), as to be almost completely negligible.

In fact, if you regard as focal for Plato anything other than art, you *ipso facto* find yourself treating art as non-focal, and usually as so marginal as to be viewed with suspicion, contempt, or almost complete exclusion from the ideal life. According to your agreement or disagreement with this estimation (which you take to be genuinely Platonic), your account will seem to others to present an almost incredibly distorted view of artistic experience, if not an almost incredibly distorted view of the thought of Plato. For Plato, in addition to whatever else he may have been, was himself a very great artist.

In our own time, it has been pointed out that in Plato's philosophizings there are many foci; and that to subordinate any one focus to others necessarily involves distortion and a consequent failure to achieve insight in that particular direction. My own interest, in the present study, is an interest in art. I therefore cannot content myself with merely assembling everything that Plato has to say, directly and indirectly, on this topic. I have to interpret what he says, in relation to the entire content of the Dialogues: so as to throw light upon the theory of art (if there should turn out to be such a theory) which is his. I make this interest focal; but I have no intention of concealing or distorting what the Dialogues may contain in the way of evidence given from some other point of view. My own bias (so far as I can myself detect it—and I have been helped a little by critics as well as by friends—perhaps critics are really friends in disguise) is chiefly in the direction of supposing that Plato really has something to say on this topic. That 'something' is (I hope) worth collecting and putting together and trying to interpret in a spirit of fairness both to Plato and to art. Previous studies induce me to regard Plato as a comparative philosopher: who compares what his predecessors and his contemporaries profess to believe, and tries to attain to a judicious balance; without any one-sided dogmatism of acceptance or rejection, but with a whole-hearted faith in the gradual evolution of philosophic truth. It is entirely conceivable that this bias may lead me, at times, into error. I try, therefore, to keep myself balanced by considering, at all points, not only the evidence which directly sustains my conclusions, but also any evidence that might reasonably be interpreted as adverse to them.

My interest, in this study, being in art, I am writing, primarily, for readers who have that interest. My interest in what philosophical colleagues may or may not think about my interpretations as throwing light upon the philosophy of Plato, is secondary. But it is there; and I try, accordingly, to make my position as clear as I can.

As far as modern books on aesthetics are concerned, I have been interested to discover that, even when they are insistent that 'aesthetics' is a very modern discipline, there are not very many (of the books I have seen) whose chapter-headings could not be used as a kind of structural framework within which the indications of the

Dialogues might well be arranged. But if I followed this suggestion, I should certainly be thought (by my readers, and by the writers of modern books first of all) to be importing an alien background and outlook which would distort the specifically Platonic features of the Dialogues. I have therefore tried, as well as I can, to preserve the characteristically Hellenic-Platonic associations of the original contexts: while at the same time not shrinking from bringing into sharp focus the central doctrine, the universal-theoretical implications of these same contexts.

I have spoken of the '*Hellenic*-Platonic associations'. I do not regard everything in the Dialogues as specifically Platonic. The interlocutors with whom a Socrates, or a visiting professor (from whatever part of the Hellenic world) converses, provide a general background which partly determines the extent to which a doctrine, conceivably Platonic, can be developed. A Socrates can hardly go much further than his interlocutors can follow him. An exceptional youth like Glaucon may be anxious to try, but the thing simply cannot be done. A philosopher like the visiting professor from Athens is only too well aware of his cultural superiority over interlocutors like Megillus and Cleinias; but he needs them as much as they need him. He provides ideas. They provide an audience and a background of experience. He defers deliberately to the limitations of their experience: constructing a 'second best', which they can partly understand and wholly approve. The modern reader can see further than such interlocutors. But even Plato cannot take his readers however sympathetic and however well trained—and (dare I add?) however modern—much beyond the limitations of their own day and age.

I start, therefore, from this general Hellenic background, sketched in outline with the co-operation and full assent of the minor *personae* of the Dialogues. Then, against this backdrop, I try to make stand out the various interpretations, hypotheses, and criticisms offered by the major *personae*: with the hope of eventually sifting out what appears to be the suggested result of the various discussions.

NOTES

1. I do not regard readers of the first group as highly sophisticated. Their views have, however, highly sophisticated defenders. Such defenders are found, chiefly

in the ranks of professors of literature (Hellenic literature); and their best-known representatives are the late Professor Paul Shorey of the University of Chicago, and the late Professor Ulrich von Wilamowitz-Moellendorff of the University of Berlin.

On the subject of Socrates and his doubts, may I refer to a recent paper of my own, entitled 'What Socrates Knows'? See *Transactions of the Royal Society of Canada*, Vol. XLV: Series III: June, 1951. Section Two, pp. 19–34.

2. I am informed that an expert on Plato, appointed to examine a Ph.D. candidate specializing in his field, asked questions so searching that the oral examination on the dissertation concluded with the questioner indicating to the candidate the precise references where answers to his questions could be found. After the candidate had withdrawn, somewhat chastened in spirit, the co-examiners, after a period of deep silence, said, 'But, Professor X, many of *us* could not have answered some of your questions!' The expert smiled and asked, 'But, my dear colleagues, who ever supposed you could? Do *you* claim to be "experts" on Plato (in addition to your other, admitted, fields of *expertise*)?' He was shocked to discover that they *did*, one and all, expect to be taken as experts on Plato. And he was amused to discover afterwards, how very many professional teachers of philosophy, and of Greek literature, would not hesitate to make the same claim. . . . *Meister, Meister, überall Meister!*

3. I have in mind the triangular pattern illustrated in the countless Madonnas, Crucifixions, and other religious paintings of the time of Raphael. Lecturers on the history of art always draw attention to this structural principle, as being derived from Plato.

F. C. Tilney, *The Lure of the Fine Arts*, Chapman & Hall, London, 1931, p. 81, says: 'It is to be doubted whether any painter actually set out to produce a picture by first deliberately adopting a triangle, a semicircle, or other geometrical device as a groundwork and then fitting his incidents on to it. . . . The usual method is for the painter . . . to think of his main incident, and to place this at once upon the canvas.' Henri (Robert Henri, *The Art Spirit*. Notes . . . compiled by Margery Ryerson, Philadelphia & London, J. P. Lippincott Co., 1923, 1930), a practising artist, giving instructions to his pupils, tells them, first to block in their larger masses, then to fit in the details. I would myself (R. C. L.) have no doubt that the square or oblong (or circular or oval) shape of the canvas itself has a prior influence upon design, and already furnishes a number of points of interest, such as its centre, its upper right-hand corner, etc., to such an extent that, in spite of Tilney's unhesitating statement, geometric forms do provide a kind of groundwork. We are also informed that the English decorative painter, Albert W. Moore, did actually, as a matter of concrete practice, paint his quasi-Hellenic figures, with their elaborate drapery, upon a pattern of points and lines, geometrically conceived. This is a matter of common knowledge.

4. So in the authoritative *Oxford History of Music*, Vol. I, by H. E. Wooldridge (Clarendon Press, Oxford, 1901).

5. An authoritative writer like Croce (*Aesthetic as Science of Expression* . . ., tr. Ainslee, Macmillan, London, 1922) insists that the artist's 'intuition', which is at the same time 'expression', is not different in kind, but only in degree, from the intuition-expression of the ordinary man. 'Each of us has in him a little of the poet, sculptor, musician, painter, prose writer. . . . That little is all our actual patrimony of intuitions or representations' (p. 11).

CHAPTER ONE

The Background of Hellenic Theories of Art

As Hellenic experience, from the tenth century B.C. onward, gradually settled into its natural groove, the first schools of reflective thought began tentatively to express their questionings and answerings in precise form. In the work of these schools we find universal acceptance of three aspects of nature which are fundamental for any theory of human art.[1] The first (1) is the recognition that the world revealed in human experience is, in all its phenomena, a changing world, a world in perpetual process, a world whose dynamic texture is fluid, like the texture of water, air, or fire. Its tissue is a tissue of motions.

A glance at the phenomena of nature, both physical and biological, made this abundantly plain. A further glance at the phenomena of human nature, social, economic, and political, made it, if possible, even more plain. *Panta rhei, ouden menei*, 'All things flow, nothing abides'. So Heraclitus: formulating, not merely what a professional school of scientists (Milesian or Ephesian) assumed as a tentative hypothesis, whose usefulness for purposes of explanation remained to be justified (if at all) by reference to its deduced consequences and their verifiability in detail, but what every intelligent Hellenic citizen naturally and without question believed to be fact.

A fundamental tendency of reflective thinking to evolve along the lines of a philosophy of the transitoriness of everything, a philosophy of the flux, of the movement underlying all phenomena of 'becoming', of apparent birth and growth, of decay and apparent death, was thus inevitable. This tendency, first formulated as a scientific hypothesis and developed into a technical philosophy in the sixth century B.C., we have had with us ever since. The evidence for it, if evidence is demanded, springs to the eye. As a theory of phenomena, it appears validated by every breath we draw, every step we take, every word we speak; by every attempt to catch the fleeting hour and express its inner secret: whether in the interlocking symbols of a poet's phrase, in the revealing chippings of a sculptor's chisel, or in the inspired strokes of a painter's brush. No one can doubt the universality, the all-pervasiveness, of its influence. A Plato absorbs it as a part of his regular education at the hands of a teacher of the Heraclitean School of Thought. So says tradition; and Plato never really admits the faintest shadow of a reason for doubting or seriously questioning its importance for life and for art.[2]

Motion, then, is the first aspect of nature universally accepted by Hellenic reflexion. With this a second aspect (2) is closely connected. In fact, if movement and its transitoriness are the obverse, this second aspect is their reverse: the reverse side of change. The sight of so much uneasy motion, of itself awakens the fancy, the hope, soon growing into a conviction: that somewhere behind these never-resting surgings there is to be glimpsed an unchanging substratum, a substance, a permanent something which is ultimate. This substance transcends (it is felt) these merely empirical comings and goings. It lends to this process—which is otherwise apparently mere process—a whence and a whither: a consummation, a meaning, an ideal purpose, a rational goal.

Ordinary Hellenic fancy, stimulated by the (doubtless inspired) phrasings of the poets, postulates, as an animistic projection of this feeling after something permanent and eternally vital, a realm of 'gods'. These 'divine' beings are pictured as ageless and deathless. They are located at first not too far away: in rushing rivers and tidal waters, in this or that mysterious cave, on the high places of Mount Olympus. Such divinities govern and direct the motions of air and water, sunshine and storm, by the sheer might of their minds: in accordance with ideal purposes immanent in those minds. They manifest their will to human beings through the mechanism of dream-imagery and trance, or through the movement of mighty oaks, whose rustling leaves murmur and whisper messages of weal or woe.

As familiarity with local geography grows, the gods become located a little further off, in the sun, moon, and planets: whose orbits they guide in such a way as to bestow upon human happenings a cosmic significance, with a sense of understanding and comfort, of companionship in a great venture, of leadership toward a more than human purposiveness and destiny.

Such fancies were supported by the Greeks finding, here and there, stones (of meteoric origin as a rule) which bore some resemblance to the human form, and could be regarded as images of this or that divinity, sent, not lightly, to command the erection of local temples with local rituals. Such a religion was fed naturally by the inspired creativity of poets. Their hymns to an Apollo or a Demeter, rehearsing the attributes of this or that great nature-power, enlarging upon its beneficence to its faithful worshippers, and culminating in ritual dances and ceremonial prayers for a continuance of protective communion, played a great part in the historical evolution of Hellenic religion. In fact, religion provided one of the more significant fields for the practice of music, of dancing, and of poetry, as arts: as arts, that is, not merely entertaining or amusing, but magical.

At about the same time, or a little later, Hellenic science began to develop: looking for an underlying meaning of events along slightly different lines.[3] The scientists looked for something less pictorial, less anthropomorphic than the gods of the poetic tradition, less subjective and fanciful. The object of their search was still thought of as concrete, but as depersonalized and generalized: as a sort of 'substance' or material power which could be used hypothetically to account for the phenomena of 'becoming' in general. That toward which they were feeling their way, approximated to a more universal principle which should not only appeal to the imagination, but should satisfy the slowly evolving intelligence of the scientist. Was one of the fluid phases of nature itself—water, air, or fire—somehow more fundamental, more substantial than the others? Could one of these—or conceivably some even more fundamental substrate, something more technical, less close to the moving surface of experience—be the original source, and possibly also the consummation, the final goal of all phenomenal changings? Could it be a sort of 'primary element', or what Aristotle was later to call 'matter' or 'material cause', of which all sense-perceivable objects, whether moving or apparently at rest, could be regarded as the transitory phases or effects?

Could it be that 'water' was the fundamental element: of which mud, earth, and stones, on the one hand, and vapour, air, and possibly fire, on the other, were temporary manifestations? Or should 'air' with its two powers of rarefaction and condensation, and with its fundamental value for all living and breathing organisms, be treated as the sought-after source and principle of explanation? Or should 'fire', itself a symbol both of power and of change, undoubtedly a chief agent of all transmutation (e.g. of earth and water into air or vapour), and definitely localizable in the sun—be treated as the most fundamental 'element' of all? Or possibly, just possibly, none of these, but some substance more remote, more infinite, more closely related (it might be) to the scientific demand for intelligibility, for rationality of explanation?

Be these things as they might (and each one had its distinguished proponents), the search for an explanatory principle, the faith in the ultimate existence somewhere, whether in the world or behind the world, which could be used to explain the world's never-ceasing motions, was a challenge to the scientists as well as to the more pictorial thinkers and the poets. The quasi-'positivist' school of Democritus, which could see in nature *no* evidence of transcendental design, but stoutly attributed all happenings without exception to 'pure chance', almost disappeared from view: surviving only in the atomist hypothesis (adopted from Leucippus), and in a few neatly phrased commonplaces. As a school of science, it was eclipsed by the brilliant success of rival schools, which did not scruple to associate themselves with the intuitions of poets and artists: glimpsing everywhere suggestions of cosmic purpose, and hints of a meaning, a pattern, a consummation, and a design accepted as intelligible by man.

Such 'sciences' are deliberately ranked by Plato with the human arts:[4] whether they follow the more concrete and materialistic (Ionian) line of explanation, or take the more abstract and mathematical (Pythagorean) direction. As for Plato himself, in the dialectical (Socratic-Eleatic) philosophizings which he partly adopts as his own, he envisages everywhere, as the final solution of the riddles of existence, and as its absolute goal, a transcendental principle of ideality and value: the 'idea of good', which is explicitly teleological.[5]

On such a view, art becomes, naturally and inevitably, the reproduction, in the medium of visual or auditory image-stimulants, of something analogous to the idea of good, i.e. to the values being investigated by the scientists and the philosophers. Thus understood, art clearly comes to include, not only painting, music, dancing, and poetry, but also science and philosophy itself, i.e. the higher, as well as the less penetrating developments of the spirit.

The third aspect of nature (3), universally felt and universally accepted by the Hellenic mind, was the fact of rhythm. The rhythms in nature, of sunrise and sunset, of morning and evening star, of waxing and waning moon, of the ebb and flow of tidal waters, could not fail to awaken attention and reflective questioning. So also with the rhythms of exercise and rest, of waking and sleeping, of growth and decay, of life and death. It was not long before the thought of a fundamental rhythm, permeating the whole world o motions, a universal law, one and the same in every phase of every kind of motion, achieved formulation. As expressed in the school of Heraclitus, this was a law of oscillation, of a vibratory pendulum-swing from opposite to opposite and back again *da capo*. As a law, this was believed to be valid throughout nature. As an explanatory hypothesis, it could be applied to the detail of change everywhere, however complex: not only to seed-time and harvest, but to war and peace, to the swing of power from aristocracy to democracy and back. It applied to economic as well as to political cycles, and to all oppositions and contrasts in life, wherever and whenever observed. In the thought of 'business cycles', we still have it with us today.[7]

Here was a key conferring the freedom of the city of reason upon all who had the courage to insert and turn it in the locks which barred the way to human progress. Here was a principle of balance, of bilateral symmetry, in things. To investigate its incidence in detail, was the task, the opportunity, of the new scientist. To portray its dominance in all structural harmonies throughout the world, transposed into the human clef, i.e. expressed in terms of the ordered rhythms of the human body and of the human mind, was the task, the opportunity, of the new artist. In such applications, the world of motions lost its first, more alien, look, its bewilderingly chaotic aspect. It took on the more friendly, more human, appearance of system, of rational meaning and humanly intelligible law.

Moreover, the discovery of subordinate rhythms everywhere soon brought out the fact of individual differences. Animal motions plainly have their own characteristic patterns, varying from species to species. Birds pattern their flight in wing-movements, fish in fin-movements, land-animals in leg-movements. Quadrupeds evolve patterns of their own; and human beings march and dance. Such ordered rhythms of human motion furnish a general basis for structuring all the specific human arts. The influence of the community or choric dance spreads itself over the whole of educative behaviour, and provides each and every medium of artistic activity, not merely with a general principle of value (an idea of 'good'), but with concrete structural patternings, whose detailed analogies in song, dance, and sentiments can be recognized as arising from an identity of underlying rhythm peculiar to the species.

Thoughts like these, still somewhat vague and suggestive, not yet hardened into compulsive dogma, or even given finality of expression, are in the air as Plato grows toward maturity. Some two, or perhaps three directional lines, along which development of these thoughts into an approximation to definitive theories, reflective philosophies of art, is beginning to take place, are already discernible as in formative operation.

One type of mentality (*a*) is perpetually attempting to account for artistic creativity by referring to objective nature. It is apparently nature which furnishes the data of the artist, the patterns among which his choice must lie, and the law which scientists are trying to formulate, the law to which the artist, if his work is to be effective, must consciously or unconsciously conform. In the interactivity of artist and nature, an interactivity resulting in art-products such as pots and pans, houses and temples, or in reproducing on a small scale, in terms of pigments, tones, or verbal expressions, the rhythmic patterns of the great world: to this type of mentality, it is quite clear that nature is and always must be the dominant partner. The function of the artist, always in strict co-operation with the latest discoveries of science, will be to give up all wayward and wishful idiosyncrasies of thought and feeling, and to discipline himself into receptivity. He will have to take humbly and thankfully whatever nature chooses to make available for his art, and to make of his faculties an unobstructive channel for nature's expression of itself.

For a theory of this general type, it will not be the artist, but, in the last resort, nature that determines the materials, the location, and the structural features of homes and temples, the chiaroscuro, the line and colour patterns of paintings, and indeed their subject-matter as well as whatever makes them into *physical* art-products. So also it is in the end nature, rather than the artist, that is fundamentally responsible for the forms as well as for the physical materials and instrumentalities of expression, in all the arts: in music and in dancing, in poetry and in prose-speech. What makes possible such a type-form as the processional march, the war-dance, the mating-dance, etc., or the epic, lyric, and dramatic patterns accepted so obediently by poets, or the nouns and verbs, the syllables and even the vowels, semi-vowels, mutes, and consonants used (according to grammarians) in speech, is, in final analysis, nature. *Wie herrlich leuchtet die Natur!*

For this type of mentality, the whole duty of the artist is to follow up the pathways opened for his use by science, and to do his best to let nature come through: in its own ways and with its own forms; exercising undistorted power over humanity on all occasions of life. Such a code for artists will fit in with the parallel tendency in general ethics, which urges human beings to follow nature in all things. In the new life according to nature, all individual and social norms will pattern themselves upon the rhythms of cosmic behaviour. Human architecture will reproduce the sheltering framework of forest and cavern. Human music will reproduce the themes of cosmic symphonies. Human speech will mimic the roarings and groanings of storm-winds, the whistlings and whisperings of zephyrs. So also in ethics; men will seek, both in individual and in social behaviour, to follow the cosmos as their leader. For the moral law budding within their hearts, they will find a sure and final guide in the courses of the starry heavens above. In a word, art so conceived and so practised will itself reveal and open up for man's use, a pathway to reality: to the reality studied in natural science, the reality feared and adored in religion, the over-arching reality of the physical world.

So much for the first directional tendency: a tendency toward 'realism', still (as Plato observes it around him) in a crude and elementary form. A second such tendency (*b*), a tendency regarded by Plato as more refined and intelligent, sees in mind rather than in nature the initiative, the priority, the creative power which calls into being a new universe, a universe of transcendental, ultra-cosmic values. To this second type of mentality, what is called 'nature' or 'physical reality' seems to be a sort of non-being, tossing uneasily in a slumber whose dream-images are without intelligible meaning. Of itself, such a world is chaotic: without system, order, or permanent structure. It is unable to provide for values anything beyond a somewhat dubious medium, a fluctuating screen against which the images of such values may, for a vanishing moment, be projected: a kind of receptacle which their forms can enter and leave, flitting in and out without gain or loss to their transcendent essentiality.

This second directional tendency is found in two well-known philosophic schools. To (1) the Pythagorean school, the physical world glimpsed by the senses is a web of pure illusion, a tissue of floating images. These are distorted copies of a reality which utterly transcends such representation, or rather misrepresentation. The sensuous world imitates the forms of the intelligible world, but the copy does not participate in the reality. The imitation is and remains valueless. The true reality, seen by the purified soul alone, is a nexus of mathematical laws. These are indeed verifiable by reference to sensuous experience. It is, however, the abstractions which transcend motion and change, the mathematical forms all carved by 'the finite' out of 'the infinite', namely, the integers of arithmetic, the regular figures of geometry, both plane and solid, which the mind apprehends as alone real.

c

To (2) the Eleatic school, the physical world is even less significant. Its phenomena constitute mere appearances: a tissue of suggestions which cannot withstand a logician's criticism. They are riddled through and through with contradictions. Both in principle and in detail, they are unthinkable: an unspeakably crude chaos, a non-being of which neither scientist nor artist can make anything finally satisfactory to mind. Space, time, motion, causation—all are equally unreal. To this school, only the completely thinkable, the utterly self-consistent, an ineffably absolute realm of ideas which would be the counterpart of an ineffably absolute thinking mind, constitutes the sole reality.

As contrasted with crude tendencies toward 'realism', the work of these two more refined schools is associated, by Plato, with the name 'idealism'. For Plato, both Pythagoreans and Eleatics are 'friends of ideas' who seek in the postulates of rational intelligence that reality which they inevitably deny to the world of sense. As far as the work of artists is concerned, it is clear that such schools will tend to take one of two directions. On the one hand, they will tend to see in the work of most artists a mere copying: a meaningless play with images. Subjective and arbitrary, such play, however absorbing to its participants, is a purely childish activity which may, indeed, amuse. It may even at times seem to promise, perhaps by its serious involvement with technique, something more than mere amusement. But in the end it is unable to extract from its premises more than those premises contain. If merely human in origin, in background, and in outlook, art remains an amusing and indeed attractive, possibly highly attractive, preoccupation. But it is a preoccupation with play, and, as such, it leads, in the end, nowhere. Its occasional pretensions to leadership, leadership into a promised realm of higher meanings, necessarily remain the merest suggestions: suggestions without conceivable fulfilment. In fact, as you can see if you regard them with a critical eye, such pretensions are, in the end, fraudulent, ludicrously so.

An idealist theory of art which follows along this line will accordingly—at least, in as far as the theorist is ambitious, seriously in pursuit of truth and genuine reality—negate, reluctantly perhaps, but with a certain finality, all claims that are made for human art as an original source of genuine value.

On the other hand, it is conceivable that a few unusual artists, recognizing the inherent futility of such play, may withdraw from the game for a while and may attain to genuine insight: penetrating to the intelligible realm of consistent meanings in which the philosopher is at home. Altogether changed by this insight, they may go down again into the twilight cave in which most men remain fettered all their lives, and may seek, by interpreting or even manipulating the images which are all that most men can apprehend directly, to use them as vehicles for conveying a genuine message: indicating some of the truths of the ideal realm.

Or it is conceivable that a few inspired craftsmen might co-operate with philosophers: using their artistic powers of image-manipulation to amplify the transcendental abstractions of the philosophers, and to clothe their skeletal outlines with sense-perceivable draperies, lending to them the semblance of life and human warmth. They might use, e.g. the isosceles triangle of the Pythagoreans, or something of the sort, to centre the shapes painted from some human grouping. By this mathematical configuration they might lead symbolically the thought of the beholder: away from the world of mere images, and toward the higher realm of pure forms. Such a suggestion would not (as in the earlier case, of imagery grouped only for its own sake), be devoid of all higher value. As a suggestion, it would be leading in the right direction: the direction in which transcendental value could really, if one looked for it with the right methods, be found.

So much for the second directional tendency: the tendency toward 'idealism'. There is also, in Plato's time (*c*) a third directional tendency. This is not, like the other two, derived directly from the world: that is to say, from motion itself, and from the search for something objective. It does not rest upon a feeling that in matter itself there is something basic, something which the poets express as a divine ordering, and the scientists regard as a dumb *nisus* within nature: a formative oscillatory process whose pulsations, with their directions and limits, can be discovered by human intelligence and formulated or otherwise expressed in terms of the triangle and the circle, interrelated perhaps by placing the triangle within the circle.

This third type of mentality is, in fact, sceptical of the alleged power of the human mind, with its brief life-span, to penetrate to anything so ultimate as 'God' or the 'secrets' of nature. This entire business of the 'gods' (so glibly elaborated by the poets), is fundamentally obscure. And as to the ultimate significance (if any) of 'nature', do not the antinomies into which philosophers invariably fall, indicate beyond reasonable doubt that 'Being or Non-being' (some call it the one, and some the other—doubtless it is all one, anyway) is fundamentally unknowable and incommunicable?

So the apostles of *the new humanism*: Gorgias and Protagoras. Abandoning forever the abstrusities of 'realism' and 'idealism' alike, as impossible and unnecessary puzzles, they set before their eager disciples a new pathway leading toward a new truth and a new reality: a biosocial truth and a biosocial reality.

In fact, for 'objective' read *social* (or *biosocial*). For 'science' read *social* (or *biosocial*) *science*: i.e. sociology and social psychology. For 'art' read *biosocial expression*: a form of linguistic in all respects social (or biosocial) in its reference, the *public* speaking or 'rhetoric' which appeals to the feelings of men in convention assembled, and sways majorities by bringing out and formulating persuasively the wishes, hopes, and ideas already in the background of their minds.

Your highest court of appeal is not the will of some old-fashioned 'god' or the 'absolute truth' of old-fashioned physical science. There are no such absolutes. There is only what a working majority, a democratic majority, will accept as its own. The new artist is a craftsman who records and amplifies his master's voice. Among the Athenians, he praises the Athenians; and his art makes the world safe for democracy by bringing clearly into the foreground of Athenian thinking, feeling, and acting, all that the Athenians, in their great democratic assemblies, regard as especially democratic: as significant, as of central importance for the Athenian way of life. For days after hearing such a patriotic oration, the Athenians go around with their heads in the clouds: better men, better Athenians in every way for having associated with the great Pericles or the great Protagoras.

The power of the new humanism is, in fact, altogether magical: as it amplifies and re-echoes the great democratic message. It tells each and every citizen that he is the true embodiment of his city; that his strength, his prudence, and his wisdom, are the strength, the prudence, and the wisdom of ten thousand: all unified, fused in the democratic melting-pot, all advancing, shoulder to shoulder, toward the glory of their irresistible destiny.

Carping criticism may conceivably call the new humanism or pragmatism a form of 'flattery'. The point, however, is that biosocial art is more broadly based, more deeply rooted, better in every way than individual art. In the new biosocial way of thinking, feeling and acting, democracy, yes, humanity itself, has at last come to stand firmly upon its own feet: finding within itself the immanent ideals which make of it what it has within itself to be—perfectly, gloriously human.

Such are the chief directions which thought in Hellas is taking, while Plato is growing toward manhood. They furnish the characteristic background, by interacting with which he gradually develops his own ways of thinking. For many years, his adherence to the Socratic method of questioning (derived by Socrates, doubtless, from the Zeno of the Eleatic School whom Plato depicts as almost Socrates's identical twin) does two things for him. It not only (1) brings out into the open and formulates clearly the idea behind each of the three direction-tendencies taken by itself: so that there can be no doubt about the origin, the nature, and the functions of each. It also (2) brings out critically the limitations inherent in each one-sided theory. It shows how and why no one of them, taken as a complete account of the matter, is acceptable.

The full Platonic idea of art, arrived at after thus elaborating and 'destroying' the hypotheses of these partial views, and so attaining to the vision of the all-positive 'idea of good', is indicated in the later Dialogues. Here the Eleatic method of analysis and synthesis is applied by Plato to discovering the complete nature of this or that concept: the concept of the statesman or philosopher-king, of the sophist, culminating in the suggested thought of a philosopher-sophist, and so on. We shall follow our author both in the Socratic and in the Eleatic direction: terminating with a quasi-Eleatic identification of 'the artist', i.e. the philosopher-artist, and a consideration of his origin, his nature, and his functions in the ideal community constructed by Plato.

NOTES

1. In the authoritative article on ART (by Venturi) in the *Encyclopedia Americana*, 1947, Vol. II, pp. 336 f., we are informed that the business of aesthetics is 'to find the common attribute of poetry, painting, sculpture, architecture, and music', and that two methods are in use, one 'objective', the other 'subjective'. The objective method proceeds by analysing 'the physical manifestations of the arts', and comes to the conclusion that 'no common attribute of words, forms, colors, and sounds has ever been found or is likely to be found'.

The author of this article omits dancing (as he says, for the sake of clarity). If he had included it (as is done by Plato, and by many modern philosophers of art), he might have suspected (as Plato, Dewey, and many others do) that *motion, rhythmic motion* is precisely the 'common attribute' which Venturi thinks is never likely to be found. For Plato's treatment of this, see p. 29 ff.

2. The theory is, indeed, treated by Socrates with a certain degree of irony (e.g. *Crat.* 440cd, *Theaet.* 152e ff.), but Aristotle is very authoritative in saying of Plato

that he was familiar with the Heraclitean teachings in his youth, and 'held these views even in later years' (*Metaph.* 987a 32 ff.).

It is sometimes supposed that Plato's 'ideas' transcend time altogether, and that his view is accordingly static, and allows no room for change of any sort. But this is exaggerated. For a full discussion of the evidence, cf. R. C. Lodge, 'Plato and Progress', *Philosophical Review*, 1946, pp. 651–667.

3. Present-day authorities (e.g. Pierre Bovet, *Le dieu de Platon, d'après l'ordre chronologique des dialogues*, Alcan, Paris, 1902, Ch. I, esp. pp. 53 ff.) tend to represent Greek science as *opposed* to Greek religion, as substituting intelligible elements and principles for a more anthropomorphic picture-thinking. I think, however, that a fundamental movement of the Hellenic mind, working its way gropingly toward something permanent underlying the world of change, developed along two parallel, or almost parallel, lines, which were gradually converging, rather than inherently opposed.

4. *Rep.* 533b–d, cf. *Gorg.* 450c–451c.

5. *Rep.* 505a ff., 540ab, etc., cf. *Phdo.* 97c f., 100b f.

6. *Rep.* 509d ff.

7. John Dewey (like many modern writers on aesthetics) somewhat similarly emphasizes the necessity, for the development of aesthetic quality, of the 'formal conditions of artistic form rooted deep in the world itself' (*Art as Experience*, New York, Minton, Balch & Co., 1934, p. 147). Chief among these are 'nature's rhythms', in which man 'participates in interacting with the rhythmic forces of nature', as he sows and reaps, celebrates his harvests and his 'consummatory victories over resistance' (pp. 147 ff.). Resistance 'accumulates energy', instituting 'conservation until release and expansion ensue' (p. 155). 'When complete release is arrived at through a succession of ordered periods of accumulation and conservation, marked off into intervals by recurrent pauses of balance, the manifestation of emotion . . . acquires esthetic quality' (p. 156). So is formed 'a rhythmically formed experience culminating in being consummatory'. It is only 'as the rhythms (in nature) become a rhythm in experience', that they become 'aesthetic' (p. 162).

If I were looking for something in Plato to illustrate Dewey's position, I should find it in the life of the model city of Plato's *Laws*. Here we have interaction with nature's rhythms (709a f.), in a community which gradually (in progressive rhythmic activities) overcomes resistance, by conserving energy and eventually expanding and releasing that energy in every phase of community life: achieving a 'fulfilment of impulsions and tensions', i.e. achieving a succession of consummatory experiences in a way which (as Plato believes, cf. 903b ff.) realizes the Platonic 'idea' of humanity.

In Plato, however, I find, what I do not find emphasized in Dewey: a conviction that art is truly this 'art of life', viz., the life of the model city itself (*Laws* 811, 817). Painting, poetry, and music are only in a secondary sense, for Plato, art. That is to say, they are 'art' precisely in so far as they are functional portions of the life of the model city. If you separate a picture or a poem from its place in the life of the group, and try to treat it as an art-work, a sort of independent 'thing-in-itself', you find the vitality tends to have faded out of it (*Phaedr.* 275c f., cf. *Prtg.* 347c f., *Symp.* 176d f.). Only in so far as you re-integrate it into the life of the model city does it really come alive again—as in the re-written traditional literature which is used in the model city (or, for the matter of that, in the ideal republic).

CHAPTER TWO

The Origin of Art

THAT motion is universal, extending throughout the environment we experience, has only to be mentioned, to be accepted at once, without question. No interlocutor in the Dialogues feels the slightest doubt about that. In fact, the opposing view, associated though it is with the teaching of the intellectually formidable Eleatic school, that 'Being' in the absolute or metaphysical sense is somehow above or beyond motion, i.e. that it remains 'an everlasting fixture', is rejected out of hand. It is 'unmeaning', simply incredible.[1]

If, now, you imagine this environmental surging of motion as existing 'once upon a time' apart from the guidance and direction of mind: you find yourself abstracting, from the environment you know, all patterning, all order and law, all meaning that a mind could grasp. You work your way to something like the utter chaos and old night depicted by the didactic poets. In a mindless multiverse, upward and downward are all one. Backward and forward are just the same.

Let us suppose that you take such a chaos as your starting-point. You now proceed to inquire what differences a guiding intelligence, with its immanent feeling for the beauty of unity, order, and balance, would make to your formless motion-swirls. You conclude without difficulty that mind, as such, introduces rhythm, ordered recurrences of patterning which an intelligence would be able, at least in principle, to formulate in mathematical terms: in a word, the kind of patterning which would seem both natural and intelligible to any member of the Pythagorean school.

As a matter of observable fact, this cosmic environment which we know, is full (as every Hellenic thinker is well aware) of such rhythms and periodicities. The stars in their courses, the ebb and flow of tides,

23

the seasonal changes, the winds, and indeed everything that we group together under the name of nature (*physis*) plainly exemplifies an orderliness, a meaningfulness, indeed, a purposiveness, which simply cry aloud for mathematical formulation. The principle of this order, in fact, is a primordial datum, something given within nature itself.[2]

Speaking in human terms, it is doubtless likely enough that the 'father and maker' of this meaningful universe is past all finding out.[3] This means that poets and scientists are at liberty to fabricate what hypotheses they please: without much hope of achieving any sort of finality. A scientifically minded mythologist can certainly construct (in his imagination) the idea of a quasi-human formative principle. By drawing on human analogies, he can proceed to deduce what precise effects such a formative principle could produce, if it set itself the task of converting the given chaos into a mind-satisfying cosmos. The non-logical content (still remaining in its inmost essence—if you can speak of 'essence' in such conditions—chaotic), would doubtless be grasped and enclosed in logically intelligible outlines. Out of such outlines would be built up, eventually, an intelligible universe of inter-implying structures whose movements would constitute an ordered system: from which many varieties of subordinate consequences could be deduced.

Something analogous to these deduced consequences could presumably—at least, in a fair number of striking cases—be approximately verified by comparison with the patternings actually observed in the behaviour of our physical environment. It would follow that, although exclusive certainty could hardly be claimed, even remotely, for any one specific hypothesis, i.e. although rival alternatives would always remain speculatively conceivable: something like a systematic general position might well—tentatively—be established. This would take the form of a mathematical physics, whose speculative constructions might interest and amuse a philosopher in his lighter hours, and would provide for his type of mentality a fair degree of intellectual satisfaction.[5]

Some such movement of thought is actually taking place in contemporary Pythagorean circles. At least, a distinguished visiting professor from Locri constructs, for the instruction and amusement of Socrates and his academic friends, precisely such a hypothetical system. Admittedly speculative, it is related, on the one side, to technical developments in solid geometry: a study attractive to the academical, although pursued with success chiefly within the Pythagorean Order. The system thus constructed presupposes knowledge of the regular solids (tetrahedron, octahedron, etc.) which can be inscribed within the sphere. This knowledge had been achieved by the Pythagoreans. The construction of these solids out of elementary triangles is typically Pythagorean; and this part of the Visiting Professor's exposition is admittedly a little esoteric: intelligible primarily to students trained in the techniques of Pythagorean science.[6]

The obscure reference to the Pythagoreans as being, not merely friends of ideas, but 'friends of God', is also characteristically Pythagorean.[7] The meaning presumably is, that the constructions of such especially favoured students are something more than a mathematician's game, a way in which intellectuals amuse themselves in their off-hours. 'God's friendship' means something further. These constructions do not have only the value of group subjectivity, the value of rules accepted (arbitrarily) by the group as binding upon them merely for the purpose of playing their game of hypotheses and consequences. They are also of objective significance. In a word, while still in part speculative, these constructions are inspired. They actually imitate or reproduce on a human scale the kind of law and order created by God. Finally, the frequent reference to sensuous verification (such as this is), is also characteristically Pythagorean; conceivably also the reference to an 'orrery', a small-scale model which reproduces approximately the observed movements of the heavenly bodies.[8]

On the other side, this movement within the Pythagorean school is deliberately related to the most deeply accepted ideals of Socrates and the Academy. The 'principle of the best' which is being applied by the visiting professor from Locri to his speculative constructions, is approximately identical with the principle of 'the good', the principle of ideality sought by Socrates in the *Phaedo* and less tentatively formulated by him, before an almost equally academic audience, in the *Republic*.[9] The application of this principle is only partial; for the content of the elementary triangles apparently remains obstinately chaotic, never actually resolved into anything completely ideal and formal. The spatial 'receptacle' is similarly factual, but is never entirely apprehensible by mind. What Timaeus teaches is a 'mythologizing', i.e. the work of a 'friend of ideas' expounding empirical science, and moving in the right direction: toward an ultimate grounding upon the principle of ideality demanded by Socrates. Hence the 'delight' with which Socrates listens to its promising suggestions; although it still remains, in the end, more empirical than a hopeful apriorist could desire.[10]

A brief outline of the relevant portions of the *Timaeus* myth follows. God is goodness. He makes whatever He touches, 'good', i.e. as like Himself as possible. That is to say, he brings out its maximum of value. Upon the datum of chaotic motility he superimposes patternings calculated to bring out its potentialities for value. These patternings are ordered in geometric forms. Fundamental among these is the form of the circle. God makes the world go round. The entire chaos is enclosed within a sphere. Its surface, thought of as revolving, constricts its content. This is forced to assume, throughout, quasi-spherical form.

That is to say (1), physical reality as a whole becomes shaped like a sphere. (2) The larger masses moving within it (the heavenly bodies) are shaped like spheres; and the orbits in which they revolve exercise, through the cycles of physical time and the physical seasons to which their regular movements give rise, a certain controlling influence upon their respective contents. (3) On the earth we find human organisms. These are thought of as (roughly) spherical in form: i.e. as fundamentally brains (with certain outgrowths of cerebro-spinal material). Going still further down the scale, we find (4) the 'elements', complexes shaped like the types of solid which can be inscribed within the form of a sphere: tetrahedra, octahedra, icosahedra, and cubes, corresponding to what we call 'fire', 'air', 'water', and 'earth', respectively. These are built up out of material which has been constrained into (5) the yet smaller forms of elementary triangles, so beloved in the Pythagorean school. Triangles are the smallest rectilinear closed figures which can be inscribed within the circle. Dissolve these triangles, the minimal or ultimate forms,[11] and you come upon unformed chaos again. You are back where you started.

Throughout the universe, motion is regularized and controlled by an 'animating principle' (*psyche*) which, as described, makes a modern reader think at first of the mechanism of a gyroscope. Two circles, one slightly within the other, and touching at two points of their circumferences, revolve in opposed directions. The outer circle (of 'the same')—corresponding, apparently, to the rational principle of identity in Aristotelian logic—normally exercises some control over the inner circle (of 'the other'), whose movements are more liable to become disordered. A principle of this type animates the movements of the celestial bodies, and indeed of human brains. Its function is, in all cases, to steady and regularize, to guide and control the otherwise chaotic motion-tendencies of its content: so as to facilitate a self-controlled contribution of something of specific value to the universe as a whole.[12]

In living organisms on our earth, their animating principle holds their content (particles of earth, water, fire, and air—referred to as its 'triangles') together in a specific equilibrium, whose mathematical formula varies from one species to another. Thus controlled, each species lives through its characteristic life-cycle, and makes what contribution it can to the life of the whole. Internally, its equilibrium is never entirely stable. The originally chaotic content (held within the organism's 'triangles' in accordance with the formula of proportion characteristic of this or that species) is perpetually trying to escape from control and to disintegrate. On the other hand, the animating central self-motion (*psyche*), superimposing the controlling forms, is perpetually seeking to achieve and maintain what the Greeks call 'self-mastery'. The resulting balance is liable to be affected, one way or the other, externally, by kindred forces in the environment.[13]

Thus, much as walking is a succession of incipient fallings, each followed by a recovery of balance: so the central self-motion always proceeds by a counter-balancing effort, which seeks to restore equilibrium. We observe this principle in operation whenever we look, e.g., at human life-processes. There is a normal cycle of exercise and rest, of wear-and-tear of tissue followed by repair and growth. If the central self-motion is too weak to ensure these recoveries by itself, it can be reinforced by external motions similar in type. Thus nurses rock babies in their arms so as to assist them in overcoming the upsets induced by the incoming stream of nutriment. Elderly dyspeptics secure similar benefits by taking a good walk, a carriage drive, or an ocean voyage. Medical men recognize in certain Hellenic dances a somewhat similar function. Rhythmic exercises affecting the organism as a whole reinforce the efforts of the animating principle, and make for self-mastery and health.[14]

Educated men observe that these rhythmic processes throughout nature are always recurrent, cyclical in character. Accordingly, they advise men of intelligence to study seriously the regular movements of the stars in their courses, and to base their lives, as far as possible, upon similar regularities and periodicities: recognizing the identity of principle which controls motions in such ways as to evoke positive spiritual values, whether in the starry heavens above, or in the moral law within. By such studies men will learn to co-operate with God in the wisest possible development of what would otherwise be vast open spaces, devoid of value. Pursued in this spirit, science, e.g. the science of astronomy, does not (as commonly supposed) make for atheism and unprincipled conduct. It reinforces, in the strongest possible way, religion and ethics.[15]

The above is not, of itself, characteristically Platonic. Most of it is explicitly Pythagorean: in origin, in background, in outlook, and in its limitations. What is especially characteristic of the Pythagorean school is the constant reference to empirical verification. The patterns, all formulated in terms of mathematical hypotheses, represent, according to the Pythagoreans, the ways in which nature observably behaves. In formulating and systematizing such patterns, the last, as well as the first, court of appeal is, always, sensory demonstration. What is characteristic of the Eleatic school, on the other hand, is precisely its transcendence of such empirical considerations. The Eleatics rely, in final analysis, upon *a priori* consistency. Their norms are based, not upon fluctuating sensory experiences, but upon ideal universality and necessity, upon transcendental logic, with its purely rational demands.

What Plato does, is to balance the requirements of these two schools, both 'friends of ideas', by making use of the principle of ideality demanded by Socrates. The rhythmic life-cycles, with Plato, are established, not by mere observation, nor by mathematical hypotheses adopted tentatively because of their descriptive factuality. Behavioural description is entirely replaced by an ideal formula, which explicitly transcends empirical verification, and claims to be connected with an absolute principle, the unhypothetical 'idea of good'. All three of these *motifs* are clearly discernible in the text of the *Timaeus*.

Plato's own interest, as is well known, is chiefly in the social and ethical consequences of such theorizings. The Pythagorean Brotherhood recommends 'imitation' of the behavioural patterns of the cosmos. Plato inquires into the value of such imitation. Surely, in the last resort, mere imitation remains as empirical as what it imitates. Its mimicry is playful, superficial, subjective, arbitrary. This may interest the Brothers. It may even help to keep them together, as a group. As a mutual admiration society, they are not as other men. They observe certain group practices. They prostrate themselves before the rising sun. They garb themselves in ritual robes. They refrain from eating beans. They share a secret pass-word, and profess to pattern their movements upon the movements of the cosmos.

Such social ritual stimulates a kind of communal dream-life. The Brothers all dream the same dream and play the same game. But such copying of behavioural patterns, however cosmic the patterns, is merely fanciful. It does not achieve contact with any reality higher than the Brothers themselves with their group posturings. A choir of eight Neo-Pythagoreans can doubtless reproduce, on a small scale, the alleged 'music of the spheres'. But does anyone contend that cult-harmonies produced in this way achieve any sort of value recognizable as such outside the meetings of the Brotherhood? Is it claimed that, as ritual, it somehow affects, by sympathetic magic, the motions of the celestial bodies themselves? Surely, the net result of all such imitations, objectively speaking, is precisely zero; although such rituals may have some slight social-psychological value for the group: in strengthening their morale, encouraging the Brothers to keep on playing their group game.[16]

As contrasted with this, the Socratic-Platonic Brotherhood (i.e. the Academy) tries to penetrate to something further: to patterns whose value is trans-empirical, guaranteed by their all being based upon something which transcends group feeling, namely, the ultimate principle of ideality itself. To form oneself upon patterns so based is so different from Pythagorean 'imitation', that the Academy uses a different, rather carefully chosen term. The academic Brother 'participates', i.e. shares directly in the values of the reality to which he assimilates himself.

Instead of reproducing superficial cosmic movements ritually and externally, he grasps their internal principle, and takes this up, directly, into his own life. He does not imitate externally the behaviour of the cosmic deities, who are doubtless patterns of holiness, justice, and wisdom. He becomes actually, *in propria persona*, holy, just, and wise: the personification of their spirit. Participating in the war-dance is not an end in itself. It awakens the war-spirit within; and the dancer's subsequent actions on the battle-field are an outward expression of the spirit which animates him. Such a life grows from within outwards, and its value is independent of the external environment, and indeed of the whole world of 'appearances'.[17]

This brings us to a position from which we can approach the subject of art, and can investigate the Platonic account of (1) its origin, (2) its nature, (3) its functions, and (4) its limitations. Art originates, as Plato insists, over and over again, (*a*) in the natural motility of animate organisms, and (*b*) in the operation of a second factor, which somehow selects, patterns, and guides this natural motility in such ways as to assist the human organism to play a more significant, a more rational part in the drama of human destiny. It is this second factor which, in the Dialogues, receives the most careful and characteristically Platonic treatment.

(1) Art originates (a) in animal motility. Young animals are, for the most part, in almost unceasing motion. They cannot stay still for any length of time. Any sort of emotional excitement produces flutterings, overt movements of the voice, body, and limbs. Animals so stimulated, react by uttering inarticulate cries. They fling themselves about, and their movements are largely spontaneous. They are uncontrolled, unpatterned, without rhyme or reason: in a word, they are non-logical, quasi-chaotic.[18]

In the human species, young children, especially boys, 'in whom the fountain of reason is as yet undeveloped', tend, if left to their own devices, to behave in the same kind of way. So do adults of the more uneducated sort, on those occasions in the human life-cycle when they relax and let themselves go. When eating or drinking (especially if to excess), when making love, when sleeping and when dreaming, many of them lapse into this primitive state. Their actions then are unbeautiful. There is something un-Hellenic, un-free, in fact, comical about such lapses from human dignity. In the weakness of disease, especially at the approach of death, and perhaps also in some forms of insanity, a similar withdrawal into merely emotional and chaotic feeling tends to take place.[19]

From this factor *alone*, nothing like art could ever originate. In the interaction of organism and environment, it is clear that the organism must be provided, from some source, with a power counterbalancing the power of the environment. Otherwise, the organism is inevitably at the mercy of the environment. In that case, it is not anything that would ordinarily be called 'art', but nature, overwhelming nature, which in fact dictates, not only the stimulating situations, but all types of response available to the organism.

Hence, indeed, arises one view of art: the widely held view of common-sense realism. According to this, animal motility is entirely controlled by natural necessity. The patternings, however simple or apparently sophisticated, assumed by the biosocial life-cycle of this or that species, are shaped, unshaped, and re-shaped, both in principle and in detail, by physical destiny: that is to say, by the external forces of the four seasons, by famine and pestilence, by disease and accident. No individual, and no group of individuals, of itself and unaided from some higher source of power, can do anything but drift with the stream: a part of the flotsam and jetsam of the flux of events.[20]

From this standpoint, it is not man, but nature, that really originates the norms and ideals of human life: factual nature with its blind causation, its non-rational concourse of what, humanly speaking, look like accident and chance. Geographical environment obviously evolves particular types of character and mentality. Every Hellene knows this, and knows also that nothing much can be done about it.[21] Again, human beings come into the world, endowed by nature with dispositions toward this or that type of character, i.e. with natural advantages or disadvantages in the struggle for a worth-while existence. Again, very little can be done about this.[22]

It is true that a rational intelligence (so far as man develops this power) tries to make the best of what it has. But as to what you have to start with, well, all the decisions are already made: by nature, not by you. You are the merest puppet of physical destiny. According to this realist-minded way of thinking, the facts of life—i.e. the biological, social, and physical environments in which man's life is cast, settle, in the last resort, everything that man apparently succeeds in doing. We cannot possibly conquer nature. We can only obey her dictates, and as we bow our heads, hope and pray for the best.[23]

What kinds of arts and crafts can human motility develop, when all controlling influences come, not from a relatively independent mind, but from nature, from factual surgings in the flux of happening? You must conform to nature. You cannot do otherwise. At best, you can, to a limited extent, perhaps co-operate. In that case, your efforts, if in a line with the directions being taken by nature, may succeed in producing 'art'—of a sort.

Birds build nests in places that are relatively safe. Many animals find shelter in forests and caves. Human beings not only seek such shelter as nature of itself provides. They co-operate by constructing, out of natural materials, artificial dwelling-places in sheltered positions. Hence the beginnings of architecture.[24] So too they group together, partly from natural gregariousness, partly for shelter and protection from obvious dangers. Hence the beginnings of village and city life, with a host of social institutions developing as natural extensions of such life. It may even be that the kind of social organization in which the elder rule over the younger, and chieftains of some sort direct the group in its efforts to win security by co-operating with nature, are themselves in the order of nature: imposed upon human beings by natural necessity.[25]

From this standpoint, common-sense realism readily accounts for the crafts or technical activities of artisans: such as building, carpentering, weaving, making pottery and utensils of all sorts. In constructing for human use this or that concrete object, such as a house or a boat, a table or bed, a cup or knife, or a piece of dress-goods, craftsmen are plainly co-operating with nature, from start to finish.[26]

So too with the common vocations of men. Farming, fishing, and hunting have the function of supplying the community with an adequate food-supply. Human reason does very little, in comparison with nature; and what little human reason does succeed in doing, plainly takes the form of waiting upon and following the directions given by nature. The various vocations connected with community life, such as retail and wholesale trading, banking and finance, transportation and civil engineering, perhaps also the immense variety of military vocations, can easily be seen to follow lines set by environmental necessity. Reason, if present, simply amplifies what nature supplies, and follows humbly where it cannot possibly take the lead.[27]

When we come to consider the so-called arts, i.e. the technical activities of the craftsmen known as 'artists', activities which produce music, painting, poetry, prose (forensic or political), etc., producing something which is not only concretely useful to the group, but is also considered 'charming' or 'beautiful'—it is not difficult to see that these activities introduce no factors that are new. They are a further extension of the same principle of necessity. Such arts minister, as language does, to the community interaction with its environment. They make this interaction more efficient.

The apparent 'idealization' found in poetry, painting, and the rest, is a mere reinforcement of the types of activity found useful in community living. These are all folk-arts. They express and enhance the folk-ways characteristic of the group. Even the deities appealed to in ceremonial dances, rituals, and hymns, are nature-deities. They represent the forces of nature with which the group is endeavouring to co-operate. From end to end, the entire effort of human craftsmanship, using human reason as a servant and interpreter of nature, is directed to forming our whole human way of living upon the ways of physical reality, upon the cosmic tissue of events which alone, in the end, exist.[28]

Such, then, is one view of the origin of human art: the view that its patterns and norms are in no sense original with man, but are all imposed upon human motility by the external forces of physical nature, the factual cosmos of which our human organisms (like other biological organisms) constitute an infinitesimal part. This widespread physical realism or hylozoism is not, however, regarded in the Dialogues with enthusiasm. It is not a view which men of philosophic intelligence feel they must or should accept. 'Persons of refinement'—persons, that is, who have received their training in the Pythagorean or Eleatic schools of thought—agree in rejecting it out of hand. Their objections, as expressed in the Dialogues, take the following form:

Materialism is a simple faith. It is unsophisticated and crude. Its acceptance is a sign of one of the lower stages of intelligence: a level well below knowledge, a level at which men accept as 'real' only what they can hold in their hands. While vigorous and perhaps convincing as long as it confines itself to the factual and sensory side of experience, 'opinion' of this type proves weak and vacillating when it comes to accounting for the higher ideas, and for the spiritual side of life generally. In fact, if we have to choose between (1) regarding matter as primary, and spiritual life as secondary, and (2) regarding soul or spirit as primary, and the physical conditions of life as secondary, critics trained in these 'idealistic' schools of thought, i.e. critics classed together in the Dialogues as 'friends of ideas', are unanimous in accepting, like Fichte in more modern times, the dogma of the priority of mind or spirit.[29]

From this idealistic standpoint, while the matter of the physical cosmos is accepted as an essentially non-logical datum, something which possesses existence, it is regarded as possessing, in its own right, nothing more. Mere motility, of itself, is structureless and devoid of value. Any patterning, any significant value-structuring, has to be imported *ab extra*. According to this way of thinking, it is not nature, but soul, the animating principle, mind or spirit, that is the independent source and origin of all values which make their appearance in the space-time world.

It is not only that closed unities such as circles, triangles, and the mathematical solids in which motility is imagined as held captive, are all mind-made. They are the creations of a mind which, by such methods, creates in its own image and superimposes its own features (so far as this is possible) upon the primordial chaos. Mind or spirit does this so as to express, so as to realize (again, so far as is possible) in such a medium the transcendent values of beauty and goodness: creating in the physical receptacle a mirror-image of its own values,

D

values whose source is within spirit itself. Order is more *charming*, more *beautiful* than disorder. Such is the standard Pythagorean teaching.[30] Unity and intelligibility are *better* than plurality without meaning or end. Such is the standard Eleatic view. The world as the mathematical physicist comes to view it, is thus a phenomenon, an appearance, an imitation or copy, a representation in regularly patterned motions, of the values (beauty, goodness, rationality) projected from within the divine mind.[31]

For idealists of the schools under consideration, the physical world constitutes an essentially imperfect copy of the divine values. These remain values for the mind that has projected them, that has superimposed its triangles and octahedra upon the chaotic motility. As far as the chaotic material is concerned, the superimposition is, and remains, external. Superimposition holds the material imprisoned, but does not succeed in transmuting it in any way. The material does not have within it anything that could respond by understanding and co-operating. It takes on temporarily this or that form, but remains fundamentally unimpressed: incapable of doing anything when the pressure is relaxed, but lapsing into its own chaotic self (if you can call such a thing a 'self'). The situation of the physical cosmos as a world under law, is something like a captured city brought by force under alien rule. The captor can create (temporarily) the external appearance of good citizenship. But he does not quite believe in it himself. (So the modern animal trainer can make tigers stand upon tubs and go through the motions he prescribes. But there is no inner understanding, no possibility of true co-operation, with a tiger.)[32]

The lesson of this (for these idealistic schools) is, that where the external world is *me on*, a form of Non-being, the empty appearance which merely mimics a world of intelligible beauty and order, the true idealist will withdraw from it into a higher realm of pure reason: curbing his natural instinctive tendencies to interact with the world, by ceremonial rituals and other practices designed to free him altogether from its influences.[33]

What is the origin of art, according to the schools of refined idealism, the Pythagorean and Eleatic schools? Art is, for them, essentially a sort of craftsmanship, passed on from father to son, from teacher to pupil. Such art is essentially reproductive, imitative, a form of mimicry. It is not, however, necessary to suppose (as realist-minded artists do) that art originates in mimicking *nature*: in producing physical replicas of what the artist touches, hears, or

sees around him. A music which merely mimics physical phenomena, e.g. imitates the environmental sounds which make life along
the water-front of the Piraeus the thing that it is—the beating of the
waves, the whistling of the wind, the creaking of ships' blocks, the
cries of the mariners—is a feeble sort of 'music'. It is as pitiable as
simple onomatopoeia in poetry, or simply holding a mirror up to
nature in painting. The creativity of such craftsmanship is crude and
cringing. It argues, in all who take it seriously as 'art', intelligence of
the very lowest order: an intelligence that reduces itself, as nearly
as possible, to zero—losing itself in a welter of feelings analogous
to the motion-swirls of primeval chaos.[34]

No, from *that* sort of imitation, sheer meaningless, messageless
mimicry, the Pythagorean artist will withdraw. Persons of refinement turn away from the merely actual, from the biosocial and
physical crudities of the environment. They withdraw into a life,
sustained by the imagination: a life which rejects the empirical
surgings of feeling and accepts the teachings of mathematical reason.
They realize the essential emptiness of ordinary biological passions,
and dedicate themselves (as far as is possible for human beings) to
what they picture as a higher life, the life of superior persons.[35]

Art helps them, sustains them in their efforts to withdraw, to die
to everyday living, and to free themselves for the transcendental
life. Art helps them in two ways (1) Through the intelligent use of
emotionally powerful imagery, it can bring home to initiates the
essential hollowness, the tragical emptiness, of everyday living. It
can show mortals as unfree, as imprisoned within their bodies, as in
a living tomb. It can picture the attempt to satisfy the desires of the
flesh as a hopeless task: the task of filling a cask by pouring in water
which perpetually escapes through holes pierced in its sides. Art can
reveal the glaring inconsistencies involved in the everyday pursuit
of pleasure, wealth, and power, the absurdity of praising the
Athenians among the Athenians, of exalting dictatorship when
before a dictator, in short, of glorifying what *is*, when to the eye of
Eleatic reason it clearly is *not*.[36]

On the positive side, Pythagorean artists can reinforce every aspect
of the Pythagorean way of life. The new marches will be ceremonial
processions of initiates withdrawing to their own place, garbed in
appropriate robes, going through the prescribed ritual, and cele-
brating their withdrawal from the senseless activities of the world
and the flesh. The new hymns will proclaim the vanity of human
wishes, the glories of a brotherhood based upon superior insight.

Technically, the new dances and the new music will originate, not in a search for merely biosocial and physical satisfactions, but in an attempt to reproduce, on a scale suited to the capacities and needs of the brotherhood, the 'music of the spheres': that is to say, a music based upon the mathematical patternings of Pythagorean astronomy. Speaking generally, the arts which make use of mathematics will be more highly esteemed than the arts which merely appeal to feeling; and Pythagorean art will be the art created by Pythagoreans for Pythagoreans, to assist all initiates in sustained self-dedication to the Pythagorean way of life.[37]

(2) Through the use, not of emotional imagery, but of mathematical and dialectical techniques, artists trained in the Eleatic school can provide further assistance toward living the life of reason. Eleatic art will construct didactic poetry: verses which will bring out clearly and distinctly the intellectual contrast between Being and Non-being. They will insist with unwearying consistency that Being *is* and Non-being *is not*. They will equate Being with Reality, an immense sphere containing whatever *is*, and utterly excluding whatever *is not*. Being is a *plenum* which, as such, utterly rejects anything even remotely suggesting a *vacuum*. In its ultimacy, Being completely excludes such forms of Non-being as space, time, motion and causality. Only the utterly thinkable is utterly real. Eleatic artists will thus, by creating a new scientific language, stripped by dialectical techniques of every suggestion of biosocial valuing, assist reason to become *pure* reason, and to contemplate itself and its own immanent ideals.

The chief example of such a master-craftsman is the great Parmenides; and the chief examples of the new trans-valuational languages are the mathematical and logical symbol-techniques in process of development at the time. These have a beauty and a charm of their own—for intellectuals, that is; and it is to intellectuals that Eleatic idealism makes it appeal. On the negative side, Parmenides is seconded by the creator of intellectual paradoxes, Zeno: who reveals challengingly the contradictions lurking in every attempt to construct a science out of any sort of union between the world of sense and the world of thought. These are not one world, but two worlds; and the Eleatic, no less than the Pythagorean, teaches withdrawal from the world of sense to the world of pure contemplation.[38]

Yet a third school of thought exercises, upon Plato and his contemporaries, considerable influence. This is the school, or perhaps we should call it the movement, associated primarily with the name of Protagoras, but including also Gorgias and the other visiting professors popularly known as 'sophists'. Representatives of this group are sceptical of any reference to an alleged 'Reality', whether physical, metaphysical or theological, as of any ultimate importance for humanity. As Protagoras insists, the subject is obscure, and our human needs cannot wait until the evidence (if any) is all in. Gorgias is doubtful whether such a term as 'ultimate reality' means anything, and especially whether it stands in any helpful relationship to what is humanly knowable and humanly communicable.

Leaders of this movement place humanity, i.e. human needs and capacities, in the centre of their thinking. They develop a 'humanism', a concrete biosocial philosophy which regards the working majority in a democracy as the proper court of appeal in all matters which are felt to be important to humanity. *Truth*, for instance, is not something which can be determined by reference to some kind of 'absolute fact' which falls outside human experience. It is simply what a majority, after discussion, agrees to accept as useful for the purposes of that majority.

Similarly, *goodness* is not something independent of human judgement, something determined by reference to the inscrutable will of Providence. It is what a working majority, again after due discussion, agrees to accept as its own objective, its working programme, its five-year plan. *The Beautiful* is not something determined by a vague reference to divine inspiration, or some kind of higher intuition. It is a pleasant form of the socially useful, accepted as such, by the democratic processes which result in a working majority. In a word, in regard to all matters which are in any way amenable to human judgement, the democratic self-determination of the group is, for all reasonable and intelligent persons, the last and highest court of appeal.[40]

For such a way of thinking, art originates as follows. Technically, the artist is a craftsman who specializes in giving pleasure: in making friends and influencing people, especially on their social side, when assembled in large groups, by suggestive control of their imagery. Such an artist is a student of social psychology and especially of what we should nowadays call the psychology of advertisement. Plato thinks of him as a producer of pleasure, a professional 'flatterer'.

His first aim is to win the interest and approval of his public. The group passes upon his value as an artist, and it is essential to him to make his work 'popular'. Thus, if he is a poet, competing in a drama festival, where the first prize is awarded by popular vote or by a decision of 'judges' who are themselves little more than a mechanism for registering popular acclaim, he will naturally play up to the gallery, and down to the groundlings of the pit. There will be patriotic sentiments a-plenty, something to touch the heart and induce the shedding of tears. There will be chills and thrills for the romantically inclined. There will be the magic of sheer poetry for the choric parts, and clever virtuoso-writing for the Messenger's speech. If the artist is a musical performer, in competing before a popular audience he will tend to emphasize everything that is showy and brilliant. His work will be ultra-modern, a miracle of technique: teeming with *tremolos, sforzandos,* and *accelerandos,* and with more than its quota of trills, grace-notes, and other meretricious ornaments.[41]

But *the* art, the democratic art *par excellence,* in which native sons like Pericles, and visiting professors like Protagoras and Gorgias are past masters, is the art of speech-making: the political or forensic oratory which enchants the soul and induces a kind of pleasure which sweeps all hearers off their feet. A good funeral oration leaves a democratic audience spellbound for days afterwards; with its head in the clouds, worshipping itself and lost in wonder before the vision of the Greater Athens conjured up by the master-wizard. A Protagoras, in a flood of words which set a-twanging every chord of the human heart, also 'praises the Athenians to their faces'. His artistic 'flattery' (if you insist) fills the minds of all members of the group with group feeling. It enhances their sense of a common origin and a common destiny. It stimulates sentiments of community enthusiasm, as all feel themselves marching together, shoulder to shoulder, under the guidance of their great leaders, in the path trodden by their fathers, and to be trodden by their sons: the path upon which the favour of Heaven so clearly shines.

And it should not be supposed that this pleasant art of the orator is *mere* flattery: that it follows where it cannot lead. On the contrary. In a democracy, the great decisions are reached after discussion by all qualified persons; and who so well qualified as the technically trained orator? His to awaken his hearers to their true selves; to tell them, if they do not yet know, what 'justice' demands of them; to show them what they really, truly, with all the pressure of their manifest destiny, want; to hold up before them the 'cause' to which they desire to dedicate their inspired efforts: the cause which is Democracy, the Beloved Community itself.[42]

So far, Plato's contemporaries are developing three distinctive accounts of the origin of artistic patterning. According to the first (1), the patterning is imposed upon human motility by external nature, by forces in the physical environment of man. Human interaction with these forces is restricted to conforming, or, conceivably, to co-operating to a very slight extent. According to the second (2), the patterning is geometrical rather than physical. It originates in the Divine activity, as God superimposes His own semblance upon a chaos empty of all inherent value. He encloses its surging motions within a sphere: in such wise that spherical motion imprisons its material content, constraining it into the forms of quasi-spherical solids, and ultimately into the shape of elementary triangles. By this technique God fabricates, at least formally, a cosmos whose patterned motions present semblances (however empty) of beauty and other values. By copying this technique as closely as he can, the human artist similarly imposes, upon the motility of human imagery, the kindred patternings of Pythagorean geometry. Such patterns (however empty of value their content may remain) prove aesthetically satisfying, as forms, to the artist. By means of this activity, he succeeds in withdrawing himself from the meaningless motion-swirls of the environment, and in associating himself, at least intellectually, with his superior Friend, the Master-geometrician, God.

According to the third account (3), the patternings of art originate in social behaviour: in the growing attempt of humanity to build up a democratic social order. The artist partly conforms to the will of the social organism, amplifying and enhancing the quality of his master's voice. And partly he succeeds also in giving to that voice a clearer tone, a more articulate emphasis, a more determinate direction: in proportion as his technical ability succeeds in clarifying and expressing the concrete tendencies increasingly immanent in democratic social living, as such.

How does Plato, as the mouthpiece of the Academy founded in honour of Socrates (its informal leader and spiritual president in perpetuity),[43] react to these three accounts of the origin of art? Like every Hellene, he accepts the account of human motility common to all three. He never questions the mission of the Hellenes to impose upon a quasi-barbarian world of social chaos the ordered patterning characteristic of a mind-satisfying social cosmos. And, in balancing these three accounts of the origin of the patterning, he accepts something from each of the three. Just as his ideal political constitution accepts something from nature, something from idealistic insight, and something from social co-operation,[44] so it is with his theory of art. Art derives, from a careful balancing of all three *motifs*, its *Lebensfähigkeit*.

From the hylozoist or realist account of the early philosopher-scientists, he derives not merely the view of universal motility, but the faith that in nature itself, however originating, there is a powerful tendency toward unity, order, and intelligible system. He is entirely convinced, for instance, that if human artists will only seek for objective guidance for their efforts as imposers of patterns, they will find that there *is*, at least partly expressed in the physical cosmos, a sort of objectivity upon which they can rely.

The 'enharmonic scale' of the 'classical' Greek music is mathematically identical in principle with the grand scale constructed in accordance with the intervals discovered between the heavenly bodies studied in Greek astronomy. A little careful research will undoubtedly discover the proper mathematical formula for a number of other Hellenic scales: of the Dorian scale corresponding precisely to the characteristic range of the young man's voice when in martial mood; and of the marching rhythms suited precisely to the young man's steps marching as to war; and the type of warlike sentiment corresponding, point for point, with the tones and rhythms of the Dorian scale. Similarly, research will doubtless discover objective correspondences between the tones, intervals, and sentiments appropriate to a revised Phrygian scale, and the tones, gait, and sentiments appropriate to men of maturer years, marching in peaceful and ceremonial mood. War-dances and peace-dances, imposed upon human motility, are in the order of nature. So are, no doubt, a few other types: the ceremonial dances in honour of this or that deity, the mating-dances approved for hymeneal occasions, the somewhat violent dances advised by physicians for acquiring emotional self-control.[45] Dances which are not in the order of nature, are, of course, to be eliminated.

So too of the differences between the sexes, of which the artist has to take account. These are definitely in the order of nature. So also of the differences between what we nowadays call 'I.Qs.'. Men, women, and children can all be ranked as 'alphas', 'betas', 'gammas', and 'deltas', i.e. as belonging to what Hellenic mythologizing calls a 'golden', 'silver', 'copper', and 'iron' class. Such differences are all in the order of nature; and Plato proposes, in all seriousness, to build upon that order.[46]

He even expects nature to provide potential carpenters, weavers, potters, and other socially necessary classes of artisan, in a mathematical proportion suited to the kind of community for which he permits us to see the blueprint. According to this master-plan, there is to be a definite concrete activity, a potentiality working itself out toward a fully developed mastery of this or that craft. Such tendencies are a part of the 'natural bent' of every little boy or girl that is born into this world alive. It is the function of the designer of constitutions to provide an opportunity for each such individual, as he grows toward maturity, if properly educated, to contribute toward the life of the whole, what he has within him to contribute.[47]

Here a question might be raised. Is not Plato's master-plan *a priori*? In that case, does not the empirical individual have to conform willy-nilly? The answer is, No. The plan is definitely in the order of nature. Plato does not teach that the State is an absolute Idea, whose realization demands certain types of occupation such as administrators, auxiliaries, artisans, and other assistants, and that therefore empirical individuals must be made to conform to these demands, denying themselves to some extent, and opposing their own natural tendencies. On the contrary: the reason for the occupational types we find is simply that men come into life born that way. The children of kings take naturally to the art of government. The children of carpenters and weavers take naturally to carpentering and weaving. In a word, nature, of itself, evolves these types. Man the administrator, receiving these types from the hand of nature, devises for them the best arrangements he can. Infancy and education, sexual attraction and married life, social stability and senescence, are all in the order of nature; and so are all typical ways of occupational living which, in the Dialogues, receive approval.[48]

Thus nature provides a few, a very few, queen-bees and potential philosopher-kings. The administrator accepts the material that nature provides, and co-operates by carefully selecting and educating a suitable leadership class: so as to enable potential leaders to realize their potentialities for leadership. It is the same with the other classes: the groups of silver, copper, and iron capacity. They are born that way. The administrator, of himself, originates none of them. He seeks only to conform, to co-operate, to discover and assist in establishing the objective norms existing *in rerum natura*, and to live according to their plain directions. To this extent, Plato is in agreement with the realist account; and a good many of his sermons are simply parables from nature.[49]

From the idealist account, he accepts the mathematics, the

dialectical consistency, and the idea of the Master-mathematician. The Divine Artificer imposes geometric patterns of the precise types discovered by his 'friends' the Pythagoreans), upon the chaotic motility: at least, so far as the inherent weakness of the material allows. In this way, He fabricates a systematic cosmic order, in which beauty and other values become expressed or partly realized. The human artist copies this technique, as well as he can, and so succeeds (to some extent) in building up a system of inter-implying forms, preferably mathematical in type. In such a system, beauty, as humanly envisaged, and other values become expressed or partly realized. Artistic patterning, to that extent, originates in mathematics.[50]

The artist-craftsman always follows his own value-judgement, such as it is. He feels after some sort of guidance or inspiration. Sometimes he is brilliantly successful, although without understanding how or why. This is illustrated by the case of 'One-poem Tynnichus'. Inspiration being, however, a chancy affair, Tynnichus was never able to repeat his one great success. Most craftsmen accordingly call upon their technique to help them over the uninspired times and places. Knowing that triangles and circles, as such, are mind-satisfying, they rather easily slip into the trick of substituting mathematical intelligence, with its tried and tested diagrams, for artistic intuition. As Plato puts it, they simply bisect what is before them, instead of feeling for the joint where nature has placed it. Such craftsmanship, unless guided aright by 'friendship with God', does not reach even the level of 'right opinion'. It is liable to construct a pattern of empty frames, a mechanical network of inter-implying parts which, however intellectually satisfying, is likely to fail when you try to capture beauty. It is silly to fish for moonbeams as if they were shrimps![51]

That is to say, from idealists of this school Plato accepts both the mathematics and the feeling after inspiration, divine guidance. He also shares the school's feeling that most craftsmanship is uninspired, an idle playing with the potentialities of this or that medium: a playing which, however technically brilliant, results in nothing of genuine value. Unlike the Pythagoreans, however, who are satisfied to leave the world to itself, while they withdraw to their 'superior' life of friendship with God, he seeks for something further.

What does this mean? On the one hand, Plato has already accepted the view that art originates in conforming to nature. He is now accepting the view that art originates in conforming to God's power of superimposing form upon chaos. That is to say, he is trying to combine inspiration and mathematical technique. It is clear that, if the diverse parts of this combined view are to achieve consistency, God, nature, and mathematical form will somehow have to be brought into positive, non-contradictory interrelationship. This could be done, e.g. by giving up the materialistic presuppositions of the hylozoists, and by making mind or spirit prior to matter. It would then be possible to maintain that the mathematical forms apprehended as *in rerum natura*, ultimately (i.e. metaphysically) transcend nature: being imposed upon the chaos by the prior power of the Master-mathematician, God.[52]

On such a view, the human artisan, in constructing houses, pictures, language, music, science, or what you will, is reproducing (whether copying from external observation, or re-creating under the guidance of internal, intuitive insight) the mathematical order superimposed upon motility by his Master, the Divine Artificer. That is to say, the human craftsman is co-operating, not only with nature, but with the Power which provides nature with its mathematical structuring. He is co-operating with God in imposing form upon matter. It may be that he is assisting, however humbly and in however petty a field, in realizing God's master-plan for humanity and for the world.[53]

Such a synthesis carries Plato beyond the position of the nature-school taken by itself, and of the mathematical school taken by itself. It remains to consider what Plato derives from the biosocial school, the humanist movement led by Protagoras and Gorgias. From this movement he derives a valuable corrective to the abstractness, the superiority, and the willingness to withdraw from biosocial problems, which characterize the idealist schools. He rejects forever the ivory-tower superiority of the Pythagoreans and Eleatics, and insists that his citizens are to remain merely human. They are never encouraged to withdraw from the problems of men, to dedicate themselves to the cult of the ingrowing soul. Even the best of men are little better than 'puppets, jerked this way and that by the strings of desire'. It is true that they cling as well as they can to 'the golden cord of reason'. But the life of the golden class is spent in the common cave. Its members use their education in the service of their fellow-men: including, not merely the 'silver' class of full citizens, but also the less privileged 'copper' and 'iron' classes, and even the slaves. 'A sad necessity is laid upon them', and they cannot decline the common task.[54]

From the humanists he also learns that human art originates in this attempt to solve human problems. It is no aristocratic art-for-art's-sake, withdrawn from the life of the common herd. It is a method, cultivated by trained and educated craftsmen, for so inter-acting with the conditions upon which human weal and woe de-pend, especially in so far as these conditions are social and can be tackled by human organization, mediated by language-symbols—as to assist in bringing about a desirable future. Art, as the humanists teach, is a way of bringing about this as yet unrealized future, by applying 'persuasion' to one's fellow-men. In a word, art is *par excellence* the practice of rhetoric in influencing the votes of a demo-cratic assembly, so as to induce co-operation leading to a successful issue.[55]

What Plato accepts from the humanists, is their end-purpose, rather than the means which they advocate. The true art, with him as with them, is statecraft: the 'royal' art which induces co-operation and friendship, weaving a variegated but closely integrated web of citizenship. In the model city of the *Laws*, Plato's administrative authorities are well aware that they are engaged in the practice of a supremely important art or craft, with which nothing, however insidious and however glamorous, must be allowed to interfere. In the *Republic*, the members of the guardian class are, above all else, 'artificers of freedom' for the entire community.[56]

In both the *Laws* and the *Republic*, Plato's administrators are also well aware that, in dealing with the less adult classes, i.e. with what we may call the 'betas', 'gammas', and 'deltas' of humanity, it would be unrealistic to expect results from a purely rational appeal, such as would be effective with the 'alphas', the golden class itself. In place of 'instruction' which clarifies the reason, it will be necessary to use non-logical forms of that 'persuasion' which stimulates *doxa*, i.e. opinion, imagination, and judgement. Thus myths and other forms of propaganda-literature, pictures, music, processional dances, and what not, forms of 'the noble untruth', will be put to work in the service of the supreme art; and only such forms of craftsmanship as are judged to be of genuine use to the community in its attempt to secure self-mastery and freedom, will be encouraged.[57]

Such 'artificers of persuasion' might, indeed, all be grouped to-gether and classed as 'rhetoricians'. But Plato's view here differs sharply from that of the humanists. The humanists know nothing higher than rhetoric: the art of persuasion which sways the votes of sovereign assemblies. As *they* see it, the rhetorician *is* the statesman.

A Pericles, a Cimon, or a Themistocles *is* the natural and proper human leader. He represents the *ne plus ultra* of human ability, whose leadership is to be accepted by its democratic correlate, whole-hearted followership. With Plato, however, it is not the rhetorician, but the philosopher, who is the true statesman. Socrates is 'the only true statesman of his time'. The technical arts of persuasion are all secondary in significance, when measured against philosophic insight. Their persuasive wizardry, their magically moving power over non-intellectuals, is undoubted. But they do not rise above the knowledge-level of *doxa*, imagination or opinion, and their crafts-manship can never be accepted as equivalent in value to the supreme art practised by the philosopher-king.[58] Here Plato combines the higher insight to which Pythagoreans and Eleatics aspire, with the biosocial interest of the humanists: to the immense improvement of both one-sided views.

To sum up: for Plato, art originates in the deliberate attempt of mankind to acquire self-mastery: to control their human motility by patterning it in ways that will prove useful in achieving the venture of humanity. Art originates, not in play or subjective self-amusement, but (1) in the attempt to apply the objective principles of structuring realized in cosmic nature. It originates (2), not in merely conforming to actual, physical nature, but in the attempt to achieve intellectual insight into the master-plan designed for the cosmos by the mathematical Master-artificer, God. It originates (3), neither in a merely empirical nor in a merely transcendental ideal-ism, but in the deliberate attempt to bring together both the facts of life and the ideals of the Master-planner—in the life of the ideal republic or model city: for the lasting benefit of humanity.

In a word, human art is properly and fundamentally the art of model citizenship, the art of self-government, statecraft: a statecraft based upon (1) natural science, (2) religio-philosophic insight, and (3) the biosocial necessities of humanity. What serves to unify, to hold in balance, these three diverse approaches to the goal, is the unique contribution made by Plato's hero and elderly friend, Socrates. Living under divine inspiration, Socrates succeeded, to some extent, in formulating the ultimate idea of 'good', and in so stimulating men of intelligence and goodwill, that they regard themselves as friends of ideas, as fellow-members in an ever-expanding spiritual 'Academy': working co-operatively, in the spirit of model citizenship, toward the ever fuller realization of that idea.

NOTES

1. *Soph.* 248e f. Cf. Burnet, *Early Greek Philosophy* (2nd edit., 1908, London), p. 15.

2. *Rep.* 523c f., *Tim.* 27d–28c, 30a, 49b–53b, 69b, cf. *Pol.* 270, 272d ff.

3. *Tim.* 27cd, 28c, 29cd, 48d, 53d.

4. *Tim.* 31b ff., 38 f., 48 f., 53b ff. (I should perhaps say that—of course—I largely accept the position of A. E. Taylor, that the *Timaeus* represents Pythagorean, rather than specifically Platonic, theory. May I also say, once for all, that references to the *Timaeus* should usually be understood as including references to Taylor's *Commentary*, and indeed to his *Translation*?).

5. Such a speculative science, resting (as it does) upon unresolved hypotheses (*Rep.* 510c. f., 511b f., 533cd), would never prove *completely* satisfying to a philosopher. It could never become an occupation for his more serious hours (cf. *Tim.* 29cd). Erich Frank (*Pl. u.d.s–g. Pythagoreer*, Halle, 1923, pp. 14–16, 117 f., 163 ff., 195) says that what Plato calls a 'myth' is precisely what *we* call *exakte Naturwissenschaft*. From this standpoint, mythological science would be parallel to imaginative literature, whose 'wizardry' always has charms, even for the philosopher, but never entirely satisfies his higher standards (*Rep.* 595b, 596c, 598d, 601b, 602d, 607c, *Phaedr.* 265c f., 275c–277a, 277e–278e (cf. 249e f.), *Soph.* 235a, *Epist.* 341c–e, *Laws* 810d–812a, cf. *Menex.* 235ab).

6. *Tim.* 53c, 54 ff.

7. *Tim.* 53d, 7–8.

8. *Rep.* 529d f., 531a f., 616c f., *Tim.* 40cd.

9. *Gorg.* 513c f., *Phdo.* 97c ff., *Rep.* 342b f., 505a ff., 517b f., 540ab, *Tim.* 29a, 3, 6, e f., 70b 8–9.

10. *Rep.* 556e, 571b f., *Tim.* 29d f., 50d f., 52b f., 57a, 61a 6, 69b, 84a–c, *Theaet.* 176a, *Pol.* 273b, *Phil.* 31d, *Laws* 691a–c. Cf. Erich Frank, *op. cit.*, pp. 99 ff., 104, 372 b.295.

What makes the scientific speculations of the *Timaeus* ultimately unsatisfactory to a Platonist (although he finds them fascinating to listen to), is that their hypotheses are grounded—like *all* Pythagorean hypotheses (*Rep.* 531bc), largely upon what is factual, empirical, guaranteed by a fluctuating sensory observation.

If such hypotheses could somehow be transcended, so that the resulting body of systematic science could be grounded upon the principle of ideality, the reasoning would then be entirely *a priori*. It would proceed from ideas, through ideas; and it would terminate in ideas: never requiring or indeed making contact with sense-perceivable fact (*Rep.* 511b f.). In such a case, we should have, not merely a secondary occupation for the philosopher's leisure (*Tim.* 59c), corresponding to the secondary interest in literature (*Phaedr.* 265c–278e, *Rep.* 595b, 596c, etc., cf. *Epist.* 341c f.), but a final, entirely satisfactory solution of the philosophical problem (cf. John Wild, *Plato's Theory of Man*, Cambridge, Mass., 1946, pp. 72–74, 199–200, 280–281).

11. The obscure intimation of *Tim.* 53 ('What is yet more ultimate than these, only God knows, and whosover is a friend of God') may be interpreted by reference to *Laws* 894a, with E. B. England's notes. Cf. also E. Frank, *op. cit.*, pp. 369–371. The triangles are generated by moving points. A point, moving in its first 'fluxion' (*auxesis*) gives a line. The line moving crosswise (= a point in its second

fluxion) gives a surface. The surface, moving toward or away from the spectator i.e. a point in its third fluxion), gives a solid. That is to say, it is always a moving point which circumscribes the chaotic matter in triangular, tetrahedronal, or spherical form.

12 *Tim.* 34b–37c, with A. E. Taylor's notes (*Commentary on Plato's Timaeus*, Oxford, Clarendon Press, 1928).

13. *Phaedr.* 245c. *Tim.* 30a, 42a–c, 43b ff., 47b f., 53a–c, 69bc, 70a, 73cd, 95c, 89a, *Laws* 653c f., 672c f., 673cd, 791a–c.

14. *Charm.* 156–157, *Phaedr.* 245, *Tim.* 43–44, 88 f., *Theaet.* 153b, *Laws* 788c f., 790c f. The practice of less well educated doctors and patients, of relying upon pills and potions, and otherwise stimulating externally mere isolated portions of the organism, is sometimes praised as a smart technical device for restoring, without delay, an upset balance. But procedures which attempt to cure one violence by a counterbalancing *violence*, tend to weaken, rather than to strengthen, the central self-motion (*psyche*). Wise physicians prescribe a regimen which affects the organism as a whole: strengthening the animating principle (*psyche*) so that, by operating from within outwards, it gradually re-imposes its controls, and so brings about a new equilibrium, restoring health naturally (*Tim.* 81 ff., cf. *Rep.* 424a).

15. *Tim.* 90a f., cf. 88c f., *Laws* 670b f., 817e, 820e–822d, 897b f., 898c f., 903b f., 966d f. Cf. also *Rep.* 500, 527d f., *Phaedr.* 247.

16. *Rep.* 529c f., 531c. For the 'imitation' and its emptiness, cf. *Rep.* 598 ff., and Aristot., *Metaph.* 987a 29 f., b 10 f. Cf. also Burnet, *E. Gr. Ph.* (1908), pp. 319 ff. Cf. also Adam's note on *Rep.* 617b 12 (*The Republic of Plato*, Cambridge Press, 1907, Vol. II, p. 453).

17. *Phdo.* 80a f., 83a f., etc., *Symp.* 209–212a, *Rep.* 410b f., 423d f., 540a f., 590e f., 611d f., *Phaedr.* 247c f., 276e–278b, *Tim.* 30a, cf. 36e f., 41b f., 90a f., *Theaet.* 176 f., *Laws* 713e, 796c, 813e f., 830e, 832, 942 f. Cf. also S. Frank 'Education of Women According to Plato' (in Lodge, *Plato's Theory of Education* (Kegan Paul, 1947), pp. 298–299. Cf. also Lodge, *ibid.*, pp. 114–137.

Further: judged empirically, the external movements of Socrates might well be thought a series of tragic mistakes; since they led, with apparent inevitability, to judicial condemnation and the draught of hemlock. But to a person of academic insight into higher values (such as we find surrounding Socrates at his death-scene), the life of Socrates shines like a transcendental beacon, pointing the way to the only true source of real value (cf. *Symp.* 216e f.).

18. *Laws* 653d f., 657c, 664d f., 672b f., 673c f., 788c f., 790c f., 815d f.

19. *Symp.* 176c f., *Rep.* 402e f., 571b f., *Tim.* 86a ff., *Phaedr.* 253d f., *Laws* 671a f., 672c f., 766a f., 793e f., 808d f.

20. *Rep.* 458c, 536a f., *Theaet.* 186b, *Laws* 709a f.

21. *Laws* 747c (cf. *Menex.* 237b f.); cf. also *Rep.* 421bc, 428d, 455ab, 474b, 475a, 490ab, 535a, *Phaedr.* 269d f., *Critias* 109d, *Laws* 655cd, 673cd, 690c, 709e f., 782e, 889a f.

22. *Prtg.* 327–328, 350d f., *Rep.* 374b, d, 434b f., 453bc, 474bc, *Phaedr.* 277b, *Laws* 654e f., 710a, 819b f., 870ab, 875b f., 904c.

23. *Laws* 644e, 656d f., cf. 654e f., 803a.

24. *Prtg.* 322b, *Critias* 116bc, *Laws* 681a. Even if we suppose Plato to have regarded a palace with its wall-sculptures (like the Parthenon friezes) as a kind of community dance frozen in marble, its architect is still dependent upon nature for his materials, and for their ability to provide shelter for the palace inmates. For a

modern parallel, cf. S. Alexander, *Beauty and the Other Forms of Value* (Macmillan, London, 1933), p. 16.

25. *Prtg.* 327 f., *Rep.* 374d, 412, 465a, *Laws* 657ab, 690a, 709e f., 714e, 715e, 879c, 917a.

26. *Phil.* 56b, *Laws* 673c, 889a f., 904c. Modern realism (naïve or 'innocent' realism, as represented in the work of S. Alexander) says much the same thing, although it selects for especial emphasis (1) the part played by the artist, as well as (2) the part contributed by nature. Cf. 'In general, when the artist paints from his image, . . . he is moulding it, in the product itself, into something . . . whose complete idea is revealed in the product itself' (S. Alexander, *Beauty and the Other Forms of Value*, Macmillan, London, 1933, p. 69). 'Every artist is in his degree like Shakespeare, who was a reed through which every wind from nature . . . blew music' (*ib.*, p. 74).

27. *Rep.* 369c f., 370d, 373b, 553cd, *Soph.* 219b ff., *Phil.* 65a, *Laws* 643b, 743d, 823f., 889d, 949e. Cf. R. C. Lodge, *Plato's Theory of Education*, pp. 33–40.

28. *Prtg.* 312, 318, *Lach.* 180c, *Rep.* 400b, 424c, *Tim.* 42c, *Crat.* 297c, 408d, *Phaedr.* 257c f., 277b ff., *Pol.* 271e f., *Laws* 644d f., 668 ff., 713d f., 799 ff., 803b f., 821, 885e, 886d, 887d f., 902b ff., 906a, 907a.

For a modern parallel to this tendency to view human art as (chiefly) a kind of craft, or as prose rather than poetry, cf. e.g. S. Alexander, *op. cit.*, pp. 16 ff., 'The greater part of what is commonly known as fine art is not art at all—but is craft . . . the greater part of our writing . . . is competent narrative or exposition, skilled but not beautiful or artistic writing such as deserves the name of literature. . . . Art grows out of craft and goes beyond it, when the worker handles his materials . . . for their own sake, and becomes contemplative instead of merely practical.'

29. E. Frank, *Plato u.d.s–g. Pythagoreer*, 1923, maintains (p. 119) that 'Plato's entire thought is, in a sense, one long Dialogue with materialism' (translation mine). Most readers believe they find this conflict in the *Crito, Phaedo, Gorgias, Protagoras*, and *Republic*. It is technically and more demonstrably present in *Theaet.* 155d f., 176, 184b ff., *Soph.* 246–248, *Laws* 885b ff., 903b ff. Warner Fite, *The Platonic Legend*, 1934, challenges the degree of 'idealism' usually seen in Plato's writings, and indeed largely denies its existence in the objective text. But see W. Becher, *Platon u.d. königliche Erziehungskunst*, 1937, pp. 15–16.

For Fichte, see *Erste Einleitung in die Wissenschaftslehre* (*Werke*, 1845, Vol. I, pp. 422–436. E. T. in Rand, *Modern Classical Philosophers*, Cambridge, Mass., revised edit., 1936, pp. 486 ff.).

The term 'Hylozoism' is used as I have used it, with reference to the early philosophers, not with the intention of suggesting a clear distinction between 'physical reality' and 'consciousness' (a later distinction), by many writers (cf. e.g., art. 'Nature' in *Ency. Brit.*, also art. 'Hylozoism'). Burnet (*Early Greek Philosophy*, 2nd edit., pp. 15–16) thinks the term Hylozoism, as used by modern writers, is liable to be misleading, by implying sharp distinctions which did not exist for the early nature-philosophers.

30. *Tim.* 28 ff., 53b ff., 69b ff.

31. *Tim.* 32e ff., 52 ff., 62d f., 81c f.

32. *Tim.* 46d f., 50c f., 57b f. For the conjunction of Pythagorean and Eleatic schools, cf. Ritter and Preller, *Hist. Phil. Graecae*, 8th edit., sect. 111, n.c., and Burnet, *op. cit.*, sects. 84, 90–96.

33. *Phdo.* 64 ff., *Rep.* 496c f., *Laws* 653c f. What Plato adds to the 'idealist' view

in the text is the specifically Socratic-Platonic 'idea' and the academic doctrine of *methexis* or participation (*Rep.* 497a, 517c f., 519c f., cf. Arist. *Metaph.* 987b 10 f.).

Plato rejects the 'idealistic' dogma of 'imitation', a 'mimicry' which is external and empty of value. It is possible (Plato teaches) to reach a degree of insight higher than that reached by these two schools of idealistic thought. For Pythagoreans and Eleatics, the extension of unity, order, and systematic law, is entirely *de haut en bas*. God doubtless enjoys the neat little system of inter-implying propositions with which He amuses His leisure hours. So, no doubt, do his 'friends', the idealists, too: i.e. the higher mathematicians of the Pythagorean school, and the contemplative metaphysicians of the Eleatic school. The intellectuals have a lovely time, playing their little game of dialectical checkers or cat's cradle. It even amuses them to discover, here and there in the empirical world, structures which seem to 'imitate', however imperfectly, the patternings constructed in the intellectuals' pure geometry. But of course they understand that all this is not to be taken seriously. Once a chaos, always a chaos. Arranging it externally into elements with mathematical interrelations, does not really change its nature. A chaos has no inwardness, and is quite incapable of understanding, co-operation, or positive, self-determined response. It cannot play the Absolute's game. However clearly you shuffle a mathematician's cards, you make no essential difference to it, none whatever.

All that 'persons of refinement' can do, is to withdraw (as far as possible) from commerce with their physical bodies, from commerce with the physical environment. Empirical living, whatever you do about it, is ultimately devoid of the slightest real value. Hunger and thirst, sex and ambition, to which the environment stimulates, are purely transitory: digressions which lead nowhere. A life of banking and banqueting, jockeying for power and junketing, gives rise, if you interact with the environment, to a lot of biosocial institutions, which it is amusing to contemplate and see through. But the whole thing is fundamentally meaningless, the clutter of the nursery which the metaphysician sweeps up and puts back into its box when the day is over, like the blocks in a child's game. Blocks they come in, and blocks they go out. All you can do, is to recognize its emptiness, and keep your mind clear of cant (cf. *Rep.* 583b–586c).

Plato's doctrine of 'participation' represents a development that goes beyond this standpoint. His teaching is, that persons of education and intelligence can do something better than withdraw to 'the intellectual place'. They can respond by co-operating with the Absolute and participating in the values which they help to create, and spread around them. Social institutions based upon the Platonic idea of Justice, with each citizen realizing his own value-potentialities in such a way as to make a specific contribution to the life of the whole community, genuinely participate in the value of ideal justice. To bring justice from its place in God's heaven, and to live in its spirit, is to incorporate it in human living; and such response on the part of leaders can assist men of goodwill in becoming truly holy, just, and wise: participating directly, while here on earth, in the life and tasks of the immortals.

In this way, the ideal blueprint, God's plan for humanity, with a place for everyone who will respond by filling that place (and so making his own voluntary contribution), holds before mankind something beyond what the Pythagoreans and Eleatics have to offer: mere negation and withdrawal. It provides a positive programme, to which all men of education and goodwill can contribute something of their own, and, in so doing, realize the highest satisfaction.

The plan can extend as far as it can meet with positive response: primarily to

E

men of the golden class, the 'alphas' educated into an understanding of the rationale of the ideal plan; secondarily to the silver class, the 'betas' of humanity, educated into an appreciation of the task and an ability to support their leaders, the 'alphas'. But thirdly, also to the 'gammas' and 'deltas', the artisans and labourers and, if slaves, also to the slaves: precisely insofar as they are endowed with minds and can respond appreciatively to the positive calls made upon their co-operative response. Beyond this, i.e. as far as the non-biological, inanimate side of existence is concerned, where there is no consciousness, there can (of course) be no understanding and no positive response. There the values are *merely* instrumental, as the Pythagoreans and Eleatics had believed.

Plato's picture in the *Laws* of the life of his model community, whose citizens are, for the most part, puppets living the best life possible for beings merely human, under the guidance of magistrates who co-operate with the divine plan, as far as this can be applied to actual flesh-and-blood human beings, illustrates the difference between his view of participation, and the Pythagorean view of withdrawal, of leaving the world to the flesh and (if any) the Devil.

34. *Prtg.* 318bc, 325e f., 327a–c, *Rep.* 396a, 397a, 596c ff., *Soph.* 233c ff., *Phil.* 55e f., 59a. Cf. also R. C. Lodge, *Plato's Theory of Education*, pp. 18–23, 28–30.

35. *Prtg.* 356cd, *Phdo.* 64c ff., 84, *Rep.* 394d ff., 475c ff., 524c ff., 531a–c, *Phil.* 55d ff.

36. *Apol.* 40c f., *Menex.* 235, *Gorg.* 523a ff., cf. 493 f., *Phdo.* 61d, 62b, 69a–d, 81 ff., *Rep.* 478a f., 586ab, *Soph.* 236e f.

37. *Gorg.* 493a, 507e (cf. *Crat.* 400c), *Phdo.* 62b f., *Tim.* 40c. For the evidence on the Pythagorean way of life, and its interpretation, see Burnet, *Early Greek Philosophy*, 2nd edit., sects. 39–45. Cf. also Ritter and Preller, *Hist. Phil. Graecae*, 8th edit., sects. 67, 82, 93, 94, with notes. For the Eleatic attitude, and especially for the tradition that Parmenides had himself been an adherent of the Pythagorean way of life, cf. Burnet, *op. cit.*, pp. 193–195, esp. p. 194.

38. The evidence for this is the poem of Parmenides, which has come down to us, and the remains (such as these are) of the book written by Zeno. For the pure contemplation of the Megarian school, and its relation to the Eleatics, cf. Ritter and Preller, sects. 288–290; also Hans Meyer, *Gesch. d. alten Philosophie* (1925), p. 127. Plato treats the Eleatics as 'idealists' (*Soph.* 246b, 248a). Burnet (who in general respects Plato's insight) thinks of Parmenides as 'the father of materialism' (p. 208), though compare what he says of Euclid of Megara, pp. 355–356.

39. Ritter and Preller, sects. 226, 235–238.

40. Ritter and Preller, sect. 227. *Crito* 44cd, *Prtg.* 318e, 323c, *Gorg.* 481d f., 482d ff., *Crat.* 385c, *Rep.* 426, 492 ff., *Tim.*, 47e, *Phil.* 67b, *Laws* 655, 658e f., 661a, 700e, 707d, 742e, 950bc. Cf. F. C. S. Schiller, 'Plato or Protagoras?' in *Mind*, Vol. XVII, p. 518–526 (1908)—also published as book (Blackwell, Oxford, 1908). John Dewey's *Democracy and Education* would, presumably, be regarded as the present-day Bible of this movement.

41. *Ion* 533d f., 535b f., *Prtg.* 326b, *Gorg.* 463a f., 501–505b, *Rep.* 386 ff., 396ab, 397a f., 425e f., 492b f., 517de, 520c f., 601 ff., *Tim.* 47c f., *Theaet.* 172c f., *Soph.* 222d. f., *Laws* 669c f., 682a, 700d f., 719c, 802d f., 810e f., 812d f., 814d ff.

42. *Prtg.* 312de, 318e, 328ab, *Gorg.* 449a, 452d f., 454b, e ff., 459a–460a, *Menex.* 234c ff., *Rep.* 493, *Phaedr.* 266d ff.

43. *Phdo.* 77e f. Cf. R. C. Lodge, 'What Socrates Knows', *Trnsctns. Roy. Soc. Can.*, 1951, Sect. II, pp. 19–34.

44. *Rep.* 431b f., *Pol.* 292c f., 310e f., *Laws* 693cd, 709c ff., 712a f., 715b, 756e f., 832b–d.

45. *Gorg.* 483a f., *Rep.* 400a, 401b f., 530, 617b, *Tim.* 35 ff., 43c f., 47d f., 53b ff., 80b, *Phil.* 17b f., 62c, *Laws* 654e f., 657a, 669c f., 672c f., 747c, 771e f., 790d f., 795d f., 812d f., 814d ff. Cf. Erich Frank, *op. cit.*, p. 155.

46. *Rep.* 370ab, 373b, 412c f., 413c f., 415a f., 423c, 453bc, 455ab, 533a, 535a f., 536a, 537a–d, 539e f., 546d ff., *Tim.* 19 3–5, *Laws* 829–831a, 904c, 908 f., 951e f., 961ab.

For discussion of the evidence on sex, cf. S. Frank, 'Education of Women according to Plato' in Appendix II to Lodge, *Plato's Theory of Education*, pp. 293 ff.

47. For discussion of the detailed evidence, see Lodge, *Plato's Theory of Education*, pp. 150–171.

48. *Rep.* 369d, 370ab, 544de, *Tim.* 17d f., 192. *Rep.* 373a f., implies that persons who specialize in painting, embroidery, working in gold and ivory, like hunters, actors, poets, rhapsodists, dancers, contractors, musicians, etc., have indeed a natural bent in the direction of their specific arts, but are NOT demanded by the 'idea' of a satisfactory community. Cf. also *Rep.* 412c f., 413d f., 415a f., 423c f., 458e, *Laws* 740e f., 772d, 929e f. But see, further, pp. 78–80.

49. *Rep.* 503b f., 537a–d, 540d f., 546, *Laws* 747a, cf. 657a, 889a f., 904c. Cf. also (for a modern treatment of this subject), Eduard Spranger, *Menschen-typen* (E.T., Pigors, 1928), esp. pp. 130–146. On the subject of the objective norms existing *in rerum natura*, as related to Plato, cf. John Wild, *Plato's Theory of Man. An Introduction to the Realistic Philosophy of Culture*, Cambridge, Mass., Harvard University Press, 1946, pp. 63, 72 f., 156–158, 203 f., 222, 270, 283.

50. *Phdo.* 77a, *Rep.* 525d f., *Tim.* 29e f., 53b ff., *Phil.* 56a, 57d, cf. 55c f., *Laws* 747a.

51. *Ion* 533e f., 534b f., 535a f., 536, *Crat.* 428c, *Meno* 93c f., 98d, *Phaedr.* 245a f., 250, 252e f., *Phil.* 51b f., 55d f., *Laws* 653c f., 657a.

52. *Tim.* 34c f., 47e f., 53b f., 69b, *Laws* 892 ff.

53. *Phdo.* 79e f., *Crat.* 388b–390e, 423c ff., 425e, *Rep.* 501a f., *Parm.* 132cd, *Laws* 653d f., 657a, 664d f., 709a f., 712a, 747d, 775e, 875b f., 889a f., 892a f., 903b f.

54. *Rep.* 375b f., 395bc, 412d f., 414e f., 415e f., 431c f., 442a f., 462 f., 501bc, 519d f., 540a f., *Laws* 644d f., 653 ff., 664, 665c, 670c f., 803d f., 810 ff., 921d f., 942a f. Cf. also Lodge, 'Plato and Freedom', *Trnsact. Roy. Soc. Can.*, XLIII, 1949, Sect. Two, pp. 90–99.

55. *Prtg.* 318a f., 328a f., *Gorg.* 449a–453a, 454c, 455a, 474b, 475e, *Rep.* 365d, 492 f., *Phaedr.* 260a, 261a f., 269d f., 271c f., *Theaet.* 167b, *Laws* 937b.

56. *Symp.* 209a f., *Rep.* 395bc, 398a, 540a f., 607a, *Pol.* 260b f., 276, 292b f., 295b, 305 ff., *Laws* 817a f.

57. *Gorg.* 452d f., 453e f., 503c, 515cd, 519a, *Rep.* 377a f., 382c, 414b f., 493, *Theaet.* 201a, *Soph.* 222c, *Pol.* 304c, *Phil.* 58a, *Laws* 663d f., 665c, 803e, 812bc, 816b f. Cf. S. Frank's Appendix II to Lodge, *Plato's Theory of Education*, pp. 288–304.

58. *Gorg.* 453e f., 503c, 515c f., 519a, 521d, *Meno* 93a f., 98b, *Symp.* 215e, *Rep.* 475c ff., 540ab, 600 f., 605a ff., *Phaedr.* 277e f.

For example, Ion, as a rhetorician of sorts (and only a rhapsodist at that, not an original composer of speeches), sincerely regards himself as essentially identical with a general, competent to direct combat practice in the field, *Ion* 541.

CHAPTER THREE

The Nature of Art, I

So far, we have considered what the Dialogues have to tell us of the *origin* of art, in a world of motion. Art originates in proportion as the would-be skilled craftsman is influenced by (1) the concrete rhythmic patternings found existing *in rerum natura*, (2) the abstractly regular patternings deduced by mathematical insight into the principle of the circle and what it circumscribes, and (3) a selection of patternings made to fit the needs of biosocial humanity. These three diverse influences are reduced to unity, or at least to a certain balance, by following the guidance of Socrates, the craftsman's son who first formulated the ultimate principle of ideality and value, and attracted men of goodwill to join, however informally, his fraternity dedicated to working out and applying the consequences of that principle.

We now pass to consider what the Dialogues have to tell us of the *nature* of art, i.e. of craftsmanship, as such. What is it, precisely, that the craftsman does? What are his functions as a craftsman, and his professional limitations? The Greek word *techne* = technique or trained skill, the activity of a professional *technitēs* (craftsman or artisan). It is applied indifferently to the trades of the carpenter and builder, or of the smith, potter, weaver, etc., on the one hand, and to the trades of the flautist, lyrist, or other musician, or of the painter, poet, or prose rhetorician, on the other. All are alike in being primarily professional activities: forms of manipulative dexterity acquired by practice, by repeated pushings and pullings applied to moving objects in a world of motions.[1]

Technical skill is acquired in the family of a *technitēs*: as an integral part of the professional life of that family. The carpenter's son, as a lad, plays with child-size models of his father's tools. He has a little hammer, a little ruler, etc., and acquires familiarity with their proper use by means of activities which are at first playful, non-professional. He imitates what he sees his father doing. This means (1) that he holds his tools as he sees his father holding the professional tools, and copies the motions of his father's hand. It means also (2) that he projects himself imaginatively into the position of (what he takes to be) a real carpenter. The movements of his hand are spontaneous. They are a form of play, and follow upon his imaginatively assumed attitude. They issue from the inside out, and are thus not purely external copyings of observed motions. He feels within himself the relation between what he is trying to do (as envisaged in his imagination) and the physical movements which lead to the results he sees before him. Eventually he develops a feeling for what movements lead to a result which he considers 'just right'. In this way he gradually acquires, not merely manipulative dexterity, but a trained empirical judgement, the judgement of the carpenter. Girls do something of the same sort, when they learn to cook by imitating what they see their mothers do in the kitchen.[2]

All this time, the carpenter's son is acting as his father's helper. This means that, at first, he merely fetches and carries for his father. But gradually he learns to hold and measure materials, to nail and cut, to make joints, to co-operate with his father in actually doing all the things that carpenters, as such, do. Before many years he will thus find himself in a position, not merely to act under authoritative direction, as a helper, but to use his judgement and direct himself. He will then be competent to work independently, to handle carpenter's tools and materials in accordance with his own trained empirical judgement.[3]

And there is something further. Carpentry is a business. By living in a carpenter's family, he will gradually have become familiar, not only with materials and tools, but also with the professional or business side of the carpenter's life. He will have become a tradesman, familiar with what is done in the trade. He will know all about customers, hours of work, fair prices, standard practices. In a word, he will have become a reasonably competent business man. He is now in a position to set up in business for himself, to marry and bring up his own family so that his sons also will learn to follow in the professional footsteps of the family.[4]

All this is very empirical: matter of practice rather than of theory. But this practical interaction with timber and nails, hammers and saws, is not the entire story. There *are* (doubtless) carpenters who remain handicraftsmen, clever in using their hands, and they never become anything more. But there is a higher level in the craft, which leads toward theory. There is a good deal of practical mathematics involved in measuring, in calculating the best use of materials and tools, and in considering how best to solve this or that problem. There is a good deal of arithmetic and geometry involved; and it is the craftsman who is able to understand and apply mathematical reasoning to his problems, who becomes a master-craftsman. He is a scientific carpenter, a master of scientific method in his field. His craft, originally manipulative, slips over gradually into the kind of science, empirical, but with a firm basis of mathematical reasoning, upon which the Pythagoreans pride themselves. A carpenter of this stamp follows mathematically exact patterns, as far as his medium permits, and you can count upon his reproducing the chief lines of a blueprint. Such a carpenter is almost an intellectual. He is liable to be called into consultation when engineering projects are under consideration. He is listened to as an expert, an authority who is more than a mere tradesman.[5]

And further: we have already noted that his craft is never isolated, tending to become a sort of 'craft for craft's sake'. It is always integrated with his life in his family, and with his life in those parts of the business community which are concerned, in one way or another, with carpentry. But this involves something we have not yet considered. It affects the whole of his work, his entire outlook upon his craftsmanship.

The patterns approved in his work depend directly, not only upon himself, but upon the recognized trade practices. The way he makes box-joints, doors and windows, chairs and tables, is prescribed for him by practices which have grown up in the course of centuries. These standard patternings are a function, partly of the craftsman's interaction with materials, partly (no doubt) of abstract mathematical deduction; but far more are they a function of the craftsmen's interaction with each other in their trade associations; and, even further, of their interaction with customers. The decision as to what patterns are professionally recognized as standard carpentry thus rests, not with the individual craftsman, except in a very few details, but rather with what may be considered the carpenters' union on the one hand, and the demands of cash customers on the other.[6]

What determines the nature of craftsmanship, as such, is thus largely (1) the medium upon which the craftsman works, (2) the abstract standards of patterning developed by mathematics, and (3) the ever-present biosocial influence of the community. All this is general-Hellenic. What Plato adds to these, as he elaborates what is involved in the 'idea of good' (as sought by the craftsman's son, Socrates), will be brought out later: after we have considered a further, somewhat different type of craft, the type illustrated by music and poetry.

The practising musician (like the carpenter) acquires his *techne* by living in the family of a professional, and practising at his craft until he acquires the degree of virtuosity he feels that he needs. Plato describes how the pupil learns to play the lyre. He sits beside his teacher, and imitates the teacher's every movement. He plays note for note in unison with his teacher, and gradually develops a sense of pitch, harmony, and rhythm, an empirical judgement of the correctness or incorrectness of the sounds his movements are producing.[7]

If he is to be an amateur, he is satisfied (as in writing) with a rather elementary degree of proficiency. For the future general citizen, it is enough if he can accompany himself in song and dance: playing the precise notes of the vocal part, one note for each syllable as sung, (and likewise one note for each movement of the dance part)— in the identical rhythm called for by the vocal pattern, which always follows the conventional standards: with only minor variations, and without flourishes, improvisations, or elaborate cadenzas of any description.[8]

If he is to be a professional, he of course goes further, much further. He then studies the concords, i.e. harmonies in which tones at different intervals (such as the fourth, fifth, and octave) are combined, in what the Greeks called 'magadizing': trying out the aesthetical effects, both in vocal and instrumental music, and in accompanying the voice with notes played an octave lower or higher, or at some other approved interval. He also introduces quite complicated variations, both in the vocal and in the instrumental part: not merely playing two or three notes of accompaniment to a single syllable, or singing two or more syllables to a single note, but suiting the sense to the sound, as well as the sound to the sense. The empirical judgement of a trained professional (like Damon) strongly approves such compositional practices, and it must be admitted that the popular judgement approves them too.[9]

The professional goes a good deal further. Greek practice had evolved a number of standardized scales: one for young men in martial mood, one for songs of revelry, one for solemn hymns to the great Gods, one for women, and so on. The 'Dorian mode' used only the rhythms appropriate for young men marching as to war. The 'Phrygian mode' made use only of slower rhythms, considered appropriate for respected citizens taking part in religious ceremonial processions; and so on and so forth. Such conventional scales are distinguished somewhat as our 'major' and 'minor' scales are popularly supposed to be appropriate for the expression of certain types of emotional experience: 'C major' being regarded as appropriate for 'cheerful' sentiments, while a funeral march should be set in a 'minor' key.

But the professional musician is well aware that such conventional rules are not, in themselves, of absolute validity. E.g. the most highly regarded of all funeral marches (Handel's March in *Saul*) is set in the key of 'C major'. Greek professionals thus do not hesitate to violate the conventions: arranging duets for male and female voices, and varying the scale and rhythms in accordance with their own developed musical judgement and taste: not even shrinking from what (to the amateur) would seem a shocking discord. Also, in preparing a composition for popular performance, professionals do not hesitate to employ trills, flourishes, and cadenzas, which would (rightly) be considered highly inappropriate for young citizen-amateurs. Here also, it must be admitted that the popular judgement tended to confirm the judgement of the trained professional, and to value more highly the taste of a Damon, who could improvise something new and original, to the taste which proved unable or unwilling to vary more than one iota from the conventional patterns.[10]

In all the above, the practising musician, as Plato says, depends very largely upon his empirical judgement, 'a certain power of guessing, given by experience and exercise', perfected by long and arduous practice. If you imagine a Greek flute, with holes cut for the various notes, and then imagine a flautist trying to play an intermediate note, for which no hole has been cut: you will see him putting his finger part-way across a hole, and listening to the sound which comes through, covering the hole more or less until his trained musical feeling assures him that the resulting tone is 'just right'.[11]

So much for the practical side of the craft. The empirical study of consonances and dissonances, of the emotional quality of scales and rhythmic sequences, takes the musician just so far: far enough for the reproduction of musical patterns standardized by professional and group approval, and for the establishment of a number of conventional rules for amateurs. But it leaves, for the inquiring mind, a number of questions of a most interesting character: questions, the answering of which leads right out of practice into theory, the kind of theory which would appeal to the Pythagorean type of scientist.

Thus, if tones are produced by air-vibrations (as any Pythagorean can demonstrate experimentally), and you can measure and count their vibration-frequencies: you can establish as a fact that there is a definite mathematical basis for each of the tones used in the standard scales. You can also study the intervals between tones, and can establish a definite formula of proportion for the various consonances recognized in Hellenic music: for the octave, for the fourth, and for the fifth. Just why the Hellenic ear should develop an absolute pitch, and should accept, as suitable for Hellenic music, only the tones produced by certain vibration-frequencies, neglecting or rejecting as unsuitable all intermediate tones (all equally possible of objective production), remains something of a mystery.[12]

But there are certain highly interesting and suggestive analogies: e.g. between the specific colours recognized in visual experience and the specific tones recognized in auditory experience; and between musical and vocal sounds.[13] Vowels, semi-vowels, and consonants, and their various combinations into syllables, words, and phrases, prove absolutely fascinating. These sounds, like musical tones and like dance-movements, are all forms of 'gesture', i.e. of expressive movement with a mathematical formula underlying its sense-perceivable rhythms or vibration-frequencies.[14] Perhaps it is because of this analogy, with its underlying mathematical basis, that words can be chanted as well as spoken, and that an instrumental accompaniment of song and dance is artistically possible; so that choral music (employing words, music, and dance-movements simultaneously, all expressing the same meaning) has become, pedagogically speaking, perhaps the most important of all the Hellenic arts. Perhaps, indeed.[15]

Questions of this sort lend themselves to empirical investigation; and Plato depicts for us, on the one hand, the experimental practitioners, 'setting their ears before their understandings', as they try to determine least-audible differences of one sort or another, and, on the other hand, the superior Pythagorean scientists, determining for all such phenomena their correct mathematical formulas.[16]

The Pythagorean scientists insist that they are just as much devoted to the facts of experience as are their simpler colleagues. But they are a little inclined (as intellectuals tend to be) to be carried away by the mathematical consequences of their own reasoning. They can see a striking mathematical analogy between the tonal intervals of this or that Hellenic scale, and other interval-ranges in the great cosmos. When Pythagorean astronomers represent the celestial bodies as all strung out along a single line, and measure the intervals which separate one from another, thus establishing a sort of 'scale' for the heavenly bodies, no great harm is done. But when the Pythagoreans proceed to discover that the mathematical basis for the astronomic scale-intervals is practically identical with the mathematical basis of the 'enharmonic' scale of the stricter forms of Greek music, it is perhaps only human, if they proceed to speculate a little.

Can we blame them if they conclude that, where small bodies, moving with such and such vibration-frequencies, produce musical tones, verifiable as such in the Pythagorean laboratory, larger bodies, moving with practically the same vibration-frequencies, must be producing musical tones too? In fact, somewhat similar tones? Of course, being beyond the range of human audibility, such alleged cosmic music is incapable of direct verification. And the thought that human music is (or at least could be and should be) an imitative reproduction of the 'music of the spheres', is undoubtedly a little more speculative than a good scientist altogether likes. Yet, the human end of the analogy is directly verifiable; and so is the mathematical part. Does not this make the conclusion, if not demonstrably factual, at least not improbably possible?[17]

Be that as it may, the mathematical method opens up a number of lines of inquiry in regions where mere empiricism is soon baffled; and it is quite clear that behind the musical practitioner with his routine production of accepted tonal and rhythmic patterns conditioning the range and depth of his musical judgement, there stands the scientist: with his mastery of mathematical technique and his uncanny insight into the intellectual implications of this question and that. Although the Pythagorean brotherhood professes to remain very close to experience, and to believe in verification (wherever possible) for their theories, who does not see that, by freeing their mathematics from the limitation to verifiable phenomena, it might be possible to go further, as a student trained in the Eleatic school would insist, much further, into the region of pure theory? Why not work out, as Plato's 'Timaeus' tries to do, e.g. an intellectually perfect system of inter-implying scales, without reference to their human audibility or inaudibility? Would not ideal music, so based, be a fitting companion-piece to the perfect system of inter-implying civic classes in the ideal republic, also constructed without assured reference to the realizability of such a system with merely empirical human beings?[18]

It remains to consider the social and biosocial influences upon the musician's craftsmanship. Living, as the musician does, in the family of a master-craftsman, he participates directly in whatever influences are at work, right there in the professional's family. The emphasis upon practice, unremitting attention to the acquisition of the musician's technique, has already been indicated. As he develops further in judgement and musical insight, he finds himself sharing, not only in the professional idealism of the skilled craftsman, but also in his critical dissatisfaction with what has already been achieved. Hence his experimentalism, his determination to advance in directions which are new, hitherto untried.[19] This leads him further: not only in practice, but especially in the direction of theory; and as to how far the professional can go, who can say?

It is here that the third factor in his development, the social and biosocial influence of the community, not merely the musical fraternity, but the community of general citizens, comes in. In preparing himself to give a public performance, the virtuoso is quite unable (at any rate until he has achieved a recognized position) to consider merely himself and his own powers of self-expression. There can be no question of 'art for art's sake'. He has to consider what his audience expects, what it will demand, what it will pay for.[20]

A musical festival in Ancient Greece is a public competition. There are 'adjudications, prizes, and public encomia'. It is vital to be among the winners; and the winner is that competitor who, for one reason or another, makes the greatest impression upon his judges. In a democracy, that means, in the last resort, the public. It is the public's applause, its cheering or hissing, that makes or breaks a man. Such a public has indeed a certain feeling for musical values. But you cannot count upon any depth in that feeling. A public audience is most easily impressed—how? By force and brilliance, by restless and exciting rhythms, by dynamic contrasts, by whole cascades of notes, by tricks of virtuosity, by clever mimicry of recognizable objects, by melodramatic stimulation of superficial emotions: in a word, by display.[21]

In order to achieve success, a young musician necessarily gives his public what that public wants. He amplifies his master's voice: exciting and soothing his public, flattering its susceptibilities, enhancing its sense of its own might, majesty, dominion, and power, practically applauding it to its face: so that an Athenian feels, How wonderful it is to be an Athenian, living in Athens, now! No young performer, if he is to make a biosocial success of his life, can afford not to cultivate the self-feeling of his community. Is it conceivable that any idealistic feeling for the higher reaches of his art, on the side of insight, can hold out against the pressure of the community, with its unceasing demand for the magical spells which keep its head among the clouds? No. Music, like rhetoric, is a community art; necessarily so.[22]

Music, that is to say, as produced by artistic craftsmen, in accordance with the professional standards of the craft, is guided by three great influences: (1) the influence of nature, with its objective rhythms and tones; (2) the influence of mathematical theory, as developed by the Pythagoreans; and (3) the biosocial pressure of the community. The first of these great influences, is fundamental, and many authorities consider it final. It forces upon the human organism (with its bi-lateral symmetry and its rather simple life-cycle) a few basic human patterns; and, in so far as its influence predominates, it makes of music a transcription, into the human clef, of the rhythms of the environment. The musician is thus a trained puppet, dancing as nature pulls the strings.[23]

The second of these influences intellectualizes music. It enables the craftsman to apprehend the mathematical formulations of the behaviour of the environment on the one hand, and of his own organism, on the other. Such insight encourages him to act intelligently and deliberately, to form his music (as indeed he tries to form his entire life) upon the music of the spheres: with an intellectual objectivity, and with the serene self-confidence which comes to those who feel that reality is on their side—that the reason in the world, and the reason in themselves, are one and the same reason. The Pythagorean musician withdraws from the crude dynamics and sensuous emotionalism of the nature-craftsman. He retires, with a few choice spirits, to an ivory tower, and devotes himself to cataloguing, contemplating, and enjoying (with a refined sense of superiority) the mysterious harmonies, the concords and discords which so plainly (to the initiate) make of every phase of existence the thing that it is. The scientific background of his Pythagorean associates confirms him in these fundamental beliefs; and his mathematical music makes him every day, in every way, a better, a more convinced Pythagorean.[24]

The third of these influences humanizes music. Some critics (and Plato is sometimes thought to be among them) might say, it vulgarizes music: robs it of its austerity, its self-discipline, its spiritual purpose, its intellectual quality; it drags music down to earth, to common folksiness, to meaningless biosocial excitement, leading nowhere but to more of the same.[25] But the humanists deny this. The humanists claim that nature's music de-humanizes. It is sound and fury, signifying nothing; nothing, that is, of human interest and value. Such music impresses. It may discourage initiative. It may leave humanity coldly indifferent. But it is not constructive. It has no positive social value.[26] So also with the abstract music of the mathematicians. It professes to withdraw men from ordinary biosocial interests; and perhaps it does what it says it does. But after all, this is merely being negative.

Music which has a definite biosocial function is not like this. It does not make of its performers stargazers or dwellers in ivory towers. It does something to fit them for peace and war. It makes them better citizens, better human beings: better in all ways of social usefulness.[27]

The music that counts, from the humanist standpoint, is the trumpet-call which brings the people together when danger threatens, when the enemy is at the gate; the flute-music or the lyrical accompaniment to festive song, which brings the people together for religion, for social recreation, and for the other purposes of peace. It is exemplified in the patriotic airs, the wedding music, folk-songs, and the like: which fill the hearts and souls of men, women, and children with the patterns of democratic humanity.[28]

What if popular music *is* sentimental, melodramatic, exciting: a sort of gathering song which is non-logical, not particularly intellectual? So much the better. That is the way people, most human beings, are; and the function of music is (and should be) to enhance the community's self-feeling: to make Sparta more warlike, Corinth more commercial, Cyrene more pleasure-giving, Athens more cultured, more many-sided in its freedom, more democratic. Music is (and should be) a form of community self-expression: drawing its strength, its meaning, and its value from the community which expresses itself therein. The influence of the community, in a word, socializes and humanizes the work of the musician.[29]

Faced with these three demands upon his craftsmanship, what does the individual musician do? The best he can, of course. He is, after all, only a puppet, drawn now in this direction, now in that. What does Plato think is the best he can do, and what are the conditions, the social and political conditions, which make it possible for him to do this best? The answer will be postponed until we have considered yet a third artistic craft: one to which Plato gives a great deal of attention. Meanwhile, all we can say is that, with Socratic idealism at the back of his mind, Plato criticizes all three influences as being too much concerned with actualities and too little with ideals; and that he seeks to discover and synthesize or balance, in accordance with the ultimate principle of ideality and value, the positive value-potentialities which all three doubtless contain.

Poetry is an outstanding example of human craftsmanship; and to discussion of its nature, its functions and limitations, a relatively large portion of many of the Dialogues is devoted. Poetry is treated as a metrical species of rhetoric, the art which uses speech persuasively, especially in addressing large popular audiences. As such, it is akin to the art of the public dancer, who sways audiences by the expressive movements of his body and its costume, and to the art of the musician, which we have just considered.[30]

In fact, it is a question whether we are right in speaking of three kindred arts. Do not the three more properly fuse, so as to form one art? To the Greeks, a poet is no mere script-writer, inscribing upon his tablet or papyrus words which might conceivably be read in private isolation, coldly and silently. What he actually writes down are lifeless marks, signs, indications, what we nowadays call the book of words. But the poet's art covers more than words. The words are written to be recited publicly, acted out by a rhapsodist, a chorus, or a dramatic cast, before an audience, with appropriate gestures. Poetry is what is called a 'co-operative' art. It requires the full co-operation (as with the art of Wagner, or of the modern cinema or television) of whole hosts of technicians: musicians, trainers, robe-makers, scene-shifters, conductors, and what not.[31]

The poet himself amplifies the message indicated by his written words. He has selected his words, not merely for their logical meanings, but for their metrical and musical qualities, for their emotional associations, for their effects in stimulating the imagination, and indeed the entire life, of his audience. He does not so much play upon words and phrases, as make use of words and phrases, together with every form of expression at his command, to play upon the audience: exciting and soothing their feelings in full range.[32] So well understood is this, that the Greek poet is frequently referred to, not so much as a script-writer or word-artist, as in the guise of a dramatist, a composer of musical drama, as the author of songs, chants, and expressive dances. It is in production, in public performance in which the entire community participates, that his words come most completely alive, and that the quality of his many-sided craftsmanship is most truly revealed.[33]

Let us begin by looking at language: of which the poet and orator make expressive use, as an instrument of persuasive eloquence. Language originates in the cries and other gestures of infancy, of adolescence, of maturity, and of senescence. These are all primarily reactions to stimulation, whether from without or from within. They are all racial rather than individual: universal-racial. Any mother or nurse, any father or wife, any physician, teacher, or intelligent citizen, can understand their import and can respond with sympathetic attention and, if necessary, assistance. Non-logical, racial, and social: the smiles and frowns of babyhood, the wrigglings and gurglings of joy, the murmurs of comfort and well-being, the breathings which betoken a lapsing into sleepiness—and, on the other hand, the cries and other movements of hunger, pain, and pure rage—are all as characteristically specific as the bleating of a sheep or the baying of a hound.

Such cries are indeed gestures: forms of communication within the species.[34] From the very first they are expressive, doubly expressive. On the one hand, as forms of motion, they perform something of the service which rocking in the mother's arms performs. They serve to release, to relax, to relieve tension. Many dances in later life have no other function. Physicians prescribe them for that precise purpose.[35] The war-cry, the mating-cry, the greeting-cry, the cry of the pack lamenting its lost leader, all these have this kind of expressive significance. To express sadness by a flood of tears, or by some more decorous ritual of grief such as an elegiac poem or a funeral oration recited *in memoriam*, is something more than merely giving way to sorrow. It is a form of exercise. It provides a suitable outlet through which the noxious element in the inner stimulus is shaken out and purged until it disappears: leaving the organism and the community the better for its passage.[36]

An art based upon these racial expressions of feeling is of directly social and biosocial usefulness. The periodic community emotionalism of art festivals, whether religious, dramatic, or commemorative, resembles the function of the regular sports meets, of whose value Plato speaks with such conviction. It eventually reconditions the participants for the sanities of regular day-by-day life and work.[37]

On the other hand, such cries are expressive also in a more objective sense. They give what Plato calls 'information', information, not merely about the state of the organism and its feelings, but about the environment with which the organism is being interactive. Such 'information', communicated to other members of the species by means of these primitive cries, and by gestures such as pointing, while 'objective' in its reference,[38] is not nearly as objective as a trained scientist would like it to be. For one thing, it is not expressed exactly, in the kind of terminology which the Pythagoreans, for instance, use in order to achieve precision in their reasoning. The medium of communication is biological and biosocial; and the information such primitive language conveys, is not merely vague. It is strongly coloured by the interests, the hopes and fears, of the interactive organism, by its racial and social bias. So completely is it thus coloured, that the information so communicated may be quite at variance with what scientists (later) believe to be the actual facts of a given situation. Thus, to uneducated common sense, seeing is believing; and a good many astronomical happenings, as interpreted in terms of crude sense-data, are popularly understood in ways which the scientific astronomer, with his more technical methods of reasoning, believes he can prove to be the precise opposite of the truth.[39]

And the same is doubtless the case with most human experiences. As seen through what we may call the human spectrum, objects are usually apprehended in ways which distort them; and the employment of everyday language (a medium useful, primarily, for biosocial communication) may be (and frequently is), from the standpoint of exact science, grotesquely misleading. From the standpoint of science and philosophy, persons who regard folk-language, with its biosocial implications, as suitable for expressing objective truth, are in the very lowest stage of intelligence. There is, indeed, in such language a reference which is objective; but it is almost hopelessly misleading and obscure.[40]

Out of such folk-language, arises gradually the artistic use of language by the orator and the poet. The orator, as such, is not particularly interested in objective truth. His profession requires that he should be competent to sway the feelings of crowds. He is not expected to instruct them: to speak as a scientist would speak to his brother-scientists. He is expected to use the kind of language that will get in under the skin of his hearers and will impinge directly upon their natural, biosocial feelings: setting in motion the action-rhythms which lead to united, community response. He becomes an expert, a practical expert, in producing this kind of response: so stimulating the action-patterns of his hearers, that they follow his lead at once, *en masse*. They do not reason, ask questions, or criticize. They simply convince themselves, by the interior force of the feelings which he awakens, that what he suggests, whether for peace or for war, is the only thing to do: the one thing that they all accept as objective—accept delightedly, tumultuously, carrying themselves along by the violence of their own glorious applause.[41]

So too of the poet. His themes are folk-themes, his imagery is folk-imagery, and his music is folk-music. His work is thus felt to be natural by his fellows. It amplifies by racial melody and rhythm the penetrative power of his message, as this 'makes its way into the inward places of the soul', and there exercises its uniquely persuasive power, its educative charm. Poets are the nation's natural teachers. It is by singing these folk-songs that members of the group, whoever they are, 'old or young, bond or free', charm themselves into the *ethos* of their folk. By yielding, with the full force of their imagination, to the poetic spell, and co-operating to the utmost in developing the non-logical, racial basis of their personalities, they become truly members one of another: welding themselves securely into a living community of feeling.[42]

And further: like the carpenter, the musician, and the orator, the poet does not stand apart from his community. He is one of those for whom he writes, the friends who sing his songs. He is a part of them, as they are a part of him. Homer is really the mouthpiece of his nation. It is the nation's own songs he writes, writes for the nation to sing, to sing to itself. His aim is (whether consciously or unconsciously) to reveal the community to itself, to assist it in expressing itself, in bringing to birth in actual, concrete social living, the aristocratic potentialities it possesses within itself. In the end, it is the community itself which is the great teacher: the stimulus, critic, and directive guide of the poet's craftsmanship; and, through his craftsmanship, of itself and of its own efforts to achieve its own destiny.[43]

Such are, in general, the views natural to craftsmen themselves: of craftsmen, and of the humanist teachers who profess to be their spokesmen. In a *Militärstaat* like Sparta, all its institutions have a military twist, a one-sided bias in the direction of the spirit which makes warriors, warriors. The poet Tyrtaeus, and the constitution of Sparta traditionally ascribed to Lycurgus, are obviously made for each other. They are two aspects, two inter-implying sides, of one

F

and the same spirit. In a cultural democracy like Athens, all institutions have a bias, a pronounced bias, in the direction of freedom and self-development, cultural self-development. Athenian poets and orators are the classical exponents of freedom: freedom of thought, freedom of speech, freedom of action, freedom of worship; freedom, if the citizens so desire, to withdraw and to pursue their ideals elsewhere. The choruses of Aeschylus, the great speeches of Pericles, the dramatic conflicts of Sophocles and Euripides, the mingling, in Aristophanes, of intense patriotism, roaring farce, and great lyrical beauty, are all integral parts, partly causes and partly effects, of the many-sided freedom which is the spirit of democratic Athens.[44]

Such is the humanist theory of the nature of poetry: a theory partly shared by Plato himself. It is clearly factual. Of the difference, amounting almost to open conflict, between the scientists and themselves, the humanists are well aware; and if the intellectuals denounce poetry as primitive and non-logical, as naïvely unmodern, uneducated, and unscientific, the poets and their humanist defenders retort by criticizing the intellectuals in their turn as disruptive influences: as unnatural, inhuman, withdrawers into ivory towers, cultivators of ingrowing souls, and the like.[45]

Mathematicians and intellectuals have, however, a more positive theory of art. They develop a language, a poetry, and a music of their own. Their mathematics overflows, with positive benefit, into every human art and craft. Their language is (of course) the technical language of mathematics itself. Mathematical reasoning has a certain persuasiveness, a convincing quality of its own. Whatever can be reduced to numbers, does not require an undercurrent of dance-rhythms and primitive folk-cries, in order to prove its case. It is convincing, however, only to mathematicians who have been trained to respond to its appeal. It does not have the especially convincing power of oratory and poetry; and in dealing with non-mathematicians, or with intellectuals who (for one reason or another) hesitate to accept the conclusions of purely technical reasoning, it requires to be supplemented by the more universally persuasive power of the orator or poet.[46]

Scientists such as the Pythagoreans are able, however, indirectly to make persuasive use (even in the form of poetry) of the language of ordinary life. A good many of their insights have social or biosocial implications; and these can be expressed in ordinary, biosocial language. And sometimes it is possible to go further. When the new scientists have succeeded in discovering the mathematical formulas which underlie the primitive rhythms and cries of nature, they can rewrite the traditional poetry: translating the vernacular into something more nearly approaching the premises and conclusions of mathematics. They can also write a new literature: translating back the sound conclusions of their technical reasoning into something more nearly approaching the vernacular. In so doing, they are guiding themselves, not by the primitive and unscientific superstitions of nature-folk, but by the latest and most sophisticated scientific hypotheses.

A music based upon a mathematically standardized scale may sound, to unsophisticated ears, a little queer. But at least it is in accord with the best scientific thought, attuned to what the world's leading thinkers are coming to believe. As such, it is obviously (to intellectuals) more acceptable in principle than the 'popular' melodramatic stuff that appeals to the uneducated. And as to this 'queerness' of the new, mathematical music, this is largely a matter of familiarity. Intensity, recency, and, above all, frequency, will enable an audience to enjoy intellectual music quite as much as 'popular' music; and where the intellectual music is, on all rational grounds, infinitely preferable to 'popular' music, the matter of its enjoyment can safely be left to sound educational training.[47]

As far as the sentiments are concerned, it should be plain that enhancement, glorification of the new way of life, the mathematical scientist's way of living, will be the new poetry's main theme. If it is true that you become a good Spartan or a good Athenian by merging your entire personality with the poetry which praises Sparta or Athens to its face: it is equally true that, if you identify yourself wholly and without reserve with the poetical glorification of Pythagorean brotherhood and the co-operative pursuit of scientific enlightenment, you will gradually enable yourself to withdraw from the uneducated stage of biosocial impulse, with its fever and fret and its primitive standards. You will leave the lowest stage of intelligence (*eikasia*), and will advance toward a higher level (*dianoia*): at which you will achieve the serenity, the confidence, the intellectual superiority of those who identify themselves with the spirit of the new science.[48]

So far, we have studied two views of the nature of poetry held by Plato's contemporaries: (1) the humanist or pragmatist view, maintained by the group of gifted authorities labelled 'sophists' in the Dialogues; and (2) the more technical view maintained by 'the so-called Pythagoreans', the scientists whom Plato regards as 'friends of ideas', almost-idealists. There is yet a third view (3), indicated in our discussion, but not yet brought into precise focus. This is the naïvely realist view, the view of the ancient quasi-'positivists', which seeks to bring out and render authoritative the objective reference: the reference to an independently existing reality. This is vaguely felt by the humanists, and is deliberately rejected, on account of its inexactitude, by the apostles of mathematical precision.

Why do both groups reject this third view, the position associated with the earlier, pre-mathematical scientists of Ionia? The humanist critics follow Protagoras, with his propagandist theory of truth and knowledge. They take their stand upon the undoubted experiences of social and biosocial living. They believe that the vague reference to something objective, with which human beings are presumably interactive in the struggle for existence, cannot be followed up and made more precise. There is no such thing (Protagoras teaches) as objective 'truth'. The propositions in which we formulate our practical beliefs cannot be judged by the degree of their conformity to some outside 'reality'.[49]

Attempts to discover the nature of a concretely existing reality, physical and existing in complete independence of the tissue of human hopes and fears (through which we indirectly sense its existence), have always (so Gorgias teaches) failed. And they always will fail. Either the alleged 'reality' does not exist 'in itself' at all; or, if we grant it some kind of transcendental existence, this falls outside human knowledge. We cannot enter into knowledge-relations with it. Finally, if, in some queer way, we do have some feeling of its objectivity in relation to ourselves: we cannot convert this utterly vague feeling into clear-cut discursive concepts. Our acquaintance is too slight for accurate description. Grant that we somehow participate in it: we prove unable to communicate this experience to others. No developed theory is possible. At all points, we are driven back upon ourselves: upon our instinctive cries and movements, our biosocial attitudes. For humanism, then, the naïve realism of early positivist science represents a standpoint which has to be abandoned.[50]

And how about the mathematical scientists? According to Plato, they do indeed believe in the empirical objectivity of the reality with which they are in contact. But the point is this: this reality can be known only *via* mathematics. Only in so far as its rhythmic structural patterns are of regular geometrical types, does reality fall within the area of what a refined mind will admit that it knows. Such knowledge is positive and empirical in its reference, but is universal and necessary, *a priori*, in its technique.

Mathematical science is technical knowledge, constructed by technicians for technicians. It is utterly beyond the ken of *hoi polloi*, the 'outer barbarians' who understand only what they can 'grasp in their hands'.[51] If, from the standpoint of mathematical science, humanism or pragmatism belongs to the very lowest stage of intelligence (*eikasia*), the naïve realism of the early positivists belongs to a not much higher stage (*pistis*). Both fall within the area of 'appearance', and completely fail to reach the level of knowledge (*episteme*). Objective knowledge is, in fact, strictly reserved for intellectuals. It is a mystery from which all non-initiates are excluded.[52]

In the Dialogues, this third view—that poetry, oratory, music, and all the arts and crafts depend upon and are somehow expressive of the positive nature of a physical reality, existing in its own right—is not usually treated with sympathy. It tends to be referred to contemptuously, as in the many suggestions that art is a form of 'mimicry': that poetry is frequently onomatopoeic, that music often reproduces the mere sounds of inanimate nature—whistling, croaking, and crashing its way to popular applause. Such mimetic art is without insight into values: into law, order, and intelligible significance. It lowers him that speaks and him that hears: levelling downward toward pure chaos.[53]

NOTES

1. It might be thought that the artistic craftsman whose medium is language, whether prose or verse, does not precisely 'manipulate' anything. It might easily be supposed that the words with which he plays his artistic game, like the technical symbols employed by the mathematical physicist of those times (Pythagorean), are not physical, objects that you could push, or pull about. Gorgias (for instance) clearly accepts this imputation. He also quite evidently feels that his own craft (oratory) is a higher form of art than any of the physically manipulative techniques. (He *might* have said, it belongs, not to the level of *pistis*, but to the higher level of *dianoia*, like Pythagorean science.) Protagoras plainly feels that rhetoric is a master-art. It is much the same thing as what in other Dialogues is referred to as the 'royal' art of governing human beings. In a word, it is the art of social and political 'weaving', which belongs at least to the level of *dianoia* (*Lach.* 188c f., 194ab, *Prtg.* 318, 328b, *Gorg.* 450b f., 452d f., 453e, 456a f., *Rep.* 530d–531c, *Pol.* 267a f., 280a f., 292d f., 303a f., 311bc).

Socrates, while apparently agreeing that the medium of language differs somehow from the physical medium of the other arts and crafts, insists upon regarding the 'master-art of persuasion' (as practised by the actual professionals of his time, though possibly not including Gorgias personally) as an art of 'flattery'. He treats rhetoric as a morally inferior craft, like the artifices of cooking and attiring, i.e. as devoid of ideal insight.

For Plato's own attitude toward the artistic use of language, whether in verse or in prose, when directed by idealistic insight (*Laws*, 811, 817), see pp. 79, 97, 125, 144, and R. C. Lodge, *Plato's Theory of Education*, pp. 150–183. Meanwhile, it may be sufficient to refer to the professional rhapsodist who (although using words) clearly handles them as forms of 'gesture', amplifying their expressiveness by manipulating his eyes, mouth, head, hands, feet, and indeed the whole of his highly trained, expressive body (*Ion* 535c f., *Crat.* 423a f.).

2. *Rep.* 421d, 455cd, 466e f., 537a, *Laws* 643bc.

3. *Rep.* 455b f., cf. 349d f.

4. *Meno* 85c, *Rep.* 349c f., 498a f., 525c, 565a, *Laws* 643b.

5. *Apol.* 22cd, *Prtg.* 356cd, *Rep.* 524c ff., 527c, 531, *Phil.* 55d f., 57cd, 59a, *Laws* 747b.

6. *Rep.* 369d ff., 372e f., 377, 386 ff., 401, 595 ff., *Laws* 801, 817d, 829d. We might compare what Plato has to tell us of the standardization of patterns in poetry, painting, and music (cf. *Rep.* 349d f., *Pol.* 299d f., *Laws* 802bc, 816c–e).

7. *Rep.* 349de, 530c f., 531ab, *Phil.* 55c f., *Laws* 812c f. For a modern example, cf. Haydn's *Il maestro e lo scolare*, a piano duet where the teacher first performs a phrase, then it is played by the pupil, and finally, by both together, in unison.

8. *Laws* 764c f., 798e–800a, 810a, 812d. Normally, music (like any other trade-craft) is handed down from father to son, in the biological family. But not only biological sons learn music. In a Hellenic community, it is possible for the sons and daughters of well-to-do persons to take lessons as amateurs, paying fees to the professional; and, in the model city, Plato envisages the State appointment of certain professionals as community music-teachers. Their function is to teach a three-year 'brief course in the fundamentals of musical practice' to all teen-age citizens (about 1,600 pupils in any given year—see R. C. Lodge, *Plato's Theory of Education*, p. 285), irrespective of the pupil's capacity and taste, and irrespective of whether their parents wish or do not wish their children to take music lessons.

This same practice, of studying a trade non-professionally, but as an amateur, paying a fee and learning the bare essentials 'as a part of liberal education', is recognized as extending, not merely to crafts like painting and sculpture, but generally: e.g. to wood-working, to weaving and dyeing, probably also to cooking and dress-making (in which the Greek housewife needed to know enough, at least, to direct her operatives, cf. *Prtg.* 312ab, 326a–c, 327a–c, *Rep.* 455cd, 475cd).

9. *Laws* 660b f., 669c f., 812d f. (with E. B. England's notes *ad loc.*—*The Laws of Plato*, 2 vols., 1921). Cf. also *Tim.* 80b, and Aristot. *Problem.* xix, 18. On the other side, cf. H. E. Wooldridge, *Oxford History of Music* (1901), Vol. I, pp. 9–13; also E. Frank, *Plato u.d.s–g. Pythagoreer*, pp. 181–184.

For a modern example of the kind of thing Plato has in mind as not unsuitable for professionals, we might think of Purcell, who, in arranging his musical accompaniments, follows (for the most part) the words, with one note of the accompaniment for each syllable of the text, but varies, with tasteful judgement: as in the song 'I attempt from lo-o-ove's sickness to fly-y-y-y-y-y-y-y i-in va-ain, since I am myself my own fever, since I am myself my own fe-e-ever and pain' (cf. *Rep.* 400a f.).

10. *Rep.* 398c ff., 424, *Laws* 655a f., 658e ff., 665a f., 669a ff., 798c f., 812b. Similarly in modern times, e.g. from Handel to Beethoven, the real test of musicianship was, 'Can the candidate improvise, create something new?' Handel frequently provided only a 'figured bass', expecting the performer to create his own accompaniment from Handel's indications. As we know, when Beethoven performed for Mozart, playing difficult compositions of Mozart's own, Mozart was not interested. It was only when he provided Beethoven with a theme, and heard Beethoven, then and there, create new and original variations upon the theme, that he took Beethoven seriously—very seriously, in fact. And we know that Beethoven, listening to the fashionable Righini improvising, inquired, 'When is he going to stop his *ewiges Präludiren*, and create music?'.

11. *Rep.* 399d, 601d f., *Phil.* 55e f.

12. *Rep.* 530c f., *Phil.* 17b f., 24a f., 26a, 56bc, *Laws* 653e f.

13. *Crat.* 423 ff., *Theaet.* 206ab, *Phil.* 51b f., *Laws* 802de.

14. *Rep.* 522cd, *Tim.* 43c f., 45b f., 64b f., *Theaet.* 153e f., 182, 186, *Laws* 669d.

15. *Rep.* 399e f., 404d f., 522c, *Laws* 653d f., 654e f., 670, 672c f.

16. *Rep.* 531a f., *Phil.* 17b f.

17. *Rep.* 617b f., with Adam's notes, *Tim.* 35b f., 80b, with Taylor's *Commentary*, and E. Frank, *op. cit.*, p. 155. Cf. also Aristot. *De Caelo*, 290b 12 ff.

18. *Tim.* 35b f., E. Frank, *identid.*, Taylor, *Commentary*, pp. 239-246.

19. *Rep.* 349d f., 397a f., 531a f., *Symp.* 187b f., *Laws* 669b f., 812c f.

20. *Rep.* 349e, 399c, 492b f., 601b f., *Laws* 700 f.

21. *Rep.* 397d f., 604e f., *Laws* 659a f., 669d, 700a f., 764d f. The 'true' use of musical festivities is to arouse community idealism and a sort of 'reminiscence' (*Laws* 657c).

22. *Menex.* 243c f., *Rep.* 396ab, 397a f., 492bc, 601b, *Pol.* 268ab, *Laws* 658 f., 700d f. For a modern instance, we have the case of Offenbach, composing 'operettas' like *Orpheus, La Belle Hélène, The Grand Duchess of Gérolstein*, etc., one after another, when he had it in him to compose something like *Les Contes d'Hoffmann*. (Cf. S. Kracauer, *Orpheus in Paris*, E.T. New York, 1938 (Knopf), pp. 345 ff.

23. *Crat.* 422e f., 434a, *Rep.* 397 f., *Tim.* 19de, 47cd, *Phaedr.* 270a, *Laws* 644d, 657ab, 668a f., 709a, 889, 904c.

24. *Phdo.* 65e f., 80e, 82c f., *Rep.* 531a f., *Tim.* 35b ff., 47cd.

25. *Rep.* 397a f., 492bc, 601b, 604e f., *Pol.* 268ab, *Laws* 658 f., 669d, 700, 764d f.

26. *Rep.* 396ab, 397ab, *Tim.* 37b 6, *Laws* 669e f., 802d 2-3, Aristot. *Pol.* Bk. V, ch. 6.

27. Or, if bad, it makes, of the performers and their hearers, worse citizens. *Rep.* 397d f., cf. *Gorg.* 501c f., *Laws* 700b f., 802a f.

28. *Prtg.* 326a f., 347c f., *Symp.* 196e f., *Rep.* 459e f., *Laws* 657c, 796cd.

29. *Gorg.* 502a f., *Rep.* 492b f., *Laws* 654e f., 659d, 796b f., 798e f., 802, cf. 669b f.

30. *Phaedr.* 258d 10-11, 265b 4, c 1-2 (cf. *Rep.* 424b f., 601ab, *Laws* 799ab, e ff., 840b). For the way in which poetry and rhetoric overlap in practice, cf. *Phaedr.* 235c, 237a, 257a, 258d, 262d, 263d, 265b, 277e, 278c, e. For the definition of rhetoric, as inclusive of poetry, cf. *Phaedr.* 271cd, *Gorg.* 450b f., 453a, 454a f., 462c f., 502cd, *Laws* 810b, 911c.

31. *Ion* 534e f., *Rep.* 373b.

32. *Ion* 535 f., *Rep.* 392b, cf. 492b f.

33. *Euthyd.* 305b, *Rep.* 373b, 607a, *Phaedr.* 234e, *Laws* 812de, etc.

34. *Crat.* 423d f., *Rep.* 397a f., *Laws* 653d f., 655cd, 791b f., 816a.

35. *Prtg.* 326a f., *Crat.* 422 ff., *Tim.* 47cd, *Laws* 790b f., 795d, 802d f., 814d f.
36. *Menex.* 234b f., *Rep.* 571b f., *Phaedr.* 244e f., 255e f., *Laws* 771e f., 790c f., 816b f. The passage from the *Republic* (571b f.) shows that *everyone* is subject to forbidden-wish dreams. Socrates teaches that such impulses have to be 'indulged neither too much nor too little', i.e. just sufficiently to encourage them to relax and go to sleep like good fellows, and to cease interfering with the higher principle of reason. In this way the good man appeases the two irrational principles, and thus ensures their not disturbing his sleep with 'lawless and fantastic dream-imagery'. It is necessary to yield to such impulses, not excessively, but 'just enough'. This is, I submit, precisely, 'purgation'.

To convince ourselves that this attitude is characteristic of Plato's respect for what is natural and necessary in our human nature, i.e. vital and non-logical rather than idealistic, we might compare the passages in which Plato accepts what he calls 'the natural bent' of mankind as usable for the purposes of idealism (by sublimation). I have in mind, e.g. *Rep.* 370bc, 371c, 374b f., 421bc, 434b, 453bc, 455ab, 458d, 474bc, 475a, 496ab, 535a, 536d, *Tim.* 18e, *Laws* 772a f., 776a, 782e f., 904c. It might be well also to consider what we find in *Prtg.* 327 f., *Phaedr.* 269d f., 277b, *Laws* 669b f., 710a, 775e, 803a.

I am conscious that readers trained under traditional academic influences may feel that my interpretation is unduly guided by Aristotle (*Poetics* 1449b 27 f.), and may be already convinced that the 'purgative' effect of art (eliminating, by the equivalent of a visit to the movies, noxious emotions which might interfere with living the life of pure reason) is characteristic of Aristotle, rather than of Plato.

I admit the force of the many passages in which Plato decries the excessive emotionalism which he associates with the traditional poetry of Hellas (e.g. *Ion* 535de, *Rep.* 386 ff., 604d ff.), and the obvious satisfaction with which Socrates speaks as though 'imitative poetry' had been entirely rejected from the ideal republic (*Rep.* 595). But I would draw attention to the fact that representative poetry is NOT rejected (in spite of the ingenious reasoning of R. G. Collingwood, *Principles of Art* (Oxford, 1938), pp. 42–52).

It is not to be supposed for a moment that Plato deliberately intends to eliminate entirely the non-logical appeal of poetry (*Phaedr.* 245a). It is only the *excessive* emotionalism of traditional poetry that needs to be corrected, by expert revision and re-writing. Plato does not intend his citizens (whether in the *Republic* or in the *Laws*) to be born, to mature, and to die as purely 'rational' beings. Their life is surrounded, from birth to death, by art, i.e. by rather carefully selected and edited art—definitely 'representative' or 'imitative' in character, and definitely giving 'pleasure', (*pace* Collingwood), i.e. the kind of pleasure 'approved by the oldest and best citizens'.

Such art is purged of *excessive* emotionalism, and the feeling that remains is ancillary to the development of civic idealism. It rests firmly upon natural and necessary (i.e. universal and quasi-instinctive) human dispositions: to which Plato is always prepared to do full justice (*Rep.* 386a, b 6–7, c 1–2, 387c 7–8, e 5–6, 389de, 390d, 392b 5–6, 395c 4–6, 396b 8–c 2, 5–d 3, 5–e 2, 397d 3–5, 398a 8–b 5, 399a–c, d 5–e 4, 11–400a 2, 401b 1–3, c 3 f.).

37. *Rep.* 399a f., *Laws* 653b f., 791a–c, 796bc, 800 f., 814e ff., 836c f.
38. *Crat.* 387b f., 422 ff., 434cd, *Rep.* 393, 597e ff., *Tim.* 19de, 47cd, *Laws* 719c.
39. *Gorg.* 492d, 527e f., *Phdo.* 109 ff., *Crat.* 421d ff., *Rep.* 382d, 493a f., 514 ff.,

614b f., *Laws* 644a f., 803c f., 821b f., 896d f., 966d f. Cf. J. A. Stewart, *The Myths of Plato*, 1905, pp. 20–51, cf. 451–456.

40. *Crat.* 391d ff., 400d ff., 423c, 428d f., *Rep.* 476b f., 479c f., 509e f., *Phaedr.* 260b f., *Theaet.* 184b f.

41. *Menex.* 234b f., *Gorg.* 452d f., 454b ff., 463e f., *Rep.* 401d f., 492 f., *Phaedr.* 271c f., *Laws* 801b f.

42. *Ion* 531c, *Rep.* 398ab, 401c f., 460a, 462a f., 463d f., 595, 598d f., *Theaet.* 152e, *Laws* 664 f., 680c. (On the other side, cf. *Rep.* 600a f., 606e, 607b.)

43. *Ion* 536ab, *Prtg.* 316d, 326a f., *Rep.* 377 ff., 404c, 492 f., 533b f., 595b, 601b, *Laws* 629a, 659a f., 660d f., 666d f., 700c f., 803de, and esp. 858d f.

Could it not be maintained, from this standpoint, that the Socratic art of spiritual midwifery, as expounded in the *Theaetetus* in the presence of Protagoras's former associate, Theodorus, closely resembles, in its functions, the art of Homer and the other Hellenic poets? Is not the philosopher, 'making music' (as he himself says in the *Phaedo*) in obedience to a divine call, and does not Plato (in the *persona* of the visiting professor from Athens) insist that the Dialogue of the *Laws* itself constitutes a dramatic poem (811c)? When he maintains that young citizens (meaning, perhaps, those destined for positions of leadership) are to be educated by studying the *Laws* and similar discussions, whether in prose or in verse, is his position so very different from that of Protagoras, maintaining that 'the principal part of education' (i.e. of education for leadership) comes from the study and interpretation of 'poetry', i.e. of discussions in verse by the classical poets who treat of moral and political excellence (*Prtg.* 338e f.)?

(Socrates, it is true, criticizes the study of poetry, as if Protagoras had intended to use it 'like a commonplace entertainment', something like our modern way of substituting a gramophone record for intelligent conversation (*Prtg.* 347cd). But this is unfair. Protagoras's expressed intention was to use an '*explication des textes*' for the purposes of moral and intellectual education; and would anyone at the present day care to maintain that such a use of classical poetry is, in any sense, an unworthy occupation for persons *in statu pupillari*?)

44. *Crito* 51c ff., *Menex.* 238e, *Prtg.* 319a, *Gorg.* 461e, *Rep.* 557b ff., *Laws* 962e.

45. *Gorg.* 502c, *Rep.* 376e f., 476b, 533b ff., 595 ff., 603 f., 607c f., *Phaedr.* 245a, 276e f., *Soph.* 249a, 266c f.

46. *Gorg.* 450e f., 453d f., 455d f., *Tim.* 53b f., *Pol.* 283c ff., *Phil.* 17c f., 25d f., 55d ff., 63d f., *Laws* 747a f.

47. *Laws* 802d, cf. 658e f., 664a f., 665b f., 667a, e f.

48. *Phdo.* 64e f., 79 f., etc., *Rep.* 510c f., 518bc, 522c ff., 601ab.

49. *Prtg.* 323c, *Theaet.* 161c f., 166d f.

50. *Rep.* 533b f., cf. Ritter and Preller, *op. cit.*, sects. 235–238 (from Sextus and from the *De Melisso*).

51. *Rep.* 531a–c, *Tim.* 53b f., *Theaet.* 155d f., cf. Arist., *Met.* 987a 20 ff.

52. *Rep.* 510c f., 529b f., 531a f., 533b f., *Theaet.* 155e, 180bc, *Soph.* 246 f.

53. *Rep.* 595 ff., is the *locus classicus* for the kind of art which does not attempt to do more than copy physical objects. A house pictured by such an artist is an imitation, not of the absolutely ideal house, but of the (imperfect) copy of that ideal, constructed by a commercial builder. Such an artist is merely playing with images, and thus belongs in the very lowest stage of intelligence (*eikasia*, cf. *Soph.* 266d).

The commercial builder is a stage higher (*pistis*), for he has produced a three-dimensional structure in which a man can actually seek protection from the elements. An architect, constructing a blueprint from which the commercial builder can work, is (as I understand Plato's position) approximately one stage higher, i.e. approximately at the level of 'the mathematical arts' (*dianoia, Rep.* 533b f., *Phil* 55d f.).

A writer like Plato, describing how ideal homes can be arranged so that life (in a model city) can be lived at what is the ideal level (for man), is at one and the same time (1) glamorizing the ideal life for man, and (2) making it seem practical. As a complete idealist, with his eye turned, now to the idea of good, and now to the Hellenic folk-language in which he is giving expression to that idea, a Plato's artistic depiction is at the highest possible stage of knowledge (*noesis,* cf. also *Rep.* 501b f.).

It is sometimes thought that Plato's criticism of the kind of art which merely copies physical objects, without further insight into the ideal, to guide the artist, is a criticism of *mimetic* (imitative or representative) art, as such (cf. R. G. Collingwood, *Principles of Art,* pp. 46–52). I think Plato's position depends, not upon distinguishing a mimetic from an alleged non-mimetic art (as to which last, Plato says, I think, not one word), but upon distinguishing four stages or levels of artistic insight. Plato says that *all* art is essentially mimetic (including language, *Crat.* 389–390). The important question is, does the artist reproduce (as so many of them do) something hardly worth reproducing—such as the image of an un-ideal house—or does he (like the inspired artist of *Laws* 682a and 811b, or like the dialectician or philosopher-artist of *Rep.* 500e f.) depict the ideal life in such a way as to stimulate us to enter upon it?

CHAPTER FOUR

The Nature of Art, II

W E have now reached a point at which we can inquire into Plato's own doctrine. In each of the three theories of his contemporaries, there is something that he is willing to accept: namely, what is most characteristic of each theory, on its positive side. Thus (1) all the arts and crafts have a human, a social and biosocial appeal. At every point they connect with and rest upon human nature, human needs, human action-tendencies. How could it be otherwise? The carpenter makes chairs and beds on which human beings can rest. The weaver produces material for tapestries and carpets for the home, and clothing for its human inmates. The musician operates with tones and rhythms which fall within the range in which human beings like to express their human feelings. The poet glamorizes human war and peace, human ambition and adventure, human loving, human living, and human dying. The painter produces or reproduces scenes which appeal to the natural, biosocial human interests.[1]

So also (2) Pythagorean science is entirely correct in maintaining that for every rhythmic recurrence in nature there exists a law or rational pattern which can be given mathematical formulation. There is no doubt whatever that the arts and crafts are all enormously improved, precisely to the extent to which it becomes possible to apply to their work exact measurement and mathematical calculation. Scientific standards and scientific methods make of art something infinitely superior to empirical groping. The difference between rule-of-thumb carpentering and scientific cabinet-making, between rule-of-thumb weaving and scientifically methodized tapestry-making, is obvious to persons of the slightest intelligence. It is also plain that the Pythagorean insight into the mathematical rationale of the various scales and harmonies used by musicians, makes of their entire art something finer than any biosocial experimenter, whose fingers are wandering idly over the noisy vents in his flute until the tone that comes through sounds 'about right' to his empirical ear, can ever hope to create. Anything like a 'grand amen' comes, not by chance, but by trained insight into law. In the same way, could anyone, without severe mathematical training, produce anything so intellectually satisfying as the antiphonies of an Aeschylean chorus, or the almost magical rhythmic equivalences of a Pindaric ode? So far, the mathematical scientist is, surely, in the right.[2]

Finally (3), if we can forget the extreme naïveté of much in Hellenic realism, is there not, in the positivist's vision of 'reality', something we should all, of whatever philosophical school, like to accept? To think of a 'reality' which somehow transcends all suggestion of our natural anthropomorphism, may seem pathetic. But it constitutes a challenge to humanism, the humanism which seeks to deny its existence.

A humanist like Protagoras believes that his relativism excludes the possibility of any 'absolute'. 'Nothing is, but thinking, social thinking, makes it so.' Quite. But he also maintains that the good orator's business is to 'make the good, instead of the evil, to seem just to social thinking', to the judgement of this or that community. He 'causes the good to take the place of the evil, both in appearance *and in reality*'. Surely we have here a suggestion that the wise counsellor *is really* better than a less wise adviser. There is a belief that good and evil, just and unjust, *are really*, in the deciding opinion of the community, distinct. Here we surely have a recognition, however vague, of an 'absolute', even if its only admitted criterion is the wavering judgement of a democratic assembly? So Socrates.[3]

Again, take the mathematicians. The conclusions of their technical reasoning *do really follow* from their premises. And while the premises themselves are (by the Pythagoreans) justified, in respect of factuality, only by reference to empirical verification; the technical reasoning, as such, is *a priori*. Its universality and necessity rest upon something presupposed: an ultimate subject which is assumed without criticism. This is a single, non-contradictory system of inter-implying propositions which is final. This is, precisely, an 'absolute', a transcendental *reality* which, like the 'Being' of the Eleatic school, is conceived as beyond question.[4]

What Plato does, is to interpret and synthesize the views of his contemporaries, balancing them against one another in the light of the Socratic criticism. What Socrates criticized, was the status of the actual, as such. This status was accepted by all his contemporaries. What Socrates asked, was whether the actual, as such, came up to the requirements of the ideal: the ideal which (at least vaguely) is at the back of all our minds.[5]

When Socrates puts a poet (for example) to the question, he finds that the poet has indeed actually, by what looks like happy chance or what is politely called 'inspiration', succeeded in throwing together a number of effective lines. The poet's reluctant answers show, all too plainly, that he is without genuine grasp of the rational principle (if any) which is involved. To the principle of the ideal, he is as blind as the rest of us. His next poem may just as well register a miss as a hit. 'Hardly one of the bystanders, but could have talked better about his poetry than he did himself', says Socrates. Small wonder that the poet's book of words, once publication has severed it from the poet himself, proves even less capable of defending itself against misunderstanding![6]

Socratic criticism, when applied to the theories of the humanists, of the mathematicians, and of the early positivists of Ionia, similarly shows that all such schools rest upon, and are satisfied with, the actual. Provided their work is successful in operation, they raise no awkward questions. If they have any vague glimpses of the absolute ideal, they prove only too willing to rest upon what they happen to have achieved, and to assume that the ideal is already sufficiently in their possession and control. The final account, developed and applied by Plato to transform and synthesize their teachings, does so by bringing clearly into the open, what their efforts presuppose, but have failed to recognize: namely, the underlying ideal.

Thus, humanists or pragmatists refer all value-judgements to group decision: to the actual decision of actual, here-and-now communities. Whatever is being planned, is 'right', in so far as the working majority of the sovereign community so decides; and for as long as a working majority continues to be of that opinion. For Plato, this means that the majority members are feeling their way, consciously or unconsciously, toward the realization of an ideal, an absolute ideal at the back of every man's mind. As Plato sometimes states the matter, a sound decision rests, not upon any chance majority, but upon an ideal majority. It is what the citizens of an ideal republic or model city, educated to judge wisely, decide. They decide by reference, not to one another, as to individuals whose votes can be counted on this side or that, but to an ideal standard, one and the same for all. It is not the number of voting citizens, but their reference to the ideal, that clinches matters and justifies the decision.[7]

Stated abstractly, this ideal is 'the good', conceived as an ultimate principle of ideality and value, which transcends the actual, as such, both in dignity and in power. It is never a mere fact, but always something better; for it serves to guide, to master, and to make fact.[8]

Stated concretely, as in relation to the theories of the humanists, it is the ideal republic or model city: the civic life in which each citizen realizes his potentialities in the service of the ideal community. Each citizen has within himself a 'natural bent', a potentiality for this or that art or craft: for carpentering or weaving, for tending plants or animals, for making money, or music, or poetry, for administration, or what not. The 'royal' art, the art of government, consists in taking persons of diverse natural gifts and temperaments and weaving them into a community of thought, feeling, and action: a community which has substantial *Lebensfähigkeit*.

In modern times, we illustrate this by reference to what a Toscanini can do with selected 'cellists, flautists and drummers. Plato refers, more directly, to his 'philosopher-king', the executive whose craftsmanship rests upon trained insight into the civic ideal, as he applies the 'idea of good' toward the solution of the problems of men in community assembled. It is the executive's business to make arrangements which will enable each citizen to realize his own 'idea', to fulfil his own best function in the life of the whole group, and in so doing to raise that life, for all members of the group (including himself), to its highest degree of humanly satisfying value.[9]

In such a community, the carpenter is no mere carpenter: no mere expert in cutting wood, hammering nails, taking measurements, and co-operating with other carpenters in manufacturing tables, beds, and houses. He is a community-carpenter. Everything he makes, and every part of his professional activity, is a part, an integral part, of the life of his community. He takes pride in his work because it has this additional value, this value for others, for the fellow-members of his community. It has this higher value, both for him and for them, because it is permeated by the spirit of civic idealism.

This is not the mere professional idealism of the expert technician, who is contented to make replicas of the ideal chair or bed thought of as existing abstractly and remotely, in God's Heaven. It is the civic idealism of the expert whose *expertise* receives recognition in his community, not merely by protection in his employment and security under the laws, but conceivably by State appointment as adviser to the legislature on all matters relating to his own craft. Whatever his status in matters military and political, where his own 'idea' is concerned, he is not merely as important as anyone else, but more important; and that status is fully recognized, recognized in principle and in theory, as well as in customary usage and in fact.[10]

So also with the rest: with poet, musician, school-teacher, with everyone whose natural bent has been developed into a technique, a socially useful craft, an art which has a place in the ideal community. When we ask, who is to write the nation's songs, we find it is always the citizen-poet, the poet whose citizenship has been proved by his actions on the stage of civic duty. It is quite recognized that others, natural or spiritual aliens to the ideal republic, may be more brilliant as craftsmen: more perfect in word-technique, better qualified professionally for the task. But unless words agree with deeds, mere cleverness is not convincing. The nation's songs are to be written by the nation's heroes. Martial music will be made by composers who have proved the quality of their citizenship on the field of battle. The hymns and temple-chants will be directed by men of mature years, deliberately selected for the position in recognition of their proved civic ability. In fact, the leaders in every field of civic performance are selected, primarily for their proved civic excellence, and only secondly for their technical competence.[11]

School-teaching is a branch of service which requires a rather special form of technical competence. Plato does not expect his born citizens to devote themselves to a teaching career. His teachers have accordingly to be imported from abroad, selected for their ability and attracted by the promise of pay and protection. But they do not receive State appointment until they have undergone a period of teacher-training which fits them for teaching the future citizens of the model city in the spirit of its citizenship. They study Plato's *Laws*, and pass an examination upon its content, showing that they fully understand and appreciate its spirit, before they can receive their teacher's certificates.[12]

So too with the traditional Hellenic poetry. This is not received, admitted to civic recognition and civic use, until it has been censored and (if necessary) rewritten so as to conform to and express the ideals of the model city; and finally, living dramatists who have perfected their technique elsewhere, are not permitted to perform their plays before citizens, until they have passed the censorship of the citizen-magistrates and have received the stamp of community approval: certifying their dramas as identical in spirit with the great drama of the city itself, its own adventure in ideal civic living.[13]

So much for the application of the ideal principle to what Plato accepts in humanism. Let us pass to consider its application to Pythagorean science, the mathematical physics of his day. In spite of the undoubted apriority of their techniques, the so-called Pythagoreans are clearly relating their work at all points to the factual, to the here-and-now, to what just happens to be so, rather than to the ideal. The actual constitutes their starting-point. It is used as a constant check upon every stage of their reasoning. And it colours their end-point, their final conclusion as to the 'emptiness' of biosocial living. This is indeed what Socrates finds to criticize in their whole outlook. They accept their hypotheses without examination. They remain ignorant of their own first principle. Their conclusion, and all intermediate steps, are constructed out of something which works, indeed, in practice. But none of them ask why it works—and none of them know. Pythagorean 'science', in a word, is a fabric resting upon convention, upon a gentlemen's agreement not to raise awkward questions about ultimates, when everything is going well. As such, it can never be regarded (Socrates urges) as meeting the requirements of ideal science.[14]

We almost need a new name for what the Pythagoreans are doing. It is, indeed, in virtue of its mathematical techniques, superior (in respect of clearness and cogency) to the arts in general, to the work of the humanists. For that work is concerned with the non-logical, with the primitive desires and opinions of men on their biological side. Such art does not look to anything further than production, technical production without insight into ideal values. Pythagorean science is better than that. But only a little better. It is a kind of dream-substitute for what science might be. Its exponents are held back by their feeling for the actual. They remain always at the third stage of intelligence, and never reach the final, the highest conceivable stage. Plato accordingly, in spite of his respect for the technical quality of their mathematical reasoning, always hesitates to welcome them as full idealists. To him, they remain, at best, only fellow-travellers, 'friends of ideas'.[15]

Precisely how does Plato propose to develop them into full idealists, to raise them from the third to the fourth and highest stage of human intelligence? He follows the guidance of two lines of thought. The first takes the direction of socialization. The Pythagoreans, as a brotherhood, have made of themselves a group apart. They have withdrawn from ordinary biosocial interests and have become specialized mathematicians: deliberately unfitting themselves for the life of citizenship. As intellectuals, they take pride in their conspicuous uselessness. They live their own life in their own way; and they have as little to do with the community, whether actual or ideal, as they can. From such an attitude and such an outlook, the community can expect—nothing. The Pythagoreans take nothing, and they give nothing; and nothing whatever can be done with them.[16]

Leaving the Pythagoreans to themselves, then, Plato makes an entirely fresh start. He develops, for his ideal community, persons whose abilities parallel those of the Pythagoreans; but he sees to it that their background and outlook are different. His candidates are oriented throughout away from barren intellectualism, and toward the broader life of good citizenship. It is from members of the 'silver' class, who are steeped from their birth in civic feeling, that he selects, in their later teens, the candidates for his leadership class. It is these, and only these, who receive the higher education which makes them at home in the world of intellectual techniques. Their characters, as shown by repeated character-tests, are fully formed upon the ideas of courage, self-mastery, social justice, friendship toward man, and piety toward God. It is as members of the community, selected by the community to develop themselves for the community, that they approach the intellectual training for which they are fitted by natural capacity. The whole atmosphere is the atmosphere of social service; and their own characters fit them for recognition of the fairness of the community's expectations.[17]

Their training, on its intellectual side, is in the same mathematical techniques as those studied by the Pythagorean brotherhood: arithmetic, geometry (both plane and solid), mathematical physics ('astronomy'), and physical acoustics. But the spirit in which they are trained is very different. They are not being trained to become scientists in their own right: seekers who follow their own curiosities and owe to themselves everything they discover, and are satisfied with the life of intellectuals, as such. Their training in scientific method is a preparation for something further. It does indeed (as it does with the Pythagoreans) enable them to develop a kind of scientific objectivity, an intellectual detachment, a freedom from the pleasure- and power-seeking tendencies of the instinctively ambitious.

But Plato's group of students acquire detachment from the one-sided ideals of the scientist too.

Their characters and their experience keep them at all times attached to the community, for which and in which they are continuing to work. They hold positions of civic and military leadership, testing themselves and being tested in all the chances and changes of community living. They learn to know their fatherland from the ground up, and acquiring deeper roots in the actual, no less than in the ideal world. In this way they remain, what the Pythagoreans have not remained—all-sided: civic intellectuals, practitioners as well as masters of theory.[18]

But—and now we come to the second line of Plato's thought—their preparation fits them to go further along the pathways of the mind than the Pythagoreans have ever gone. Where the Pythagoreans stop, Platonists continue. Pythagorean science catalogues and formulates the behaviour-patterns of the actual world. Plato's students go further. They ask why, why, why? Why is it that these patterns—or rather, the patterns foreshadowed and indicated by the actual patterns—are the way they are?

What is it about the numbers 12 and 6, the numbers 12 and 8, the numbers 8 and 6 (or however the scientists formulate the concords recognized by the Greeks), that makes them, in themselves, harmonious? What is the underlying ground of the relation between human music and human dancing, on the one hand, and human music (and dancing) and human language, on the other? Why is it that we differentiate this or that colour in the entire colour-range, and distinguish it from its neighbour colours? How is this related, and why, to the distinctive tones in music, the distinctive vowels and consonants in language, or the distinctive dance-rhythms of folk-dancing, and to the distinctive, racial nature of the human individual? What is it that makes one proportion of earth, water, fire, and air capable of sustained existence as a human being, whereas another is capable of existence as an ox, a tree, a bird, or a fish? What is it that makes certain atom-whirls rather than others, eventually come to existence as the relatively regular orbits of the celestial bodies? Why are these things thus?[19]

Everywhere the Socrates-minded student sees problems: problems which take him further than cataloguing the phenomena of our world. In particular, pursuing the Socratic maxim that the unexamined life is not worth living, he proceeds to examine the life of the scientist himself. He relates the sciences (usually studied separately) to one another, and particularly inquires, first, into their intellectual interrelations, and finally into the ultimate basis—the ultimate intellectual, ideal basis—of their common presuppositions.

This is Socrates's old quest of 'the good': the ultimate principle of ideality and value. It was glimpsing this that made Socrates himself give up the one-sided life of a scientist, to which he had previously felt drawn.[20] As contrasted with the work of the scientists, this vision assumes the aspect of a concrete all-embracing science, perfected by being grounded finally in its own immanent principle: a single science, completely transparent to a well-trained mind. Such an ideal scientist should be able to traverse the entire intellectual realm from end to end. He should prove able to start from any point and, by sheer persistency, by the use of severely intellectual methods, to reach any other point. The actual would be not simply accepted (as by the Pythagoreans), but understood: understood in its relations with each and every science and each and every art. All problems would be envisaged as connected (*via* their own presuppositions), not only with one another, but with the ultimate principle of all, the unhypothetical first principle, tentatively named by Socrates 'the (idea of) good'.[21]

Such a science (embracing all the sciences and all the arts) would not be merely descriptive, depictive. It would be normative. It would include the social as well as the natural sciences, and would culminate in what Plato calls the 'royal' art, the art of government. This, as Plato imagines it, would bring together in fruitful co-operation, the arts of the humanists and the sciences of the mathematicians, in a single master-art: the art of the ideal executive, the 'philosopher-king'.[22]

We now pass to a brief consideration of the Socratic ideal in relation to the alleged 'reality' of the naïve realists or early 'positivists'. These are at the second of the four stages of intelligence: the stage (*pistis*) at which men accept as 'real' only what they can see with their eyes and grasp with their hands—i.e. the concrete actualities of the physical environment. This whole stage is thought to stand to the stage beneath it, the stage of the humanists (*eikasia*), somewhat as 'reality' stands to 'its appearances'. Socratic criticism points out that physical reality of this sort, itself stands in the relation of 'appearance' to something higher, namely, (1) the underlying laws of phenomena, as studied in the natural sciences, and (2) finally, the absolute ideal of an 'ultimate' reality: to which even the conclusions of the technical sciences stand in the relation of 'appearances'.[23]

Phenomena (things we can see and hold), as Socrates regards them, are factual enough. To the eye of sense, they are perfectly real. But to the eye of the mind, their alleged 'reality' is very imperfect, riddled with contradictions. You cannot think of beds and tables, of mud, hair, and dirt, or even of sunlight and the star-spangled firmament of heaven, as constituting *ultimate* reality. They are fluctuating and impermanent, without logical universality and ideal necessity. There is nothing there for a mind to seize and hold in its purely rational grasp. They are not substances, but floating adjectives: flitting in and out of the intelligible realm, in which they have no abiding-place.[24]

Phenomena are appearances, images generated from a tissue of seething motions, when these happen to come into interactivity with the fluctuating processes of our organs of sense. The 'physical objects' of positive science represent a temporary cross-section of these two processes in the moment of their interaction. Such 'objects', together with the 'physical space' in which we endeavour (vainly) to assign to them something more than a relative location, and the 'physical time' in which we try (equally vainly) to assign to them something more than a relative dating, are—as any member of the Eleatic school is prepared to demonstrate to all comers—not really thinkable. Such 'objects' belong to the realm of 'non-being': which is almost identical with absolute chaos.[25]

As contrasted with this physical 'reality', Plato indicates the kind of reality that an absolute Mind could accept as ultimate: a reality thinkable through and through. Only the kind of reality which would satisfy, not a mere intellectual's 'mind', but a completely developed soul or spirit, is ultimately acceptable.[26]

All the rest, humanist art, intellectualist science, the positivist search for the 'reality' embodied in immediate appearance, culminate in the notion of an ideal society: a community of co-operating souls or spirits, following intelligently and wholeheartedly the guidance of the Master-soul or Master-spirit, God. In such a world, the 'idea of good' takes concrete form as the Divine Plan which contains, ideally speaking, a place, i.e. a definite function, for every person and every thing which can in any way respond to the Divine appeal, by co-operation. The more than human agencies which doubtless guide the stars in their courses, the well-meaning statesmen who direct the destinies of nations, the lesser artists and scientists who are pursuing ideal beauty and ideal truth, each in his chosen field: all are alike participating in the ideal life, realizing their own value-potentialities and supporting and being supported by all the rest. Such is the master-plan, whose reality is ideal: ultimate and absolute.[27]

In such a world, what is the nature of art, ideal art? It is exemplified in what the ideal artist does. Let us consider a few of Plato's own pictures of the ideal craftsman, pursuing his chosen art under the conditions of life in the ideal republic or model city. Let us take, first, the creative author. Plato regards himself as a prose-poet and teacher: a writer with a message, a propagandist for the ideal life. He composes original philosophical Dialogues, which invite to fellow-membership in the Academy all who feel within them the call to idealistic self-education, and are able and willing to respond.

Plato's invitation is not addressed to everybody; not to the Hellenic equivalents of Tom, Dick and Harry, the membership of the Drones' Club; not to *hoi polloi*, the countless semblances of humanity who serve another's will, or serve a will which they call their own, but it drives them with relentless energy into a maelstrom of meaningless motions, of activities and counter-activities without ideal *wohin*. His invitation is not addressed to slaves, handworkers, office-workers, or money-makers: to the busy, busy men of the world, who toil so strenuously for a superficial success along this line or that, but remain blind to all questions of deeper import.

It is addressed to a Glaucon or Adeimantus, a Simmias or Cebes, a Cleinias or Megillus: to men of good family and goodwill, who have both the time and the inclination to reflect well and to choose their course after deliberation. Such life begins in the late teens and early twenties. It is renewed in the thirties, in the forties, possibly in the fifties. Even in the sixties, it is not too late. It is to men whose life is thus beginning, or beginning again, whether their powers of insight are manifestly in the opening bud, in full flower, or just before the final harvest, that Plato's message is addressed.[28]

The content of the message is, in principle, simple. It is a call to a serious and holy life that is at the same time a joyous, playful, and utterly human life: tugging at every cord which moves the human puppet to laughter and tears, yet holding at all times fast to the golden cord of reason. The ideal life for humanity is depicted for us most fully in the *Republic* and *Laws*. And yet, in spite of the infinitely varying uniqueness of Plato's writings, in which of the Dialogues does not the contrast of the actual (with its suggestion of pure comedy) and the ideal (with its sense of the tragical in life, even in a life of high purpose) succeed in transmitting the self-same message?

Think of the *Phaedo*, depicting the anxious and solemn farewell of the Socratic intimates to the leader who is participating in their researches for the last time on earth, and the anxious and solemn welcome to the new leader who is momentarily kept from them by sickness. The thought of the ideal society is never absent, and its central tenets are brought out and vigorously re-affirmed. At the same time, while tears are not distant, there is humour, cheerfulness, yes, and laughter for the little touches of comedy in the human puppets, our noble selves.

Think of the *Meno*, with its solemn sense of immortality and of the new society which is dedicating itself to plumbing the depths of *a priori* knowledge. Socrates's persistent irony in the face of human pretension, his outrageous selection of an untutored slave to reveal to thoughtless freemen what they are too 'torpified' to see for themselves: all this exhibits the same humour, the same seriousness, and the same message, as the *Republic* or the *Laws*. It is sometimes thought that Plato's 'secret' is Socrates. It would be closer to the mark, to realize that it is the ideal society: indicated, indeed, not only in the Dialogues, but also in the *Epistles* which are still read.

What the artistic writer does, when thus inspired by idealistic philosophy, is, to write Utopias: i.e. to make the life of the ideal society seem (as indeed it is) attractive and acceptable.[29] If he composes hymns to the Gods, or makes up stories about men and women, these all, in a variety of ways, stress one and the same theme: the glory of citizenship in the ideal community. In fact, what differentiates the ideal author from the well-known traditional writers, is that, while they, one and all, celebrate the actual cities of Hellas, the traditional heroes and the traditional gods, 'praising the Athenians to the Athenians', or (like the Spartan Tyrtaeus) composing a Spartan war-song for Spartan men: the ideal prose-poet glamorizes the ideal citizens of the ideal city in which he has achieved membership. He composes prose-poems which will confirm *seine Menschen*, his fellow-citizens, in their community idealism. Such is the primary work of the philosopher-artist in the field of literary craftsmanship.[30]

In a secondary way, if a given writer is less originative, he can and should devote his powers to editing and to some extent rewriting the traditional literature of Hellas: so as to adapt it to the needs of the new community. Working on a committee of expert literary craftsmen, under the leadership of a philosophically trained chairman, he can see to it that the traditional material is touched up a little here, toned down a little there: permeated with community idealism, in such a way that the new 'Boy's Homer' (like the modern *Télémaque*), the new 'School Euripides' (like the *Athalie* or *Phèdre* of Racine), and the rest, can safely be put into the hands of eager youth, with perfect assurance that they will edify, fostering the spirit of heroism, of self-mastery, of comradeship, of piety, and all other virtues of good citizenship.[31]

In yet a third way, if a literary authority happens to be still less originative, but with perhaps greater critical powers, he will prove able to assist with his advice (like the modern publisher's reader) the committee of censors: which has the duty of determining whether the newest creations of local poets, and perhaps also works composed by foreign poets, are sufficiently imbued with the spirit of community idealism to be admitted to local publication. This kind of service, whether formally or informally, is performed by members of the writers' guild everywhere: with a view to enforcing or raising standards of professional craftsmanship. Why should it not be performed in the ideal city, with a view to enforcing or raising standards of community idealism?[32]

In these three ways, the union of philosophy with the art of creative and critical writing will ensure that whatever works do succeed in receiving publication in the ideal city, are entirely worthy. The productions of authors will never be left in the lowest stage of intelligence (*eikasia*), which merely plays aimlessly with effective imagery; never in the almost equally low stage (*pistis*), which merely reproduces blindly the sounds and sights of the physical world; never in the third stage, the stage remarkable for professional technique, where the craftsman chisels out lines of flawless correctness which win prizes; for, when you look closely, you realize that the supreme insight is not there. You are dealing, not with a true idealist, but only with some 'friend of ideas': some prize-poet like Agathon, some son of well-conditioned parents, like Glaucon, who do not yet quite see their way.[33] No, the philosopher-artist in this field, like the philosopher-artist in the field of government, raises his craft to the highest level of all: the level being permeated by insight into the 'idea of good', the ultimate principle whose power transmutes every kind of human activity, making it an integral part of the ideal life.

If we look at other forms of philosopher-artist recognized by Plato, we find this position confirmed.[34] As 'philosopher-craftsmen' are recognized, not only the founders of the ideal community, but all members of the 'golden' class of full guardians in the *Republic*:

the 'artificers of virtue'.[35] There are also included all higher magistrates in the *Laws*, i.e. all members of the great Nocturnal Council (which contains the heads of almost all departments of administration). On the evidence of the text, we must accept as included a good many persons who, while not officially magistrates, are in the employ of the community, and accept the position, and adopt the idealist attitude expected of public servants: such men as the philosopher-lawyer,[36] the philosopher-physician,[37] and the philosopher-teacher;[38] also the philosopher-interpreter (of oracles, etc.).[39] In view of the evidence, it appears that the philosopher-author[40] (here the propagandist, rather than the poet we have considered above) and the philosopher-musician (composer rather than performer)[41] should also be included.

There are even indications that such callings as that of the sailor, pilot, and engineer, and even of hotel-keeper, are capable of developing a taste for public-spirited service of idealistic philosophy; but Plato deliberately withdraws from pressing this suggestion.[42] It is to be assumed that such unsuspected auxiliaries of the ideal life are somewhat analogous to the militia, the 'silver' class of the *Republic*. If it is insisted that they fall more properly into the 'artisan' class, it should be recognized that, in the *Laws*, all members of this class participate directly in the spirit of community idealism; although, as a class, artisans are not required to exhibit the higher philosophical insight. Something of the sort is true even of the slaves: in so far as slavery is actually practised in Plato's Utopias. At least, there is no doubt that some degree of community idealism is expected; and arrangements are contemplated which would lead to official recognition and reward (including enfranchisement) in the case of public-spirited loyalty and service beyond the line of duty.[43]

All these occupations or crafts found in the ideal community are (1) grounded upon non-logical action-tendencies which can be of great social utility. They are (2) developed (whether by repetition and habituation, or by the application of mathematics) into techniques which make them of even greater social utility. And finally (3) they are formed upon ideal reality: i.e. upon the ideal patterns discovered by scientific research and applied to human uses. In so far as they are permeated by the spirit of community idealism, all such arts become integral parts of the ideal life for man. It is indeed only in so far as they achieve this, that they rise above the level of meaningless play-activities (*eikasia*) and reach the level of the highest conceivable significance for man (*nous*). Ideally speaking, it is the nature of art to become thus functional in the ideal life: i.e. in the life of the ideal community whose spirit is sufficiently indicated in the *Republic* and *Laws*, and which constitutes, as Plato sees it, the highest good for man.[44]

NOTES

1. *Rep.* 533bc.
2. *Rep.* 531ab, *Phil.* 17 f., 26a, 51b f., 55d f.
3. *Theaet.* 172ab, 177d f., 179b.
4. *Theaet.* 163a, 180d f.
5. *Gorg.* 482c f., 521d f., *Rep.* 505d.
6. *Apol.* 22a f., *Phaedr.* 275d f., *Theaet.* 164d f., 166a f., 169d f., *Parm.* 128de. S. Alexander thinks *great* art is like a living organism detached from its parent. It is *lebensfähig* in its own right.
7. *Gorg.* 471e f., 473d f., *Rep.* 493b–d, *Theaet.* 174a ff.
8. *Rep.* 505e f., 507b ff., *Tim.* 29e f.
9. *Gorg.* 502d f., 506c f., 513d f., *Phdo.* 98 f., 99c f., 100a, 101d, *Rep.* 433 f., 441d ff., 455d f., 466d, 474bc, 540ab., *Pol.* 304 ff., *Laws* 773d 4–5, cf. 739b, 785b 8–9, 807b, 835d–941d, 964d ff.
10. *Crat.* 389a, *Rep.* 428c. For the status of artisans in the model city, see *Laws* 745a, 847b, 850, 914c, 920a, 925e.
11. *Laws* 799ab, 811c f., 829c f.
12. *Laws* 804c f., 811d f., 813b f.
13. *Laws* 817a f. It would be a mistake (I think), to assume that such regulations are not intended primarily for the protection of persons *in statu pupillari*, or approximately so. Plato does not intend to shackle or otherwise hamper creative artists by regulations which we would not ourselves approve at the present day.

The whims of artists (and they *have* whims) are *always* subject to effective criticism: (1) at the hands of brother-artists (cf. the contemporary professional criticisms of Haydn, Mozart, Beethoven, Brahms, *et al.*). In our own day, writers seeking publication are *always* subject to the criticism of 'publishers' readers'. Or in music, a Tschaikovsky's ideas of what should go into a piano concerto are subjected to the (very severe) criticism of a practising virtuoso like Rubinstein. Such criticisms always annoy the creative artist enormously. It is extremely rare for criticism to say: 'Where he [Beethoven] is not orthodox, it is safest to conclude that orthodoxy is wrong' (*Ency. Brit.*, 14th ed., Vol. 3, p. 321). As a rule, the artist pockets his pride and rewrites his composition until professional criticism accepts it.

There is also (2) the general value-judgement of the community itself. From this there is no escape, or any final appeal. It is this which eventually decides the reputations of the great artists themselves. Artists frequently protest against it (cf. *Prtg.* 352de); but, just so long as art is a form of communication, and has a social side, there can be no doubt that some feeling for what the community will accept, constitutes a definite part of the creative artist's outlook. Plato is quite as well aware as ourselves that any governmental attempt to dictate to creative artists what they shall and shall not do, would be 'the death of art' (*Pol.* 299e). Incidentally, *all* regulations for artists in the model city are framed by joint boards, upon which the artists themselves have full representation (cf. *Laws* 657a f., 659d, 660a, 738b f., 764c f., 772a f., 799a, 801c f., 802a f., 809, 811b f., 812c f., 816bc, 817d, 828ab, 829c f., 848d f., 894). The philosophy-trained magistrates merely act as chairmen, who represent the general community spirit, and give the effect of law to the results of research (or other recommendations) on the part of the joint committee. This is the regular way of doing business in the model city, in every field of activity except the military field.

14. *Rep.* 510c f., 527a, 529b f., 531a f., 533b–d.

15. *Soph.* 246–250 (with Lewis Campbell's Introduction to his edition of the Greek text, Oxford, 1867, pp. lxxiv–lxxv). Cf. *Rep.* 531e.

16. *Phdo.* 64a ff., *Rep.* 519c f.

17. *Rep.* 413c f., 498b ff., 503, 537.

18. *Rep.* 501d f., 537d, *Tim.* 29cd, 59c. The details are worked out in the *Laws*, e.g., 760b ff., 813d, cf. *Rep.* 416d f.

19. For such 'problems' and their effect upon the inquiring mind, cf. *Phdo.* 96 ff., *Crat.* 387b f., 388b f., *Rep.* 425a f., 444d, 510c f., 524 ff., 530b f., 531e f., 533a f. 537cd, *Theaet.* 185c f., 206d, *Laws* 794 ff., 818b f., 894a, 967d f.

As to the numbers 1, 2, 3, 4 (out of which the number 10 is constructed, the whole being represented geometrically—in the form of the right-angled triangle associated with the Pythagorean brotherhood), and their relation to 'the whole heavens' which (as Aristotle observed) the Pythagoreans regarded as 'a harmony and a number', there was doubtless some speculation even among the Pythagoreans themselves. It is, however, with the name of Speusippus (an Academic) that the chief mass of *spekulatives Hirngespinst* (Erich Frank) is associated. The suggestion that each species exhibits a specific law of proportion (between the elements of fire, water, earth, and air, of which it is composed), and that this number, a constant for each species of living beings, exercises a controlling influence over the motion-patterns (walking, skipping, and running, for human beings, flying, for birds, swimming, for fishes, etc.) characteristic for each species, and, in the case of human beings, determines their 'natural' (apparently, non-logical) marches and other forms of folk-dance, on the one hand, as well as of their corresponding songs and other forms of 'vocal gesture' on the other, together with some feeling that it accounts also for the apparent correspondence between the colour-range and the tonal-range of human sensation—I find nowhere concentrated and reduced to an uncompromising statement of theory. But the 'nuptial number' in the *Republic*, and the vague but significant statement in *Laws* 967d f., cf. 747, make one realize the enormous extent to which Plato's thought is influenced by such underlying mathematical analogies; and there is a great deal of suggestive evidence, here and there in the Dialogues, indicating that the Pythagoreans were not the only educated men with an eye open for underlying mathematical analogies extending over the entire range of human experience.

20. *Phdo.* 96 ff.

21. *Meno* 81cd, *Rep.* 507b–511d, 517b f., 532a f., 533c f.

22. *Rep.* 540ab, *Laws* 951e f., 964d f., 967d f.

23. *Rep.* 510 f., 533a f.

24. *Rep.* 597a ff., *Tim.* 37d–39d, 45c f., 50b f., 52a f., *Theaet.* 156 ff., *Parm.* 130c f.

25. *Tim.* 49a f., 50b f., 53b.

26. *Soph.* 249a f.

27. *Symp.* 209a f., *Rep.* 395, 397e, 433 ff., 463d f., *Tim.* 47 f., *Laws* 846d f., 963b f. Cf. W. Becher, *Platon und Fichte: die königliche Erziehungskunst* (Fischer, Jena, 1937), who is perfectly clear, not only that the position of *Führer* (in Plato) rests upon *Leistungsfähigkeit*, but also that *every* member of the State is *Leistungsträger des ganzen* (pp. 26–28, 33, etc.).

28. *Rep.* 498a f., indicates that what happens to most men, if the invitation is not accepted while they are still young enough to respond with fresh growth. But the *Laws* indicates that old age, especially when it has behind it a mature experience of men and laws, is never too old to co-operate with the idealistic spirit and to reinforce the message (*Laws* 969bc, cf. *Rep.* 328d f., 498e f., 499e f.). In Megillus and Cleinias we have a concrete representation of the late ('sabbatical'?) pause, in which experience withdraws for a while to refresh its idealism (cf. *Rep.* 498bc).

29. Cf. *Laws* 811c f.

30. *Laws* 664b ff.

31. *Rep.* 377b ff., *Laws* 800a, 801a f., 802a f., 810d f., 811b f., 817b f., 858d f., 957a f.

32. *Rep.* 379a f., 386a f., 401, 595 ff., *Laws* 829c f.

33. *Rep.* 533a.

34. The following passages all refer to 'philosopher-artists' or 'philosopher-craftsmen', over a fairly wide range of artistic activities: *Gorg.* 503 f., *Symp.* 211c f., *Rep.* 402b f., 484ab, 498c–502c, 520bc, *Phaedr.* 265d, 270b, 271 f., *Theaet.* 273e f., *Phil.* 62a, *Laws* 660a, 661c, 662a, 663b f., 709b ff., 718de.

35. Such executives are always regarded by Plato as genuine artists, as contrasted with journalists, painters, and other craftsmen, who produce (at best) a mere 'image' (in an alien medium) of the real thing. Thus, if Homer had actually functioned as chief executive of some city, as law-giver, educator, or someone who had really *done* something of social value, instead of merely playing cleverly with images of these useful activities, he would have been a philosopher-artist. The art of life, of social living directed by the idea of good, is the real thing: the practical side of the philosopher's art or craft. If journalism, painting, etc., are used in the service of that art, they too participate in its reality (like Plato's *Laws* and the more inspired parts of Homer). Cf. *Rep.* 395bc, 599d ff., 606e f. (cf. also *Rep.* 389d, 390d, 607ab), *Phaedr.* 276 f., *Laws* 810e f., 817a f., 858d f.

36. *Symp.* 212a, *Rep.* 409 f., *Laws* 702b, 751c, 753a, 951–953d, 957, 966c–967e, 969a f. Solon and Lycurgus were traditionally regarded as authorities of this type (*Laws* 858c f.).

37. *Symp.* 176b f., 185d ff., *Pol.* 292c ff., *Laws* 709 f. Acumenus and Eryximachus are examples of the philosopher-physician referred to in the Dialogues.

38. The philosopher-teacher is one of the highest group of guardians in *Rep.* 540b. In the *Laws*, where he is one of the very highest magistrates (964c), he is probably to be equated with the minister of education (the most important of all the great offices of State). As such, he exercises supervision, rather than undertakes classroom work.

39. For philosopher-interpreters, see *Laws* 774e, 828b f., 845e, 865 f., 871c, 873d, 916c, 958d (cf. *Rep.* 458c, *Laws* 770b f.), and 964bc.

40. The philosopher-author is a propagandist for the ideal community. He produces suitable compositions in prose, as well as in verse, which will be chanted regularly by the citizens of the model city. He will specialize in hymns to the gods

and encomia of famous citizens. This is not formal script-writing, attaining to a very low level as 'patriotic' literature. Plato expects it to be genuinely inspired, with the highest conceivable community ideals.

'Such is the magic of the new literature, and so varied its appeal, that the new citizens are revitalized, thrilled. The new literature helps them see things in their ideally true colours, name them by their ideally true names, realize their transcendental significance in ideal living. Each day is a new and rather special sort of Christmas Day. Each citizen is a new embodiment of the spirit of the family group, a rather special Odysseus or Nestor. Each wife is a new and rather special sort of Penelope or Andromache. And each child is a very special sort of little Telemachus or Nausicaa. The glamour of such names expresses the inner significance of the race. It whispers hope, inspires courage, and breathes prayer: that the new spearhead of the race may prove worthy of the name he bears. As the citizens associate more actively with the storied heroes of the race, they become more genuinely fellow-citizens of the ideal community whose home is in heaven' (*Prtg.* 326a f., *Crat.* 397b, *Rep.* 591c f., *Phaedr.* 252d f., *Theaet.* 176a f., *Phil.* 39c f., *Laws* 816ab. Cf. also Sophocl., *Ajax* 550–551, *Iliad* Z 476–480.—The passage quoted is from R. C. Lodge, *Plato's Theory of Education*, p. 178).

41. In the *Laws*, choral singing plays a great part in the educational system. The musicians who compose the chants which are sung and danced, are not (presumably) citizens. For no regular citizen of the model city devotes more than three years to a 'brief course for musical amateurs'. This course qualifies him to take part in the temple chants and in the monthly solo and choral competitions (for which he receives further training at the hands, presumably, of members of the music-teachers' association). The adjudicators at these monthly contests are all experts (*akroi*), i.e. non-civic musicians receiving State appointment for their *expertise*. Plato thinks of a select group of such experts (composers) set to discover, by research, the mathematically objective bases for the community-approved scales. Such persons are like Damon. It is made perfectly plain that, while non-citizens, such experts operate under the direct authority of the minister of education, and that the authority which they exercise is considerable. The very best of them undoubtedly correspond to the philosopher-author; although their philosophy (such as this is) is perhaps not (as a rule) derived from attendance in the dialectic class open to higher magistrates-to-be. They seem to be a superior kind of quasi-Pythagorean. (See *Rep.* 402 ff., *Laws* 764–766, cf. 657a 7, b 1–2, 659d–660a, e 9, 661a 5, c 5–8, 662b 4, c 5, 663bc, 772a, 799a, 801c f., 811b f., 828, 829c f., 833e, 835a, 936a).

42. *Gorg.* 511c–512d, *Laws* 831e, 918b f.

43. *Laws* 653 ff., 775c 2 f., 812b f., 881c. The tendency is to accept into full spiritual fellowship (however informally) all who are capable of responding co-operatively to the call of the ideal life.

44. *Symp.* 209a ff. Generally speaking, it is only the superior guardian class that guides itself entirely by reason. And here too, its membership is recruited entirely from the 'silver' class. This silver class of regular citizens, both in the *Republic* and in the model city of the *Laws*, is entirely surrounded, from birth to death, by community art. In all it feels, says, thinks, and does, it is influenced by the all-pervasive suggestions of that art.

CHAPTER FIVE

The Functions of Art, I

I F we collate the passages in the Dialogues which discuss the various activities referred to by the Greeks as 'arts', we find, universally accepted, a definition of art as 'productive'. The characteristic function of art is to produce. The function of architecture is to produce buildings. The function of agriculture is to produce food. The function of weaving is to produce garments. Carpentry produces implements of wood, cobbling produces shoes. Painting produces pictures, poetry produces hymns and dramas, rhetoric produces speeches. Music produces accompaniments (rhythmic, harmonious, melodic) to song and dance. In a word, each 'art' has a specific, community-recognized function.

In general, the Greeks do not go much beyond this sort of definition. It is the starting-point and also the end-point of their reflexion.[1] But the questioning minds presented to us in Plato's Dialogues go a great deal further.[2] The simple-appearing definition of art as 'productive' contains more factors than are visible at first sight; and, according as questioning minds emphasize this factor or that, we find them developing the definition along a variety of distinct lines.

Thus, to some minds (1) it is immediately obvious that, in order to produce overt art-works, the artist, whatever his art, is co-operating with nature. To construct a palace, an aqueduct, or a simple home, the architect or builder is dependent, at every step, upon concrete materials: ranging from marble or stone or timber to the simplest forms of brick and plaster. These are his data, without which he cannot operate; and in final analysis they come to him from the hand of nature: objective, factual nature. Similarly the farmer requires soil, rain, sun, and air, as well as suitable seeds and plants. The cobbler requires wood or leather. The painter requires pigments, the musician, chords of varying tension, the poet, words.

These data, in every case provided by nature, have to possess a structure suited to the specific function of the artist, if they are to furnish him with an appropriate physical medium. Without the co-operation of nature, he can produce nothing.[3]

To other minds (2) it is even more obvious that the artist, whatever his art, co-operates with a given community. He constructs (in a sense) to order: to satisfy a given community's need. There must be some kind of economic demand for the artist's products: whether these are disposed of through the common mechanism of corn- or fish-market, or are brought by expert middle-men to the attention of wealthy connoisseurs. No one constructs aqueducts, church music, or epithalamia *in vacuo*. As a professional, the artist either has a signed contract in hand, or a public competition in prospect, success in which will bring him fame and other suitable emoluments. He gives his public, or at least tries to give his public, what it wants: amplifying, as artistically as he can, his master's voice. This attitude toward the artist and his function is connected, in the Dialogues, not only with the science which comes from Ionia, but with the humanism associated with the name of Protagoras.[4]

To yet other minds (3) it is clear that what makes an artist an artist is his technique: his mathematics, his logic, his scientific method. The popular mind calls this 'inspiration', and refers the whole matter to the guidance of the gods. But the refined intelligence which looks beneath this 'inspiration' can see that there is a method in the artist's alleged 'madness': a method to which the 'friends of God', i.e. the Pythagoreans and Eleatics, can give a specific name—the name of mathematics or dialectic.[5] To minds of this stamp, it is only too plain that what makes an artist an artist is neither objective nature, nor the biosocial interests of man, but the artist's technique. Without his selection, his ordering and re-arrangement of elements so that they enhance each other, the potentialities of artistic value would remain for ever slumbering in the bosom of unconscious nature, of a Being indistinguishable from Non-being; and society would know nothing of them beyond the vague intimations of the formless dream of 'a Good'.[6]

Let us investigate the functions attributed to art in each of these three schools of thought. (1) To the scientist who studies the tissue of objective factual motions called, in its collectivity, 'nature' or 'Being', it is at once obvious that nature constitutes a fundamental reality, to which man has to conform, if he is to survive, to succeed in living through the human life-cycle.

To a Heraclitus, the fundamental law of nature, the law of which all other laws, norms, and rules which work successfully, constitute subordinate phases, is the law of the pendulum-swing, the law of rhythm. Backward and forward, upward and downward, day and night, life and death, peace and war: everywhere we observe alternating phenomena which illustrate this fundamental fact. It is a fact which artists, like all other men, must take into account. In a word, the primary function of art is to conform to nature, to the fundamental fact of rhythm.[7]

Consider the farmer. Commercially, his function in the human economy is to grow plants for human uses, especially for food. If he is to be successful in this, he must follow the rhythms of the natural life-cycle of his plants. He must respect the seasons: sowing in the Spring, harvesting in the Fall. He must see to it that each species of his plants receives proper attention to its objective needs in the way of alternating rhythms of sunshine and shade, of watering and drainage, of enriched and fallow soil, of exposure to and shelter from, frost and wind.[8]

It is doubtless true that only God can make a tree. Creation is God's prerogative. But that does not mean that there is not much that a skilful farmer can do. He can select the seeds he plants, and the place of their planting. He can cultivate and prune, can fertilize and weed: so that his tender seedlings are neither choked nor permitted to straggle and run wild. By conforming to nature, the farmer can grow for timber; or he can construct a hedge, an orchard, or a windbreak. He can even call into being a garden, a landscape on which his eye can rest with pleasure.

If he is very determined, he may try to grow figs on thistles, or attempt other experiments in plant-breeding. But, whatever his immediate aim, he will soon discover, that, for success, it is essential for him to study and follow throughout the objective, factual rhythms observed in nature. His activity as an artist is, in fact, a copying and imitating, a varying rather than a creating. His productive function is not (like God's) primary, but secondary. Give him his data, and then he will do what his art enables him to do skilfully: i.e. what faithful observation and humble experimentation show to be both possible and useful. But the limits toward which he can operate successfully are all set, not by himself, but by nature.[9]

It is the same with all other arts. Consider, e.g., the art of painting. As discussed in the Dialogues, the general opinion is that painting is primarily a representative art. Its chief function is to imitate: to copy, to reproduce the visible aspects of some physical object. So far, the painter's function resembles the function of the sculptor and even the carpenter. They differ in that the carpenter produces a three-dimensional wooden replica of the object: a replica whose proportions are either identical with those of the object, or are based upon the precise mathematical measurements of a sliding scale; whereas the sculptor and the painter have to substitute the eye of the beholder for the measuring instruments of the artisan. The sculptor and the painter (and this is of the essence of their arts) produce something whose proportions *look* 'right' to the beholder, and *suggest* the precise mathematical proportions of the original.[10]

Where the position of the beholder has to be taken into account, the artist has to practise distortion, to induce the effect desired. In a large statue, seen from below, the nearer parts (judged by the eye) look larger, the remoter parts, smaller, than exact measurement would show them to be. These deficiencies (for so the artist considers them) have to be remedied by slightly diminishing the size of the nearer, and increasing the size of the remoter, parts. In a picture (the extreme case which limits the artist to two dimensions), if the painter is to suggest the third dimension and appropriate proportional relationship of all parts, he has to make a large number of distortions of perspective, shading, and colouring. None of these is (as a rule) a matter of precise measurement. They are matters of trained empirical judgement: somewhat as a Greek flautist (or in modern times a violinist) has to feel his way, using his fingers and his ear, toward what will *sound* like the 'right' pitch of his notes. As is well known, in modern as in ancient times, an artistic painter, using these tricks of distortion, can not only suggest the third dimension and appropriate proportions competently. He can deceive a careless beholder into imagining that the artificial images before him are the actual physical objects which they merely indicate or depict.[11]

The possibilities of such suggestion are by no means limited to the mathematico-physical proportions of the object being reproduced. If we consider, not merely the optical organ, the physical eye of the beholder, but the eye of his 'mind', including the entire range of his experience, the scope of suggestion at once becomes very great indeed. A beholder accustomed to seeing two friends always together, can readily be induced, on seeing a picture of the one, to conjure up in his mind a corresponding picture of the other. Indeed, the mere name of Simmias is enough to suggest, to a member of the Socratic circle, a mental image of Cebes.[12]

The painter can, in point of fact, count upon a good deal in the way of such associations, memories, and expectations. But from the standpoint of Ionian science, both the painter and the beholder are limited by their experience to the physical environment. It is factual nature, with its physical surfaces and its physical pigments, which makes possible the art of representative painting, and, in the end, determines how far the imitative artist can go.[13]

In the other arts, the situation is strikingly analogous to this. In music, the trained ear of the auditor corresponds to the trained eye of the beholder in pictorial art. Musical tones are analogous to the colours of painting; and a melody is a kind of tone-picture, a physical model (constructed of tones, harmonies, and rhythms) of some part of the tissue of objective motions in the physical world. In language, the letters (vowels, consonants, and mutes), together with the syllables and words to which these (according to grammarians) give rise, are expressive of certain types of motion. They are analogous to the tones in music, the colours in painting, and indeed to the expressive movements of Greek dancing: so that the poet or rhetorician, with his artistically selected phrases and sentences, is giving us a kind of gesture-image or word-picture of the physical world.[14] The rhythmic words parallel and even coalesce with the rhythmic tone-structures of the accompaniment. Or, if we consider the Greek chorus, we see that the verbal rhythms coalesce with the rhythms of interpretative Greek dancing. In fact, in Classical times, the three arts (of poet, musician, and choreographer) characteristically combine in a single representative art: not unlike (in principle) the modern music-drama associated with the name of Wagner.[15]

In all these species, the generic function of art, from the standpoint of Ionian science, is to construct, in some selected physical medium, a copy or model of this or that physical object. This object (again, from the standpoint of Heraclitean science) is a portion of the rhythmically patterned tissue of motions which constitute the events of the physical world. It is thus the rhythmic motions of the physical world which lend to artistic representation its data, its patterns, its scope, and its objective significance.[16]

Let us now consider the function of art, from the standpoint of *humanism*: the standpoint associated in ancient times especially with the name of Protagoras. This position has an almost overwhelming appeal for the citizens of a great democracy, such as existed at Athens. It is accordingly expounded and criticized in the Dialogues, defended

H

and re-expounded by Socrates, re-criticized and finally (it would seem) incorporated into Platonism itself: when Platonism at last decides to come to terms with the world of actuality.[17]

This is the standpoint which takes life and growth, rather than a static science of nature, as fundamental. In a world of change, the growing organism, with non-logical impulses, struggling continuously for survival, provides not only the premises, but also the conclusions of any sort of wisdom which desires to be practical. The patterned activities of peoples, the rhythmic gestures and cries from which the representative arts gradually evolve, all arise in this struggle. As groups and individuals seek to live through the various phases of the biosocial life-cycle, they co-operate in coping with their problems. Their efforts, at first matters of blind trial and error, eventually culminate in some sort of success. This stamps into the cultural background and outlook of the group, the patterns of communication which prove satisfactory.

From this standpoint, all ideals are empirical. They represent human lines of attack, community plans of action, experiments whose import is humanly biosocial. All ideas are empirical hypotheses, cues to action. You try them out, and observe what happens. If you like the consequences, you have found something that works. This you call, justifying your hypotheses. But your test, your validating criterion, is always, what proves satisfactory to the dominant group: never, anything 'absolute'.

There are no 'absolutes'. There is no Reality with a capital R: any more than there is Truth with a capital T, or Knowledge with a capital K, or Beauty with a capital B. In fact, Ionian science, in so far as it aims at an alleged 'factual objectivity', is pursuing a pure will-o'-the-wisp.[18]

Consider a concrete example. A public speaker is successful when he wins applause; when the plan he advocates is adopted by majority vote; when its biosocial consequences prove satisfactory to the group. A Themistocles, a Pericles, or a Cimon, is a great statesman. On the humanist theory, his 'greatness' is a function of the estimation in which he is held by his fellow-citizens. If his plans for repelling invasion, for collecting contributions, for putting up useful and impressive public buildings, are adjudged acceptable (not only in the hearing, but in the outcome), his fame is established. But if the invasion is not repelled, if the courts decide that he has mismanaged public funds, if the enemy pulls down his 'long walls' and imposes a war-indemnity, the self-same 'great statesman' becomes, almost over-night, a 'discredited politician', with nothing before him but exile, poverty, or death.

In such a world, the really 'great' men in every art are, quite simply, those whose leadership achieves popularity. They work for the cash rewards, the esteem, the prestige which become theirs. They judge merit by biosocial consequences—as who does not? And among those consequences, winning friends while influencing people ranks among the most highly valued. In a democracy, this is elementary. Such is the primary, the generic function of art.[19]

The voice of wisdom (of practical wisdom, that is), as interpreted by a Protagoras or a Gorgias, urges the practice of this generic art, the art of salesmanship, advertisement, or persuasive flattery: the art entitled 'rhetoric'. This art, based upon experimental methods, teaches how to sway the ideas of men in convention assembled: how to formulate such men's own blind purposes, stimulating them with well-selected slogans, convincing them that the sovereign people can do no wrong. It is suggested that, while in the political field there are no absolute 'rights' or 'wrongs', 'truths' or 'falsities', there *are* such distinctions as 'better' or 'worse'. The really clever statesman is the speaker who utilizes his mastery of effective slogans to induce the people to vote for a policy which they will consider satisfactory, not merely for the moment, but 'better' also in the long run. That is to say, he reinforces convincingly the long-range beliefs of his auditors as to their own cultural significance and destiny. These constitute the screen against which he projects the images characteristic of his particular art.[20]

Thus Protagoras, although professionally a mere teacher (sophist) interested in securing his professional fee, has enough social tact to keep at all times the respect of his audience. He claims and wins, under all conditions, their sympathy, approval, and esteem. His coming is awaited with eagerness. When he walks, the ranks divide before and close behind. When he opens his lips to speak, the silence is profound. When he comes to an end, the applause is deafening. Even when defeated in argument, he continues to retain the centre of the stage. As the acknowledged eminent authority, he can afford to disclaim envy: as he gracefully prophesies, for his young opponent, a brilliant future.

So too, the 'great' dramatists, those who win the prizes awarded, in effect, by popular vote, have to be a little careful about what they put into their plays. A ritual costume, revealing the 'secrets' of the Mysteries, can cause trouble. A patriotic chorus, on the other hand,

will ensure the happiest results. A depiction of serene old age coming
to one who has served his country well, a continuous suggestion that
gods and hereos are watching over the destiny of the homeland, that
the apparent sorrows and even catastrophes of men are leading, by
mysterious ways, to the accomplishment of some deeply satisfying
purpose: all this sort of thing will provide the members of the audience with an opportunity to project themselves into the life depicted
for them, a life broader, deeper, and richer than the daily round and
common task. Even the virtuoso-writing which gives a well-graced
actor his chance to stimulate the entire range of emotions in his
audience: so that they will shed tears of pity and will experience de-
lightful shudders at the horrors being enacted before them; this will
stir up the audience to vote the prize to the drama whose emotional
dynamics expand and contract the feelings of all who are subjected to
the spell. Their sense of being alive had been enhanced, and a good
time has been had by all.[21]

It is the same with all the arts. Every artist, from cabinet-maker to
flautist, from candlestick-maker to epic poet, is a professional. He
has something to sell; and whether that something is technically good
or bad, if he is to make sales, he will have to be a practitioner, in a
democracy, of the over-all art of salesmanship. His generic function,
therefore, will be: to enhance the community's life-sense, to stimulate the sources of its positive self-feeling, and (at best) to give it a
lead in the direction of its manifest destiny in the world of claims and
counter-claims. Such an art is not so much objective as biosocial. It
seeks to attain its ends, not by conforming to impersonal fact, but by
persuasively organizing the community's will-to-thrive.[22]

Let us now pass on to consider the function of art according to the
third school of thought, the mathematical or logical school represented by the 'friends of ideas', i.e., the so-called Pythagoreans and the
Eleatics. These 'idealists' agree in disregarding, on the one hand, the
crude empirical senses (which mean so much to the Ionian scientists),
and, on the other, the crude empirical, quasi-instinctive feelings
(which mean so much to the humanists). Such 'idealists' construct a
more 'refined' world: an intellectual's world, a tissue of inter-
implying geometrical or dialectical patterns. Plato groups them together, largely because their patterns, whether geometrical (Pythagorean) or dialectical (Eleatic), are (in both cases) based upon the fundamental conception of ideal unity (the 'one').[23]

In such a world, the medium of art is no longer anything as primitive, as close to the soil, as the language of instinctive feeling which

plays such a part in Homeric poetry and Periclean rhetoric. It is the more refined, technical language of the mathematical sciences, with their arithmetical and geometrical patterns, and of logic or dialectic, with its intentionally standardized concepts and categories.[24]

While relatively abstract, this intellectual medium of expression, as found in use in the 'idealist' schools of Plato's time, is not final. Its intellectualization never reaches the level of 'pure' reason. It belongs, in fact, to the third, rather than to the fourth stage of intelligence, and is (according to thinking in the Academy) somewhere midway between the world of appearance (sensuous or emotional) and the world of ultimate, metaphysical reality. The mathematical sciences are explicitly accorded by Plato a status somewhere midway between the humanistic 'arts', and the absolutely final science of metaphysics. The logical or dialectical science cultivated by the Eleatics, is given approximately the same degree of provisional rather than final, absolute certainty and truth. As long as their ultimate assumptions remain unexamined, such disciplines cannot be thought to belong, entirely and without remainder, in the metaphysical realm of pure reason. They participate, to a slight but material extent, in the twilight uncertainty that surrounds all empirical art.[25]

The general function of mathematical and logical technique, is to raise an experience out of the realm of blind, empirical groping (in which assertion and counter-assertion are equally possible), and to introduce it into a realm in which definition, exposition, and proof (or disproof) are possible. This is the realm of clear-cut ideas.[26]

In the world of Heraclitus and of Protagoras, everything is in motion, in a state of becoming. You can never truly say that it 'is' this, and 'is not' that. It is in process of change, entirely devoid of identity. Heraclitus characterizes this by saying that 'you cannot step into the same stream twice'. The water will have flowed on. A later writer corrects him by saying that, in such a world, you could not step into the same stream *once*.[27] There is no sameness at all, either in 'you' or in 'the stream'. Where everything is in a state of flux (*panta rhei*), there are no 'things', and clear-cut ideas are without any point of reference and application. In such a world, thinking, mathematical and logical thinking, would be futile, without concrete application. The 'friends of ideas' have accordingly devised a technique calculated to withdraw humanity from the Heraclitean and Protagorean world, into a realm where the arts of the mathematician and the logician are at least possible.[28]

In this technical world of the 'idealists' of Plato's time, then, the generic function of art (i.e. of intellectual technique) is *to clarify ideas*: to raise experience to the intellectual level at which clear and distinct thinking, resting upon carefully defined terms and their classification and division into systems of inter-implying data, seems to have before it a vista of endless progress. The possibility of pursuing almost limitless lines of implication is, in fact, so fascinating to its discoverers, that such 'idealists' never stop to inquire into the basis (if any) of their detailed researches. They merely go on their way, rejoicing.[29]

From such a world, Heraclitean-Protagorean motion is utterly banished. Physical space, time, movement, change, causation—all such terms are, to the new intellectualism, devoid of metaphysical status and meaning. But the new metaphysics has its own terms, all charged with a new, non-empirical significance.

Thus in the world of ideas, the 'friends' of such abstractions discover a new type of movement. This is the kind of movement characteristic of inter-implication: the movement of thought from premises (assumed hypothetically) to the conclusion or conclusions which such premises imply; and again from a position (hypothetically assumed) to the premises which would seem to account for such a position. There are evidently many lines along which thought can move; and a school interested in the principle of unity readily makes vague over-all assumptions: e.g. that ultimately all ideas are 'one', i.e. form inter-implying parts of a single, all-containing system.

But the Eleatic idealists of Plato's time are like the Pythagorean scientists, in that they merely assume, without serious examination, the validity of such working hypotheses. What work has been done (by the great Parmenides himself), is unsatisfying. It seems to terminate in a maze, a multiplicity of downright contradictions: unsolved paradoxes, passed for further investigation to the more promising members of a younger and conceivably more profound body of thinkers. Meanwhile, there is no doubt that implication possesses a characteristic type of motion, utterly distinct from anything expounded by Heraclitus and his fellow-Ionians.[30]

So also, in this new world of ideas, 'idealists' are rapidly discovering new and superior principles for organizing, classifying, and relating ideas. In place of the (largely empirical) category of cause-and-effect, they discover the more transcendental category of ground-and-consequent. This also possesses a form of movement quite distinct from anything in the Heraclitean 'flux'. Instead of the empirical concept of space, where everything is external to everything else, they discover the 'place of ideas', which is devoid of externality.[31] Ideas are not outside of, above or below, to the right or left of, one another. Instead of empirical time-flow, these 'idealists' discover eternity or absolute duration. These 'ideas' and their interrelations are not affected by empirical time. They endure eternally.[32] Any well-trained member of the new school of thought which assumes the validity of such concepts, can devote himself to this sort of transcendental contemplation: in perfect confidence that, by thus withdrawing from the empirical world, with its unending and (to intellectuals) unmeaning flux and reflux, he is achieving a new and transcendental sort of 'highest good', a serenity of mind, a peace which utterly passes the understanding of a Protagoras, a Gorgias, or a Callicles.[33]

Friends of this new way of ideas are not without feelings: the feelings appropriate for intellectuals. Their feelings are startlingly different from Protagorean feelings; but how much better grounded! Such human weaknesses as are indicated by the terms, pity, fear, hate, and love, are (of course) finally excluded from the consciousness which has achieved the new transcendentality. But intellectual satisfaction in solving intellectual puzzles, transcendental pride and joy in transcendental achievement, intellectual approval of other friends of ideas, a sense of comradeship in a common cause, and a sense of profound superiority when they look upon the blind gropings of less well-schooled mortals: feelings of this type are obviously present with them.

It must be wonderful (they feel) to be friends, not only of ideas, but also of God: to enter, *via* their technical use of understanding, into the Divine Mind; to live, move, and have Being (transcendental Being) in His life, His movement, and His Being![34] This sense of superiority, developed further by the Stoic School (for which Plato's abstract idealists are unconsciously laying the foundations), needs no further elaboration here. To Plato's Socrates, and to the visiting professor from Athens, there is always something slightly ludicrous about such pretension and such self-confidence. That beings who are, and remain (in spite of their technical achievements) merely human, at best mere puppets, playthings of the veritable Gods, should convince themselves that they are as Gods, knowing both good and evil, and having within themselves the entire range of the Higher Experience, is more than faintly absurd. The references to this side of 'idealism' in the Dialogues are accordingly gently ironical.

There is a suggestion that thinkers of this stamp are almost too 'refined' to be taken seriously: that they suffer from a 'holier-than-thou' complex. Only God Himself could be as wise as members of this school profess to be![35]

In such a school, what is the function of art? As we have said, to clarify ideas. But it is a great deal more than that. Art is always productive, creative of this and that. Idealistic art, the art of abstraction, of technique, is creative of theorems and incipient systems, of branches of mathematics and symbolic logic, developed along many lines, without much regard to their empirical significance and applicability to the problems of men. Idealistic music, for instance. This is so refined in its abstraction from empirical conditions, as to be inaudible to mortal ears. The Pythagoreans deduce a 'music of the spheres'. But it is too transcendental to be susceptible of anything like empirical verification. So too, as compared with the pictorial arts which enhance life in a Protagorean world, they develop abstract diagrams which appeal to intellectual intuition and can be used (doubtless) to teach lessons of transcendental value. The place of empirical poetry is occupied by the form of communication (evolved by Zeno) known as 'dialectic'. The empirical wizardry of a Homer or a Pindar is superseded by the altogether magical technique of the new *a priori* reasoning, with its promise of transcendental thrills.[36]

Here, then, in the work of the three philosophical schools, we have three distinct theories of the function of art. Its function is to produce (1) physical replicas of the rhythmic motions which constitute the physical cosmos, or (2) enhancement of community egoism in such a way as to influence the community will-to-thrive, its will-to-control others, or (3) abstractive techniques which will substitute on all occasions, for the instinctive vitalities of common sense, the *a priori* constructions of mathematics and logic. According to these ways of thinking, an artist is generically (1) a humble copyist, (2) a persuasive public speaker, or (3) a formal logician.

While these are primary, the generic functions of art and the artist, we find Plato, in the Dialogues, interested far more in other, secondary, more specific effects. He is especially interested in the educative and ethical consequences of the primary functions: in their influence upon the development of men and women into good citizens, and (in some cases) into good leaders. From this standpoint—which is quite different from the standpoints of the Ionian scientists, of the humanists, and of the abstract idealists—his Socrates and other representatives of philosophic insight not only criticize all three theories of the generic function of art, but also have something new to offer: something less extreme, better balanced, a more satisfactory account of the artistic function—in an ideal, or nearly ideal, human community.

Let us proceed to follow Plato, first, in focusing our attention upon the educative and ethical effects of art in the view of the three schools of thought; secondly, in bringing out the negative force of the Socratic or quasi-Socratic criticism; and thirdly, in investigating the new positive theory of the function of art in an ideal community which Socrates (in the *Republic*) and the visiting professor from Athens (in the *Laws*) set before us.

NOTES

1. *Symp.* 205bc, *Rep.* 533a, *Soph.* 219c. To say that the builder builds, the farmer farms, the weaver weaves, etc., is a simple and 'safe' definition in terms of function. As long as you stick to such definitions, you cannot easily be refuted, or go wrong in debate. Similarly the youthful members of Plato's (informal) Academy, as depicted in the Dialogues, have a pronounced tendency to stick to what we might call 'Lesson I' in the Theory of Ideas (cf. *Phdo.* 100b f., *Parm.* 130, *Rep.* 504e f., *Phil.* 14d ff.).

2. In Plato's Dialogues, the authorities whose theories go so far as to awaken questioning, are not (as a rule) native sons of Athens. They are visiting professors (from Abdera, Elea, Leontini, Locri, etc.). In only one Dialogue (the *Laws*) is the characteristic visiting professor represented as a native Athenian. And *he* is represented as a travelled man. It is *Ionian* science, humanistic life-wisdom, Pythagorean mathematics, Eleatic logic-chopping, which furnish the themes for discussion. In a word, it is usually by interacting with theories derived from sources outside the Greek peninsula, that the outlook of the Platonic Academy is developed in breadth, depth, and precision.

3. *Laws* 657a, 709a f., 747c, 829b f. For 'words' see pp. 106–107. Cf. *Crat.* 386a, 430b, 434a. Perhaps the technical difficulty in securing suitable pigments, had something to do with the relative paucity of colours used in early Hellenic paintings. Thus we are told (F. C. Tilney, *The Lure of the Fine Arts*, Chapman & Hall, London, 1931), pp. 91–92, 'According to the elder Pliny, the Greeks in the earliest attempts used but four pigments: white, yellow, red and black. . . . The later days of Zeuxis, Apelles, and Protogenes (included blue and green too). . . . The colour sense of Apelles was already five centuries . . . removed from that of Homer' (cf. also, *ibid.*, pp. 22, 95, 101).

4. *Prtg.* 325c f., 342d, *Gorg.* 501e f., *Euthyd.* 289d f., *Rep.* 365d, 377b, 397 ff., 476c f., 492d, 493a, 600, 602b, 605a, *Tim.* 19cd, *Pol.* 268ab, *Soph.* 235d f., 236a, *Laws* 643bc, 656d f., 659d, 663d, 664b, 681c, 700a f., 720b, 793a, 812b.

5. Aristot., *Met.* 986a 15 ff., Alex. Aphrodisias in Arist. *Met.* I 6, p. 55 Hayduck (cited in Ritter and Preller, *Hist. Phil. Graecae*, 8th edit., sect. 76, with notes). Cf. Ritter and Preller, sects. 78, 82, 328.

6. *Prtg.* 338e f., *Gorg.* 503a f., *Tim.* 68b f., with Taylor's *Commentary* on 68a 4–7, *Phil.* 12d, 26b, 51b f., *Laws* 709b–d.

7. *Crat.* 401d, 402a, cf. 440, *Theaet.* 152e ff., 179d f., cf. Aristot. *Met.* 1010a 13 f., Ritter and Preller, sects. 32–34, 40, 41, 43–44, 47. Cf. also Burnet, *Early Greek Philosophy*, (1908), pp. 167 ff., esp. sect. 79.

8. *Rep.* 369c f., 370d, 420d f., *Soph.* 219b, *Phil.* 56a, *Laws* 643b, 743d, 760e, 842 ff., 915 ff., 949e.

9. *Theaet.* 149de, *Soph.* 265b ff., *Phil.* 55d f.

10. *Crat.* 423d, *Rep.* 596d ff., *Laws* 663c, 667e ff. Cf. Tilney, *op. cit.*, pp. 63, 109, 'In Art, feeling is everything, demonstrable truth nothing. We want things to *look* right; that is essential. Whether they *are* right or not is of minor importance.' This author believes that this necessary distortion 'is not generally known'. It is at least [R.C.L.] very frequently repeated in works on aesthetics.

11. *Rep.* 476c, 531ab, 598, 601c f., 602c, *Phil.* 55d f., 57d, 59a, *Laws* 889. In one of the large Chicago galleries on Michigan Boulevard, each room is provided with a longish table in the centre, around which, if you look in at the door, you will sometimes see two or three people standing. As you look down a long corridor, into the room in which the corridor ends, you see such a table, with three persons (apparently a mother with two small children) standing behind the table. It is not until you enter the room that you discover that what you have actually been seeing is a picture, so painted and hung as to give you this illusion. In this one room, there is no physical table.

12. *Phdo.* 73d f., *Phil.* 38c f. Cf. Croce, *Aesthetic as Science of Expression* . . ., p. 18. Tilney, *op. cit.* p. 223, writes: 'There is an airy magic in a fine picture. . . . The mind does not receive a record passively, but explores a suggestion actively. At a proper viewpoint the spectator reads into the work all that he knows and feels and desires, and it is on this co-operation that the painter counts.'

Tilney, apparently, confines this to the art of painting. But I [R.C.L.] would suppose, partly from the suggestion of Locke (*Essay* II ix 8—Molyneux's problem), and partly from my own experience (cf. the poet Heinrich Heine's description—in the fragment entitled *Florentinische Nächte*—of the pictorial associations aroused in him by music) that something of this sort is true in *all* the arts, including the art which Tilney explicitly excludes (sculpture). What psychologists call 'perception', i.e. the interpretation of *sensa* with the help of our memories, indicates that the experience is quite universal in scope.

13. It is because the physical pigments are made up of the same four elements as the rest of the physical world, and are similarly coloured, that it is possible for the painter to use them in such a way as to reproduce the physical aspects of other physical objects (*Laws* 889). A picture is a kind of model (not unlike a carpenter's or a sculptor's model) of the physical object: reduced (in appearance) from three to two dimensions, but definitely suggesting (to the eye of the beholder, from a given position) its more obviously three-dimensional original (*Rep.* 598a f., 601a f., *Phil.* 42a, 59ab).

14. *Crat.* 423a–424e, *Laws* 816a; cf. *Theaet.* 202 ff., *Soph.* 253a. Croce, in the 'General Linguistic' part of his *Aesthetic as Science of Expression* . . ., criticizes the efforts of grammarians and similar persons to reduce language to 'parts of speech',

and even more if they try to reduce it to words, syllables, letters, and sounds. As Croce views the matter, language is 'expressive', and it is its expressiveness, upon the whole, which lends significance to what mechanical analysts (later) distinguish as 'parts'. For Croce, the whole is NOT made up of the alleged 'parts' at all. It is essentially 'indivisible' (see esp. pp. 2–5, 8, 11, 20, 108, 143, 146–151). 'If expression be indivisible, the physical fact in which it externalizes itself, can be . . . subdivided. A painted surface, into lines and colours, groups and curves of lines, kinds of colours; a poem into strophes, verses, feet, syllables; prose into chapters, paragraphs, headings, periods, phrases, words. . . . The parts thus obtained are not aesthetic, but physical facts, arbitrarily divided' (p. 108).

15. *Rep.* 398d, 399e f., *Laws* 653 f., 655d f., 657d, 658e f., 669b f., 790d, 814 ff.
16. *Rep.* 397a–c, 399e f., *Phil.* 17b f., 56a. I refer to Heraclitus, as representative of Ionian science, partly because of his importance in its development (cf. *Theaet.* 179d), but chiefly because of his influence upon Plato (cf. 242d). The *Timaeus* and the *Theaetetus* make this abundantly clear; and we know from the evidence of Aristotle (*Met.* 937a 36), not only that Plato was educated in the Heraclitean doctrine, but also that he 'retained these views in his later years'. (Modern critics [e.g. Wilamowitz] suggest that this is not factual, but is probably an inference from the fact that Plato wrote a Dialogue entitled *Cratylus*. But surely [R.C.L.] it is perfectly grotesque to suppose that a modern knows more on this point than Aristotle, who was actually present, and apparently makes a simple statement of what looks like fact.)

From this standpoint, any art-work is a patterned interplay of rhythms, reproducing something objective: e.g. an orrery, a planetary map, or a symphonic presentation of the music of the spheres are a carpenter's, a painter's, and a musician's 'imitation' of one and the same object—the physical motions studied by the astronomic scientist.

17. For exposition and criticism, see *Protagoras, Theaetetus,* and *Rep.* I, etc. For the re-exposition by Socrates (who leaves the position unrefuted), see *Theaet.* 166 ff. For the re-criticism, see the *Sophistes* (in connexion with which, John Wild, *Plato's Theory of Man,* Cambridge, Mass., 1946, esp. pp. 271, 280 ff., is helpful). For the probable incorporation into Platonism, see the *Laws,* which (as I understand it) expounds, not the life of *transcendental* idealism (of the *Phaedo* and *Gorgias*), but the 'mixed life' of the *Philebus*: which represents a balance (like the model city of the *Laws*) between idealism on the one hand, and realism and humanism on the other. For the relation to Athenian democracy, see esp. *Rep.* 338d f., 557 ff., *Laws* 700b–701b.

18. This is the position of Protagoras, as maintained in his book *On Truth* (discussed by Socrates in the *Theaetetus*), and supported by various passages in the *Republic* (e.g. 492–493).

19. *Meno* 93b–95a, *Gorg.* 455e ff., 473c–486d, 503c, 515c–517b, 518d f., 521a f.
20. *Rep.* 493a–c, *Phaedr.* 261c f., *Theaet.* 167b f.
21. *Ion* 535, *Rep.* 595c, 604d ff., *Laws* 669b f., 700b f. Cf. Aristot., *Poetics* 1449b 27, 1454a 24–30, *Eth. Nic.* 111a 10, with Burnet's note.
22. *Gorg.* 450d f., 452d f., 454e ff., 463 f., *Menex.* 234e f., *Rep.* 492 f., *Phaedr.* 261cd, *Theaet.* 166 ff., *Laws* 700b f.
23. *Rep.* 510d ff., 522e ff., 531, 533b f., *Soph.* 242d ff.
24. *Rep.* 522 ff., *Tim.* 53b ff., *Theaet.* 185c f., *Soph.* 248c f., 253 ff.
25. *Rep.* 531, 533 f., *Parm.* 134 f.

26. *Rep.* 525 f., 529 f.

27. See Aristot., *Met.* 1010a 13 f. (The 'later critic' is Cratylus.) The grouping together of Heraclitus and Protagoras, in connexion with the changing world, the perpetual 'flux' of things (in spite of their differences in other respects), is Platonic (*Theaet.* 152 ff., 156 ff.).

28. *Crat.* 439d f., *Rep.* 523 ff., 529b f., 531a–c, 533b f.

29. *Rep.* 509d ff., 522c ff., cf. *Phaedr.* 265d f., 268 ff., 277bc. Perhaps we should add *Parm.* 137 ff.

30. *Euthyphr.* 11cd, 15a, *Meno* 86, *Crat.* 420bc, *Phdo.* 78c, 100, *Rep.* 510, 530c, 583e, *Tim.* 40bc, *Phaedr.* 245d, *Parm.* 135b–136d, *Laws* 897c f., cf. 891e f., 894e f., 896a, c, e f.

31. *Rep.* 510c–511c, *Tim.* 37–39d, 49–58c, *Phaedr.* 247b f.

32. *Meno* 81b f., *Phdo.* 97c ff., cf. *Parm.* 141, 151d f.

33. *Phdo.* 64c–69, cf. *Gorg.* 512d f., 521d f.

34. *Tim.* 53d.

35. *Meno* 81b f., *Rep.* 505bc, 506cd, *Tim.* 51e, 53d, *Phaedr.* 278d, *Soph.* 216a, 242 ff., *Laws* 644d f., 803c f.

36. *Rep.* 509bc (Glaucon remains at the level of 'understanding'—*dianoia*—which is at the level of Pythagorean science, *Rep.* 531, 533). *Parm.* 135d (Zenonian dialectic, like that of Parmenides, proceeds, upon the assumption of hypotheses, i.e. remains at the level of *dianoia*). Cf. also *Meno* 83, *Tim.* 53c ff., 80ab.

CHAPTER SIX

The Functions of Art, II

EXAMINED as to its value for education, ethics, and politics, the functional effect of art is clearly seen (in the Dialogues) as, to assist in 'developing right opinion'. That is to say, the artist provides reinforcement for the attitudes considered 'right'. He assists in developing the children of well-conditioned parents into good citizens and (in some cases) into good leaders.

Speaking generally, in Ancient Hellas, a 'good' citizen corresponds to a typical member of Plato's 'silver' class of civic auxiliaries. He is the steady character who is loyal to his community under all conditions. Rich in what Pareto calls 'Class II Residues', he is naturally (i.e. by disposition, even without specialized training), both in background and in outlook, a conservative. In times of peace, he can be trusted to observe and indeed to enforce respect for law and order. He will stay happily in the home town. He will rise politely when his elders put in an appearance. He will listen respectfully to what age and experience see fit to say. In time of war, he will trail his pike, marching in disciplined silence, and resolutely obeying his commanders. In a word, he will live up to the good old Homeric tradition of soldierly behaviour: with perhaps just a side-glance of admiration at the methods of modern Sparta. Never an intellectual, he will live and move in an atmosphere of comradeship, and of loyalty to community ideals. The Achaeans in Homer greeted their leaders' directives with universal acceptance; and so does he.

There is one further point. The community to which the 'good' citizen feels loyal, is never (in Ancient Hellas) anything vague, general, or abstract. It is concrete and very actual. His ethical and political outlook, while considered 'good' in the home town, will appear, to members of other communities, always a little imperfect and one-sided. But no one would ever dream of calling a typical

Hellene 'a man without a country'. He is never 'a good citizen' in general. His citizenship is always intensely specific. He is a good Athenian, a good Theban, a good Corinthian, a good Spartan: and proud to be what he is.

The universal Hellenic view is that the atmosphere of the arts, in the midst of which such a citizen lives, influences his attitudes very directly. If his biosocial environment is that of an artisan, a carpenter, weaver, or potter, this will tend to condition his attitudes so that he too (like his father and brothers) will become an artisan, a carpenter, weaver, or potter.[1] If we turn to such arts as painting, poetry, or music, we shall find things much the same. The general rule is, like father, like son. Carry analysis a little further, and everyone can see that two factors are involved. In each and every case, there has to be (1) some degree of natural capacity and interest, and (2) some degree of training supplied by the conditioning environment. If the environment supplies suitable training, and the individual does his part by supplying suitable capacity and taking sufficient interest: there is genuine interaction. The combination of both factors leads to the finished carpenter or potter, the finished painter or poet, as a result.[2]

Our first question is, assuming that art somehow influences the development of opinions considered 'right' for an Athenian or a Corinthian carpenter, poet, or musician: How does the adoption of the realist-minded attitude of Ionian science affect the work of artists? First and foremost, it reinforces respect for all rhythmic forces that are objective, factual. Given a modicum of natural ability, it is the second factor, the pressure of environmental forces, repeated and intensified, that seems all-important. The trainee's nature is docile. He adopts a receptive attitude. He opens himself to objective nature and becomes an unresisting, an integral part of his world. He conforms to *what is*, and pulsates with its rhythms.

The physical climate, for instance, of his home town exerts a definite influence, not merely upon his physical characteristics: upon the colour of his eyes and hair, upon his stance and the proportionate development of his muscles. It affects the development of his interests and ideas. It fixes, within certain limits, his character. The heat or cold, the dryness or wetness of his surroundings, the contours of the land upon which he walks: all such things affect him directly. Mountaineers are demonstrably different from plainsmen and from longshoremen. They not only look different. Their characters and dispositions are different. The ideals thus developed (in mountaineers, plainsmen, longshoremen, etc.) are clearly an important part of the opinions considered 'right' in such localities.[3]

So also with the social climate, the moral atmosphere of this or that community. Here art can copy the processes of nature, reinforcing the effect of natural rhythms by the rhythms of song and dance, by the rhythms of military drill, by the rhythms of cultural training. If every civic institution stresses, in all that is said and done, the values of the life militant: after a while you have the *ethos* which makes of Sparta the thing that it is—a *Militärstaat*. If every civic institution emphasizes commercial values: after a while you have the *ethos* characteristic of Corinth. If every institution stresses the values of freedom, of democracy, and of culture: after a while you have the moral atmosphere of Athens. In such ways, art reinforces the influence upon character of the physico-social environment.[4]

So much for a general answer to our first question: as to how the adoption of the attitude of the factual scientist affects the work of artists. We now approach our second question: as to what it is in human character that is thus influenced; and as to how art effects its influence.

According to Hellenic thought, there are three natural tendencies upon which nearly everything in a man's character depends. These are the powerful non-logical impulses connected with eating, drinking, and sex. They are what Plato calls 'necessary' appetites. In some degree they are universal. Every human being feels their power. And to some extent a positive response to their promptings is necessary: if the individual is to survive and to do his part toward ensuring the survival of the community. Hence the importance, to the community, of 'right opinion' in such matters.[5]

Properly controlled and guided by respect for the growth and prosperity of the community, these appetites are of direct ethical value. But if uncontrolled, if permitted to run to extremes, any one of these three may develop into what Plato calls 'a wild-beast appetite', which may prove ruinous to community and individual alike. Eating and drinking to excess, if habitual, unfit a man for performing the duties of citizenship; and excessive sex-indulgence (especially if in ways contrary to the natural use) may bring about the almost complete disintegration, both of the community and of the individual.[6]

The problem, therefore, for anyone interested in constructive social ethics, is to discover in what ways, and to what extent, art can be used to reinforce what the community regards as 'right' in respect of these three impulsive tendencies: that is to say, to reinforce the virtuous habit of temperance. From the standpoint of factual (Ionian) science, it is a question of how to condition the child, the youth, and the adult: so that he will acquire at least enough of this virtue to qualify as a 'good' citizen. There is no question of intellectualism, or of over-straining toward some kind of ascetic idealism. It is a question of *habitual conduct*. An occasional lapse, e.g. (according to Hellenic opinion) may prove unavoidable. So long as it is only occasional, it probably does no great harm—especially if a decent concealment is practised. The question is, how to acquire and strengthen temperance *as a habitual virtue*: to the extent and in the ways regarded as 'right' or 'honourable' in this or that actual community.[7]

Greek experience regards as acceptable, three main ways of reinforcing the degree of temperance considered practicable. The first is by outdoor sports, i.e. by the regular, community-approved field-exercises which keep a man physically fit. It is obviously impossible for a man who weakens his body by excessive self-indulgence, to excel in outdoor sports; and it is perfectly clear that a man who keeps 'in training' is accustomed to practising a somewhat rigorous degree of temperance.[8] The second is by public opinion. If a community seriously approves (however informally) usages considered 'right', and severely disapproves of practices considered 'wrong', its influence upon individual citizens is undoubtedly very great. 'The eye of the rulers is always upon the young'; and the young, conscious of that eye, behave accordingly.[9] The third is by community education: formal education in community values, leading to respect for community laws, rigorously enforced.

In all three of these, there is a certain place for art. But it is especially in the third, i.e. in education in the institutional system of this or that community, that art plays its greatest part. As Plato says, art 'both conditions and charms the youth into temperance'. Let us consider, in a few typical cases, how the arts recognized in a Hellenic community 'condition the youth into temperance' by means of education.[10]

Take the art of carpentry. This produces wooden utensils: bowls, plates, tables, weavers' shuttles, and the like. But it also trains men to become carpenters. This training may be chiefly technical: as in the case of sons being trained to carry on the paternal business. Or it may be liberal: as in the case of sons of well-conditioned parents, who acquire a little knowledge of the art, not to practise it for pay, but as amateurs, for purposes of general education.

In both cases, this training, whether technical or liberal in intent, takes place within the artisan's family circle. The child plays with 'mimic tools'. Later, he becomes 'father's helper'. Very gradually, by doing this and that, partly to order, and partly by imitation of what he sees others doing, he learns the approved use of actual tools, and eventually becomes a competent carpenter. By this method of learning, however, he is always more than a mere technician, a manipulator of wood and of instruments for working with wood. He has acquired the biosocial outlook, the professional bias of the ancient equivalent of the carpenters' union. He feels, thinks, talks, and acts like a professional. In fact, he *is* (in most cases) a professional. It is the same with the art of pottery, and indeed with all such arts.[11]

The point is this: whatever the technical instruments mastered, whether the hammer, saw, and plane, the potter's wheel, or the weaver's loom, he is also learning to act as a happy, useful, and loyal member of the professional family: a family in which steady work, competent craftsmanship, and respect for the usages of the trade, are absorbed as part of the artisan's cultural atmosphere. Excessive indulgence in eating, drinking, and sex, is no part of such an atmosphere. That sort of thing is left to the idle rich.[12]

In the artisan family, steadiness and hard work are the rule. In such ways, i.e. partly by interacting with the objective nature of the several kinds of wood and iron used in the trade (in which he has to conform to that nature, if he is to succeed as an artisan), and partly by conforming to the economic, social, and biosocial usages customary in the professional group, he is becoming conditioned for a life of useful activity in the community. He is at all times learning to live with his fellows, to share their ideals as well as their tasks, and to be an acceptable member of the group. That is to say, life in such a family is factual preparation for good citizenship, so far as the artisan is permitted to acquire citizenship in this or that Hellenic community.[13]

In all the arts and crafts, the objective factors operative in the environment, both physical and social, produce this same kind of effect. They condition men for 'temperance and justice', i.e. for living in a stable society. Let us now glance at such arts as dancing, poetry, and music, which are closely interconnected. Dancing is sometimes treated as a subordinate form of gymnastic, concerned with patterns of rhythmic motion, exercises which have a direct effect upon the health of the body. At other times, dancing is treated as a subordinate form of music: as the rhythmic accompaniment of folk-chants, reinforcing, through gesture, the message of the words chanted. In this second form, there may be a very direct influence upon 'the health of the soul', i.e. upon character.

Military drill, for instance, associated with chants expressive of a patriotic attitude toward defensive warfare, especially in the community-approved war-dances, can be very effective (as the Spartans have found) in developing the habitual civic virtue of courage. Processional marching, when associated with chants praising the civic deities who bring peace and prosperity to the community, especially in the community-approved peace-dances, can be very effective in developing a positive attitude toward temperance and justice, i.e. respect for community law and order.[14] Certain other dances, whose motion is perhaps a little wilder, are thought (by medical opinion) to provide aid in controlling the non-logical phobias which arise in the organism in a variety of untoward circumstances. Such dances assist in reinforcing the civic habit of overcoming fear and presenting a bold front on all proper occasions.[15]

Harmony and melody, as used by the musical composer to reinforce the message of the approved chant-words, in association with the dance-rhythms, particularly as found in the choral music approved by this or that community, are also very helpful in reinforcing the approved community *ethos*. These three arts, viewed from the standpoint of factual science, can provide an insidious atmosphere which finds its way into the internal rhythmic structures of the organism, and conditions habit in the approved ways.[16]

Thus we realize how, always considering the matter from the standpoint of Ionian science, the objective factors of the environment interact with objective tendencies present in the organism, and how that interaction can be given a one-sided twist toward militarism, commercialism, or the adoption of faith in freedom and liberal culture. It is (from the standpoint under consideration) always a matter of objective conditioning. You hammer away at producing the attitudes a community accepts as desirable; and, in the end, you bring all your citizens into step. They accept the word of the community, partly because it conditions, and partly because, by its artistic wizardry, it charms them. They march forward, wheel to the right or left, and come to a halt, as one man: reacting always with the habitual responses built up in them by *the arts, which are all forms of physical drill*. The man of good habits is the good citizen. You can count upon the well-drilled man to react in the ways approved in Sparta, or in Corinth, or in Athens.[17]

Let us now ask, how *acceptance of the humanist attitude* associated with the name of Protagoras or Gorgias affects the work of artists toward developing and strengthening the civic virtues approved in this or that community. We have already seen that the scientific attitude treats all arts as ways of conditioning, as forms of *physical* drill. That is to say, it emphasizes the *objective* factor, the overwhelming influence of the factual environment. Acceptance of the humanist attitude emphasizes the *social* (or biosocial) factor, the relation of the dominant group to the individual.

'Parents naturally stamp upon their children and grandchildren their own institutions.' Parents reinforce their admonitions in the family, as teachers do in the school (which is regarded as an extension of the family), by the use of corporal punishment. And magistrates in the city (also regarded as an extension of the family—and school) reinforce the requirements of the community laws with appropriate punishment for defaulters. But this is rather extreme. Actually, the gentler and more frequently used method is by 'the muses and the gods of contests', i.e. by music and gymnastic: in a word, by the mild but pervasive influence of community art.

From the humanist standpoint, the arts are never regarded as extended forms of *physical* drill. They 'habituate', it is true; but not by mere intensity and frequency, as such; i.e. not by a mechanical conditioning which beats down the individual will. The arts are more subtle in their pervasiveness. They are social and biosocial: parts of the family and tribal background and outlook which permeates the entire cultural atmosphere of the group. They get in under the skin of individual group-members, and *make them want to do*—whatever the community regards as proper. The individuals *want* to be members of the group, in good standing. It is all *voluntary*.

This is true of all the arts, including carpentry, weaving, and pottery, quite as much as poetry, painting, and music in all its branches. A young man, brought up so that his natural bent is progressively developed by the insidiously social and biosocial promptings of his community, does not feel that he is being used for another's purposes. He does not feel drilled and forced, willy-nilly, to do this and that to satisfy someone else. On the contrary: he has within him something which wants to be a good carpenter, a good painter, or a good musician. He identifies himself with this inner want. He welcomes the experienced co-operation of teachers, parents, and his elders generally. Are they not assisting him to become himself, and at the same time (this is the beauty of it!) to become a valued member of the community, whose needs his art enables him to satisfy:[20]

Thus the public speaker, influencing people and inducing the civic assembly to vote overwhelmingly for policies likely, in the long run, to work out for the community's good, is doubtless achieving an envied success. Is he not a great leader, a statesman? But he is also, by subtly praising the Athenians to their faces, and employing all the sure-fire slogans about freedom, democracy, and the manifest historical destiny of Athens, flattering his audience. He is satisfying the inner need of every citizen of that great city and country to feel himself important: a man playing (by his vote, if by nothing further) a decisive part in world-events. Like the patriotic poet or the popular Homeric recitalist, he exercises, in the practice of his art, an almost hypnotic influence, which is altogether magical. He feels inspired. His audience is similarly carried away. Everybody shares in the enhancement of self-consciousness achieved, and a wonderful time is had by all.[21]

Similarly with the musician, the 'celebrity artist' who makes of himself an immense success with a democratic audience. He enjoys his own virtuosity, of course: like the modern Vladimir de Pachmann, with his murmured '*Ach, welche Virtuosität!*' But it is the effectiveness of his performance *upon the audience*, which is the final criterion of his success. It is the people upon whom he is really playing. His ability as a technical musician is used as an instrumentality for stimulating their emotions over a wide range: so that they too, each and every one of them, participate in the feelings excited and eventually gratified, soothed by his skill. They go away from the concert sated and enthusiastic: feeling that they too have played their part in the success of the great occasion. They have realized themselves as sensitive artists: artists skilled in appreciative discrimination and criticism, fellow-citizens in a great and honoured musical community. There has been something in it for them too. Their sense of significance has been most agreeably titillated; and, like the audience which has been excited and exalted by a great public speaker, they do not come down to earth again for some time.[22]

It is the same with the painter. He produces flattering portraits of his sitters and paymasters, and memorials of the historical or legendary greatness of his community. Everyone who can in any way appreciate the niceties of the painter's art, feels his own ego flattered into expansion and growth. It is the same with the embroiderer, with the weaver, with every successful professional artist and crafts-man. All forms of art, as the humanist sees them, involve a sort of mutual back-slapping, co-operation in telling the world what fine fellows, what clever and ingenious artists, what highly-to-be-envied fellow-citizens we cultured and free-speaking Athenians really are! Art is the chief enhancer of community morale. *Vires adquirit eundo.*[23]

In a word: the humanist standpoint regards the effect of art as being fundamentally social or biosocial. The artist experiments. He tries out what is most effective with his audience: flattering its self-feeling until he can practically induce it to adopt whatever views and opinions he thinks it should adopt for its own benefit, in the long run. His criterion throughout, however, as to what is likely to prove beneficial, is not physical, but social or biosocial. His morality is group-morality, civic morality; and his art is civic art: the art that accepts, stimulates, and enhances with its wizardry, not an external and impersonal factuality, but the vital impulse, the confidence in its own historical destiny, which induces an Athenian, a Spartan, or a Corinthian, to live his community's life and dree his community's weird.[24]

Let us now inquire in what ways the *adoption of the idealist attitude* (associated with the Pythagorean and Eleatic schools) affects the work of artists in stimulating the development of opinions con-sidered, in this city or that, 'right'. These schools substitute for the physical factualities of Ionian science, and for the quasi-instinctive action-tendencies of Protagorean humanism, the abstract and highly technical patterns of mathematics and logic. At the same time, by remaining at the level of 'understanding' (*dianoia*) which assumes (without examination) certain principles, and verifies deductions from these principles by reference to experience of sense-perceivable fact, these idealist abstractions fail to achieve the finality sought, e.g. by dialecticians of Plato's Academy.

When this abstract idealism is applied to the arts, the arts all be-come so much applied mathematics and logic. Instead of depending upon the trained empirical judgement which guides itself by artistic feeling and good taste, Pythagoreans and Eleatics apply severely intellectual reasoning-patterns, and reach conclusions whose con-sistency, both with one another and with their premises, is suscep-tible of strict proof or disproof. Proof or disproof, that is to say, within the artificial limits of ideas guaranteed by the primary hypothesis, the unproved assumptions of this or that departmental science.

The painter or sculptor no longer asks how his products look to the eye. He uses an appropriate instrument, and applies exact measurement, in the Hellenic equivalent of a millimetre scale. The musician no longer accepts the artist's ear, with its sense of absolute pitch, harmony, and rhythm, as in any degree final. He substitutes precise mathematical formulas and equations. Heard melodies may be empirically sweet; but those unheard, provided they follow the mathematical rules, are sweet in a different sense—a sense transcending aural judgement. They are more profound, more significant, more satisfying to the intellect.

It is the same with the work of the carpenter, the weaver, and the potter. Substitute mathematical measurement and logical method for rule of thumb: and you at once have a superior form of art. Idealism, transcending the opinions which rest upon sensory experience, is at all points superior to the blind workings of non-human nature, and to the almost equally blind reachings-out of instinctive feeling. In fact, the degree of spiritual value which attaches to the work of *any* art is in direct proportion to the extent to which that art admits of mathematical and logical direction and control.[25]

Let us now apply this to the social arts or social 'sciences', as they are sometimes (rather optimistically) called. It is in so far as such disciplines admit of statistical techniques, geometrical diagrams, and the reasonings of the logician, that they are approved by the so-called Pythagoreans and by the Eleatics (as by a Pareto in our own day). A practising social psychologist of the humanist school can go only so far. He sets out, with the greatest audacity, to influence the opinions of men in large groups. He has acquired a certain knack, a practical dexterity in dealing with this or that biosocial situation. But his 'knowledge' (if one can call it that) is both empirical and imperfect. The most celebrated practitioners, men like Themistocles and Cimon, have come to grief in the end. Their technique (such as it is) has proved inadequate. Even if helped out by the impressiveness bestowed by the study of Ionian science (as in the case of Pericles), it has proved unequal to the task.[26]

What the abstract idealist recommends, is that all social problems of any degree of complexity shall be handled, not by trained guesswork in out-guessing rivals and in conforming to 'the temper of the House', even though such guesswork has a few years of 'experience' behind it. On the contrary: such problems should be handled by trained intellectuals, experts who have a genuine technique, and can reduce social behaviour to mathematical patterns. Thus, a good table of population statistics, based upon observations recorded over a long period of years, and with conclusions definitely verifiable at all empirical points, will be indispensable when real intellectuals are called to the work of administration.

Suppose it is decided, e.g. to administer, using the new techniques, a community of 5,040 males between the ages of twenty-five and eighty. It is possible to calculate (from such a table) how many births will be required, in any given year, to keep up the number; i.e how many marriages will have to be fruitful. It can similarly be calculated how many children of pre-school age will have to be provided with suitable playgrounds, how many children in the primary, and how many in the secondary, schools will come under the guidance and control of the minister of education; how many men will be available for the armed forces, for the various magistracies, and for the priesthood. The precision of such calculations will be of the very greatest benefit to all programmes which fall within the scope of the social and biosocial arts. It will take away the reproach of vagueness and uncertainty usually levelled against these arts, and, in the event, will prove indispensable to any serious attempt at expert administration.[27]

We now turn to consider *the Platonic position* as to the generic function of art, and its effectiveness in strengthening such community-approved virtues as courage, temperance, and justice. First, we focus our attention upon the negative aspect of the Platonic position: the criticisms directed (by his 'Socrates' and other representatives of philosophic wisdom) against the positions maintained by those who accept (1) Ionian science, (2) Protagorean humanism, or (3) Pythagorean and Eleatic idealism.

In so doing, we understand that Socratic negation is never one-sided and final. It is never intended to be simply destructive. It is always a first step toward removing hindrances to constructive interpretation of the position under examination. In actual fact, in the Platonic Dialogues a position apparently refuted forever is frequently revived and stated more persuasively, either by a convinced adherent of the view apparently refuted, or by some member of the informal Academy which so often surrounds Socrates, or even by Socrates himself. And the re-statement is not always, or even usually, refuted. In some form, it tends to be taken up into what we can regard as Plato's considered position.[28]

The quasi-electric shock induced by having one's lurking inconsistencies suddenly brought to light, is something like the effect produced by modern psychoanalysis. It is educative and curative. It frees one from excessive self-confidence. Anyone who has evolved, from somewhere within himself, a first formulation of a theory, is naturally inclined to accept it as 'true'. He has a naïve faith in the truth-value of his judgement, as such; and this first formulation looks good to him. He tends to believe, with a conviction which seems to him intuitively 'right', that all who think otherwise, must surely be 'wrong', and their views, in so far as they do not agree with his own, 'nonsense'. This conviction, if allowed to stand, obstructs the way to any further development.[29]

Socratic criticism is usually directed, not against the position, as such, but against the obstruction, against the naïve confidence that the first formulation is 'right', and precludes further inquiry. There is no reason why further development (when this is rendered possible by destroying the first naïve assumption that finality has already been achieved) should not follow along the lines already indicated in the first partial formulation. There is no reason why such development should not reach conclusions more firmly based: conclusions including, perhaps, something of the apparently opposed positions which have hitherto been rejected with contempt, and without adequate examination.[30]

In a word, Socratic criticism is usually directed against a rigid formulation of this or that position: and against the conviction that an extreme form of the position, maintained in a formula which can only be repeated *ipsissimis verbis*, is the only possible formulation. That is why Socrates is unwilling to listen to, or to participate in, criticism of the written word (e.g. of the published phrases of this or that poet or thinker), taken *au pied de la lettre*.[31] He prefers to deal with a person, a person who is present and can express himself flexibly, so as to meet questions which subtly vary the situation, to deal with which the formula was originally devised. By such questioning (frequently borrowed by Socrates from other critics, of whom his words are 'only an echo'), it is not difficult to reveal to any flexibly-minded exponent of this or that position, that a first formula is not the only possible formulation, and may easily not be the best. Something must be devised which will meet the new criticisms. Without such re-formulation, the position stands refuted.[32]

When a representative interlocutor who maintains this or that position, is being questioned, Socrates (or some other exponent of Platonic wisdom) does one of three things. (1) He brings up in-dividual (but not untypical) cases which cannot be accounted for on the position as formulated, but clearly necessitate revision of what is now seen to be an over-hasty generalization. Thus Laches's firs formulation of a definition of Courage, by reference to 'the man who does not run away, but remains at his post and fights against the enemy', is shown to need revision by reference to (*a*) the cavalry, who sometimes 'fight flying', and (*b*) the Lacedaemonian infantry, who, at Plataea, 'fled' and then (when the ranks of their pursuers were disordered) 'turned like cavalry, and won the battle'.[33]

(2) He takes a leaf from Zeno's book, and shows, *more Eleatico*, that a formulation assumed, without examination, as sound, may lead to two plainly contrary consequences, and therefore requires very considerable reconsideration and revision. Thus Gorgias, a 'good' rhetorician, defines the art of rhetoric as the art of persuasion, in public, about justice and injustice. He maintains (*a*) that his art is productive of the greatest good, and that he teaches his pupils to become 'good' rhetoricians like himself. At the same time, he complains (*b*) that certain trained rhetoricians do in fact, sometimes make a 'bad' use of their art. This inconsistency between the 'good' and the 'bad' consequences of the art, as defined by Gorgias, is very clearly brought out by Socrates's questions, and Gorgias accepts the necessity of further consideration.[34]

Finally (3) the critic shows how accepting a given formulation as beyond question, may prevent him from appreciating the merit of methods (also regarded as acceptable) which plainly lead to other formulations, inconsistent with the first. Thus, it is brought out that acceptance of the Heraclitean account of motion (as essentially a to-and-fro pendulum-swing), if applied to intellectual thought, would make nonsense of the Socratic method of ideas. It is similarly shown that acceptance of Parmenides's formula about the non-existence, unthinkability, and unspeakability of motion, would make nonsense of the Socratic use of ideas. There are a number of criticisms of this type: advanced sometimes by Socrates, sometimes by representatives of the wisdom issuing from Elea.[35]

Let us now focus our attention upon the more positive aspects of the Platonic position. No positions formulated and discussed in the Dialogues are just silly, wrong-headed, to be rejected out of hand. The problems with which they deal are significant problems. Take the position of the Ionian scientists. While nagging questions and sly insinuations can shake a man's confidence in his first naïve formulation of what is involved in the conception of objectivity, of factuality, of *Dasein*, does anyone really doubt that, after all, there is really 'something there'? Not Socrates. Not even the abstract idealist, Timaeus: whom we find playing happily with his intellectual's blocks, his tetrahedra, octahedra, icosahedra, and the rest. Naïvely formulated, what 'is there' is said to be crude and non-logical. Even the Divine Artificer, playing at world-building with these same blocks, can only partially reduce the original world-stuff to mathematical form and logical order. Even reason can only very partially apprehend the underlying material upon which the shapes of the blocks are superimposed.[36]

This underlying material (studied by Ionian science) is the 'primordial chaos' of the poets, the 'wild-beast appetite' lying in wait behind the urbane appearance of self-control which marks the good Hellene, the tendency toward disease, disintegration, and death, that lurks in even the healthiest of organisms. You cannot quite think it. You cannot give it adequate formulation in logical propositions. It is structureless, lawless, meaningless. It is an offence to the logic of Parmenides. It is a perpetual problem to the ethics of the good citizen. And yet: there it is. What do you propose to do about it? In some way or other, objectivity has to be accepted and taken up into the final philosophy. An aesthetical grouping of tetrahedra, an unearthly ballet of bloodless categories, may amuse the intellectuals for a while. But, in the long run, a philosophy which is going to satisfy human beings will have to find room for 'reality', for an 'objectivity' that is something more than the inter-implication of technical propositions in a logician's universe of discourse. Somewhere, it will have to rest on—well—fact.[37]

Or take the position of the humanists. It is only too easy to poke fun at it. All you do, is to assume another position, the position of factual science, or the position of the 'friends of ideas', or what you will; and from such a position, you will have an easy victory—if no one is present, to point out what you are doing, with your *petitio principii*. To account for 'truth' in terms of social or biosocial consequences, or to attack the value of abstract logic by arguments themselves abstractly logical, can easily be made to look like nonsense. Anyone can pick holes in such logic, and can have a good laugh at the absurdities of humanism.

Socrates, after picking holes in the logic of Protagoras's formulation (in his book, *On Truth*), grows ashamed of himself for poking fun at a man after he is dead and no longer in a position to reply. It is not altogether sporting. After all, Protagoras was a great man; and a little of that sympathy and insight (of which philosophers speak) will see that the great man had, after all, a great message. Socrates then projects himself into the *persona* of Protagoras, and reconstructs his position. This position, he leaves standing.[38]

For Socrates himself believes (like Protagoras) that the reality studied by Ionian science is obscure, and that life is too short to spend in pursuing what may be a will-o'-the-wisp ('truth'). He too believes in the priority of the practical reason: the proper study of mankind is (surely) man and ethics, human ethics. He too believes that there is a 'better' and a 'worse' for human beings; and he too makes it his business, his especial business, to persuade (as far as he can) his fellow-citizens to follow the 'better' path. He too is convinced of the value, in seeking that path, of investigating the consequences, the social and biosocial consequences, of a proposed course of action. He too, although mathematics has for him an intellectual fascination, does not really believe that, in the world of practical affairs, *pure* mathematics is much use. 'Have you ever', he asks Glaucon, 'known a mathematician who was good for anything' (i.e. a man of sound practical judgement)? 'No,' is the reply, and the reply is left, unquestioned.[39]

Thus, while the Protagorean formulation of the humanist position has certain flaws, the position itself, when restated so as to avoid such deficiencies of exposition, is (humanly speaking) acceptable enough. It fits into the movement toward a more inclusive philosophy of values, which Socrates himself advocates. It is consistent with the common-sense attitude of Socrates toward biosocial satisfaction ('pleasure'), in spite of the extent to which this common-sense attitude is sometimes elaborated (among humanists) into the full-blown theory of 'hedonism'. The highest good, in the end, must contain, in its value-including 'mixture', ingredients taken from the teachings of the humanist school—although the formula, it is true, has to be somewhat amended.[40]

Or take the position of the 'friends of ideas'. This too can be attacked, if you simply assume a different set of first principles; or if you pick out flaws in this or that person's formulation of the view. The Pythagorean brotherhood, in its 'superiority', does raise an ironical smile. The Eleatic account of 'Appearance and Reality', with its uncompromising assault upon common sense, readily awakens unconcealed jeering. The abstractions of this school can so easily be made to look like thought-webs, floating adjectives without local habitation or substance, the merest make-believe. Ordinary people always feel a little queer about metaphysics; and if you can make it appear that it is the metaphysicians who are being queer, the joke is (of course) on *them.*

Here too the Platonic critic, while fully conscious of the flaws in the current formulations of idealism, is completely convinced that there is something in their position, something profoundly significant. It may be necessary to save 'ideas' from their 'friends'; for, without 'ideas', adequately understood—well, where are you? The earlier, abstract formulation may fail, may show flaws. But what you have to do—for you cannot do without intellectual technique—is to re-formulate the position, to base it upon a principle which is not just assumed, but is *un*hypothetical: a final ground.[41]

So too with Pythagorean mathematics. They are indispensable. Their weakness is in the loose, over-hasty reliance upon sensory experience, as if it could provide them with sufficient verification. Mathematical propositions apply to sensory experience undoubtedly; but it is pitiably weak, to try to ground them upon such experience. You can conceivably ground empiricism upon the *a priori*. You cannot possibly ground the *a priori* upon empiricism. Ideas, whether mathematical or logical, can only be grounded adequately upon—whatever it is, which is the principle of ideality. This, however, is the idea of good. This, and this alone, can be the final ground.

At the same time, the idea of good cannot be treated as a mere abstraction: just another bloodless category. It must be integrally connected with the whole of experience: on its empirical no less than on its transcendental side. Grounded in metaphysics, mathematics (and indeed the entire realm of the ideal) must be capable of application also to the physical world, the world of things you can touch and see; and also to the psychological world, the world of images, of sensations and emotions, of value-feelings and the struggle for a worth-while life-cycle.[42]

What is needed is thus a philosophy which proceeds by successive re-formulations of the fundamental aspects of experience: (1) its factuality, its reality which is discovered by the seeker who employs an adequate technique, heuristic hypotheses starting with sensation and used as stepping-stones toward the final principle of ideality and value; (2) its human quality, its significance in terms of the sensations, the emotions, the instincts, of a single species: *homo insipiens*, at best a mere puppet of the Gods, forever striving after an ideal perfection of his essential imperfectibility; (3) its ideal quality, its intellectual significance, a rationality tempered, however, always with 'music'—

i.e. with the human, all-too-human arts, and with the sense of an ever-present, inexorably extra-logical factuality.[43]

In a word, what Socrates proposes, is to retain what is positive in the work of all three great schools of philosophy: in spite of their mutual inconsistency, which is so easily demonstrated. He proposes to keep on with the gradual re-formulation of the chief thesis of each school: diminishing, to some extent, the misunderstandings which arise from faults in the form of expression. He does not believe that the differences of the three schools will gradually disappear: so that eventually a synthesis can be effected. On the contrary, the work of criticism will sharpen and accentuate the differences. But he does believe that a certain practical balance can be achieved: never final, always flexible and progressive, a 'mixed life', to which each and every philosophical school can make its positive contribution. Actually, it is in its future history, that philosophy, human philosophy, can expect gradually to work out its growing destiny. The life of reason is not (as the abstract idealists supposed) something apart, something withdrawn from human life, and superior to common humanity. It is simply the fuller, richer, but always human life: which retains everything of value in human experience. It is in the progressive history of culture, a cumulative development of human values, that it realizes its idea.[44]

How does this apply to the theory of art, and its effect upon the community? Plato is a persistently severe critic of the artists whose productions he discovers in the world around him. In an ideal Platonic community, very little of what has satisfied the actual communities of his day, could possibly be retained (he insists), without a good deal of revision. So many artists have been contented, childishly contented, with an achievement which is only technical, a mere shadow of what it might conceivably have been. The poets of the ancient world have learnt to express themselves in verse-patterns (often 'a little outrageous', at that): contrasting and unifying exciting images into a kind of word-picture which proves attractive to—the kind of people who read poetry. It proves attractive, at times, even to the scientifically educated, who really know better, but have nothing better to read. The musicians have learnt to fuss around with scales and harmonies which no one really understands; and what does it all amount to? A tumultuous rush of rhythms, a confused brutish noise called 'modern music': all discords, trills, and clever jangles. Unless you provide it with a book of words, or at least a programme guide, does anyone know what it is all about? Except that it excites vast audiences, and stimulates a confused emotional response![45]

And so of the other arts, painting, embroidery, weaving, carpentering, and the rest. Have the artists any genuine insight, a message of their own? Or are they not, almost all of them, contented to accompany, to enhance, to amplify—anything, whatever you give them for a theme? A carpenter will construct out of wood, anything whatever the cash customer who is proposing to use his productions, cares to demand. Simply set your theme, *any* theme (good, bad, or indifferent) for competition, and offer a prize. The appropriate purveyor of flattery will amplify it for you in prose or verse, with or without musical or terpsichorean accompaniment: in embroidery, painting, or sculpture, anything you care to ask for, and in whatever style happens to be in fashion. As long as an opportunity is provided for playing a technician's game with rhythmic contrasts, for what more does he, as a master of technique, ask?[46]

From the standpoint of factuality, are not all the arts imitative? And of what are they imitative? 'Reality,' you say. Yes, but of what reality? Well, what they supply is related, of course, to what audiences demand; and what audiences demand is related to their degree of education, character, and vision. Children call for puppet-shows, young people for dance-music (with a biosocial reference), or possibly for romantic tragedy. Men of a certain age ask for epic poetry. If you are giving a party, you provide *Trinklieder*, songs of revelry, the light stuff furnished by flute-girls: whatever you think will make the party 'go'.[47]

If your guests insist on being more intellectual, one of them will soon suggest a theme for conversation, or for clever after-dinner speechifying. The rest will respond with common sense, popular science, brilliant nonsense, word-artistry, or (it may be) even with philosophy disguised as sophistry. Each will profess to be reproducing, in this genial expression of his own disposition and interests, significant features of 'reality'. But who does not see that a good deal of revision will be required, if the 'reality' conceivably underlying such artistic play, is to be brought into clear focus, and genuinely apprehended by the intellect? Does any part of what they say claim to be expressive of authentic truth? Is not the truth, rather, heavily veiled, and is it not obvious that the artists are really more interested in the veils than in what they conceal? For the most part, artists are concerned to 'imitate' (as the phrase is), rather than to unveil the reality which a philosopher (perhaps) may glimpse here and there.[48]

Or, take the standpoint of humanism. At first sight, it might seem that the arts, especially the 'humanities' (as so many of them are called), give a humanist all he needs to ask: a picture of human beings with their needs and their powers, their hopes and their fears, their dreamings and their overt doings. Many a humanist accordingly professes to make such arts central in his scheme of education for citizenship. But who does not see (at least, when it is pointed out to him by a Socrates) that these arts are, for the most part, superficial froth: a form of escapism from the facts of life? You dress up and go sit at a play or a concert. You visit a fashionable art-exhibition. Your senses are titillated, your emotions are stimulated, perhaps exhausted, your judgement is agreeably flattered. But is there any evidence that adults, when assembled in large numbers, are in a mood to appreciate or understand truth (if they should, by some chance, hear it), or that any artist of intelligence really tries, under such conditions, to do much beyond working on their feelings with clever flattery? Surely, the evidence is all the other way.[49]

And yet (a philosopher would say) there must be *some* way in which art might conceivably make a worthy appeal to the senses and emotions of citizens—or at least to the worthier, the older, more experienced, and more serious amongst them. It is all very well to talk of banishing from the ideal community the type of art created to appeal to the idle, the frivolous, and the sinisterly interested. But in an ideal community (furnishing, surely, an ideal audience for the right kind of artist), there must be room for—an ideal type of art: the type that would be just right for, e.g. the 'silver' class of the *Republic* or the model citizens of the *Laws*. That is to say, while earlier efforts (in the empirical cities of Hellas, which have 'just grown') at expressing the artistic influence, may have proven largely unsatisfactory to philosophers, this is, surely, not a ground for banishing art, as such. It is a ground for improving upon the work of earlier artists, and so attaining to an art which shall really be worth while.[50]

General citizens (Plato's 'silver' class) are not an academic group of intellectuals. They have not reached the high level of philosophic insight into principle, the level at which men can be trusted, without guidance, to govern themselves wisely. They live at the level, not of knowledge, but of opinion. What they ask of their leaders, is guidance: so that their opinions shall at least be 'right'. This means, in harmony with what the experience of the best and wisest members of the community judges to be 'right'. Like Glaucon and Adeimantus in the *Republic*, or Cleinias and Megillus in the *Laws*, general citizens do not, of themselves, possess the insight which reveals truth and enables men to construct at least the outline of the divine plan for humanity. But they are prepared, and indeed anxious, to follow a leader whose character and intelligence they can appreciate. They not only accept his conclusions. They insist (in both Dialogues) that there should always be a place, within the constitution of an ideal community, for such a leader.[51]

The leader occupies the position of president of the Academy: what would nowadays be called head of the community's 'brains-trust'. That is, he is an expert adviser to the government. All higher magistrates are trained in such an academy: trained in law and philosophy. The administration is carried on by mixed commissions, whose chairmen are dialectically trained magistrates, and their other members are citizens (or approved sojourners) who have achieved the level of right opinion, and can be trusted to support the government under all conditions.

The opinion which is judged to be 'right' is, by this mixed administration, carried down, not merely to the silver class, but also to the copper and iron classes, and (so far as possible) to the slaves in the model city. Members of the golden class (all higher magistrates) are 'artificers of freedom'—not only for themselves, but also for each of the other classes; for these, in living their characteristic life, guide themselves by right opinion. While the magistrates are the *official* agents for enforcing what civic opinion regards as 'right'—i.e. are the duly constituted authorities to whom new or doubtful cases are referred—right opinion also receives the unhesitating support of every member of the silver class, i.e. of all free citizens. From the *Laws* it is clear that this acceptance and support penetrates yet further. It permeates the non-civic classes encouraged and permitted to live and work in the model city. These classes include the 'metics', the aliens attracted to take up residence by the opportunities open to men of ability in the model city; i.e. the teachers, the business men, the artisans. It also includes, as far as possible, the slaves. *Every* last member of the community, 'old or young, bond or free', never ceases from 'charming himself' into acceptance of the opinions considered 'right'.

It is precisely here that art realizes its potentialities for civic usefulness. Art can be the mirror of good citizenship, the communicator and amplifier of right opinion. As Plato directs its use, art supplies the *ethos* of the model city with its constant overtones, its characteristic cultural atmosphere. Each citizen breathes this in. It is as natural as living. Each community member, at each and every phase of the human life-cycle, finds it so. The day starts early, with the good housewife arousing the household and sending the children off to school. In the morning, each member of the community (old and young, bond and free) does his work: *his* work, the work which constitutes his positive contribution to the economic, moral, and social life of the community; the work which justifies his claim to citizenship (or at least to residence) in the model city. During the rest of the day, there are processions to the temples: whose services follow the approved traditional ritual of worship and prayer. There are community sports, in which the young participate directly, and their elders vicariously: leading up to the monthly field-days, in which the whole community renews itself and re-dedicates itself to its high purposes.

For the artistically competent, there are further cultural opportunities, as they practise the approved arts of music, of dancing, and of poetry; and for the intellectually competent, there are always the higher studies of mathematical science, of dialectic, and of the principles of administration. For those called to the actual work of administration, there are committees which discuss and make recommendations, later embodied into community law by the appropriate law-making bodies. This work may, and in the highest governing bodies does, continue far into the night: while the regular citizens obey the suggestion of civic right opinion, by sleeping soundly, in complete confidence that everything is under control.

In each of these activities, it is the rhythms of art which set the tempo and establish the patterns of civic life. It is art which channels the animal instincts of humanity into pathways where they lose their wild and socially disintegrative tendencies, and become drives of community usefulness. Art transforms the stealth, the greed, the irrational individualism of the hunger-impulse, into the well-regulated community *syssitia*, the meals of citizens where all partake together.[53] Art takes the powerful thirstiness of the individual members of the group (an impulse which, left to itself, could easily weaken reason, character, and respect for the orderliness and dignity of civil life), and transforms it into the social institution of the *symposium*, a well-regulated banqueting at which many interests of the community are not only retained without loss, but are strengthened and furthered.[54] So also art takes the even more powerful urges of sex (which, left to themselves, are the most socially disruptive of all natural drives), and, by song and dance, and by established tradition, sublimates them to community usefulness, and even supplies a touch of poetry, with its overtones of idealism.[55]

What is this art which succeeds in building up and reinforcing right opinion? Is it the art which seeks to strengthen the already strong *influence of the external world*, and to turn citizens into un-protesting portions of the rhythmic tissue of events? Is it the art which seeks to disentangle and clarify *the biosocial impulses natural to man*, and to turn citizens into more highly cultured eaters, drinkers, and lovers? Is it the art which seeks to amplify *the master-voice of reason*; to intellectualize the citizens, and turn them all (so far as possible) into superior persons, members of a kind of *ultra*-Pytha-gorean brotherhood: a group of serious thinkers who converse only with a Pythagoras or a Parmenides, a Pythagoras or a Parmenides who converse intimately only with each other and (if they eventually decide that there *is* such a being) with God?

The answer is, both No and Yes. No, in so far as each of these types of art claims to exclude the others. Yes, in so far as, in and through their divergencies, these types of art can be interwoven, held in a state of balance. Plato's community is not one-sided. It is all-sided: holding in a state of balance all the tendencies which keep it alive and human. A community in which the highest good is, not this or that, but the 'mingled life' that contains everything which holds positive value for humanity, the 'balanced' life—requires a similarly balanced art: an art which does justice to every side of life and reinforces its value-producing potentialities.

The Platonic 'idea of good', his principle of ideality and value, is not exclusive, but inclusive. The divine plan has a place for everyone to pursue his natural bent. The gods in heaven do not quarrel, but co-operate; and the plan calls for men to do the same. In the model city, every kind of activity natural to man can, by appropriate administration, be so interwoven with the rest as to realize a maxi-mum of positive value. In such a community, the functional effect of art is to clarify, confirm, and further the ideal plan for humanity: permeating the silver class, the copper class, and the iron class, with appreciation and affection for the ideal so clearly envisaged by the golden class. All citizens (and other members) will co-operate in realizing the value-potentialities implicit in humanity as constituting *via* their participation in the life of the model city, an integral part of God's world, the world of spirit.[56]

NOTES

1. *Prtg.* 328a, *Rep.* 421d, 466e f., *Laws* 643a–c. Pareto, *The Mind and Society* (E.T. 1935), sect. 91, cf. sects. 364, 1786, 2031.

2. *Prtg.* 327a f., cf. 318bc, *Rep.* 370a, 374–376c, 412c f., 415a f., 423c, 537a, *Phaedr.* 269d f., *Laws* 643a f.

3. *Menex.* 237e f., *Tim.* 22c f., 24cd, *Critias* 109d ff., *Laws* 679b f., 745b f., 747de. The part played by such environmental conditions in the social, moral, and political life of Athens, is conspicuous in its history.

4. *Rep.* 550d ff., 557b ff., *Laws* 628d–637e, 700b f., 709a f.

5. *Rep.* 558d f., *Laws* 771e f., 782d f.

6. *Charm.* 155d, *Rep.* 403a, 571b f., *Laws* 636b f., 645d f., 835c ff.

7. *Laws* 783a f.

8. *Rep.* 404d f., 458d f., *Laws* 835e f.

9 *Laws* 646e f., 663e ff., 836a.

10. *Laws* 635b ff., 641d, 642a, 645b, 659d ff., 670d f., 673e.

11. *Laws* 643a f., cf. *Rep.* 421d, 466e f., 537a.

12. *Prtg.* 312ab, 326a f., 327a f., *Rep.* 405 ff., *Laws* 643e f., 696a.

13. *Rep.* 406d f. In the model city, artisans are not permitted to acquire citizenship. Their numbers are regulated by the magistrates (acting as chairmen of committees of appropriate experts). While they are, at times, called in to give expert advice to legislative committees, their residence-permit depends always upon their continued good behaviour (*Laws* 846d f., 850a f. Cf. *Prtg.* 319b f., 322d f.). Compare also *Laws* 765a f., where the reference to 'experts' in music (if taken in connexion with 812c f., where the experts are 'music-teachers', not citizens, and 810e f., which insists that no citizen shall take more than the three-year short course for amateurs) seems to imply that music-teachers (who are 'foreigners imported for pay', *Laws* 804d, 813e) are 'metics', i.e. belong to the artisan class of craftsmen. At the same time, being selected for their *expertise* and also for their understanding of the institutions of the model city (*Laws* 811d f.) by the minister of education, who gives them public employment, they have almost the status of paid officials of the community. Cf. the respect paid to Damon in *Rep.* and *Laches.*

14. *Laws* 654 ff., 664e f., 672e f., 795d f., 798d ff., 814d ff.

15. *Laws* 790e f., 815c.

16. *Rep.* 377c, 395c ff., 400e ff., 522ab, *Laws* 665a–c.

17. *Rep.* 518e, 522a f., 619d, *Tim.* 47cd, *Laws* 633b f., 655d f., 663e f., 792e, 889a f.

18. *Prtg.* 325d, 326c f., *Rep.* 421c f., *Laws* 681c, 720b.

19. *Lysis* 208d, *Prtg.* 326ab, *Rep.* 376d ff., 401b f., 522a, *Laws* 653b ff., 783a, 838c f.

20. *Prtg.* 325d f., 326b, *Phil.* 58b, *Laws* 653c, 656d f., 663d f., 864e f. The 'preambles' (which are the artistic side of the Laws--see *Laws* 722d) appeal to voluntary co-operation (*Laws* 718de, 719e f., 720d ff., 880b, cf. *Rep.* 396bc, 430a 5, 433a 6, 499e f.).

21. *Prtg.* 315ab, 337c f., *Menex.* 234c f., *Gorg.* 456a f., 463 f., *Phaedr.* 261c f., *Symp.* 177b f., *Theaet.* 167b f.

22. *Menex.* 235b f., *Ion* 535b f., *Rep.* 401c f., *Laws* 658d ff., 700 f., 817b f.

23. *Euthyphr.* 6c, *Prtg.* 347c f., *Gorg.* 463, 501 ff., *Crat.* 432b, *Rep.* 373ab, 377bc, 424a, 425a, 444c, 602d, 605a f., 608ab, *Phaedr.* 245a, cf. *Critias* 107b f.

24. *Prtg.* 327a f., *Menex.* 235d f., *Crat.* 432b f., 434ab, 439cd, *Rep.* 338d f., 401, 425a f., 492b, 493a, *Theaet.* 167b f., *Phil.* 58b, *Laws* 625d ff., 628e f.

25. *Rep.* 520c, 521d ff., 524d f., 526a, 527bc, 529a ff., 533b f., *Phil.* 55d f., 57d f., 59a f. Moderns tend to think of exact measurement as mechanical, as excluding originality, the touch of individuality which issues in something new and unique, distinctive of each artist. (Cf. Croce, *op. cit.*, p. 136, 'Art is intuition, intuition is individuality, individuality does not repeat itself.)' But the ancients have no such thought. It simply never occurs to them. The mechanical age is too far off in the future, and Hellenic artists always, as a matter of course, express their individuality. Cf. Tilney, *op. cit.*, pp. 207, 215, 'Although Athens uttered many thousands of vases . . ., there is never one that is a copy of another. Tracings and patterns were never used. Every one is an original, and unique. Even to-day they exist in many thousands.'

I myself [R.C.L.] suppose that this statement of Tilney's goes a little too far. It is reasonable to conclude that, as in the Greek publishing factories, a single model was 'copied' simultaneously by many workers—much as in our modern art schools; but (of course) with individual differences. I rest this conclusion on the use of the term *paradeigma* in Greek. It means, precisely, a painter's (or sculptor's) model. Cf. *Rep.* 500e, 592b, *Tim.* 28c, *Parm.* 132d. The individual artist 'assimilates himself'—with all his individual characteristics—to the model. That is precisely why the 'copies' are all so different. I suppose the Pythagorean point of view is illustrated in the work of the modern naval architect, who uses all the mathematics he can, in designing vessels for this or that purpose; but his finished designs are characteristically different from the designs of rival architects attacking the same problem.

26. *Gorg.* 454e ff., 503c f., 515c f., *Rep.* 493a f., *Phaedr.* 270, *Theaet.* 167b f., *Phil.* 58b.

27. *Laws* 747, insisting upon the value of statistical methods as applied to *empirical* social problems, is definitely in the spirit of the 'so-called Pythagoreans' (of *Rep.* 531, 533). The so-called 'nuptial number' (*Rep.* 546b f.), definitely transcends empiricism, and is presumably not Pythagorean. It is therefore not considered here. For vital statistics, and their empirical applications in Plato's writings, see, further, R. C. Lodge, *Plato's Theory of Education*, Appendix I ('Numbers in the Model City').

28. *Lach.* 194a. Gorgias's view of the function of rhetoric, and its relation to justice in the community, apparently refuted in *Gorg.* 461a, is taken up again by Polus; and (after Polus has apparently been refuted) yet again by Callicles, with increasing vigour of conviction. The position of Thrasymachus, apparently refuted in *Rep.* I, is revived again in *Rep.* II by Glaucon, seconded by Adeimantus (these are presumably members of the informal 'academy' which is familiar with the main theses of Socratic idealism (*Rep.* 505a, 507a f., 596a f., cf. *Phdo.* 72e ff., *Parm.* 130c f.). The position of Protagoras, apparently refuted in its formulation (1) by Theaetetus, and (2) by Theodorus, is revived by Socrates himself (*Theaet.* 166a–168b), and is then left unrefuted. (Attention to this last is particularly drawn by the late Prof. F. C. S. Schiller, 'Plato or Protagoras?', in *Mind*, N.S. Vol. XVII, 1908, pp. 518–526. Also in book with same title, pub. Blackwell, Oxford, 1908.)

As to 'Plato's considered position', I understand this to be 'the mixed life' or balanced life treated as the *summum bonum* in the *Philebus*, and represented in the *Laws* by the 'second-best polity', viz., the model city. There are many passages, e.g. from p. 309 to the end of the *Politicus*, treating the art of statesmanship as an art of 'weaving together' types of character which, logically regarded, appear mutually exclusive, and quite a number of passages in the *Republic* too, which support this view of the balanced life as Plato's 'own'.

29. *Lach.* 188d f., 194a, *Gorg.* 457c f., *Meno* 80ab, *Soph.* 230b f.

30. *Theaet.* 150b f., cf. *Lach.* 200a f. Socratic criticism (e.g. of Charmides, Protagoras, Gorgias, Callicles, Thrasymachus, *et al.*) is almost always directed against the first formulation, with the idea of stimulating the interlocutor to improve upon the formulation, to make it clear and precise. What Socrates does is (in all cases I have examined), to question unproved assumptions, i.e. to 'destroy the hypotheses' (*Rep.* 533c).

31. *Prtg.* 329a, 347b, *Phaedr.* 275c f.

32. *Prtg.* 347c f., *Phaedr.* 275e f., *Theaet.* 157c, 160d, 161b, 162a, 164d f., 166d, 168b, 169a f., 171c, *Parm.* 135b f., *Soph.* 217d f.

33. *Lach.* 190d f.

34. *Gorg.* 451d f., 461a, *Meno* 84a f., *Parm.* 130c ff.

35. *Crat.* 439 cf., *Parm.* 129b–135e, *Theaet.* 161e f., *Soph.* 259e f.

36. *Tim.* 48 ff.

37. *Crat.* 396a ff., 422c f., *Rep.* 571b f., *Tim.* 53b f., 81 ff. (For the chaos, cf. also *Phdo.* 72c, *Gorg.* 465d.) The 'ideas' are not *purely* formal. Still less are they merely 'imaginative make-believe' (as is maintained by P. E. More, *Platonism*, 1917, Ch. VII, pp. 182 f.). They are *'patterns fixed in nature'* (*Parm.* 132d), and in investigating their various divisions and interrelations, the dialectician has to find 'where the joint *is*', and not divide just *any*where, as 'a bad carver' might. (See *Pol.* 262b f.) The 'earth, water, fire, and air', which the Divine Artificer's solid geometry carves out of the pre-existent chaos, are *factual* potentialities. (Cf. *Rep.* 528b f., *Phaedr.* 265e, *Pol.* 262b f., 265a, 283d, 284a, 285a f., 287a f., *Phil.* 58a.) This is perhaps the chief thesis of John Wild, *Plato's Theory of Man*, Cambridge, Mass., 1946. His subtitle is 'An Introduction to the Realistic Philosophy of Culture'.

38. *Theaet.* 166a ff.

39. *Euthyphr.* 6b (cf. Euseb., *Prep. Evangelica*, ed. Gaisford, 1843, XIV 3, 7), *Apol.* 29b f., *Crat.* 425c, *Phdo.* 96 ff., *Rep.* 462 ff., 531d f., 612b f., *Phil.* 55c f., *Laws* 689c.

40. *Prtg.* 353–358, *Rep.* 412a, 581d ff., *Tim.* 48a, *Pol.* 309 ff., *Phil.* 59d f., 61 ff.

41. *Rep.* 508e f., 510c ff., 531 f., 533, *Parm.* 135.

42. *Rep.* 533b f., 540a, 546a, *Tim.* 81b f., *Parm.* 134, *Laws* 747a f.

43. *Rep.* 546e, 548c, 549b, *Phaedr.* 273e f., 278d f., *Phil.* 62 f., *Laws* 644d f., 802a f., 803b f.

44. *Pol.* 283d ff., *Phil.* 20b f., 22 f., 61b ff., cf. *Phdo.* 77e f. Cf. also R. C. Lodge, 'What Socrates Knows', Royal Society of Canada, *Order of Proceedings*, June, 1951, p. 14.

45. *Prtg.* 339b, 347b f., *Gorg.* 501–504a, *Rep.* 600e ff., 605c ff., *Phaedr.* 277e f., *Laws* 658 f., 700 f., 719a f., 811b f., 812c f.

46. *Euthyd.* 289d f., (cf. *Alc. I* 108), *Rep.* 297c ff., 596d ff., 601c ff., *Laws* 656c f., 657d f., 660a, d f.

47. *Prtg.* 347cd, *Symp.* 176, *Rep.* 397a d, *Laws* 657e f.

48. *Symp.* 176e ff., 198d f., *Rep.* 377b ff., 401, 611c f., *Laws* 801 ff. Wilamowitz regards the speech attributed by Socrates to Diotima, not as philosophy disguised as

sophistry, but as, largely, pure sophistry (Wilamowitz, *Platon*, 2nd edit., 1920, Vol. I, p. 380). He refers to 208c of the *Symposium*—and why not? But Socrates states, at the end of his account (*Symp.* 212ab), without qualification, that he is *persuaded of the truth* of what Diotima has taught him.

49. *Ion* 531bc, *Prtg.* 325e f., *Gorg.* 502bc, *Rep.* 475c f., 492b f., *Phaedr.* 265d, *Laws* 658e f., 700b f., 810d f.

50. Many readers conclude from *Rep.* 595a, 607b ff., that poetry and other representative arts are (with the exception of 'hymns to the gods and praises of famous men') (see 607a) to be completely excluded from the education of the silver class (cf. e.g. Croce, *op. cit.*, p. 158, who sees in these passages an attack upon art as such); and such readers conclude from *Rep.* 522ab that all forms of music are presumably dropped from the education of the golden class, when this is separated from the silver class. But it should be perfectly plain that the silver class is intentionally surrounded, from birth to death, by a cultural atmosphere which is provided by art. Art is really all they can take in; and they breathe it in at every moment. It invigorates them and colours their entire outlook upon life (*Rep.* 401c f., *Laws* 653 ff., 800a ff., cf. *Pol.* 277 cd).

The art which is approved for civic purposes is not the casual creation of *any*one who happens to feel inspired to express himself as a poet, painter, or musician (cf. *Ion* 535e f.). It has to be approved by 'the experience of the oldest and best', as expressive of the community *ethos*. But the modern reader, when he finds art referred to as restricted to 'hymns and encomia', tends to understand this in an unduly narrow sense. In Plato's way of writing, *all* approved artistic patterns are 'consecrated to the appropriate deity', *more Egyptiaco*. This means that processional dances are an extended sort of 'hymn' to Apollo (or some such deity), while military marches, military dances, and the virgins' dance in armour, are a sort of 'hymn' to Ares or Athene. Even the rather wild dancing approved for medical purposes (*Laws* 790d f.), is treated as a kind of divine service. Just how the lampooning of each other by licensed satirists (*Laws* 816d f., 935c f.), and the comic uglinesses, not to mention the presentations of the seamy side of life (for external observation, not for imitation), are to be interpreted, is not quite clear. They would hardly come under the title of 'encomia', or of 'hymns' to Apollo or some other approved deity. But it is quite plain that the well-educated citizers are expected to be able to recognize vice, when they see it, as well as virtue (*Rep.* 378a, 396a, 402 f., etc.), and there might conceivably be a somewhat indirect reference to service of Dionysus or Marsyas—or possibly Hygieia?

(The new literature demanded by Plato is exemplified by the Platonic Dialogues themselves, *Laws* 811b f.)

51. *Rep.* 412ab, 497c, *Laws* 769c, cf. 969 *ad fin.* (I suppose this position is strengthened by comparing the way in which Plato thinks of the higher kind of physician, who is superior to his own written prescriptions, and is able to apply his mind freshly to any problem in the field of medicine. Cf. *Pol.* 293ab, 295c f. For further discussion of the complete evidence, see R. C. Lodge, *Plato's Theory of Education*, pp. 42-44, with the accompanying notes (p. 58).)

52. *Laws* 665c f., 810e f., 817d f. Cf. R. C. Lodge, 'Plato and Freedom', *Transact. Roy. Soc. of Canada*, XLIII, 1949, pp. 91-101.

53. *Laws* 636, 780b f., 782e f., 806d f., 842b.

54. *Laws* 639b ff. For our modern usage, cf. the banquets with which many an otherwise highly respectable club closes its work for the year.

55. *Rep.* 459e f., *Laws* 771e f., 835d ff. Plato is not under the illusion that *all* art, art *as such*, has a good civic influence. This is indeed believed by modern authorities of the calibre of Max Schoen. See his *The Enjoyment of the Fine Arts*, Philos. Libr., New York, 1944, p. 20, 'An Art work cannot be anything but wholesome in its influence. . . . It raises the self to a realm of experience cleansed of the dross and dirt, the strife and struggle, the back-biting and back-sliding, which often . . . are the substance of day-to-day existence. . . . No one can leave . . . a great performance of a great play or symphony without feeling that he has been in touch with perfection; that for a moment which was also an eternity, God was truly in His Heaven. This is good at its highest because it is life at its best.'

Sir Arthur Sullivan, in a lecture which has been published, maintained that it was impossible for music to have any but a good influence. (Some of the extant 'songs of revelry', as of the dance-music (largely from *Roberto il Diavolo*) associated with the *Can-Can* dance—and indeed a few compositions of Mozart, were certainly not designed by their composers, to have a good moral influence. They belong to the group which Plato deliberately excludes from performance in the presence of the young.)

56. *Rep.* 412c, *Tim.* 87c f., *Pol.* 309 ff., *Phil.* 61 f., *Laws* 903b ff.

CHAPTER SEVEN

The Limitations of Art: How to Meet Them, I

THE Hellenic artist produces physically overt objects considered by human beings useful or charming. Objects such as beds, houses, chariots, ships, or the fisherman's nets, the weaver's shuttles, the carpenter's hammers, etc., are all primarily useful. Objects such as a hymn to Apollo, an interpretative dance, an embroidered or painted representation of the Battle of the Titans or the Rape of Proserpine, or (for the matter of that) objects such as the circles and squares, spheres and cubes, of geometric science, are primarily charming or beautiful. There is nothing to prevent an object designed primarily for use (e.g. Achilles's shield or Penelope's bed) from possessing *also* accompanying charm or beauty. So too there is nothing to prevent a palace, a tapestry, or a ceremonial dance (or, for the matter of that, a triangle, circle, or tetrahedron), designed primarily to charm, from having *also* quite definite uses in daily life. Why should there be? But, in general, the distinction between the artisan's products which are primarily utilitarian, and the artist's products which are primarily charming or beautiful, is justified by a glance at the facts of the productive life, in Hellas as elsewhere. Human art produces objects which possess one, at least, of these values.[1]

In producing such objects, the artist feels himself to be transmissive, rather than in an especial sense creative, of the values which are associated with his work. The carpenter who manufactures a bed, large enough and strong enough to stand up to the treatment to which beds are ordinarily subjected, and at the same time soft enough and inviting enough to induce restful slumber: does not create the need for repose after the day's work is done, or the desire for a good bed. He simply accepts the facts of life, and puts his abilities to work in accordance with the requirements of the situation.

The resulting concrete bed represents his contribution to A's or B's having a good night's rest. The carpenter, in a word, is simply one link in a chain. He fits on to the link before him, and connects up with the link which follows.

So also the portrait-painter does not in any way create the conditions in which portraits are considered socially desirable. He merely sets his abilities to work, and produces what the occasion calls for. The resulting picture represents his contribution to A's or B's simple-minded egotism, or should we call it his love of some sort of immortality? In the same way, the poet who composes (to order) an epithalamion or epinikion, does not in any sense invent the institution of marriage or of horse-racing. He merely makes his characteristic contribution to the pomp and circumstance of the occasion: enhancing and glamorizing the feelings associated with such institutions. Like the carpenter, he is a link in the chain of events: a chain which he does not set in motion, although his work does help it to continue.[2]

In being transmissive, rather than creative, of values, the artist has, in the first place, to put himself *en rapport* with the value-opportunities of the occasion which provides for him the determining link. To the artistic mind, there are always many such potentialities inherent in a given situation. Where a layman might see nothing but a block of marble or a piece of timber, the artist is apt to see, in the veining of the marble or the graining of the timber, something like a bust of Athene, or a table or stool. His imagination is full to overflowing, of such schematic patterns (within the range, doubtless, of his experience), and he is always open to the suggestions of this or that object. The artist is sensitive, perceptive, ready to follow the guidance of his vision. As the Greeks express this, he is 'inspired', from a source prior to his own artistic activity. He places himself and his technical powers at the service of this 'inspiration', whether this takes the form of an image as concrete and specific as the requirements of a technical blueprint, or remains somewhat vague and in the back of his mind, an influence which he thinks of as 'the Muse'.[3]

In the second place, the artist never stands alone. He has to put himself *en rapport* with his fellow-artists. A carpenter who has been through the mill, growing up in a family of professional carpenters, playing with mimic tools, becoming his father's helper, at first in play, but later in earnest, eventually becomes a master-workman. By the time he becomes the head of another family of carpenters, he is an artisan to his finger-tips. He has associated with carpenters all his life, and is highly sensitive to their professional outlook: to their accepted methods and their highly critical standards. In order to win their friendliness and to keep their respect, he has to make himself one of the group, a hundred-per-cent. artisan. If his fellow-carpenters are contemptuous or jealous, they are in a position to make fun of him and his work; and a word spoken out of season can easily spoil his prospects of professional advancement. It is much the same with artists whose aim is primarily to charm or enchant, rather than to be crudely useful. A poet, painter, or musician who does not win and keep the respect and friendship of his professional associates: so that they feel that his work and his success is in a sense the work and the success of the group to which they also belong, is headed for trouble in his professional life.[4]

In the third place, the master-artist has to establish a certain *rapport* with his professional assistants and collaborators. He has to pass on his inspiration to them: if their work is to be transmissive of the values held in his vision. Many, if not all, of the activities recognized in Hellas as 'arts' are of a collaborative nature. They require the co-operation of numbers of expert fellow-workers. Such arts as carpentry, pottery, and weaving are family arts; and the head of the family counts upon the active assistance of sons (and, in some cases, of apprentices) who are born (or adopted) into the family business.

The same is true of the art of the sculptor, the painter or embroiderer, and (possibly to a slighter extent) of the musician. Poetry in Hellas is understood to be a kind of master-art: employing the services (as in modern show-business) of large numbers of *virtuosi*, including soloists, choruses, and other types of artist. In Plato's Dialogues it is made plain that the work of a master-composer can be ruined if he meets with poor co-operation in the way of delivery or interpretation on the part of rhapsodes or readers; much as in modern times an acknowledged masterpiece like Beethoven's violin concerto can be so rendered, even by a player of repute, as to be a complete failure at its first performance. In Hellas the work of a poet or prose-writer is never read silently. It is spoken aloud, acted out, amplified with expressive gestures. With the entire group of his collaborative assistants, the master-artist has to be very careful, if he is to be sure that they will be transmitting the values he wishes to have transmitted.[5]

In the fourth place, the artist has to place himself *en rapport* with his audience, i.e. in the last resort, with his community, his public.

His contemporaries, however, are not the final link in the chain; for they too transmit—to posterity—the values they receive from him. His community, his public, thus extends far into the future; particularly so if, like Thucydides or Plato, he is writing consciously *für die Ewigkeit.*[6] If his artistic powers, both of perception and of expression, are truly great, his work will be repeated like Homer's: reinterpreted both in form and in content so that generations yet unborn, and indeed centuries of new readers, will derive inspiration from the original source, and will pass it on to their successors, enriched with the growing experience of the race.[7]

If the artist is one of the great ones, his work will express, not merely a particular flash of inspiration, significant only for his own time and place; but an inspiration of universal human significance. For him, the determining link is not merely some influence which immediately precedes and stimulates his artistic reaction. His work transcends the temporal order, and enters a realm in which what determines him is the entire chain of links, past, present, and indefinite-future. A Homer or a Shakespeare at his best is thus the living spirit of poetry; much as a Thucydides is the living spirit of history, a Beethoven is the living spirit of music, or a Plato is the living spirit of philosophy. The work of such artists never loses contact with the well-springs of inspiration. Long after the original artist is dead and buried, his work will continue to receive renewed appreciation, understanding, and interpretation. It is, in fact, only in the future evolution of culture that it will achieve its still growing fulfilment.[8]

In the fifth place, the artist has to keep *en rapport* with his medium of expression. A boat-builder has to be very careful what kinds, and what cuts, of wood he uses for this or that part of his boat. A painter has to be very careful, not only about his pigments, but also about the preparation of the surface upon which he is proposing to spread the final coat of paint—if any coat of paint is ever really 'final'. And this is true, whether he is merely painting a red barn, or whether he is painting the picture of a red barn.

So the poet has to be extremely careful, not merely about the words and idioms he selects and pieces together, but about how he relates his verbal medium to his musical medium, and to the choreographical medium of expression, over which his responsibility as a composer also extends. Developments or changes in any of the media of expression will require corresponding changes in technique. In classical Greece, for instance, development in the art of cutting planking called for very different techniques of boat-building from those in use in Homeric times. Again, in classical times, the Hellenic language had developed to such a degree of complexity and refinement, that a would-be sophisticated poet needed to be something of an etymologist. At any rate, his work called for a degree of understanding unknown in earlier days, when Greek was not 'taught' at all. With all such developments in his medium of expression, the artist, if he is to be a master in his chosen field, must keep in the closest possible contact.[9]

Finally, in the sixth place, the artist has to be at all times *en rapport* with the instruments of which he makes use. These tend to be fairly numerous, and new or improved ones are being invented all the time. Someone invents, let us say, an ingenious gadget for straightening wood. That is something no Hellenic carpenter can afford to be without. Someone else invents a 'panharmonion', a new way of fastening lyres together so as to provide an instrument on which you can play music in *all* the keys. Professional musicians at once experiment with it: to see how far it fits in with the 'modern' tendencies in Hellenic composition. They are sensitive to the imperfections of traditional instruments, and are always on the look-out for something better, something which will increase the range, the force, or it may be the delicacy of musical expression. With all such innovations, the professional of course keeps in the closest possible touch.[10]

In each of these respects, from the search for inspiration to the use of instruments of expression, the artist is liable to many and severe limitations. He is limited, in the first place and at all times, by his own degree of artistic aptitude. He is more sensitive, more perceptive of values than the ordinary man. But such sensitivity has its degrees; and even the very greatest artists are not always on the heights. At his best, Homer is beyond praise. All you can say is that he is a genius, a man inspired. But there are certainly times when inspiration lags, and Homer nods. Is the Catalogue of the Ships inspired poetry—or a literary man's substitute for a good card-index? And look at the things to which Socrates objects: the melodramatic thrills and chills, the unmanly howls and coarse laughter, the lack of dignity and even decency![11]

An artist is limited, severely limited, by possessing merely human powers. He tries to throw himself into a receptive mood, and calls upon the Muse to 'come through' and take charge of his work. But the impetuosity of youth, the confused turbulence of emotion both in adolescence and in manhood, and the weakness of old age, all limit his openness of mind; and what 'comes through' is often far short of the ideal spirit of poetry.[12] The same is true of the philosopher. However great his abilities, he remains all-too-human; and, precisely to that extent, his inspiration will at times fail him. His senses, his imagination, his memory, his power of reasoning, his insight, will vary. At the best, his perception of values, his contact with the ideal source of inspiration, will be wonderful. But how often he will be—not at his best![13]

This means that the artist, at times, will be relatively insensitive to the message he is trying to convey. If his inspiration is indirect, if it comes to him through reading, through studying and interpreting what he reads (e.g. in some earlier poet or prose-writer), difficulties of grammar and syntax, or of the unusual words selected by his author, may seriously mislead him. In that case, he will misinterpret his author's ideas. He will fail to realize the original vision. The quality of the interpretation will correspond to the insight of the interpreter; and if there are many interpreters, some wilfully and others involuntarily deficient in insight, there will be many interpretations, perhaps all differing and all fallacious, of one and the same poem.[14]

Or, where the degree of inspiration achieved fails to penetrate to a complete understanding of what is involved in the original situation; we may have occasion to observe something like the almost grotesque blindness to the potentialities of a great theme shown in the *jeux d'esprit* of an author of the calibre of Lysias. You may think of this sort of thing as clever nonsense. But the nonsense is none too clever, at that. If an artist is lacking in perceptive delicacy, almost anything can happen. It is as if a carpenter proved unable to understand a foreman's blueprint.[15]

Socrates finds such deficiencies all too common among Athenian artists. When he puts the poets to the question, inquiring into the message they are trying to convey, he finds them easily confused. They become emotional, and prove quite unable to explain passages from their own writings. Socrates does not doubt that there is some inspiration there; but when he finds hardly a person in the audience, but could talk better about the poetry than the poets themselves, he is shocked. It is only too obvious that their vision is unsteady, and hardly qualifies them to pose as the teachers of Hellas. They may be sensitive, but they are not sensitive enough.[16]

This weakness of perceptive delicacy does not occur only among artists of the highest degree of sensitivity. It is found all along the line. An artist's artistic colleagues, his fellow poets, painters, and musicians, or (if you insist) his fellow carpenters, potters, and weavers, can develop something of a blind spot toward values other than those which appeal to their own particular inspiration. An artist's work is easily misunderstood; and professional jealousy, with envy and malice leading to downright misrepresentation, can be pretty deadly as limitations to an artist's effectiveness.[17]

Again, the collaborators directly concerned with transmitting the artist's vision to his public (the solo *virtuosi* of one sort or another, the choruses, the numbers of craftsmen concerned with the many detailed activities which constitute the fringe of show business in ancient Athens) can fail, at this point or that, to appreciate or to understand the values which it is their professional business to transmit. It is hard, if not impossible, to keep their perceptive delicacy, their openness to the artist's inspiration, always at concert pitch. It is not necessary to stress the possibility of sinister factors; of envy or malice. A little stupidity, plain ordinary human dullness and inattentiveness, is quite enough to limit severely the effectiveness of any performance which is dependent upon the mental alertness of merely human assistants.[18]

Or consider the audience: the playgoers, the concertgoers, the throng of visitors to the picture-salons. There is no doubt about their enthusiasm. They bustle from one exhibition to the next, and rave about everything that takes their fancy. There is no doubt about the volume of their responsiveness. What thunderous applause, what joyous outcries![19] There is no doubt, even, about the perceptive acumen of some few of these enthusiasts—as individuals, that is. But once men become members of an audience, the social side of their experience tends to do something to their judgement. They become swayed by crowd-psychology, by confused mass-feeling.

Only too easily they believe themselves to be an *élite*, representative members of an artistic, economic, social, and political community, a theatrocracy. They are in the position of critics, of judges who have to be approached humbly by the artist whose work is being subjected to their judgement. They are superiors, able to confer or withhold favours. In their hands, whether for good or ill, they hold the professional fortunes of all who appear before them. If those hands are to clap, to bestow their favour, their life-giving favour: such audiences expect to be considered, to be flattered. They expect to have their feelings titillated, to have their emotions stimulated. In a word, they expect to have themselves, with their sovereign import in the scheme of things, expressed, recognized, and acclaimed. Does not their verdict ensure to the artist who expresses them to themselves, praising the Athenians to their faces, his prestige as an artist, together with his patrons, his pay, his public, and his encouragement to continue along his chosen path?[20]

By having to conform to such standards, the standards of a theatrocracy, the artist feels himself severely limited. Of the strictly artistic quality of his judges' sensitivity, he tends to feel more than doubtful; and yet, there it is. He is forced to put himself into their hands; and perhaps has to tone down his inspiration to what such an audience is willing to accept. A discouraging position for a man of independent ability and insight![21]

So much for the limitations associated with the perceptive side of the artist's work, with its degrees of delicacy, of insight, of inspiration. We now turn to consider the limitations associated with the other side of his work: with his technique, and his power of controlled expression.

NOTES

1. Very modern authorities, with one voice, insist that the distinction of 'useful' and 'fine' art is modern. It is a distinction not found at all in the ancient world. A slightly older writer, like S. H. Butcher, whose book, *Aristotle's Theory of Poetry and Fine Art* (London and New York, 1895) is still widely used by students of art as well as by students of Aristotle, uses the term 'Fine Art' without the slightest hesitation, in dealing with Aristotle's theories. He is of course well aware that the *phrase* 'fine art' is not Hellenic. But he regards the Hellenic term *mimesis*, usually translated as 'imitative arts' (in a usage found in Plato and even earlier), as meaning much the same as what a modern means by the term 'fine arts'. (See esp. pp. 115 ff.) Later writers, however, like R. G. Collingwood, *The Principles of Art* (Oxford, 1938), in a work regarded as so authoritative that librarians in great cities tend to place it on the reference shelves of their general reading-rooms, insist that 'The Greeks had no conception of what we call art, as distinct from craft' (p. 5). They of course distinguish poetry from carpentry, but merely as they would distinguish pottery from carpentry, i.e. as a different craft.

I hesitate to seem to disagree with the eminent authorities of our time, of whom the late Professor Collingwood is undoubtedly one. It is of course certain that the Greeks often think of architecture, sculpture, painting, music, and poetry, as 'crafts'. They *were* crafts. But I certainly find, in the text of Plato, many passages which seem to mark a distinction greater than the distinction of one craft from another craft.

I have in mind, particularly, the many passages dealing with the subject of inspiration. Poets, painters, and musicians, claim to be inspired, and Socrates is among the very first to grant that claim, in fact, to insist upon its validity. I cannot find much evidence that carpentry, pottery, and weaving, or the kind of painting that paints an actual barn red (as contrasted with a picture of a red barn as part of a landscape), are regarded as inspired. It is doubtless true that the Hellenic equivalents of the medieval guilds regarded themselves as stemming from a (probably mythical) 'founder' of some sort. But I do not find artisans (in spite of Socrates's pronounced respect for their undoubted *expertise*) regarded as inspired, in the same sense that a Homer is so regarded. There is here one great difference.

A second difference between arts and crafts is the very great importance ascribed, in the Dialogues, to the *educational value* of poetry, painting, music, and dancing. These arts are *indispensable in educating for citizenship.* I cannot find that such crafts as the craft of the carpenter, weaver, or potter, are similarly regarded. They *can* indeed be studied amateurishly, as a part of general education; but they are *not indispensable for citizenship.* In fact, professional practitioners of these crafts are deliberately excluded from citizenship; and the citizens are explicitly forbidden to practise any of these crafts professionally. The craftsman's type of *expertise* is, indeed, sharply distinguished from *paideia*, the type of education suited to the development of free men. This is a second great distinction.

In view of the undoubted evidence for these two important distinctions, I am inclined to think that Mr. S. H. Butcher's view is more nearly in accordance with the facts, than the view expressed by so many of our most modern writers in the field of aesthetics.

2. *Ion* 535e f., *Rep.* 597d f.

3. *Apol.* 22c, *Ion* 536a f., *Crat.* 396d f., 399a, e f, 407e, 428cd, *Symp.* 196d, *Phaedr.* 234c f., 235c f., 237ab, 238cd, 263d, 265b, *Tim.* 27d f.

4. *Lach.* 184b f., *Prtg.* 316d, 327a f., *Rep.* 406a ff., 421d, 466e f., 537a, *Phaedr.* 235e f., *Laws* 643e f.

5. *Lysis* 204d, 206a f., *Charm.* 162d, *Ion* 534e f., *Prtg.* 312ab, 325e f., *Gorg.* 482bc, *Rep.* 373b, 466e f.

6. *Phdo.* 78a, *Rep.* 497cd, *Laws* 811c f., cf. 765d f., 769e, 858c f., 880d f., 957d, 964d f. Thucyd. *De Bell. Peloponn.,* I 22, 4.

7. *Ion* 535e f., cf. *Prtg.* 338c–347a. I have in mind the perpetual reinterpretation of Homeric themes, not only in the work of the Greek tragedians (*Rep.* 595c, 598d, cf. *Theaet.* 152e. Cf. also Athenaeus, *Deipnosoph.* 347e), but in the work of Elizabethan and classical French tragedies, and also of modern operatic composers, and even of very modern novelists such as Anatole France. Alexander, *Beauty and the other Forms of Value* (Macmillan, London, 1933), p. 99, refers with approval to Coleridge's idea that a great poet is able to 'give his work the organic coherence of a living thing. . . . The poem is an organic thing . . . its separate parts are limbs of the whole'. (The words are Alexander's, but the idea is surely [R.C.L.] much older than Coleridge, as the allusion to the *membra poetae* (of Horace) is presumably intended to imply.) Alexander thinks of a great, vital poem, as living on, after its inspired writer has passed on, with a life of its own, like an independent organism. Plato thinks of the 'life' of, e.g. the Homeric epics, as sustained, (1) by Homer, (2) by Aeschylus and his brother dramatists, (3) by all subsequent readers and writers, who take up the themes of Homer into their own life, and sustain them out of their own living force. Apart from someone lending to them such creative, living force (out of his own life), the poet's book-of-words is a maimed thing, if not utterly dead (*Phaedr.* 275c f., cf. *Prtg.* 347d f., *Theaet.* 163de, 166 f.).

8. *Ion* 535c f., 536b f., *Phdo.* 77e f.

9. *Prtg.* 328a, 340 f., *Crat.* 391d ff., 418a f., 424d f., 425d f., *Rep.* 398c f., 399e f., 501a f., *Tim.* 47cd, *Laws* 653b f., 655 f., 659d f., 664e, 669b f., 672d f., 769a f., 812cd. Cf. *Ency. Brit.*, 14th edit., arts. BOAT, SHIP, where the development since Homer (*Odyss.* V) is outlined and explained.

10. *Rep.* 399c f., *Phil.* 56c, *Laws* 669b f.

11. *Rep.* 377d ff.

12. *Apol.* 39a, *Charm.* 154b f., 155d, *Ion* 535b f., *Prtg.* 334d f., 336a f., *Crat.* 384b, *Phdo.* 65a ff., *Phaedr.* 228a, *Laws* 644e f.

13. *Rep.* 487cd, 489d f., 490e f., 536cd, 602e ff., *Laws* 803c, 886b ff., 907d ff. Croce, *op. cit.*, pp. 11, 13-15, maintains that the difference in artistic sensitivity between a great artist and an ordinary man is merely 'extensive, quantitative'. There is 'identity of nature between (the great artist's) imagination and ours . . . *Homo nascitur poeta.* . . . Some men are born great poets, some small'.

Alexander, on the other hand, notes a rather widespread difference between craftsmanship (shown in competent prose-writing, with analogies in the other arts) and artistry. 'Art grows out of craft and goes beyond it, when the worker handles his materials not only as a means of reaching a certain practical end but for their own sake, and becomes contemplative instead of merely practical' (Alex., *op. cit.*, p. 18, cf. pp. 17, 20, 24, 25, 27, 35, etc.).

14. *Prtg.* 338 f., 347c f., *Phaedr.* 275d f.

15. *Phaedr.* 242d f.

16. *Apol.* 22a f., *Rep.* 606e f.

17. *Lach.* 184b f.

18. *Lysis* 204d, 206a f., cf. *Ion* 535e, *Gorg.* 456c f.

19. *Rep.* 475c f., 492b f.

20. *Apol.* 34c ff., *Ion* 535e, *Menex.* 234c f., *Gorg.* 463 ff., *Rep.* 426b f., 590b f. *Laws* 667b f., 669b f., 701a f., 722a f.

21. *Rep.* 492cd, 493d, cf. 397a f., *Laws* 700d f.

L

CHAPTER EIGHT

The Limitations of Art: How to Meet Them, II

WE now turn to consider the artist's limitations in respect of technique, his power of controlled expression. This is no mere matter of *self*-control. It involves his control over the physical environment: over the medium in which he expresses—whatever he expresses, and over the instruments he uses, as well as over the human beings with whom, as he works, he interacts. This sort of control requires something different from intuitive vision, however 'inspired'. It requires a degree of knowledge, of factual science.

The medium in which the artist works is thought of as a rhythmic tissue. It is a complex tissue: constructed, in the last resort, of the four elements popularized in the development of Ionian science, namely, fire, water, earth, and air. The painter, for example, exercises control over colours. What, from the standpoint of science, are colours? They are 'effluences of fire'. More particularly, they are forms of 'flame', i.e. of the heatless glow which is one species of 'fire'. To prepare colours technically for his use in painting, the artist extracts certain dyes from plants or animals, or selects certain pigments. These are ultimately all, as thus extracted, forms of 'earth'. He mixes these forms of 'earth', for his use, with 'water' (or with some form of 'water', such as oil). He then places these mixtures, using appropriate instruments, upon his canvas, and they dry in the 'air'. Some of the colours used come to him directly from nature. Others he obtains by mixing the given colours until the intermediate shade he obtains satisfies his artistic feeling.[1]

In preparing such mixtures for his use, the artist is in no sense 'creating' their colouredness. Only God can do that. There is doubtless what we might think of as a secret mathematical proportion, some kind of formula relating Red and Blue to Purple, or the

146

pigments of Blue and Yellow to Green, etc., etc. And it is not unreasonable of the Pythagorean scientists, with their dream of discovering some day the numerical formulas which they believe to
underlie every phenomenon observed in nature, to speak as though
the discovery of colour-formulas is merely a question of detailed
research. Perhaps it is. But meanwhile the formula remains God's
secret; and the human painter's analytic-synthetic technique, applied
to the pigments found in nature, while he may like to think of it as
his attempt to imitate something like God's formula, remains (for
the time being) very empirical: a matter, largely, of trial and error.[2]
   It is much the same with the musician's control over tones. Here
the Pythagoreans are on much firmer ground. They have really
succeeded in learning how to formulate the mathematical interrelations of some of the harmonies used in Hellenic music. There is
more than a suggestion that the tonal intervals of Hellenic scales are
related to the intervals which separate the planets studied in Pythagorean astronomy, with a proportion which is positive and direct.
And there is a hope that persistent research into tones and rhythms
as related to this or that 'virtue' (as certain martial rhythms and tones
are related to 'courage'), will before long succeed in establishing
standardized scales and patterns excellently suited to building up
human character for the purposes of good citizenship (model-city
style).[3] But, for the time being, musicians have to continue composing empirically: depending upon the discriminations achieved by
the human ear, and trying things out, to see how they sound, until
they hit upon something which 'sounds right'.[4]
   The point is that, while the artist (ideally speaking) should know
all that science can teach him, if he is to exercise competent control
over his medium; science at present is not in a position to tell even
a Damon quite as much as he hopes, one day, to learn from it. In the
meantime, the artist is still thrown back, largely, upon his artistic
sense: i.e. upon expert trial and error. He has to mingle his pigments
until the effect 'looks right'. He has to vary the position of his fingers
on the vents of his flute, until the effect 'sounds right'. His alleged
'knowledge' thus turns out, in practice, to be still largely a matter of
'guesswork'. It is a kind of knack derived, a little haphazardly, from
simple experience: guided by standards emerging, partly from somewhere within the artist as an individual, and partly from a kind of
gentlemen's agreement as to what he and his brother-artists will
accept as 'just right'.[5]
   So much for the artist's knowledge of physical science. This is

clearly in an undeveloped state; well below, for the most part, the level attained by the carpenter, the weaver, and other utilitarian artists. For these are able, to a considerable extent, to make use of the assistance supplied by exact measurement and mathematical reasoning. In a word, precisely where the artist needs something different from vague intuition and inspiration, we find him severely limited. He is still hardly beginning to emerge from the most elementary level of value-feeling.[6]

The artist also requires knowledge of psychological science. Is he any better off here? It is quite obvious (as soon as a Socrates points it out) that if the artist's business is 'to enchant the soul', i.e. to attract, stimulate, and influence his audience: enhancing their experience and transmitting to them his divinely inspired message; he will need to know something about, let us say, audience psychology. If human beings, whether as individuals or as members of an audience assembled in a group, fall (psychologically speaking) into distinct types, A, B, C, . . ., open only to corresponding types of artistic influence; it is plainly vital for the artist to know something about these types, both theoretically and practically.

The artist, that is to say, not only needs to be well grounded in the theory of types. He needs to know, very clearly, what each type is, and to be able to distinguish it from the other types which, to an untutored mind, seem to resemble it. And further: he has to be able to distinguish, very clearly, the corresponding types of art. He has to know precisely how (and why) this type of painting, of music, of oratory or what not, affects 'type A' positively, and 'types B and C' negatively. He also needs to know what kind of difference it makes if his audience is restricted to one or two individuals, rather than expanded to a crowd. Such knowledge is only theoretical; but the distinctions have to be kept clearly and firmly in mind, if the artist's message is to be expressed in a way which is true to type.[7]

And yet further: the artist has to know how to apply all this knowledge in practice, if he is to be successful. He needs to have a good deal of experience of audiences, and he has to keep his wits about him. He needs to be able to recognize clearly and accurately with what type of audience he has to deal: so that he can proceed to set before it only the kinds of pictures, of music, or of speeches, which will prove most effective. It is not much use playing classical music to an audience of ultra-modernists, or trying out a Punch and Judy show on the community *élite*! A touch of 'the abstrusities' heightens the effect of your speechifying, if delivered before an audience of cultured Athenians. But it would be worse than wasted if you tried it on a group of Cretans or Spartans.[8]

There is no doubt that every successful artist (whether carpenter, poet, or statesman) needs something of these kinds of knowledge. There is no doubt that, since the arts have all grown up empirically out of practical human needs, successful artists in every field have somehow picked up a certain amount of practical psychology. But the question arises as to whether the professors have succeeded in developing a scientific psychology of types: something clear, exact, and objective, on which the artists can rely.

And there is always the further question raised by Socrates, as to whether, if there *is* any such scientific knowledge, it can be communicated. Is it capable of being taught? By reference to the textbooks of his period, Socrates shows that, behind a fearsomely pretentious nomenclature, the professors conceal an almost complete lack of insight into the really important questions. There is, as yet, no scientific psychology of the kind desiderated.[9] And on the practical side, Socrates (as ever) remains unconvinced that the trial-and-error efforts of a few audacious experimenters in this field, can, within measurable time, be reduced to a teachable system of scientific doctrine.[10]

That is to say, for the time being, would-be successful artists are, at all points, thrown back upon their common-sense intuitions— which have the status of 'guesswork'. This is the very lowest stage of what, with the uneducated, passes for 'knowledge'. It is nothing more than 'opinion'. Mostly, this consists of images flitting in and out of their minds, dim foreshadowings of this or that. The suggestiveness of such floating imagery is eked out here and there by a meagre practical experience—the kind which is not yet raised by mathematical technique to the level of inter-implying system. Experience, guided by a judgement which becomes skilful through giving painstaking attention to matters of detail, gradually raises the artist (when at his best) to the level called by Plato 'right opinion'. Music, feeling after the right balance of tones, is full of such empiricism. So is medicine, feeling after the right balance in which health consists. The art of the farmer is not in much better case, and the same is true of the art of the pilot and of the general.[11]

'Right opinion' is about as far in the direction of knowledge, as most artists, at least, most of the artists who aim at charm, at enhancement of experience, seem willing to go. A painter is perfectly willing to paint a 'Cobbler at his Last', without knowing a thing about either cobblers or their lasts. So long as he puts on canvas a texture of forms and colours which 'looks good' to him, and to others equally ignorant of cobbling, he is satisfied. Similarly a speaker who has developed the power of the word, seems even to pride himself upon not having to learn the truth about the matters on which he offers persuasive advice. As long as the stream of phrases issuing from his lips 'sounds good' to him, and to listeners equally ignorant, he is more than satisfied. Simply because he can string words together and can fill the minds of an (ignorant) audience with plausible and convincing imagery, he will not hesitate (although entirely unqualified by training or by experience) to offer prescriptive advice on questions of medicine, of generalship, and of statesmanship; in fact, on anything whatever.[12]

Such voice-wizardry is a dangerous gift. It not only leaves a man in his ignorance. It keeps him there. He thinks that he already knows enough for his purposes. He prides himself on not needing to know more. In fact, he may be in that most noxious state of ignorance, which thinks it actually knows, when it doesn't. You can always tell a clever journalist, but you can never tell him much![13]

The artists who use exact measurement and apply to their problems the calculations of mathematical science, are in much better case. They are not subject to the limitations inherent in 'opinion' (whether 'right' or not). They reach a level of knowledge which, however partial and imperfectly based, is at least far clearer and far more reliable than 'opinion'. They know what they know, and, to a considerable extent, how they know it.

A carpenter who uses practical geometry in his work, not only has experience. He has technique. His mathematical reasoning, practical and restricted though it is, takes him outside the class of mere artists and handicraftsmen. As far as clearness and cogency of reasoning are concerned, he belongs in a higher class: the class of applied scientists. In fact, you might regard architects, engineers, and statesmen who have learned to apply statistics to problems of human administration, almost as lay brothers of the Pythagorean Order. For the Pythagoreans too, although famous as mathematicians, are really, for the most part, applied mathematicians. They ground themselves at all points upon empirical verification; and they hesitate to initiate or pursue inquiries leading in the direction of transcendental speculation, by means of 'pure' reason, into the absolute basis, the ultimate presupposition, of their various disciplines.[14]

It is not too difficult, to imagine the artists who aim at charm or beauty, eventually rising above the biosocial beauties of this earth: the glamour-boys and glamour-girls, the forest streams and moonlit lakes, the external trappings of power, might, majesty, and dominion. To human experience, these things are beautiful, undeniably so. Indeed, who would have it otherwise? But their charm is relative. It varies with time, place, and circumstance; and, although most artists never dream of transcending the range of their ordinary, biosocial experience, and the world has not yet learned to pay attention to what lies beyond;[15] any intellectual realizes that science has a still higher source of charm, of beauty which can almost be regarded, not as relative, but as unconditioned.

There is about mathematical reasoning, a satisfying depth, as well as clearness and cogency. It is far more persuasive, at least to intellectuals (i.e. to men of trained rational judgement), than the smiles and tears, the passionate affirmations and negations, of the crude senses and emotions. The straightness glimpsed behind a straight line drawn by the hand, the roundness glimpsed behind a circle drawn upon paper, the utter squareness and cubedness indicated by the models you can touch and see—all such experiences open to the mind's eye a new world of inter-implying regularities of figure, whose charms do not fade at dawn, or lose vitality with the passing years. It is the realm of the ideal, whose truths are unvarying and eternal, and its values transcend relativity.[16]

The artist who beholds this vision, realizes the power, as well as the fascination, of abstract thinking. As he grows into something of an intellectual, his work gradually takes on the quality of abstract art. If he still retains the artist's interest in depiction, he tries to present to the senses the inner meaning, the inter-implying laws, of the phenomena which formerly attracted him by their sensuous beauty. If a painter, he tries to suggest, in and through his pictorial art, the symmetry and measuredness, the orderliness, the intelligible quality, the symbolic significance, of what is selectively presented to the eye.

He may attempt this by introducing what (to the eye of sense) looks like distortion, an apparent distortion which he could justify by appealing to exact measurement, or at least to a system of inter-implying mathematical rules.[17] Or he may deliberately, in a professedly 'abstract' art, distort and rearrange the features of the given, so as to bring out even more sharply the inner significance of what he sees.[18] He may even go so far as to paint what, to the artistically untutored eye of common sense, looks like a queer pattern of geometric structures: triangles, rectangles, and cubes—a pattern, however, which to the trained scientific intelligence may indicate the profound insight, not merely of a 'friend of ideas', but of a 'friend of God'.[19]

Similarly with the intellectual musician. The ordinary citizen, who has taken only a short course for amateur performers, cannot understand anything more complicated than a hymn-tune or a military march. He feels, indeed, something of the charm, the biosocial charm, of popular music; but it is doubtful if he really understands it. To men like Cleinias and Megillus in the *Laws*, music is 'just noise'. Without programme notes, or a revealing title, they do not really know what it is all about.[20] The more advanced musician, however, i.e. a man like Damon, interested in mathematics and physical acoustics even more than in what appeals to the untutored ear of common sense, expresses himself in rhythmic patternings which bring out something far deeper than amateurs can begin to appreciate. Can it be that such a musician has become almost a Pythagorean, a scientist composing scientific music for his brother scientists?

Be that as it may, such mathematical or abstract music appeals, not so much to the ear, as to the mind. The tones which such a musician demands, are perhaps hardly producible on the traditional instruments of Hellas; and the scale-patterns upon which he insists, are unfamiliar to the ordinary run of concertgoers: unfamiliar (it may be) even to professional instrumentalists. But to listeners who have the mentality to understand, the pure inner glow of the impassioned truth-lover, the deeper meaning, is there. The work of such artists points dimly but unmistakably toward an even deeper development of art, toward a perfection beyond what anyone but a philosophical idealist could hope to appreciate.[21]

So also with the intellectually trained statesman. The magistrates of Plato's model city are administering laws made, not for purely rational beings, members of some noumenal realm dreamed up by some one-sided idealist, but for quite ordinary citizens, resident aliens, and slaves: i.e. for creatures made of human flesh and blood.[22] Yet the magistrates appeal, as far as they can, to intelligent understanding and voluntary co-operation. They expect to be met halfway by public-spirited self-control on the part of those whose civic life they are elected or appointed to guide. At all times, they are prepared to reason sweetly, to explain to all who are both able and willing to apply their minds, why this or that ordinance has been passed, and how it is calculated to benefit the community as a whole.

They point out that their own work is subject to higher revision and control, and that the constitution contains positive provisions for its own periodic amendment.[23] However, when among themselves, they tend to make use of dialectical reasoning. At least, it is by statistical information and scientifically correlated generalizations that they are primarily influenced. They constitute, in fact, a brains trust of trained social scientists; and there is a suggestion that their attitude is influenced, not merely by the facts of life, but by a hope of achieving, some day, yet further insight into the principle of ideality itself.[24]

Even at this third level (*dianoia*), which is higher than all but a very few human beings can hope to attain,[25] the artist still feels himself limited. It is true that his technique raises him above many of the earlier limitations. He is no longer blind when he stretches out, reaching after values which prove satisfying to a delicately perceptive nature. He understands clearly what he is trying to do. He has achieved a fair mastery over the technical methods which enable him to succeed: with his medium, with his fellow-workers, and with his community. He is in the position of a Pericles, a Euripides, an Apelles, or (in our modern world) of a Mozart or a Beethoven. These are the advantages of 'science'.[26]

But, even at this high level, he finds that human art remains, at best, an imperfect thing: an affair of lights and shadows, of checks and balances, of fallings and recoverings. He meets with suggestions and intimations of a beauty, a perfection of charm which goes beyond what can be imputed to science. Every now and then he glimpses (and perhaps at moments achieves) a beauty which transcends the tried and tested formulas of human science. It leaves him amazed: attracted and hoping, yet baffled.[27]

Perhaps the ideal is essentially elusive, never altogether realizable in human art. Perhaps he is straining after a perfection characteristic, not of human, but of divine art: making yet one more vain human attempt to know the unknowable.[28] Let us imagine him penetrating yet further into the secret formulas of nature; or at least into some humanly intelligible symbol of them. Would that make him still more of an artist, at least on the perceptive side? Or would it (in the end) take him entirely beyond the inherent potentialities of art? Would it turn him into a 'friend of God': a lover, no longer of this imperfect world, but of divine wisdom—in a word, a philosopher?[29]

In the Dialogues, the highest reach of any profession tends to be discussed in this sort of way. The 'royal' art, the art of the statesman, is envisaged (ideally) as the art of the *philosopher*-king. Of this art, Socrates is the only practitioner of his time. But, as everyone knows, Socrates is 'fey'. He lives, not in our world, but in the realm which transcends our world, 'God's Heaven', where nothing imperfect is to be found. He lives among ideals which are absolute: beauty, justice, goodness, truth. He is trying to relate these to our world. But can anyone say that his work is a success?[30]

The case is similar with the other arts: with the art of the philosopher-lawyer, of the philosopher-physician, of the philosopher-mathematician, of the philosopher-educator.[31] It is similar with the philosopher-writer, whether he writes poems, or (like Plato) prose-dramas.[32] It is the same with the philosopher-rhetorician, the philosopher-musician, and the philosopher-painter. In the upper reaches of their arts, all such practitioners are philosophers: fellow-members of some academy of the spirit, at home with one another, and with Socrates, their leader.[33] But do they remain, also, statesmen, physicians, mathematicians, musicians, and painters? Are they able, somehow, to bridge the gap which divides the actual from the ideal? Or does their transcendentalism disqualify them for seeking anything as empirical as success in our world of claims and counter-claims?[34]

Let us attempt to answer this question by reference to the evidence. Plato thinks of the philosopher's calling as being like the poet's calling. It is a holy estate, requiring divine inspiration.[35] But among men, the position of wisdom-lover (like the position of poet) seems altogether wonderful. It is honoured. Consequently, many individuals, desirous of being honoured above their fellows, try to get themselves regarded as Thales was regarded, or Lycurgus, or Solon: the 'wise men' of antiquity.[36]

They give up the practice of the arts in which they have been trained. They even withdraw from the activities of civic life. They profess to commune with the absolute. They claim to be accepted as oracular authorities. They put on airs like prophets and priests and possessors of a more than human wisdom.[37] Such men, as Plato refers to them, are in many cases quite unqualified (either by character and natural intelligence, or by trained insight and education) for their lofty profession. Their ambitions exceed their abilities, and they have simply mistaken their true vocation. Their alleged 'wisdom' turns out to be spurious, a tissue of monstrous sophisms; and, as they cannot do what they would, and will not do what they could, their lives are wasted. They prove utterly useless, both to themselves and to the community.[38]

While many feel themselves thus called, the *élite*, the genuine lovers of wisdom, are very few. They too feel within themselves an impulse to give up the practice of the arts and sciences in which they have been trained. They too would like to dedicate themselves solely to the pursuit of 'wisdom', whatever that might prove to be. They enjoy taking all knowledge for their province and being spectators of all time and existence; and they feel reluctant to come down again into the cave and mingle with their fellow-citizens: engaging (like their fellows) in the trivial round, the common task.[39]

But, while many talented artists and scientists apparently feel, at times, impelled to give up the practice of the arts in which they have achieved a degree of success, and to devote themselves to this life of pure contemplation: the genuine philosophers are not permitted (by their education) to follow this impulse. Not for them the ivory-tower life! They are compelled to descend again into the cave, and, with a spirit renewed by contemplating the philosopher's vision, to 'do *their* work'. This means, to apply their powers as trained artists enlightened by philosophy to the service of their fellow-men.[40]

After a period of bewilderment in which their eyes, accustomed to the bright visions of idealism, find it hard to adapt themselves to the twilight obscurity of unidealistic actuality, they learn eventually to see distinctly, both (1) the ideals and (2) the facts of human life. For the remainder of their mature working years, they devote themselves to artistic creativity for the good of the community: each working along the lines in which he is especially competent.[41]

Take the man who has been trained in the arts of administration. He is now, not a pure, but an applied, philosopher: a philosopher-statesman, i.e. a statesman enlightened by his contacts with philosophy. Precisely as a painter looks, now toward his model and now toward his medium, painting in this feature and painting out that, until he produces the best likeness he can of what he sees in the model: precisely so does the philosopher-statesman look, now toward the idea of good, and now toward the social institutions of his fellow-citizens. He retouches here and remodels there, until he has wrought into the tissue of their living all that he sees in his vision of the ideal republic, or (at the very least) all that he thinks they can make their own, of the institutions of the 'second-best' model, the community outlined in the *Laws*.[42]

With his trained knowledge of the facts of life, the philosopher-statesman realizes that ordinary men and women can hardly be expected to respond directly to a purely rational appeal. They can be induced, it is true, to feel something of the attractiveness of his vision. But it would be too much, to expect them to see it as clearly as he sees it, with a full sense of its beauty and power. His vision has to be translated for their benefit; expressed in ways which they can appreciate and accept. He has to appeal convincingly to their senses and emotions.

It is here that art, with its trained ability to enhance experience, to present ideas which might otherwise appear cold and abstract, in forms which feel intimately warm, concrete, and alive, comes in. The average citizen, the ordinary commercial worker, and the slave, to be influenced effectively, have to be approached non-logically, through stimulating their instincts, their imaginations, and their emotions.[43]

To stir up their courage, you give them, not only discipline and drill; you give them martial music and the anapaestic battle-chants of Tyrtaeus. To induce temperance, docility and controlled follower-ship, you do something more than address them in accents of command. You prepare for their use, solemn ceremonies, and ritual hymns to the great Gods who guide and protect human life, and are the authors of all our blessings.[44] The non-logical rhythms of such art introduce a measuredness, an orderliness into civic life, and confirm what tendencies in the direction of rhythm and harmony are already present within the citizens.[45]

The philosopher-statesman thus requests the co-operation of his brother-artists: whose gifts lie, not in the field of administration, but in more specific fields. Some of them are masters of tonal rhythms and harmonies. Others exercise mastery over words, the words of prose and of poetry. Yet others have power over the lines and colours of pictorial art. Yet others are experts in the fields of hygiene and gymnastic training. If the artists to whom he appeals are themselves philosophers (like Damon the philosopher-musician or Plato the philosopher-writer), these will have beheld, each in his own specific way, the same vision that enlightens the philosopher-statesman. They will be glad to respond to his request.[46]

A Damon and his musical colleagues respond by perfecting the scales, harmonies, and rhythmic patterns best calculated to stimulate the central principle of self-motion which animates each citizen. Citizens so stimulated will of themselves grow into living models of the civic virtues. For these civic virtues (courage, justice, temperance, comradeship, piety, and the like) are largely acquired by processes of self-habituation; and the community music makes it both natural and easy for the citizens to habituate themselves to the community *ethos*: to 'charm themselves into' good citizenship. All the songs and all the dances, all the chants and all the choral services in the temples, are consecrated to this purpose; and it is confidently anticipated that, where Apollo and the Muses grant their divine aid, community life will eventually become a civic analogon of some great Terpsichorean Symphony, a choric-symphonic ballet (classical style) entitled 'Model City Ballet'.[47]

So also Plato and his fellow-writers respond by perfecting the technical patterns of the art of philosophical dramatics: in ways calculated to induce all competent readers to join the new school of reflective citizenship. Here each student feels his way toward as much rational insight as is possible for him. All will develop at least 'right opinion', an appreciative attitude toward the rationale of the model city; while those who learn to understand clearly and distinctly the principle of ideality will go further. They will create or edit utopias. They will compose encomia of the gods and of famous men. And they will so express themselves through their art of literary dramatism, that the citizens, as they act out the new dramas and chant the new processional hymns, will project themselves imaginatively into their rôles. They will assimilate themselves to the parts they portray; and in reality as well as in idea, will find themselves triumphantly marching home to God, in the steps their fathers trod.[48]

So also with the philosopher-educators. They will teach their pupils in the spirit of reflective citizenship. Whether we look at the military sports with their community field-days, or at the cultural training, both literary and musical, with its community festivals, or at the severe legal, scientific, and dialectical studies, calculated to prepare select students for administrative service of the community: the influence of philosophic insight upon the teaching is as pronounced as in the cases of the philosopher-statesman and the philosopher-writer. It also operates in the same direction. The philosopher-teacher tries to pass on what he knows. He tries to bring up his pupils to become as like himself as possible: each living, according to his individual lights, in the spirit of membership in the ideal community; each 'doing his own work', i.e. making, to the community life, the individual contribution for which, by ability, natural inclination, and education, he is best fitted.[49]

It is the same with the philosopher-physician, the philosopher-lawyer, the philosopher-priest, and all similar members of the higher professional classes. All co-operate in applying their specific arts, enlightened by philosophy, to the service of the community. All help to raise the tone of community life, as nearly as is possible in dealing with fallible, human material, to the level of the ideal which, as philosophers, they all understand. All are alike members (whether formally enrolled in this or that administrative council, or not)[50] of a quasi-Platonic Academy. Whether formally or informally, they work together as 'artificers of freedom': functioning like *daemones*, the guardian spirits who mediate between heaven and earth, and interpret God's ways to man. How does the authoritative Hesiod phrase it? 'Holy spirits upon earth, authors of good, averters of ill, guardians of speech-gifted men.'[51]

To a certain extent, the group morale of such mature leaders is participated in by those highly promising members of the rising generation who have been selected to co-operate with their seniors: the elder statesmen who constitute the 'Council of the Areopagus', the highest administrative body in the model city. The juniors have not yet themselves seen the vision. But each functions as a junior executive to some one of the seniors, such as the minister of education. Meanwhile, each proceeds with his studies, and each associates with all the rest.[52] As the well-known *Epistle* expresses it, 'When teacher and pupils of philosophy associate intimately in their researches, so that their life is one life; in this continuous merger of personality, something happens. As an inner glow kindles and becomes a leaping flame: even so the philosophic spirit within the soul comes to a spontaneous birth; and it develops and grows by self-nurture.'[53]

To a slighter extent, the same spirit doubtless develops in those intimately co-operative committees (legislative, executive, or advisory), in which so much of the public work of the model city gets done. Here one of the seniors functions as chairman. The body of the committee is made up of experts in this or that field (some citizens, some non-citizens) who proffer factual information and make recommendations on matters where their particular experience renders them especially competent. It may be in agriculture, in commerce, in physical hygiene, in technical music, in the detailed usages of religion, or what not. The philosophically trained chairman provides the philosophy. The other committee-members discuss the details. The committee as a whole comes to a unanimous conclusion. In such co-operative activity, it is expected that the non-philosophical members will at least develop 'right opinion': coinciding in spirit, although hardly in quality of insight, with the knowledge of their leaders.[54]

It is barely conceivable that here and there some retail tradesman, hotel manager, or what not, might come to understand, not only the technical side of his business operations, but its 'philosophy', its significance and ideal function in the life of what is thought out as a 'model' city. In such a case, we should undoubtedly have a philosopher-retailer, philosopher-innkeeper, or what not. But while the case is theoretically conceivable, the visiting professor from Athens (who is leading the discussion) regards the eventuality as unlikely and (as contrasted with alternative possibilities) as, on the whole, undesirable.[55]

Philosophy has, in the model city, still wider fringes of influence. The entire life of the regular citizens, of the resident aliens, and of the slaves too, is so permeated by it, in all that is said, thought, and done, as each 'does his own work' in the community, that all are members one of another. All reach the level of 'right opinion'. 'Young and old, bond and free [we are told] never cease from charming themselves' into enthusiastic acceptance of their individual functions in the scheme of things. One and the same spirit pervades and unifies the life of the entire group, and penetrates, with enthusiastic acceptance, to the details of their living. To precisely that extent, the specific arts practised by this or that individual are enlightened (as far as the mentality and education of the individual render this possible) by philosophy.[56]

In such a community, this is about as far as art can be expected to go, as it seeks to overcome its limitations. The limitations which are matters of sheer ignorance, stupidity, ill-will, and lack of education, are (as far as possible) in process of being transcended. To a philosopher, many of the difficulties of a merely *common* sense, simply cease to be problems. He sees right through them, as an adult sees through many of the problems of children.

But the members of the model city, from lowest to highest, are after all only human. They are not as gods, and nothing can make them so. At best, they remain God's puppets. They cling as well as they can to the golden cord of reason. But do they ever really succeed? Do they ever do more than approximate, very gradually, toward the artistic realization of their vision? Are they ever quite able to make, of their dream of 'a good', a perfect waking reality? For human beings, the process of waking is difficult and lengthy. It stretches indefinitely into the future; and its end is only dimly envisaged.[57]

In final analysis, then, we still have our four levels of artistic development, each with its characteristic limitations. These are:

1. The level of instinctive and emotional feeling for what has 'charm' for human beings. Here artists attempt to produce, by trial-and-error methods, images of the structural patternings associated with such charm. This is the Protagorean or humanistic level of art (*eikasia*). It does not rise above 'opinion'.

2. The level of faith in the over-arching importance of a physically objective world. At this level, artists attempt to produce physical copies of physical things and events. They belong to the class of handworkers: guiding their activity by the 'feel' of things in their hands (*pistis*), without the aid of mathematical theory. Like the early scientists of Ionia, they also do not rise above 'opinion'.

3. The level of mathematical technique applied, however, without insight into its principle, to the empirical world. Here artists attempt to construct mathematically correct models of physical reality. They may be like the higher type of artisan who constructs and applies mathematical blueprints; or like what Plato considers the slightly higher type, the Pythagorean scientist who constructs, e.g. an 'orrery' or model of the planetary system. Such artists transcend 'opinion', and achieve (in *dianoia*) the lower reaches of 'knowledge'.

4. The level of dialectical or metaphysical insight into the principle of ideality. Here philosopher-artists attempt to apply the idea of good to the whole of human life, in the closest realizable approximation to utopian perfection. This level (*nous*) attains the higher reaches of knowledge.

The characteristic limitations of each level are partly overcome by advancing to the next higher level. Instinctive feeling becomes enlightened by being brought under objective control. Physical productivity becomes enlightened by being brought under exact mathematical methods. Departmental knowledge becomes enlightened by being brought under insight into the final unifying principle of value; and the whole, when directed from above, becomes as free from limitations as is possible in dealing with (1) human material, and (2) a physical, space-time medium. It is wonderful, what art can do, when the artist is finally enlightened by philosophy. But even so, art is an essentially imperfect activity: in which achievement never quite catches up with its own idea.[58]

One question remains. Have we been describing a process of
etiolation: in which, as one advances from the lowest to the highest
level, something of human value is, at each successive step, lost?
Does the realistic handworker lose his humanistic qualities? Does the
mathematical student unfit himself for handwork and physical
activity? And does that *rara avis*, the 'philosopher' or lover of
transcendental wisdom, become a mere otherworldly dreamer: lost
to natural human feeling, lost to workaday duties, lost, even, to the
claims of science? Does he become reason personified, a reason so
abstract, so 'pure', that it thinks only—itself? Are philosophers just
—philosophers?

Many persons think so; and the evidence of the Pythagorean and
Parmenidean schools can easily be so interpreted. And there is,
further, always the natural impulse of an ultra-refined thinker: to
withdraw from crude realities which interfere with his thinking.
But as Plato finally views the matter, the artist who approaches the
higher reaches, loses nothing of human value. In achieving the
philosopher's vision of the principle of ideality, he grasps the *ens
realissimum*. It is all pure gain. In winning his own soul, he has not
lost, but has won, the world also. Transcendental idealism ensures
physical realism; for the soul, with its transcendental insight, is
essentially 'prior' to the motions of the space-time world.[59]

'In achieving the vision, the artist loses nothing, but gains everything.' Precisely how is this done? In the first place, the process of
achieving includes everything of value. Those selected to be members of the leadership class, from which the higher guardians come,
are already the most outstanding members of the 'silver' class. This
means (1) that they possess *all* the natural aptitudes (physical, moral,
social, intellectual) which are considered desirable in a man.[60] It
means (2) that these natural abilities have been developed by education in music and gymnastic, to the highest level attainable with
human material. These young men and women have proved
themselves, again and again, in severe tests of character and of
intelligence. They have shown that they have 'taken the dye of right
opinion' so that, in them, it is indelible. They are living patterns of
all the civic virtues, and are especially qualified for the higher
intellectual disciplines which are designed to set the coping-stone on
the arch of their education.[61] At the same time, this intellectual
training is carefully balanced by further physical, moral, and administrative experience. When, at the age of fifty, the very best of them
are finally selected to contemplate the vision of 'the good', they are

M

in no sense 'etiolated'. They are well-rounded, well-adjusted, fully mature citizens. They incorporate *all* the excellences which are found in human nature at its best.[62]

In the next place, after the vision has been achieved, and the fifty-year-old members of the 'golden' class set themselves to guide and direct the destinies of their community so as to realize 'the good': they do not in any sense withdraw from life. As 'artificers of freedom' to the entire community, they furnish the chairmen of *all* committees which govern the public life of their state. They retain, that is, their intimate connexion, not only with education and with all matters of war and peace, but with religion, with art, with commerce, with agriculture, and with every other activity of the group.[63]

In the *Republic*, they are granted vacations to refresh their grasp of the vision and so to re-condition themselves for 'their work'; and they are finally permitted to retire from their arduous administrative labours, in order to enjoy a little leisure at the last.[64] In the *Laws*, the sketch of the minister of education (most important of the great offices of state) makes it plain that these highest guardians are to be married men, fathers of families, and presumably also citizen-farmers (at least before and after the period of their magistracy). In both Utopias, it is only citizens who have excelled on *all* sides of life (a very full life), who are chosen as representative directors of the community's way of living.[65]

As to *how* the vision of 'the good' assists the philosopher-statesman, the philosopher-artist, and the other types of philosopher, to do their specific 'work', we are given three accounts. The first is by reference to the painter, already considered. He looks now at his model, and now at his painting: working away at the painting until it more nearly resembles what he sees in the model.[66] The second is more abstract. The dialectician, with his insight into the final principle of ideality, works over the hitherto ungrounded assumptions of the sciences, until these become integral parts of one fundamental science, with their conclusions eventually raised to the status of inter-implying universals. He proceeds 'from ideas, through ideas; and in ideas' the process terminates—without at any point losing itself in the indefinite multiplicity of individuals.[67]

The third is more concrete. The artist whose art is statesmanship, in applying the principle of ideality to human affairs (which of themselves might easily tend toward chaos), uses three forms of the ideal principle. The first is beauty or charm: secured by balancing the parts or elements within a whole. The second is symmetry: the principle of balanced measure, which ensures this beauty or charm. The third is truth: which ensures objectivity.[68]

Applying these three ideas, the philosopher-statesman mingles the various value-potentialities inherent in humanity. He thus develops a form of social life which does justice to all the parts: by so balancing them against one another that their contrasts (within a single unifying whole) enhance the values of all. Pugnacity and timidity (for instance) are, in themselves, inconsistent, mutually hostile elements of human nature. The royal art shows its power by so weaving them into the concrete texture of community living, that each, losing its one-sidedness, becomes an integral element within the balanced life of the whole.[69]

That is to say, from Plato's point of view, the function of the arts is (ideally) to assist humanity in its venture: in practising the true art, the art of ideal living. In a community so organized that there is a part for everyone to play relatively to the harmonious well-being of the whole, each individual can follow his natural bent, and at the same time make his maximal contribution toward the life of his fellow-citizens. In such a life, broadened, deepened, and enhanced to the maximal degree by the contributions of all, each achieves the greatest quantity and quality of happiness possible for man. The limitations of the arts, which can be indefinitely reduced by education and goodwill, are the limitations inherent, partly in humanity, and partly in the space-time environment.[70] For their gradual reduction in a more nearly universal determination to co-operate in realizing the life of the ideal community, Plato looks toward education: continuing into an indefinite future.

NOTES

1. *Meno* 76d, *Rep.* 429 f., *Tim.* 67c f. (with Taylor's *Commentary*), *Theaet.* 153a f., 156a f., *Phil.* 12e, 51cd, 53ab.

2. *Crat.* 424e f., *Rep.* 586c, *Tim.* 68b f. (with Taylor's *Commentary*). Tilney, *op. cit.*, p. 22, maintains that 'the philosophers of antiquity made no provision for Colour in their theories of Beauty, possibly because they did not know Colour as we know it'. I cannot see that Tilney's position here is entirely consistent with the evidence (from Plato's Dialogues) referred to in the present context, and indeed elsewhere, wherever Plato's account of colour is discussed.

3. *Rep.* 377b, 399 ff., 410a, 498c, 520d, 530, 617b (with Adam's notes), *Tim.*

35 ff., 43c f., 47d f., 67ab (cf. Erich Frank, *Plato u.d.s–g. Pythagoreer*, p. 155), *Phaedr.* 250b f., *Phil.* 17b f., 62c, *Laws* 655d f., 657d, 658e f., 800 f., 814d ff., 817d, 828a, 829d.

Frivolous and indeed vicious exhibitions are sometimes attended, for their educative effect only. They enable the young to appreciate (by contrast) the value of their own more serious institutions. But such attendance is always a matter, not of participation, but of external observation (*Laws* 816c f., cf. *Rep.* 395b f., 409).

For further discussion of all the evidence on these points, see R. C. Lodge, *Plato's Theory of Ethics*, pp. 446–454, *Plato's Theory of Education*, pp. 66–85.

4. *Rep.* 530d f.

5. *Rep.* 349d f., *Phil.* 56a, *Laws* 769ab. I would like to suggest a comparison with the committees of experts (in the *Laws*). These, acting under the chairmanship of a philosophy-trained legislative authority, set up the standards as to what shall and what shall not be done (in the model city) in the fields of their specialized *expertise*. The matter is not entirely unlike the way in which Socrates's companions in the condemned cell, themselves being in the position of members of the 'silver' class of the *Republic*, look to Socrates as in some sort their leader, as if he were a member of the 'golden' class, guiding them so that they can 'hold fast to the golden cord of reason' (*Phdo.* 77e f., cf. *Laws* 644c ff.).

6. *Rep.* 597d ff., *Phil.* 55d f. Cf. A. E. Wiggam, *Exploring your Mind with the Psychologists*, New York, 1928. Bobbs-Merrill. (Interview with Dr. Catharine Cox Miles.)

'On the whole, poets . . . rated a little lower (than scientists) in persistence, balance, and soundness of common sense; and where action and thought are dependent upon reason they did not rate high' (p. 154, n. 27).

7. *Rep.* 493a, *Phaedr.* 270c ff., 277c.

8. *Phaedr.* 269d f., 271e f., *Laws* 658b f., 680c, 802c f.

9. *Rep.* 492 ff., 533b f., *Phaedr.* 261 f., 266b ff. Cf. Jowett, *The Dialogues of Plato*, Vol. IV, pp. 175–191 ('On the Nature and Limits of Psychology').

10. *Meno* 76d, *Rep.* 493a–d, *Tim.* 68d, *Theaet.* 153a f., 156a f.

11. *Phil.* 55e f.

12. *Gorg.* 456a f., 459a f., *Crat.* 424a, 430b f. (cf. *Ion* 541), *Rep.* 597e f., 598b f., 600e f., 607e f., *Critias* 107b f., *Pol.* 277b f. Cf. R. G. Collingwood, *The Principles of Art*, pp. 11, 46–52, 65, 78 ff., on 'amusement-art'.

13. *Meno* 84a f., *Rep.* 596b f., 598b f., *Soph.* 229b f., 233d f., 234a, 236a f. Polus is an example of the 'clever journalist' (see *Gorg.* 462bc).

14. *Apol.* 22c f., *Rep.* 510c f., 529–531, 596b, 597a, 599c f., *Phil.* 55d f.

15. *Euthyd.* 281a, 289a f., *Symp.* 211d f., *Rep.* 495c ff.

16. *Symp.* 210e ff., *Rep.* 526d f., 528b f., *Tim.* 53b ff., *Phil.* 51b f., 56c f., 64d f.

17. *Soph.* 235d f.

18. *Crat.* 431b f., *Soph.* 235e f.

19. Cf. *Tim.* 53b ff.

20. *Rep.* 397b f., 399a f., 475cd, 601b, *Phil.* 55c f., *Laws* 669d, 700a f., 802c, 810a, 812a f.

21. *Symp.* 187a f., *Rep.* 530d f., 617b (with Adam's notes), *Tim.* 47cd, *Phil.* 17e. For the inaudibility, see *Rep.* 530bc, *dianoiai lepta, opsei d'ou*. For the 'perfect system of scales' and its attempted use by practising musicians subsequent to Plato, cf. *Tim.* 35b f., with Taylor's *Commentary*, and E. Frank, *op. cit.*, p. 155; also H. E. Wooldridge, *Oxford History of Music*, Vol. I, pp. 7 ff.

22. *Rep.* 472b f., *Laws* 739c f., 746a f., 781a f., 783a f.

23. *Laws* 718b–723a f., 945c f. The training in music and gymnastic generally, prepares for voluntary acceptance of the community laws (*Laws* 663b ff., 812bc, etc.).

24. *Laws* 737d f., 740b, 747b f., 784, cf. *Rep.* 546. See also R. C. Lodge, *Plato's Theory of Education*, Appendix I ('Numbers in the Model City').

25. *Rep.* 510b f., 530e f., 533a f.

26. *Phaedr.* 268c f., 270a, e f.

27. *Ion* 534b, *Symp.* 211d f., *Rep.* 472d, 500e f., 586c, 598b, 602cd, *Phaedr.* 245a f., 248d, 249cd, *Pol.* 277bc, 299de (corrective to *Phil.* 51b f.), cf. *Laws* 769a f.

28. *Rep.* 472b–473a, *Tim.* 28e f., 37e f., *Parm.* 134a f., 141de, *Phil.* 62ab.

For a striking modern illustration, cf. Balzac's attitude toward transcendentalism (with him, practically identical with 'philosophie') on the part of artists, in his volumes entitled *Études Philosophiques*. I have in mind particularly his story of the painter who, trying to express something which, on empirical canvas, is probably inexpressible, kept painting out the outlines, and then trying, by further re-painting of lights and shadows, to bring out the spiritual quality of his subject. Eventually, while (at moments) a very sensitive and sympathetic spectator *almost* imagined he could catch a glimpse of what the painter had talked about: when he looked more closely, there was nothing there but a confused mass of pigment. The inexpressible had, after all, not been expressed.

29. For the transcendentalism, cf. *Phdo.* 64a ff., *Rep.* 479e, 496b, 519c f., 529 ff., *Phaedr.* 245a f., 248c f., 249c f., *Tim.* 53de.

30. *Apol.* 28e f., 31d f., 37e f., *Gorg.* 512e, 521d f., *Phdo.* 78a, 69a f., *Symp.* 175a, *Rep.* 506d f., 533a, 540ab, *Parm.* 130c f.

31. *Symp.* 176b f., 185d ff., 212a, *Rep.* 524e ff., 540b f., *Pol.* 292c ff., *Laws* 957, 964b f., 966c f.

32. *Rep.* 470e, 472d f., 484cd, 510e f., 540a f., *Phaedr.* 269d, 270a, *Laws* 629 ff., 666c f., 736c f., 802bc, 811c.

33. *Phdo.* 78a, *Rep.* 472d, 484c f., 540a f., *Phaedr.* 270 ff.

34. *Phaedr.* 245a f., 249c f., *Theaet.* 174a f., *Phil.* 62b.

35. *Ion* 534b f., 536a.

36. *Prtg.* 342e f., *Crat.* 398b, *Rep.* 495c, 599d f., *Phaedr.* 258b, 278cd, *Laws* 690a–c, 858c f.

37. *Rep.* 495d, *Pol.* 290c f.

38. *Rep.* 490d f., 496a.

39. *Rep.* 490e f., 484e f., 495ab, 496b f., 504c f., 517d f., 519d, 520a f.

40. *Rep.* 395bc, 484c f., 494b f., 499b f., 500d f., 519–521c.

41. *Symp.* 211d f., *Rep.* 515c ff.

42. *Rep.* 484c f., 500e f., 517c f., 540a f., *Laws* 739a–e.

43. *Prtg.* 325c f., *Rep.* 376e–377c, 378de, 395b ff., 522ab, *Tim.* 47cd, 88b f., *Laws* 653b f., 672cd, 673cd, 788e f., 789d f., 790c f., 791e, 815e f. For further discussion, see R. C. Lodge, *Plato's Theory of Education*, pp. 150 ff., 287 ff.

44. *Ion* 533d ff., *Rep.* 399a f., 459e f., *Laws* 633a f., 664b f., 670d f., 814d ff., 828 ff.

45. *Prtg.* 325d f., *Rep.* 401 f., 601b, *Tim.* 47c f., *Laws* 659d, 782e f., 802c f., 812c f.

46. *Lach.* 180c, 197d, 200ab, *Rep.* 400b, 424c, *Laws* 811c f., 964b ff.

Many authorities see a certain identity between the vision of beauty (*Symp.* 210e ff.) and the idea of good (*Rep.* 511b f.). Cf. A. Fouillée, *La philosophie de Platon. . .* (Paris, 1869), p. 353, P. Natorp, *Platos Ideenlehre* (Leipzig, 1903), pp. 172, 173, A. E. Taylor, *Plato the Man and his Work* (New York, 1927), pp. 230–231, U. v. Wilamowitz-Moellendorff, *Platon*, 2nd edit,.Vol. I, pp. 388–391.

47. *Rep.* 400 ff., 458d f., 518de, *Laws* 653b f., 664b ff., 803de, 835d f.

48. *Rep.* 413d f., 427b, 540a f., *Laws* 713d f., 738bc, 759cd, 828a, 838d f., 880e f., 927a f., 950d f., 964d f. Cf. R. C. Lodge, *Plato's Theory of Education*, pp. 114–137, for further discussion.

49. *Rep.* 421bc, 519c f., 521b ff., 540a f., 592ab, *Pol.* 297b, *Laws* 735a, 811d f., 818a, 964bc, 965a, 967d f.

50. *Laws* 951d f., 961a f., 962c f., 964b f.

51. *Symp.* 202d f., *Crat.* 397e f. (cf. Hesiod, *Works and Days*, 120 ff.), *Rep.* 395bc, 468e f., 540a f., 592ab. Cf. R. C. Lodge, 'Plato and Freedom', *Transact. Roy. Soc. of Canada*, XLIII, Series III, 1949, pp. 87–101.

52. *Laws* 951c, 961ab.

53. *Epist.* 341b f., cf. *Phaedr.* 276b f., *Laws* 968d f.

54. *Laws* 657a f., 659d f., 738b f., 764c f., 772a f., 799a, 801c f., 802a f., 809, 811b f., 812c f., 816bc, 817d, 828ab, 829c f., 848d f., 934, cf. *Prtg.* 319bc. This evidence is (I think) inconsistent with the contention (e.g. *Jour. of Education*, 1945, pp. 58, 164, 224) of critics like Messrs. Lauwerys and Neurath, that Plato's government is 'totalitarian'. Incidentally, Plato hates a tyrant.

55. *Laws* 918b f.

56. *Laws* 664 ff.

57. *Rep.* 412a, 424a, 425ab, d, 427a f., 458c, 497c–e, 500cd, *Pol.* 294a–c, 295ab, 300c–e, 301bc, *Laws* 645b 6, 769b f., 875cd, 880de. Cf. R. C. Lodge, 'Plato and Progress', *Philos. Review*, 1946, pp. 651–667.

58. *Rep.* 471e f., *Laws* 709a f.

59. *Rep.* 540a f., 612a f., *Phaedr.* 245c f., *Tim.* 89e, *Laws* 894 ff.

60. *Rep.* 484c f., 487a, 490a–d.

61. *Rep.* 400d ff., 412d–414a, 487a, etc.

62. *Rep.* 395bc, 540a f., cf. R. C. Lodge, *Plato's Theory of Education*, pp. 220 ff.

63. *Rep.* 540b, cf. *Laws* 656c f., 659a f., 660a, 738b f., (the legislator 'has not despotic power', see 739a 6), 764c f., 772a f., 799a f., 801c f., 809 ff., 816b f., 828a ff., 848e f., 934b, etc.

64. *Rep.* 498bc, 504a, cf. R. C. Lodge, *Plato's Theory of Education*, pp. 108–109.

65. *Laws* 659b f., 715cd, 729d f., 730e, 755a ff. (The mode of election is 'in a mean between monarchy and democracy', 756e), 759c f., 765d f., 919d f., 945e f., 961a, 964b.

66. He first constructs an outline, and gradually fills in the details, as experience indicates. *Rep.* 472d, 484c f., 501a f., 540a, *Pol.* 277b f., *Laws* 769a f., 934c (cf. *Crat.* 430bc, 434a).

67. *Rep.* 511bc, *Soph.* 252e ff., *Phil.* 12e f., 15–17a.

68. *Phil.* 61b f., 64b f., cf. *Gorg.* 507e f. For the balancing of parts within a whole, cf. *Rep.* 401c f., 443c, 444c f., 484b f., 589a f., etc., *Tim.* 88b f., *Laws* 693d, 694a, 701e f., 746cd, 756e, 773a f.

69. *Pol.* 309b ff., *Laws* 628a f., 691e f., 693d f., 712c f., 756e.

70. *Apol.* 37a, *Prtg.* 318ab, 356d, *Gorg.* 458b (cf. *Euthyphr.* 15d), *Phil.* 55a f.

CHAPTER NINE

Mimesis

A PUZZLE dogs the footsteps of all who seek to understand what Plato has to say about art. It arises in connexion with Book X of the *Republic*. Many readers believe that the first part of this Book is a downright attack upon art, as such. They think Plato is attacking artistic make-believe, as distinct from the utilitarian craftsmanship which turns out pots and pans, wall-drapes, and the latest thing in Hellenic roofing. Others feel that it is part of a considered attack, continued elsewhere, upon what is called 'amusement art', the art which has no aim beyond entertainment. Such art titillates the senses and emotions. It flatters and encourages the egoism of men in convention assembled. It reduces humanity to its lowest common measure: a childish theatrocracy incapable of appreciating the life of reason. Yet others feel that Plato is attacking art, only in so far as art is *mimetic*, impersonative rather than narrative in method. It is the *mimesis* (they feel), the projection of the self into this or that feature of the person or situation being represented, which makes the philosopher's attack upon make-believe and upon entertainment art, both possible and (from the philosopher's standpoint) inevitable.[1]

For each of these positions there is plenty of evidence; not only in Book X of the *Republic*, but also, as soon as you look for it, elsewhere in the Dialogues. There is a tendency to treat poetry as a form of 'rhetoric', and accordingly to classify poets with the sophists (whose master-art is rhetoric); and thus to criticize the entire class so formed, as operating by make-believe rather than by rational instruction.[2]

There is a further tendency to adopt, for purposes of criticism, the standpoint of the so-called Pythagoreans, whose mathematical technique (such as this is) places them one rung higher on the ladder of knowledge than the artisans, and two rungs higher than the artists —who are then denounced as occupying the lowest rung.[3] It is particularly obvious that the writer of Book X regards this technical attack with considerable complacency;[4] and, if this were all, the position taken in Book X would involve no particular 'problem'. We should all agree that (for whatever reason) Plato is taking a grotesquely narrow view of what we regard as 'art'; and that his criticisms have to be written off as unfortunate aberrations on the part of an otherwise profound philosophical intelligence.[5]

But the puzzle arises precisely from this: that elsewhere throughout the Dialogues, sometimes quite incidentally and without the slightest hesitation, deeper and (to the modern reader) more immediately satisfying views of the nature and function of art are indicated, and, if formulated, are (quite as a matter of course) accepted by all who are participating in the discussion.

Thus, in the entire range of the Dialogues, from the *Ion* and *Meno* to the *Laws*, and focused with especial clearness in the *Phaedrus*, we find the universal Hellenic view of art as divine in origin, referred to without question. There is a suggestion of irony here and there. But that the artist is somehow 'inspired', is nowhere, even remotely, challenged. In fact, the view is insisted upon, and its consequences are carefully drawn out.[6] Art is everywhere regarded as the gift of Apollo and the Muses: a precious gift, to be sought by prayer, in a spirit of sincere humility. The artist throws himself, with all his trained powers of expression, open, completely and without reserve, to the divine influence: following whithersoever it leads.[7]

The artist is exalted, inspired, rapt; carried far beyond the confines of common sense and the austere restraints of a scientific method which demands empirical verification. He is conveyed (who knows how?) into the mysterious region which lies back of beyond; and what is there vouchsafed to him as he maintains contact with his holy guide, is welcomed with thankfulness and solemn joy. It is like the oracular responses vouchsafed to the prophetic medium, the priestess at Dodona or Delphi who is in a receptive state of religious ecstasy.[8]

On his return to the world of common sense, the artist is still, for a time, under the influence. He remains dazzled by the transcendent brightness of his vision. He proves unable to express his insights in ways which seem intelligible to common sense. Put to the question before a critical audience, he stutters and stammers, and appears distraught. Not one of the bystanders, but could answer the questions better than he can. This is true of the poets put to the question by Socrates.[9] It is true of Socrates himself, when put to the question by

Parmenides.[10] To many a modern reader, Plato's vision of the 'ideas', when subjected to the unsympathetic *ex cathedra* criticisms of an Aristotle, appears equally confused.[11]

And yet: if this is the way in which the higher truths upon which mankind depends come (by revelation, by inspiration, by divine guidance), are not the artists—after all is said and done—in the right? Is it not common sense, with its readiness to ridicule what it fails to understand, that really needs to be put to the question: until it achieves a proper degree of humility, and learns that enlightenment requires sympathy, and that the first crude thoughts of common sense could be, and probably are, wrong?[12]

Here, then, we have two opposed views of the value of art; whether it is imaginative art, amusement art, or mimetic, impersonative art, that is in question. Each view is widely held and deeply rooted in the tissue of thoughts which constitute the main body of Platonic doctrine. Yet the two views are manifestly inconsistent; and the inconsistency appears to be felt by Plato himself.[13] We are faced by a genuine puzzle. How (if at all) can it be solved?

Plato himself is very careful, throughout his whole attack, to use repeatedly the adjective, *mimetic*. It is mimetic art that is under fire, and it is mimesis that is somehow what is fundamentally amiss with the work of the artists being excluded from Plato's Utopia. The term is subjected to a sort of definition; and it is as so defined that mimesis appears liable to criticism in Book X.[14]

Elsewhere, however, Plato feels no need to criticize. Mimesis is frequently mentioned without the slightest suggestion of disapproval of any sort. Indeed, mimesis appears to be of fundamental positive value in Plato's theory of education: whether education is vocational or professional, or whether it is moral or intellectual. The education for character and citizenship outlined in the *Republic* and *Laws*, rests very heavily upon mimesis, and indeed upon mimetic art.[15] Even the education for leadership, severely intellectual as most of the curriculum is made to appear, does not entirely eschew the aid which mimesis has to offer.[16] In a word, the puzzle of the two inconsistent attitudes as to the value of art, centres right here, in the term 'mimesis'. We shall therefore subject this term to special study: including in our investigation, not only the treatment in Book X of the *Republic*, but the treatment in other parts of the *Republic*, and in other Dialogues as well.

The term *mimesis* is used (1) in a general, and (2) in a special sense: by Plato as by other Hellenic writers, from Homer on. In the general sense, any sort of artist (from carpenter, potter, or weaver, to painter, musician, or poet) may be said to 'mime', i.e. to 'imitate' or represent whatever he is trying to produce. He is attempting, using physical elements (earth, water, fire, air), to construct a physical replica of this or that physical object. He is not trying, as a rule, to make the thing itself. *That*, he leaves to God. He is trying to make a copy of it: a physical object which, in greater or lesser degree, 'imitates' or resembles its original.[17]

Thus, a sculptor produces a three-dimensional copy of (e.g.) a human figure. This copy may conceivably prove (when tested by measurement) to be mathematically exact. It may resemble its original in length, breadth, and depth, in circumference, and in the proportion of its parts to one another. Or it may merely *look* exact. It may be shown (by measurement) to be distorted. The Hellenic sculptor applies paint to his figure: so as to make it resemble, even more exactly, its original.[18] Similarly, a painter produces a highly flattened version of (e.g.) the same human figure. He reduces it to what we might call two dimensions, and so distorts the proportions of its parts, by tricks of perspective, that (at a distance and in a poor light) it looks very like the statue or its original. It might, indeed, if viewed by a child or a careless spectator, be mistaken for the statue, or even for the man.[19]

So too, the poet presents a word-picture of (e.g.) the same person. He uses the gesture-tendencies implicit in linguistic expression so as to indicate what the person he is naming stands for, his meaning or idea. For instance, if the person is a king, an intelligent word-artist summons to his service words like 'monarch', 'ruler', 'leader', 'commander', and a whole host of adjectives and verbs whose associations call to mind kingly attributes.[20]

There is a somewhat less intelligent use of words, such as a punster or an inferior word-artist might bring to bear. He might select words, not primarily for their intelligible sense, their meaning, but for their sound-effects; for what technicians call their 'onomatopoeic' value. Thus, instead of writing, 'The heroes sat at meat in the shade,' a professional rhetorician (priding himself upon his mastery over the descriptive resources of language) will write something like, 'What time, in the Elysian fields, the breezes whisper and whistle through the tree-tops: as they sway them to and fro, shading gently the heroes seated at the banquet.' So too even a Plato adapts to his aid the artifices of alliteration, when he writes of the effects of 'much music, poured unceasingly through the funnel of the ears. The virtuoso warbles and wails and weakens his soul, until he becomes but a feeble wielder of the lance.'[21]

In the case of a great rhetorician like Lucian, or a great writer like Plato, sound will always be kept in due subordination to sense.[22] But children and other persons of immature taste and incomplete education will carry the mimetic tendency involved in such words as 'rattle', 'crash', 'bang', 'smash', etc. (in their Hellenic equivalents) to extremes. They will imitate the crowing of cocks, the bellowing of bulls, the yapping of dogs, the neighing of horses, the bleating of sheep. They will reproduce, as well as they can, the sough of the wind, the hiss and roar of breakers, the rumbling of thunder, the creaking of ungreased wheels and ship's blocks, the whistle of a boatswain's pipes, and other noises reminiscent of the water-front. It is all mimetic, very much so. But mimicry of this type belongs to the very lowest level to which art can sink. It is deserting sense altogether, and is verging upon downright imbecility.[23]

What is there about mimicry of this type that makes it 'wrong'? Why is it 'childish, uneducated, tasteless'? Precisely how is it being contrasted with an intelligent use of words, by a word-artist who is reproducing the meaning, the idea, rather than sound-effects? Not but that sound-effects can properly be used to amplify the meaning of an idea. They may help to bring home the meaning, to persons who find abstract thinking too hard for them. We have here a reference to a pre-supposed scale of values. What is this scale?

Let us look over the range of what can be mimicked: copied, imitated, or reproduced by the poet or other artist. (1) At the lowest level, we have simple mimicry. You can imitate, copy, reproduce, or mimic, the superficial appearances of things. In such mimicry, you give an impression of what a given thing *looks* like, *sounds* like, or *feels* like. You pay little or no attention to what the thing really *is*, in itself, in *rerum natura*.

At this level, your copy may (*a*) be a 'good' copy. It may resemble, very closely, the superficial aspect you are mimicking. The gesture or sound you make, and the gesture or sound the thing makes, may be practically indistinguishable.[24] Or (*b*) your copy may be just 'fairly good'. It appears, in general, like the object. But there are discrepancies in matters of detail. Looking carelessly, you might confuse it with the object. Looking closely and intelligently, you would be able to see which is the imitation, and which is the real object.[25] Or finally (*c*) your copy may be 'poor'. The differences, that is to say, between it and its original are so considerable, that without further specific assistance hardly anyone would be able to guess what you are trying to reproduce. Some childish drawings, some forms of '*art moderne*', fall into this class. In some modern music (as Plato's visiting professor from Athens says), there is excitement, rapid movement, lots of noise. But does anyone know what it is intended to portray? Not without a title (or some other literary or pictorial —i.e. non-musical) assistance. When an artist has to call upon artists in some other field to tell the public what he is trying to express, surely, his own art is failing to do its proper work. This is art at its very poorest: imitation that, even as mimicry, fails.[26]

Be that as it may (i.e. whether your technique is good, indifferent, or poor), so long as you confine yourself to mimicking superficial appearances, your mimesis remains at the level called by Plato *eikasia*. It is superficial play with imagery. Childish, really. A little undignified as an occupation for adults. Like 'letting go' at an informal party and dancing on a table or taking part in a roaring farce: anything for a laugh.[27] Possibly a little (a very little) of this sort of thing has its place with human beings. Maybe, like some of our less creditable wish-dreams, it provides a needed relaxation of tension, a favourable pause (as it were) in living a strenuous adult life. Perhaps its contrast enhances for us the value of more serious things. Entertainment art—if you care to call it that—if harmless, has a certain place in the balanced life of the citizen. But that place is not a high one; and such art should never be taken seriously, or be over-done.[28]

(2) Let us now go a little higher up the scale of what can be imitated by an artist. Instead of mimicking some superficial aspect, you might produce a physical replica of the physical thing. Thus, a scribe makes a copy of a manuscript, or a sculptor produces a replica of this or that human form. Here also your technique can be good, indifferent, or poor, according to the faithfulness with which you reproduce the details of your original. In judging the value, however, of such copies, the standards of criticism tend to be severe. Have we not all ample experience of the things which such copyists try to reproduce for our use? Where we are in a position to compare the copy directly with the original, we soon know how good or poor it is. An authentic copy may have a very definite value for us. Such art is obviously useful; and for utilitarian art, so long as it involves honest work and does not pretend to be more than it is, Socrates, the artisan's son, has no criticism. The artisan is worthy of his hire.[29]

(3) Let us go yet higher. Instead of simply copying the external,

physical appearance of the object, the artist may try to penetrate to something deeper. He may guide himself by some system of inter-implying rules acceptable to poets, or painters, or musicians. He may follow some system which is mathematical or quasi-logical. He is then definitely a technical, professional artist.

Members of the Pythagorean brotherhood, for instance, construct a small-scale model of the celestial bodies. This is mathematically exact. Such an 'orrery' is useful, if not indispensable, for purposes of scientific demonstration.[30] An artistic poet or sculptor may try to represent, not this or that human form, but (by means of an idealizing symbolism) the spirit of Zeus or Apollo, of Athene or Aphrodite. This is expressed, indeed, by means of a formal pattern which follows quasi-human proportions. But the whole is enlarged, and its dignity and power are enhanced; so that you can see through the physical medium to its superior nature.[31] This is partly a matter of craftsmanship, partly a matter of inspiration. It cannot be explained otherwise.

So too the higher kind of poet tells us, not merely what this or that human being actually said or did on this or that occasion (this would belong to the *second* level of mimesis, discussed above). He can tell us (again, with a mixture of craftsmanship and inspiration) what the (mythical) hero Odysseus and the (mythical) goddess Athene said to each other in Ithaca, and how each, looking into the other's eyes, saw, beyond all disguise, the ideal spirit of wisdom. He can tell us, not merely the human, but the divine names of things. He can transmit to us the great legends upon which Hellenic religion builds its temple-cults.[32] In fact, his poems (when revised by the most competent human authority that reason can conceive) may safely be used to educate into the spirit of idealism, the generations of citizens yet unborn in the ideal republic and model city.[33]

Whether Plato's own Dialogues belong here, at this level of mimesis, along with the (revised) poems of Homer, Tyrtaeus, and Solon, not to mention minor artists like 'one-poem Tynnichus', is a little uncertain. It may be, that the Dialogues belong to a still higher level. So also of the music of the ideal city. This includes the marches, battle-hymns, and encomia which idealize the actions of famous heroes; the processionals and solemn action-dances in honour of the greater deities: to whose favour the creation and preservation of the humanly ideal city is ascribed.

All alike are inspired.[34] Whether we place them at this third level, or higher, depends, in the last resort, upon whether we believe that

Plato has proceeded beyond the point admittedly reached by his hero, Socrates. Socrates will never admit that he has actually apprehended the final vision of 'the good'. He can describe the road which leads to it. He is quite sure of what is to be seen there—*if* one succeeds in reaching it. But, for himself, it remains always the land of promise: lying a little beyond his ken. It is something to be inquired after by his successors in the future history of philosophical investigation.[35]

If Plato remains at this level; if he is still (like Socrates) a seeker and a leader of seekers (and many authorities believe this to be the case), then his Dialogues and their contents (however inspired) do not rise above this third level. Perhaps he would rank them a little above Homer and the best of the traditional literature of Hellas; for these writings need revision, while his own, highly novel, species of reflective drama, does not.[36]

If, however, we are to suppose that Plato himself realized at least enough of the vision to predict the future course of philosophy, and that his writings from the *Republic* to the *Laws* represent his deliberate attempt to re-make human institutions in the light of the vision, we must come to a different conclusion.[37] In that case, both his Dialogues and the consecrated songs, dances, and marches prescribed (at least in principle) for the ideal republic and model city, are to be regarded as belonging to a level definitely higher than can be attained by anyone who remains at the third level.[38]

In any case, what especially characterizes mimesis at this level, is its permeation by the higher kind of reality: the reality of the 'idea'. For it is this that the higher kind of artist (whether Homer at his best, or Plato in his later Dialogues) is endeavouring to represent. In fact, with the help of inspiration from above, this is what he succeeds in incorporating in his work. At this level, the musician is not simply amusing himself by throwing together tones and harmonies in this or that type of rhythm until he hits upon something which sounds good to him: i.e. gives pleasure both to himself and to others. He is reaching out with his human pseudopodia into what is beyond human control. He is projecting himself wholeheartedly toward 'the veritable Above'. He is feeling after guidance, entrusting himself to what he believes to be higher spiritual powers; and he feels that he is somehow receiving that guidance.[39]

In so feeling, he is aware that he might conceivably be mistaken. Human beings have believed this sort of thing before, again and again; and they have frequently, at least, been deceived. Is it

conceivable, for instance, that what Homer tells us about Zeus sending a lying dream to Agamemnon, or that what Hesiod tells us of
the doings of Uranus, Cronus, and Zeus, can be either logically or
theologically correct?[40] How is one to know whether what feels like
inspiration is or is not to be trusted? Humanly speaking, the final
test would seem to be, consistency with the vision, the idea of good.
What Plato actually tells us, however, is that the final court of
appeal, 'the one sure criterion', is 'the writings of the legislator'.
These are the regulations of Plato's *Laws*, regarded as embodying
'the experience of the wisest and best'. That is to say, these formulate
the most reliable and authoritative human experience which can be
brought to bear. In coming to this conclusion, Plato believes that the
discussions of the *Laws* can be taken as 'inspired, like a poem'. What
agrees with these, is to be accepted. What disagrees, is to be rejected.[41]

(4) Let us pass on to consider the next stage: which (with Plato) is
final. This is the highest level to which human reason, when naturally
gifted and adequately schooled, can attain.[42] If you list and classify
the objects which mankind has agreed to regard (e.g.) as 'beautiful',
you find that you can arrange them in a sort of value-scale. Thus the
beauties of nature (whether animal, vegetable, or mineral) would
usually be ranked below the beauties found in humanity; whether at
the more nearly animal level of glamorous youth, or at the level of
character at which the animating principle expresses itself in noble
actions, or at the more intellectual level at which a fine mind sees its
way through puzzles and apprehends fundamental principles. But
when you have before you the entire list, you can hardly fail to
observe that there is not one of them, whose 'beauty' is not relative
to circumstances of time and place, of background and outlook.[43]

You do not doubt, that, however 'relative' the beauty, it is, in its
way, genuine. However empirical, there is something about the
beauty of such things which presumably goes deeper than the
surface. From somewhere in the back of your mind there emerges
gradually the thought of a beauty which would not, like these
empirical beauties, prove transitory, changing, relative to circumstances. It would be a beauty that would be permanent and absolute;
something in which the mind could rest with complete satisfaction.
It would be, not hypothetically beautiful, beautiful under such-and-
such conditions, but beautiful unconditionally, in itself.

This could not conceivably be one of the 'things' in the series
regarded as beautiful. It would have to transcend the particularity of
particular things, as such. It could be nothing but the law of the

beauty manifested in all of them; the universal principle, imitation of which, or participation in which, lends to them the degree of beauty which is genuinely present in them. In a word, this would be the ideal principle of beauty: whether (as practising artists tend to think) what is known as 'symmetry' or 'measureliness', what Pythagorean science calls 'the mean', or possibly something yet deeper, harder to formulate.[44]

Similarly, if you list and classify the objects which mankind has agreed to regard as 'good', you find that you can arrange them in a sort of value-scale. Thus: wealth, health, and physical strength would usually be ranked below the dispositions of character known as 'virtues' (courage, temperance or self-control, justice, etc.). These again would usually be ranked below the various excellences which indicate the presence of a fine mind (good sense-organs, good memory, quickness and accuracy of apprehension, etc.).[45] But when you look over such 'goods', you can hardly fail to see at once (if a Socrates asks you) that there is not one of these whose 'goodness' is not relative to all sorts of circumstances.[46]

At the same time, in regarding a good income, good looks, good health, a good memory, etc., as 'good', mankind is pretty well agreed that (however 'relative' the value of such things, however difficult to explain their value to a questioning mind like that of Socrates) their 'goodness' is genuine. You cannot explain it away. However empirical, it somehow goes deeper than the surface of things. It connects with 'reality'.[47] From somewhere in the back of your mind, there emerges gradually the thought of a goodness which would not (like these empirical 'goods') prove transitory, mutable, relative to circumstances. It would be a goodness which would be permanent and absolute; something in which the mind could rest with complete satisfaction. It would be, not hypothetically valuable, good under such-and-such conditions. It would be good unconditionally, in itself.[48]

This could not conceivably be any one of the 'things' regarded as good. It would have to transcend the particularity of particular things, as such. It could be nothing but the law of the goodness manifested in all of them; the universal principle, imitation of which, or participation in which, lends to them the degree of value which is genuinely present in them. This would be the idea of good, the principle of ideality, as such. In practice, Socrates has been tending to equate this with 'knowledge'. He has been maintaining that all values, and all 'virtues', are dependent, for the degree of their 'goodness' or value, upon knowledge, insight, wisdom.[49] But in the *Republic*, Socrates expresses dissatisfaction with this position. For, if you ask, 'Knowledge of—*what?*', you find yourself defining 'the good' as 'knowledge of—the good'. In a word, you are defining it in terms of —itself. But such a position is patently absurd.[50]

It is necessary, therefore, to push the analysis yet further. What is being looked for, is a principle of ideality which shall be, at one and the same time:

(*a*) An ideal of knowledge as an inter-implying nexus of clear-cut conceptual meanings. This will provide the human inquirer with an ideal standard. By imitating this, he will prove able to take the confused tissue of inconsistent and unsubstantiated suggestions (which is the first product of his empirical sensings, imaginings, hopings, and fearings), and convert it gradually into something more nearly approximating to a logically self-consistent system—in a word, to *knowledge*. By mimesis of this ideal, the inquirer gradually becomes a genuine *knower*.[51] Otherwise, as Protagoras had maintained, there could be no such thing for man as 'truth' or 'knowledge' or 'objective value'.[52]

(*b*) A principle of intelligibility which renders objects knowable, i.e. capable of being objects for a knowing subject. Participation in such a principle ensures to objects an intelligible structure: whether mathematical (as the Pythagoreans believed) or logical (as the Eleatics maintained). For if reality on the one hand, and the knowing mind on the other, were not somehow commensurate, i.e. if the field of *what exists* fell outside of the field of what is thinkable, then (as Gorgias on the one side, and Parmenides on the other, both maintained) 'knowledge' would be impossible: an entirely empty ideal.[53]

(*c*) The principle of ideal reality, i.e. the principle, participation in which makes the physically or socially actual, to the precise extent of such participation, at last achieve genuine existence.[54]

The way this principle operates, is relatively simple. The entire soul has to turn away from the merely superficial and empirical. It has to turn toward (and to imitate wholeheartedly) the transcendental ideal of a reality which is, in all respects, perfect. Only so do we assimilate ourselves to that reality. In so far as we participate in that reality, we become truly real in every phase of our living: as individuals, as citizens, and as human beings. This mimesis is the highest possible form of art. It is the art of life, in which we project ourselves imaginatively into the position of perfect citizens, perfect members of a perfect community, and live accordingly. Each of us thus does 'his own work'. He makes, to the community, the contribution which, by natural inclination and by education, he is best qualified to make. In this way the life of the community is, to the highest possible degree and to the greatest possible extent, enriched. To co-operate in realizing this highest possible human good, is the noblest of arts, the most valuable use of mimesis.[55]

In so living, the Platonic artist makes use of all he has learned from Ionian science, from Protagorean humanism, and from Pythagorean and Eleatic technique. From the Ionians, he has learned respect for physical objectivity. From Protagoras, he has learned to accept the natural, instinctive wants and emotions which characterize human beings. These 'necessary' appetites, and the over-all attraction to social living, he attempts to weave into a complex tissue: a 'mixed' or balanced life which allows, to every legitimate interest, a suitable place in harmony with the rest.[56] From the Pythagoreans and Eleatics, he is learning all that can be of use, in the way of mathematical and logical technique, toward administering a community designed to make realizable a maximum of positive value.[57] In a word, like the painter perpetually applying selected colours so as to produce, upon his canvas, the best and most harmonious interpretation of 'the heavenly pattern' of his object,[58] the Platonist who imitates and seeks to reproduce the ideal, so directs his life as to make of it a significant part of the onward march of events, of culture and of science, toward the goal for humanity designed, in ultimate analysis, by—God.[59]

The above completes our account of mimesis in the general sense. But Plato uses this term also in a secondary, more specialized sense and this specialized usage is highly characteristic of his way of thinking. To copy objects has a very important effect upon the person who sets himself to copy or imitate—and doubtless also upon all persons concerned with the mimetic process. In fact, we can distinguish two kinds of effect. The first (*a*) we can call 'expressive'. The second (*b*) we can call 'assimilative'. Let us consider these, at first, separately.

(*a*) In mimesis (as in *aesthesis*, sense-perception), we have two factors, one objective, the other subjective. The artist, in interacting with the object he is imitating, puts something of himself into the picture. This makes the resultant art-work, not just *a* picture, but *his* picture. It is only partly objective. It is the object-as-seen-by-the-artist, *his interpretation or impersonation* of the object. In fact, if we look closely at an art-work, we find it can tell us (perhaps) even more about the artist than about the object. We can discover a good deal about the artist's methods, about his degree of insight, about his entire background and outlook. In a word, in mimesis, i.e. in impersonating, merging his personality with, a given object, the artist, however well or however badly he succeeds in reproducing the object, is inevitably *expressing himself*.[60]

The modern reader finds a striking example of this in the work of Plato himself. Plato indeed insists that, in his Dialogues, the reader will find, NOT 'opinions of Plato', but only an impersonal portrait of Socrates, suitably embellished. Modern scholars, however, believe that, by imagining themselves as writing the Dialogues (i.e. by projecting themselves into Plato's creative rôle and thus merging their own spirit with the spirit of their author), they can feel as Plato felt. They believe that they are accordingly in a position to report (after careful introspection) what Plato's 'own' opinions really were. Such imaginative constructions are highly subjective. But scholars believe that there is no substitute for sympathetic study, checked (of course) by the techniques of objective scholarship. Everyone smiles a little at Schleiermacher's confidence in his *platonisches Gefühl*. But that is only because Schleiermacher was, now and then, demonstrably wrong. On the other hand, everyone speaks with respect of Wilamowitz, when he uses this same method; because, it is thought, the great 'dean of classical scholarship' may be right.[61]

In any case, nearly all readers come to the conclusion that Plato's 'secret' is not entirely concealed. In writing the Dialogues, he quite certainly (they feel) expresses himself. However, in Plato's case the merger seems to be so complete, that in his self-expression, not merely Socrates comes alive. Hovering around the fringe of his *dramatis personae* (representative, as these are, of nearly every side of the life he is discussing), we find the poets, soothsayers and priests, the gods and intermediate daemonic forces, of his homeland. We find, in a word, not only his own balanced philosophic outlook. We find also the entire background which goes into making him what he is: the unconscious spokesman of the spirit of Hellas, of its literature and arts, its myths and religion, no less than of its science and philosophy.[62]

That is to say, the self which the artist expresses in the mimetic (= impersonative) process, is not merely, and not primarily, his educated self. It is not, primarily, the rational personality which decides, after due deliberation and comparison of alternatives, just what 'reason' suggests that he should put into his picture or poem. This comes out quite clearly when Socrates puts the poets and other mimetic artists to the question. Very much that is in their background, and somehow gets itself expressed in the final result, is non-logical, racial. Of much of this, they are not themselves aware.[63]

And yet, such factors are at all times demonstrably present. The various species of animals all have specific ways of expressing their simpler, more racial, feelings. The inarticulate squawks and grunts of birds, beasts, and human beings, in situations which awaken feelings of hunger or sex, of fear or triumphant rage, are entirely characteristic and easily recognizable. They are quite as characteristic as the movements of head and tail, of wing or limb, with which, on such occasions, they react. By means of such cries and gestures, living beings release the feelings natural to their particular species, and communicate these feelings to their fellows.[64]

In the case of human beings, this means that the art-work, the picture or copy, is always a biosocial picture or copy. It is always something of specifically human interest to human beings. Human language is folk-language. Human literature is folk-literature. Thus, if you look at the content of Homeric poetry, what do you find? A biosocial mirroring of the various sides of human life. You find ambition, glamour, and display. You find comradeship, passionate love, and the warrior's heroism. You find aristocracy and radicalism, valour and craftiness, tenderness and downright brutality. You find the charm of youth, the majesty of maturity, the weakness of age, mitigated by the power of experience and wisdom. There is something in such poetry for everyone: for father and son, for father and daughter, for husband and wife, for master and slave. Even for the gods (if those all-too-human gods read their Homer), there is much to enjoy: as well as something to pardon, in the well-meaning but humanly distorted picturing of the life of the Olympians.[65]

So much for the first, the 'expressive' effect of art. In expressing himself, in releasing, that is, his personal and racial feelings, the artist does something to the object. He humanizes it, transcribes it, as it were, into the human clef. Let us now consider (*b*) the second, the 'assimilative' effect of mimesis. In assimilating himself, the artist does something, not to the object, but to himself: something quite different from merely releasing feeling. He merges himself with the object, projects himself into it. In imaginative sympathy, he participates in its nature. His feelings become directed from without. They are subdued rather than released. In so far as they take on the nature of the object, they become objectified.

A great deal depends upon the nature of the object to which the artist assimilates himself. Suppose he projects himself into a wild, frenzied dance, in honour (if one can call it that) of the god Bacchus. He lets himself go: inviting alien, non-Hellenic forces to take control. In thus impersonating the god Bacchus (as the god is believed to be under such circumstances), he is practically ceasing to be a self-determining Hellenic citizen. Gone are his temperance, his sense of reverence and justice, his feeling for prudence and wisdom, perhaps even his disciplined, civic courage. Useless for warfare, useless for the works of peace, he is becoming even as the Barbarians. From the standpoint of the ideal republic and model city, he is almost a total loss.[66]

And we must not suppose that such mimesis is without permanent effect upon character. The lover of vicious dances is assimilating himself (whether he knows it, or not) to the vices he delights in portraying, acting out by impersonation. He is acquiring, from the objects he copies, a secondary nature; and before its growing power, his original, primary nature is soon helpless. A man has to know something of the seamy side of life. That is certain. But his knowledge should be an external affair: contemplative rather than assimilative. If the object imitated is bad, antagonistic in spirit to the regulations of the model city, mimesis is dangerous. It should be rigorously eschewed.[67]

On the other hand, if the object impersonated is good, virtuous, altogether admirable, mimesis is thoroughly approved. Imagine a group of young maidens, dancing in honour of the virgin goddess, Athene. Armed with spear and helm, in ordered rhythms they portray the virtues and accomplishments of the goddess to whom, in spirit, they assimilate themselves. Civic courage and the beginnings of wisdom as an accepted life-guide become, in this merger of persons, theirs. Mimesis of this sort is an essential activity of every inmate of the model city.[68] In the effort to flee from the ills of life, and to become holy, just, and wise, assimilation to the nature of the gods whom all revere, is indeed the standard method.[69]

And this is true, not only in religion and in hero-worship, where the virtues are contemplated as in human or quasi-human form. There, the nature and power of assimilative mimesis are easily understood. Wherever there is personal love and devotion, it is not difficult or against nature, to assimilate oneself to the object loved.[70] But something of the same sort occurs in connexion with attitudes and objects which many would regard as non-human, as impersonal, and as leading away from the worship of the gods and the practice of the divinely approved virtues. Consider (e.g.) science, at which orthodox piety sometimes looks askance.

The scientist is not necessarily a sceptic and an atheist, a follower of the cult of hedonism. In fact, the severe study of science disciplines to a much-needed objectivity, the human spirit. Science rescues us from the fever and fret of merely biosocial desires, concentrated with narrowing interest upon petty, non-logical issues. Science broadens and deepens our outlook, and bestows upon us a serenity such as, perhaps, no other human activity can give.[71]

In particular, contemplation of the starry heavens above, with their ordered patterns, their intricate but assured measures which no star ever over-steps, exercises an especially beneficial effect upon the imaginations of the young. As their open minds contemplate in awe and wonder, some sense of the profoundly impersonal purposiveness of the great universe steals into their hearts: and transmutes, with its utter objectivity, the slowly maturing moral law within. Youthful spontaneous action-tendencies, hitherto only too ready to follow any strong impulse, gradually become organized. They become built up, like a sound constitution, into a system based upon respect for freedom under law, impersonal, objective, cosmic, a true image of the ideal.[72]

That is to say, in Plato's ideal theory, the object imitated and reproduced is 'good'. In the model city, mimesis assists us in our human task of assimilating our selves to what is best in the environment: social, theological, physical, and ideal. Under the pervasive influence of great art (especially when selected, revised, or originally created in the spirit of idealism), we learn to appreciate, to love, and to accept wholeheartedly, the idea of good. Is not ideality the ultimate base of everything that we are prone to regard as 'beautiful'?[73] While leaving to others the persistent probing of that base, i.e. to our metaphysical specialists in the 'golden' class, do not the rest of us (who remain in the classes of 'silver', 'copper', and 'iron') feel, with every fibre of our being, that our life-problem is finally solved? In a community resting upon this base, where the constitution provides for each a place (securely grounded) in which, while following his natural bent and making to the community a contribution which is his very own, he at the same time enjoys a balanced life, enriched with the similar contributions of his fellow-citizens—do we not feel absolutely at home? Could even God think out for humanity a better plan?[74]

In an admittedly imperfect city like Athens or Sparta or Corinth, mimesis of the community *ethos* would simply amplify and extend the imperfection. In a community like the ideal republic or model city (where every institution is as ideal as thought can conceive and humanity can accept), mimesis of the community *ethos* amplifies and extends the degree of perfection which is humanly attainable. The human actors throw themselves wholeheartedly into their civic rôles, for which they are supremely well cast. The result is an ideally satisfying drama; a mimetic life which realizes the perfection of art, a mimetic art which realizes the perfection of life.[75]

Let us sum up Plato's account of mimesis. The nature of man is essentially mimetic. His life is the life of a puppet: dancing and giving utterance to a few characteristic cries, according as nature and the environment pull the strings. The puppet responds blindly to the promptings of instinct. He uses what intelligence (if you can call it that) develops within him, chiefly in making his responses more concentrated. This makes them more discriminating, more efficient, more purposive—but hardly more enlightened. The various arts and crafts evolved in his way of living are all relative to his rather simple animal and human-animal needs. They appeal to his natural impulses, his 'necessary appetites'. They intensify and enhance his natural enjoyments, perhaps also his natural pains; for in most human activities the enjoyment (however enhanced) tends to be mingled with pain.[76]

The community life usually referred to (by those who accept Glaucon's contemptuous criticism) as 'the city of pigs', illustrates the highest to which the simple mimetic life, of itself, tends to evolve. This is a folk-life, with its folk-habits, its folk-meals, its folk-labour, its folk-songs and dances, and its folk-religion.[77] In these folk-activities, the men, women, and children give expression to their social, tribal and racial impulses, by imitating, projecting themselves into, and merging themselves with, the life around them. It is all very natural. It is even charming. But it is also quite blind: devoid of philosophic insight.[78]

The community life demanded by Glaucon, and criticized by Socrates as 'the city in a state of inflammation', illustrates the highest to which the sophisticated mimetic life, the life of culture, of art for art's sake (as exemplified in the culture-city, Classical Athens), can be expected to evolve. This is a highly sophisticated life. It has artistic banquets in honour of some prize-winning poet. It possesses a highly organized and differentiated industrial economy. It can point to a famous array of painters, sculptors, writers, and composers; not to

mention its brilliant *virtuosi* and their attendant train of minor
executants and assistants; and not forgetting its magnificent temples
with their elaborate processions and cults.[79]

In this life of artistic sophistication, a band of cultured citizens and
foreigners go the round of the theatres, art-galleries, and concert-
halls. They take time out to discuss the latest scientific discoveries, and
generally turn themselves into the intellectuals of Hellas. Such a life is
stimulating, tremendously so. It is also quite charming. But (as a
Socrates views it) it remains, in essentials, unenlightened. It is still
'blind'. It is devoid of philosophical insight into the 'idea'. It fails to
connect with 'the veritable Above'.[80]

Examples of a more highly specialized kind of community life,
specialized in the intellectual direction and enjoyed by rather small,
but highly select groups, are furnished by the Pythagorean brotherhood, and by such societies as the Eleatic school of philosophy.
These are regarded by Plato as 'friends of ideas'. That is to say,
Platonists feel that they are what we nowadays call 'fellow-travellers'. They are indeed 'idealists', although only to a limited extent.
They go along with Platonists, but only just so far. The members of
such groups are mimetic: in the sense of disciples forming their way
of living upon the *ipse dixits* of the Master, and merging their personalities with the *persona* accepted as representative of the spirit of
the group. But they remain a little detached from humanity. They
are withdrawn from the life around them, into a one-sided and
'superior' intellectualism of the ivory-tower sort; so much so, that
representatives of Plato's Academy think it both possible and
necessary for lovers of wisdom to go a great deal further.[81]

Plato's puppets 'hold fast to the golden cord of reason' (so that
this becomes dominant in their lives), but without detaching themselves from the natural impulses and just claims which keep them
human. They are thus able to develop a well-rounded way of living.
This does full justice to natural inclination, to individual capacity, and
to social, economic, and physical, as well as to theological, needs.
The 'mingled or balanced manner of living' is (for such puppets) the
rational life: the life which participates directly (humanly speaking) in
the idea of good.[82] Such a life is through and through mimetic. The
individual puppets throw themselves wholeheartedly into every
phase of the life designed for them in the model city. By seeking the
natural outlets for their energies provided in the life of full citizenship, they realize what they have within themselves. In so doing,
each is also playing his most suitable rôle in the community drama.

Thus all together realize, not only their implicit dream, but also the ideal plan for humanity designed from eternity by their true Master, God.[83]

The mimesis of the citizen differs sharply from the mimesis of the common artist in Hellas. That is why Plato criticizes the one and supports the other. The artist usually believes that he is fulfilling his function as an artist, when he creates objective art-works. He points with pride to a picture, a statue, a piece of music, a poem. But from such works, he can and does detach his personality: as he goes forward to the creation of further art-works, all equally detachable. When so detached (as Socrates points out), the creative vitality may seem to have gone out of the artist,[84] or out of the work which he called into being and then left to carry on for itself.[85] But beyond such creation, the Hellenic artist has no further conception of his function. That is why he is precisely on the level of a carpenter, weaver, or potter. He is completing a technical job to order, and is marketing the product through the recognized community channels.

The Platonic artist is not like this at all. He does not fabricate detachable objects which can be handed around, exposed for sale, and perhaps be unfairly criticized and thrown upon the scrap-heap. His creativity is an integral part of the community life. What he contributes to that life, is his active citizenship. This is a living and growing thing: interpenetrating with the life and growth of his fellows. His babyhood life, his neighbourhood-child life, his schoolboy life, his life of military service, his life as husband and father, as magistrate or priest, permeated in principle and in detail by the spirit of model citizenship—that is what he imitates, copies, produces, and identifies with his full personality. From the community life he is never detached, and it is never detached from him. It lives in his life and in the life of his fellows.[86]

To make the difference more explicit, consider the following: In Plato's community (as in other communities) there is frequent need of artists of some sort. Someone has to design and build the community temples and civic homes. Someone has to construct the ploughs and other instruments. Someone has to weave the garments which the citizens will wear. Someone has to design and embroider the robes carried in solemn procession to the goddess Pallas Athene. Someone has to construct the shields and spears and other implements of war. Are not these (it may be asked) detachable objects—in the model city, quite as much as in historical Sparta, Athens, or Cnossus? Again, does not someone have to put together the words of the sacred chants, the rhythms, harmonies, and tones of the hymns and marches required in the model city? Does not someone have to string together the funeral orations, the encomia of citizens who are (for one reason or another) being elevated to the position of community heroes? Are not such things 'detachable objects'? Could you not hand them around and conceivably (if they had an economic value) expose them for sale, or (if they were judged to have no value) throw them on the community scrap-heap?

The answer is as follows: (1) As far as the work of artisans is concerned, Yes. In the model city (much as elsewhere), detachable objects, ordered and paid for, will of course be required. But such objects are not constructed and exposed for sale by *citizens*. It is foreigners, 'metics', who construct and sell all such things. These are temporary sojourners, not permanent members of the community. Citizens do not make bricks or pots or ploughs or shields. They order these from workmen, and pay for them. No citizen practises any utilitarian art; especially, for pay.[87]

(2) As far as the work of artists is concerned, the answer is, No. The stories, hymns, march-tunes, and the rest, which are current in the model city, are not the work of individual citizens, celebrated as 'artists' and paid or praised for the professional quality of their productions. They arise out of the community living, and are, one and all, *mimesis* of the community *ethos*.

Thus, the literature used in the model city is adapted for community use by being rather thoroughly re-written. It is doubtful, when Homer's committee of revisers had finally completed their work, whether Homer (for instance) would have recognized that he had had anything whatever to do with the moral stories (each inculcating at least one approved civic virtue) depicting the ideally perfect Olympians who are so superior to all human weaknesses, the insufferably heroic heroes, the ideally manly men and the ideally womanly women—which he would hear being put before the young. Could there conceivably be any place for that rather immoral glamour-girl, Helen of Troy, or even for the goddess Aphrodite, not to mention that ancient week-ender, the all-father, Zeus—in the impeccable themes he would find being retailed in the model city? And would Homer have been able to recognize the new Odysseus, as morality personified, with no unscrupulous wiliness, no crude violence, and no casual girl-friends?

It is hard to say. But, much as the work of individual scientists tends to sink gradually into the impersonality of systematic science;

so, in the model city, the productions of individual poets, after they had been worked over in committee (directed by a magistrate), so as to become representative of the all-dominating community *ethos*, would tend to become integral portions of the approved corpus of national literature. In the end, it is the community, rather than the individual citizen, that persists; that continues to live and breathe in the approved poems, laws, and philosophies which it informs and inspires.[88]

That is why the poets retained for service in the model city are not distinguished masters of the written word, or even especially talented versifiers. They are amateurs. They are veterans who have themselves played a part in the deeds they relate. They are men whose pride and joy it is to be good citizens, to have served the community well. It is the same with all priests and magistrates. The chief question before the electors is always, Have they conformed, throughout their life, to the spirit of the laws? Are these candidates, in every fibre of their being, representative of the spirit of the model community?[89]

Composing verses or march-tunes is merely a part of the way in which A or B pursues the life of model citizenship. It is precisely analogous to the way in which C or D looks to his farming, or E or F performs his military service, or G or H serves as junior executive or as priest. The life of the community is everything. The life of the individual, except in so far as he 'imitates', i.e. copies, projects himself into, merges and identifies himself with, the life of the ideal community for man, is—nothing. In the sports festivals, in the encomia and funeral orations, the community is (in the end) honouring, encouraging, and re-conditioning for life—itself.[90]

In other words, Plato is constructing a city, not of artists (as the word is understood elsewhere in Hellas), but of citizens. That is why, in Book X of the *Republic*, he criticizes artistic mimesis, as understood by Homer and his fellows. It is because, for Plato, mimesis is not something external, the work of a clever journalist talking or writing about what *others* do. In the end, it is identical with the life of action itself, the life of model citizens. Their civic drama is not something you go to see in a theatre or art-gallery. You see it on the streets, in the homes, and in the council-chambers of the model city itself. If Plato's own Dialogues have any merit, it is that in them the laws, the structural principles, and the spirit of the model community come alive and express themselves: express themselves so that all can understand, appreciate, approve, and live accordingly.[91]

NOTES

1. Cf. R. L. Nettleship, *Lectures on Plato's 'Republic'* (ed. Benson, London and New York, Macmillan, 1901 and frequently reprinted), pp. 340 ff., 'Plato has set himself to write an indictment of art . . . like a controversialist. . . . The whole passage remains rather an attack upon certain developments of art than an adequate theoretical treatment of it.' Cf. also B. Croce, *Aesthetic* . . . (tr. Ainslee, 2nd ed., Macmillan, London, 1922), p. 158, 'Plato, author of the first, the only really great negation of art . . .'

For the especial emphasis upon *mimesis*, cf. R. G. Collingwood, *The Principles of Art* (Oxford, 1938), pp. 46–52. 'That Plato attacks and excludes *all* poetry [is a] myth. He is really attacking *mimesis*—amusement-poetry, representative art—not the non-representative kind.' Cf. also pp. 11, 78 ff.

There exists a vast literature upon this topic. It will be observed that I am confining my references to the most widely known and most unquestionably respected authorities.

2. *Ion* 535b f., *Prtg.* 316d f., *Gorg.* 454d ff., 502a f., *Phaedr.* 277e f.

3. *Prtg.* 356d f., *Rep.* 509e f., 597b f., 602b f., *Phil.* 55d f.

4. *Rep.* 595a, 608b.

5. Cf. Nettleship, *op. cit.*, pp. 343, 345, 'not a true account of artistic production', p. 346, 'harsh and ludicrous', p. 353, 'not adequate'.

6. *Apol.* 22a, *Ion* 533d f., 542, *Meno* 81a, 99b f., *Phaedr.* 245a, 265b, *Laws* 682a, 719b. This is regarded as holding good, not only of poetry, but of all the higher arts (cf. *Symp.* 295b).

7. *Ion* 535a f., *Crat.* 428c, *Laws* 653c f., 719b.

8. *Ion* 533e f., *Meno* 81a, 99b f., *Phaedr.* 244a f., 245a f., 247b f., cf. 248de, *Laws* 738c.

9. *Apol.* 22a f.

10. *Parm.* 130d f., 131e, 133a f., 135a f.

11. Arist., *Eth. Nic.* 1096a 18 ff., *Metaph.* 990a 35 ff.

12. *Gorg.* 473d, *Rep.* 517d f., *Phaedr.* 244d f. The Socratic method proceeds deliberately to prove the wrongness of our first crude thoughts, cf. *Meno* 80a f., *Rep.* 487a f., *Theaet.* 150b f., *Soph.* 230b f.

13. *Rep.* 401c f. (cf. *Laws* 653d f.) is hardly consistent with the position in Book X (cf. Jowett, *The Dialogues of Plato* . . ., Vol. III, pp. clxiii, clxv–vi, 'Plato seems to waver between two opposed views.' *Rep.* 607c f. seems to conclude that the 'proof' in Book X, however satisfying technically, is hardly to be regarded as final.

14. This is especially emphasized by Collingwood. The evidence of *Rep.* 595a ff. is entirely decisive, as far as it goes. The 'sort of definition' is found in *Rep.* 596d ff. The mimetic artist fabricates 'appearances', 'semblances', imitations, not of the 'idea', but of the imperfect 'copies' fabricated by artisans. The passage contains, for contrast-effect, a reference to the 'real' artist (i.e. the philosopher-artist), who knows what he is imitating (namely, the 'idea'), and creates 'realities' (*Rep.* 599a f., cf. *Symp.* 211e f., *Phaedr.* 276e–278d).

15. *Rep.* 395c, cf. *Laws* 643, 653c f., 655d f., 664e f., 672b f., 830 f. For further discussion of the entire range of such evidence, cf. R. C. Lodge, *Plato's Theory of Education*, pp. 116 ff.

16. For the evidence, and discussion of its interpretation, cf. R.C.L., *op. cit.* pp. 128 ff.

17. *Crat.* 431c ff., *Rep.* 596 ff., *Soph.* 265b ff.

18. *Rep.* 420cd, 529d f., *Soph.* 235d f., *Laws* 668d f.

19. *Crat.* 434a f., *Rep.* 598a f., 601a, 602c f., *Soph.* 236a.

20. *Crat.* 392d ff., 422d f.

21. *Rep.* 411ab, Lucian, *Vera Historia*, Pt. II, *ad init.*

22. *Rep.* 398d, 400a, d.

23. *Crat.* 422d f., 423cd, 424c f., 426c f., *Rep.* 396ab, 397a, cf. *Laws* 700d f.

24. *Crat.* 422e f., 432c f.

25. *Crat.* 431b ff., *Rep.* 601 f., *Soph.* 235d.

26. *Crat.* 429a, *Laws* 669d.

27. *Menex.* 236d, *Rep.* 510a, 597d f., 602b, 606c, *Phaedr.* 230de. Cf. *Herodot. Historia* VI 129.

28. *Rep.* 571b f., *Laws* 657e ff., 667d, 797b f., 816d f. R. G. Collingwood tends to identify the mimetic arts (as ordinarily understood) with 'amusement' arts to 'entertainment' arts, and accordingly criticizes them adversely (*op. cit.*, pp. 11, 51 f., 78 ff.). He could doubtless point to the definition of 'amusement' arts (*Pol.* 288c) in confirmation.

But I venture to think that this is only a partial truth. It may be true of the work of *actual* painters, musicians, etc., in Plato's view. But it is not true of the *revised* work of artists whose gifts are being guided toward the support of community idealism in the ideal republic and model city.

Plato's view is that children and other persons of imperfect education and immature judgement are incapable of apprehending clearly and distinctly the higher truths. They have, accordingly, to be assisted by what they *can* appreciate: *viz.*, the mimetic arts. These appeal to their sense of pleasure, their feeling for amusement and entertainment. *Via* this appeal, the mimetic arts gradually fit members of the 'silver' class (and doubtless also of the 'copper' and 'iron' classes) to 'charm themselves' into appreciating the beauty of reason; i.e. into accepting idealistic regulations, even without fully understanding the intellectual justification for what they are accepting.

As artificers of right opinion, the mimetic arts are indispensable, and their ability to amuse and entertain is helpful. It is only when divorced from the right direction, that pleasure-seeking is deprecated. There is no art for art's sake, or amusement for amusement's sake, in Plato, that is, in the philosophy of which he approves (cf. *Rep.* 377a f., 425a f., 537a, *Laws* 653 ff., 793d, 796bc), although he never objects to a little 'harmless amusement'. In general, art is, for the sake of the good; amusement is (directly or indirectly) for the sake of the good.

29. *Apol.* 22cd, *Crat.* 424d, 430b, *Rep.* 510a, 515c f., *Critias* 107, *Soph.* 235d f., *Laws* 668d f. A virtuoso flautist has experience of flutes. He knows what makes a physical flute usable or not, for his purposes. He can indicate to the manufacturer how the flute should (physically) be constructed. It is only when he uses his flute as a musical artist, trying to reproduce (e.g.) the song of birds, or to stimulate religious emotion, that he may sink to the lower stage of intelligence called *eikasia* (cf. *Rep.* 601d, *Phil.* 56a).

30. *Rep.* 349d f., 510b f., *Tim.* 40d.

31. *Rep.* 611c f., *Soph.* 235d f., *Laws* 653c f., 665a f., 668d f., 682a. Cf. further, R. C. Lodge, *Plato's Theory of Ethics*, Ch. XI, esp. pp. 333–334.

32. *Crat.* 391d f., *Symp.* 209d f., *Rep.* 388 f., 390b f., *Phaedr.* 245a, *Laws* 738b f.

33. *Rep.* 377c ff., 386a, 389d f., 401b f., *Laws* 657a f., 664a, 716b f., 801c ff., 817d f., 828a f., 829c f., 909e f.

34. *Rep.* 399a f., 607a, *Laws* 802, 811c.

35. *Apol.* 33b, *Phdo.* 78a, *Rep.* 506b ff., 533a.

36. Wilamowitz, *Platon*, 2nd edit., Vol. I, pp. 723–724; R. C. Lodge, *Plato's Theory of Education*, pp. 159–170.

37. *Rep.* 540ab, *Laws* 969cd, *Epist.* 324b ff.

38. *Rep.* 511b f., 533a, 592, *Epist.* 341c f.

39. *Rep.* 399e f., 411e, 500e f., 531c, 584d f., *Tim.* 35 ff., 47d f., *Phil.* 17cd, *Laws* 653c, 656d f., 670e f.

40. *Rep.* 377c ff., *Laws* 719, cf. 656 ff.

41. *Rep.* 401a f., *Laws* 658e f., 801d, 811c f., 817a f., 858e f., 957d.

42. *Rep.* 507b, 509b, 533a, 540a.

43. *Symp.* 210a ff., *Rep.* 479a, 480a.

44. *Symp.* 211d f., *Phil.* 64d f., cf. R. C. Lodge, *Plato's Theory of Ethics*, Ch. XIX.

45. *Laws* 631d. For discussion of the entire evidence *re* value-scales in the Dialogues, see R. C. Lodge, *Plato's Theory of Ethics*, pp. 175–341, esp. Ch. VIII.

46. *Euthyd.* 279–282d, 288d–290d, *Rep.* 505 f.

47. *Symp.* 211c f., *Rep.* 505e f., cf. 484c f., 500cd, 520bc, *Laws* 681b f.

48. *Rep.* 505 ff.

49. *Euthyd.* 281de, and the evidence of the 'Socratic Dialogues of Search'.

50. *Charm.* 169b f., *Euthyd.* 292e, *Rep.* 505b f.

51. *Rep.* 508c f.

52. *Theaet.* 152a f., 166d ff.

53. *Rep.* 508e f., *Tim.* 53b f., *Parm.* 133b ff. For Gorgias, see Ritter and Preller, sec. 237 (fromSextus, *Adv. Math.*, 78–79).

54. *Phdo.* 99e f., *Rep.* 509b, *Tim.* 50c.

55. *Rep.* 521c ff., *Theaet.* 176.

56. *Rep.* 443c, 558e f., 571e f., 585e ff., 589a f., *Phil.* 61b ff., cf. *Pol.* 309b ff., *Laws* 772d f.

57. *Rep.* 546, 587 f., *Laws* 747a f., cf. R. C. Lodge, *Plato's Theory of Education*, App. I ('Numbers in the Model City'). *Parm.* 130b f., is usually interpreted as ascribing a certain degree of originality to Socrates in respect of dialectic. But there can be no doubt that the philosophical exploitation of conceptual techniques, as such, originated in the work of the Eleatic school. And the 'torpifying' effect of the Socratic elenchus is simply (as Burnet states) due to applying to ethical questions the method which Zeno had invented as a weapon against the Pythagorean hypothesis of the identity of mathematical and physical units (cf. *Parm.* 128b f.). Zeno and Socrates (in this Dialogue) seem to understand each other like identical twins.

58. *Crat.* 424d f., *Rep.* 484d, 500e f., 540a, *Laws* 739c f., 769a f.

59. *Rep.* 592, *Laws* 644d f., 903b f.

60. *Ion* 535d f., *Rep.* 600e ff., *Phaedr.* 263e f., *Laws* 653d f., 719c, 815d f., etc.

61. Cf. e.g., Paul Friedländer's *Platon I* (Berlin and Leipzig, 1928), which is dedicated to Wilamowitz, with the characterization of W. as *daimonios* (i.e. like Socrates, 'divinely inspired', superior to the technicalities of a merely objective scholarship). I myself feel a great respect for the quality of Platonic insight shown (as a rule, throughout his *Werke*) by Schleiermacher, as well as by Wilamowitz

and by Friedländer himself; and I suppose that Plato would like to be approached and interpreted in this spirit (cf. *Phaedr.* 245a).

62. For the evidence upon which this paragraph depends, cf. R. C. Lodge, *Plato's Theory of Education*, pp. 1–9.

63. *Apol.* 22a f.

64. *Crat.* 422e f., *Rep.* 493b f., *Tim.* 40a, *Laws* 653d f., 672b f., 673c f., 815e f.

65. *Crat.* 400d f., 425c f., *Rep.* 363b ff., 377b ff., *Laws* 801a f.

66. *Ion* 534a *Phaedr.* 253a, *Laws* 790c f., 815c f.

67. *Rep.* 394d f., 401a f., 409a f., 603d ff., *Laws* 653c f., 656d f., 659d.

68. *Laws* 796c f., 813e, 814d f.

69. *Theaet.* 176a f.

70. *Prtg.* 325d f., *Symp.* 209, *Rep.* 396bc, *Phaedr*, 252d f.

71. *Rep.* 500bc, *Laws* 821 f.

72. *Rep.* 500c, 590e f., *Tim.* 47a f., *Phaedr.* 269e f., *Laws* 967a.

73. *Symp.* 201c, 206a, 212a, *Phdo.* 100c, *Rep.* 452e, cf. *Lysis* 216d.

74. *Laws* 903b ff.

75. *Rep.* 394e ff., 400e f., *Laws* 811c f., 817a f., 858e f., 957d.

76. *Rep.* 533b, 558e f., 586b f., *Pol.* 274b f., *Phil.* 35e f., 41c, 45 ff., *Laws* 644d f., 803c f.

77. *Rep.* 369c–372d.

78. *Pol.* 272.

79. *Prtg.* 314c ff., 337d f., *Gorg.* 447 ff., *Symp.* 176e ff., *Rep.* 372e ff., *Laws* 778c f.

80. *Rep.* 475c ff., 484bc, 586a f., *Laws* 700e f.

81. *Rep.* 505a f., 529b ff., *Tim.* 51d f., *Soph.* 242d ff.

82. *Gorg.* 507e f., *Rep.* 443c, 540a f., 589a f., 592, *Pol.* 309b ff., *Phil.* 22, 60d ff., *Laws* 693d, 694a, 701e, 756e, 773a f.

83. *Rep.* 395c ff., *Laws* 903b ff., cf. 817b f.

84. *Ion* 535d f.

85. *Prtg.* 347b f., *Phaedr.* 275d f., *Theaet.* 165e f., 171c f., *Soph.* 243a f.

86. *Rep.* 395 ff., *Laws* 664e ff., 817b f., etc.

87. *Rep.* 395b f., *Laws* 743d f., 846d f., 850, 919c f.

88. *Menex.* 234e f., *Rep.* 377b f., 386b ff., 397d, 401, *Laws* 802, 817d, 829d.

89. *Laws* 715c, 729d f., 730d f., 829c f., 919e, 945e f., 948a, 951d f., 961a, 964b, cf. *Rep.* 540a.

90. *Laws* 657c f., 658e f., 738d f., 771d f., 800c f., 813d f., 815d, 816b f., 817c f., 828a, 829b ff., 835b, cf. *Menex.* 234e f.

91. *Rep.* 599 ff., *Phaedr.* 275e f., 277e f., *Laws* 817b f. It has long been known that the *Republic* and *Laws* are, fundamentally, treatises on education, which succeed in doing what they talk about, *viz.*, educating their readers. Cf. Further, Dewey, *Art as Experience*, p. 7.

CHAPTER TEN

The Judge in Matters of Art

WHO is regarded, in the Dialogues, as a competent judge in matters of art? Is it (1) everyone (the many, or the people), i.e. every normal human being? Is it (2) the interlocutor, i.e. the individual singled out by a Socrates for questioning, to explain (if he can) his aesthetical value-judgements? Is it (3) the man of general experience, who has personally viewed and studied many, many art-works, before arriving at his opinions? Is it perhaps (4) the technical artist himself, the fabricator of art-works, with his judgement standardized by interaction with the opinions of fellow-artists? Or is it rather (5) the citizen (of the 'silver' class), or, possibly, the trained magistrate (of the 'golden' class)? Or finally, could it be (6) the dialectician or philosopher proper? For each of these classes, we can find evidence, in this or that Dialogue. Let us consider their claim to competence of judgement, taking each in turn.

(1) Everyone. Value-judgements in matters of art are made by young and old, rich and poor, bond and free. But they differ enormously. What gives pleasure to the young (for instance) simply bores older persons; and what gives pleasure to the old, bores young children. Adolescents, again, despise 'kid-stuff'. They have outgrown playing with dolls. And as to what the grave and reverend seniors profess to admire, adolescents can hardly bring themselves to believe that it is alive. The traditional epic narration is so deadly dull! For themselves, they just love the thrills and passions of melodrama—with possibly an occasional lapse into the resounding belly-laugh of comedy.[1] To adolescents, unbalanced and undignified feelings are the genuine stuff of life;[2] although perhaps the really coarse laughter and the more abandoned dances are more wholeheartedly enjoyed by men who have lost their standards: the vicious and the *déclassés*, the drunkards, the cheap foreigners, and the slaves.[3]

There is no question that everyone makes such judgements. Everyone knows what he likes, i.e. what 'charms' or gives him pleasure; just as everyone knows what tastes sweet to him, or what tastes bitter. Suppose you try to concede 'competence' to everyone who makes such value-judgements. The difficulty is, that A tends to differ from B, C, and D, and that the differences may be great, as well as irreconcilable. If, then, you say that everyone has a 'right' to make such judgements, to take himself as 'a measure of all things', the only conceivable agreement in sight is, surely, an agreement to differ. But such an agreement, in the last analysis, takes all meaning out of such terms as 'competence', 'right', and 'measure'. If your value-judgement means nothing or less than nothing to B, C, and D, and *vice versa*; if, in other words, there is nothing at all normative about the aesthetic value-judgement, you might as well give up before you start. For you are clearly not going anywhere; neither you, nor anybody else.[4]

A Protagoras, who accepts these premises as his starting-point, rejects this conclusion. He believes that he (and the pupils to whom he reveals his secret) *can* 'go somewhere'. Although individuals differ, and have an inalienable right to differ: if you look around, you will observe the formation of loose groupings of like-minded persons. In a large city like Athens, you will find there are enough persons of like-minded tastes to support, e.g. the ancient equivalent of a Punch-and-Judy show,[5] or a sort of Talkie,[6] or a theatre for the legitimate drama.[7] You can always get a crowd for a torchlight relay race, if on horseback,[8] for an exhibition fight in armour,[9] for a lecture on self-improvement, or even for the better-language movement.[10] There are enough like-minded persons to support confectioners' shops, fashion shops, and shops which cater to more questionable tastes.[11]

About the judgements of such groups, there is, of course (from Protagoras's premises), no question of absolute truth or falsity. In a democracy, such groups are all equally free to judge precisely as they see fit.[12] But you can make a fair living by catering to the tastes of such groups. In fact, where people are swayed by their feelings, you can study a little social psychology, and acquire (from attending Protagoras's classes) the power of the word. You can then proceed confidently to sway the feelings of this or that group. You can find your account either in doing this yourself,[13] or perhaps (like Protagoras) in teaching the art to others: passing on the secret of how to win friends and influence people. This is quite practical. There is real money in it.[14]

It is possible also (as Protagoras believed) to go further in the direction of theory. You can follow along the line which rests upon social 'science', i.e. upon psychology and sociology. You are catering to the natural appetites of people. As human beings (whether as individuals or as members of groups), people have 'natural', i.e. factual, quasi-instinctive wants, interests, and aims. You can count upon them. It is upon these that you play, when you work your way toward the kind of success which awaits the accepted social leader.

You set yourself, therefore, to study the behaviour of *homo gregarius*. It is all very empirical—and why not? But, if you plan to be a master of men, able to forecast the direction of public taste, and perhaps to be able to help it along (to your advantage): you will find it pays to be able to tell, e.g. the Athenians what the Athenians love to hear. You speak to them of their great history and manifest destiny as the cultural leaders of Hellas and of the world. You praise them to their faces for their love of freedom: the freedom to think for themselves, to speak for themselves, to judge and (in general) to judge and behave. Anything that seems to harmonize with their behave—in their undoubted group competence—as they see fit to 'historical destiny' will tend to be adjudged 'better', 'nobler', 'more beautiful'. With a little knowledge of what you can count upon from the group, you will find this tribal view of valuation—in spite of the occasional shifts of fashion which occur in a democracy—works, upon the whole, very well.[16]

Not to know this, is to be naïve. In matters of art, whatever the art, it is what the group, the larger group, the people or the many, think (or can be induced to think), that sets and maintains the standards. Such groups never doubt their own competence and sovereign authority.[17] If, then, you are an artist, and desire to make an economic and a social success of your art, you obviously have to give the people what the people want, or think they want. You 'flatter' them (if you do not object to this term)—how? By enhancing, reinforcing their confidence in what they believe to be their manifest destiny (*viz.*, of cultural leadership). In other words, whatever your special art (medicine, painting, music, or what you will), you cannot, if you plan to make a success of your life, neglect to cultivate this further art: the art of advertisement or 'flattery'—i.e. the social psychology and influential rhetoric taught by professionals like Protagoras and Gorgias. This is the regular highway to practical success.[18]

'*Practical* success'? Yes, and its significance for art too is greater (a Protagorean would insist) than you might, at first, be inclined to suppose. You might think it easy to question the public's *expertise* in matters of art. The public doubtless (you might say) knows what it likes; but is what it likes, *art*, real art, art as such? Is not the public's knowledge (you might ask) really confined to registering and re-porting upon its own degree of satisfaction? Imagine a mediocre artist, well trained in the social techniques of Protagoras. All that the public would know, would be that its senses and emotions, including its feeling of self-importance, were being agreeably titillated. The public's 'judgement' would simply be its reaction to these emotional thrills and chills. It would be something like a fever-patient's reaction to the taste of a draught of wine.[19] In a word, such 'judgement' is not necessarily (or even probably) a reliable index to the *artistic* value of the stimulus as music, as poetry, or as painting. Is it not perfectly possible (you ask) for a good artist to fail to win popular acclaim? Is it not equally possible for the prize-winners at the festivals to be, artistically speaking, like Agathon in the *Symposium*, obviously second-raters? Is not (in short) popular success one thing, and artistic success something else?[20]

To this question, the answer from the humanist standpoint is simple. In this or that special case, humanists concede your point. But in the long run, and over a wide area of judgement, they say, No. It is not true. In the long run, what humanity likes and acclaims as art, *is* art. Popular judgement, by and large, is sound; not merely in the case of 'popular' art, the so-called 'entertainment' or 'harmless amusement' art; but in the case of 'great' art, 'classical' art, too.[21]

Art which appeals only to a few, to a special clique, is not great art. Art which is truly great as art, will in time succeed in appealing to humanity in general. Look over the history of art. Look over the list of names universally acclaimed as 'great', and you will find this true beyond reasonable doubt. In the final analysis, 'the many' means everyman, humanity itself. So understood, 'the many' *are* the best judges of poetry and music, in a word, of the art that charms. The individual is (and remains) free to judge as he pleases. It is only in so far as he uses his freedom in such a way as to reject the superficial bias, the one-sided pull of this special interest or that, and lets the universal-human within him come through and decide for itself, that his judgement becomes normative. It is a folk-judgement of the folk-value of folk-art. This is the humanist position championed by Protagoras; and in this position, the conclusion is not inconsistent with the premises. Both premises and conclusion (as drawn by Protagoras) may be taken as sound.[22]

(2) The interlocutor. A Platonic Dialogue is (speaking generally) a discussion in which two or more persons, one the questioner, and the other (or others) taking the position of the interlocutor, participate, frequently before an audience. It is usually assumed that the discussion is of interest to the audience, and that the audience is directly concerned in having the discussion proceed in an orderly and systematic manner.[23] Discussion should bring out clearly the implications of this or that hypothesis, and should tend toward some sort of final conclusion.[24]

It is expected of the questioner, that he shall possess sufficient insight into method to lead the discussion competently;[25] while the minimal requirement for an interlocutor, is that he shall be co-operative in his replies, answering the questions in such a way as to assist the questioner in conducting the discussion toward a reasonable conclusion.[26] It is not expected, that is to say, that he will answer ambiguously or insincerely, on the one hand, or with pretentious dogmatism, on the other. He will be loyal to the requirements implicit in philosophic discussion, and will regard his answers as always subject to further questioning (in a friendly spirit) and elucidation.[27]

That is to say, the discussion is a quasi-academic affair. It is partly of social, but primarily of intellectual, benefit to all participants. The audience benefits by vicarious participation in the discovery and establishment of reasoned truth. The questioner benefits by receiving, with the help of his interlocutor, at least co-operation toward a step-by-step exposition and confirmation of a hypothesis or thesis in which the questioner is interested. This is the position taken by the visiting professor from Elea;[28] and even Socrates expresses delight when the responses of a Theaetetus indicate acceptance of Socrates's own opinions—opinions which Socrates has not yet formulated. Theaetetus's bright answers, hesitating a little as they seem, at least save Socrates the labour of further discussion![29]

What is the benefit to the interlocutor? It too is partly social, though primarily educational. Like the administrative co-opts of the Nocturnal Council, the interlocutor is selected for his natural ability; and he benefits by being co-opted, taken up into the company of more mature minds, and by being given, whenever needed, a friendly, helping hand.[30] It is stated that his rapid growth in *a priori* insight is at first vague and dreamlike. Left to itself, this insight is liable to lapse.[31] But with repetition of the friendly guidance, it eventually becomes an integral part of the interlocutor's nature. In favourable cases, he soon acquires competence to think, question, and decide for himself.[32] There is a yet further benefit, of a more moral sort. Being induced to face almost continuously the weaknesses and inconsistencies inherent in his hitherto untrained thinking, the interlocutor is learning modesty and self-criticism. His mind is being purified of its naïve tendency toward dogmatic self-assurance: the greatest obstacle to spiritual growth.[33]

In matters of art, the selected interlocutors represented in the Dialogues are unusually well informed and unusually intelligent. A Glaucon or a Phaedrus, participating in a discussion led by Socrates, never shows the slightest difficulty in understanding and accepting suggestions, as to which, at the present day, some of us might feel a little hesitant. The same is true of Protarchus and Philebus, not to mention Socrates himself, when being taught by Diotima.[34] The interlocutor, then, when matters of art come under discussion, shows himself especially gifted, especially able to reveal what is at the back of his mind. In a word, his judgement exhibits universal-human quality, so far as this can be tested by the devices which ensure dialectical consistency. The interlocutor's judgement is, in content, about the same as that of 'everyone' (as previously considered). But it differs in being deliberate, i.e. justifying itself against questioning and criticism.[35]

(3) The man of experience. The strength and weakness of aesthetic experience are discussed in a number of passages. It is clearly recognized that the amateur, the concertgoer or enthusiastic frequenter of the Athenian picture-galleries, is a person of very considerable experience in matters of art. He is well aware of the kind of thing he likes, and the kind of thing he dislikes.[36] So too it is certain that members of Plato's 'silver' class, whose life is perpetually subjected to artistic influences (selected for their effects upon his ways of feeling and thinking), are at least equally saturated with the kind of appreciation which comes with experience.

The effect of art-works, impinging upon the appreciator all day and every day, is to saturate him with 'right opinion'. He feels, thinks, speaks, and acts, in matters of art, as it is believed that a man of experienced judgement *should* feel, think, speak, and act.[37] That is to say, the universal-human valuation-tendencies at the back of his mind are confirmed and amplified as a result of his observations. Intensity, recency, and, above all, frequency, do their work. These condition young and old, men and women, to play (unhesitatingly and with deep personal and group satisfaction) the parts designed for them in the human drama.[38]

But that is all. Experience alone, however intense in matters of art, and however frequent, does not necessarily develop independence of judgement, or originality of critical insight. Experience does indeed train the feelings. Directed experience may train the feelings aright. But the resultant judgement is merely right 'opinion'. The experienced man knows (if you can call this opinion 'knowledge') what is right and what is wrong. But he cannot tell why.[39] For development of the higher sort of insight into the 'idea', something more than experience of art-works, however extensive and however continuous, is required.[40]

(4) The artist. In matters of art, the judgement of the practising artist, especially when standardized by interaction with the judgements of his fellow-artists, is of great value. What a Sophocles thinks of dramatic poetry, what a Pericles thinks of political oratory, are always to be considered with respect, if not always treated as finally authoritative.[41] The individual carpenter, weaver, or potter, as a professional, of course accepts and obeys the regulations adopted by his professional associates. So (doubtless) does the layman. At least, the employer of artisans, whether an individual or the community, is concerned that professional standards of work shall be lived up to, in all respects. In the utilitarian arts, this is elementary.[42]

With artists whose aim is 'beauty' or 'charm', it is much the same. Poets and painters, offering their work in competition with other poets and painters, have a lively sense of the standards of technical achievement expected in their particular fields. While creating works which no layman could hope to rival, professionals observe certain general rules of technique. No stringed-instrument player (for example) would attempt to tune the chords of his instrument more tightly or more loosely than is the standard practice of his fellow-musicians. Anything else would be despised as trickery rather than musicianship. There is, in fact, a degree of tension which the trained ear of the professional accepts as 'just right'.[43] So also, when it comes to selecting expert adjudicators, the nominations which musicians are willing to accept, are normally in the hands, not of laymen, but of those professionally interested in music. That is the way things are; and it is the way things should be.[44]

However, when it comes to open festival-competitions, the musician subjects himself to the judgement, not only of his fellow-artists, but of the community at large. On such occasions, the musician (however undoubted his musicianship) may feel compelled, in order to achieve popular acclaim, to soft-pedal, here and there, his own artistic judgement. In fact, wherever (for reasons over which he is unable to exercise control) 'judges' of some sort are set over him—judges who represent something other than the artistic judgement of his peers—he knows that he may have to defer to their authoritative requirements. But if he finds it prudent, at times, to let virtuosity take the place of sound musicianship, he still knows that he can count upon a certain measure of sympathy and understanding from his fellow-musicians, who are doubtless present in the audience. He feels that his reputation as a competent professional is still largely in their hands. And there it is relatively safe; provided he does nothing likely to awaken the forces of jealousy and slander which (in human critics, however technically expert) are always, to some extent, present.[45]

The judgement of the professional artist can, however, be deeper than this. Its validity is not really confined to matters of mere technique. The artist who respects the judgement of his fellows, is always aware that sound artistry is only one of the achievements they expect from him. There is the further matter of inspiration.[46] If he is a sincere artist, he is expected to live up to the gospel of 'art for art's sake', and to believe in 'all for art, or the world well lost'.

If he lives up to this further expectation, he will close his ears to the siren whisperings of Protagoras. He will despise the employment of extraneous methods of ensuring popular success. He will resolutely trust to his artistic feeling, his inspiration and his technique, to win for him in the end, the measure of success which deservedly comes his way. The genuine artist is thus something more than a mere professional, doing a good job for good pay. He keeps before his mind's eye the vision of something higher than empirical success in this or that actual community. His idealism is transcendental, and looks for guidance to a power which is only partly of this world.[47]

(5) The citizen. To the modern reader, the Platonic 'citizen' seems (at least, at first sight) distinctively different from 'everyman' or 'the many'. 'Everyman' is clearly an individual. He is free to come to his own independent decisions in matters of art. He does not dream of having to conform to any given set of rules—whether such rules are thought up by artists, or are imposed by some other kind of authority. He just says what he feels and thinks. Given a mass of such individual reactions to situations considered aesthetical, it takes a sort

of sifting-out process, using analysis and synthesis and possibly also formal statistics, to extract and formulate the general features of an alleged universal-human judgement.[48]

As contrasted with this, 'the citizen' is, surely, never an individual. He is a type: with the general outlines of his aesthetic judgements pretty firmly pre-established. In Hellenic life, this is obvious. If you are an artist, travelling with your wares from one community to another, you subject your work to the judgements of the citizen-body. You do not expect a civic audience to give you an unaided judgement: an honest-to-goodness, man-to-man verdict. You address them always as 'Men *of Athens*', 'Men *of Corinth*', 'Men *of Sparta*', or what not. You keep in mind their political background and outlook, their traditional place in cultural Hellas, and the like. Hellenic citizenship is, in this sense, always specific, typed, standardized. You know what to expect, and you act accordingly.[49]

So also with the Platonic 'citizen'. He is a member, not of an actual, but of an ideal community. The cultural outlines of his community are somewhat inflexible, standardized, typed. He is never just 'a human being', but always a full-time member of Plato's 'silver class'. That is to say, he is a farmer-citizen, with a background of military service. Trade he leaves to others (operating under specified regulations). In all matters of aesthetic judgement, he defers to what he likes to think of as 'right' opinion. If something new in the way of art comes to the model city (e.g. a show by a travelling dramatic company), the model citizen never thinks of seeing this and deciding for himself whether he likes it or not. He waits to see what the local pundits (a carefully selected committee of artists headed by a highly educated magistrate) decide for him. That is the way things are done, practically everywhere in Hellas. The only difference is that, in the model city, they are done for him rather better.[50]

When we look a little more closely, however, we find that the alleged difference between (a) everyman with his independent judgement and (b) the citizen who apparently never makes an independent judgement in his life, is not as great as we might, at first glance, tend to suppose. At least, if we look at the content of the universal-human judgement toward which everyman is (perhaps unconsciously) feeling his way, and the content of the 'right opinion' to which the citizen looks for guidance, we soon realize that the difference approximates to zero.

What the silver class regards as 'right', *is* right; as right, humanly speaking, as human judgement can be. 'Right opinion' is not an artificial set of rules imposed arbitrarily from above. It represents the best that a combination of inspired artistic insight and experienced wisdom that has been to college, can discover. It is true that members of the silver class do not share directly in the technical insight and the inspiration of the artist. It is true that they do not understand the metaphysical grounds which influence the philosophy-minded magistrates. But they do feel, with every fibre of their being, that the final conclusion expresses something that they are more than willing to accept for their own. It is precisely right, just as it should be.

That is to say, right opinion is identical in content with the universal-human judgement. If there *is* a difference, it is only that the product of artistic insight *plus* philosophic wisdom is a little clearer, a little more distinct, and rather better grounded (no doubt) than the judgements of a number of chance individuals.[51] But there is no sense of externality, of compulsion, of inferiority in the face of superior authority. The citizen accepts gladly and wholeheartedly, in matters of art as well as in all other matters, the arrangements being made to ensure that his opinions in matters of art shall be, not chancy affairs, but fundamentally reliable: in a word, 'right'.[52]

So far, it might be supposed that the citizens possess and are using common sense. Their judgement in matters of art (it might seem) is not exactly original or profound. It is simply well tutored, and reposes largely upon a canny acceptance of what they feel to be for their ordinary, everyday advantage. In a word, their common-sense utilitarianism makes of them (it might be said), not artists, but 'Philistines'.[53] But this supposition would not be in accordance with the complete evidence. The citizens are throughout represented as amenable to artistic considerations. Hence the 'preambles' which precede every major regulation. Hence the obvious fact (as soon as you look at it) that their entire life, from the cradle to the grave, is lived in an atmosphere of art; and that this life is itself regarded as an art, as the most genuine and significant of human arts.[54] In fact, if an 'inspired' judgement is defined as a non-logical value-judgement accepted as coming from a higher-than-human spiritual source, mediated (as a rule) by almost any number of human links (all of whom, down to the very last recipient, being regarded as themselves inspired), then the citizens can be trusted to feel that their community judgement is more than utilitarian common sense.[55]

There is no doubt that Socrates, in the *Republic* as elsewhere, is himself inspired.[56] There is no doubt that the visiting professor from Athens (in the *Laws*) is to be regarded as similarly inspired.[57] It is quite clear that, by means of their inspired regulations, they are transmitting their inspiration (in the form of right opinion), first, to their interlocutors, and finally to the citizens of the silver class. It might even be insisted that this inspiration is being transmitted (partly by the behaviour of the model citizens themselves) to the personnel of the copper and iron classes, and even (so far as such persons are capable of appreciating their blessings) to the slaves.[58] The citizens, at any rate, both men and women, feel, with every fibre of their being, that the community life in which they participate, is inspired. They feel themselves members, not merely of a 'model' city, but of the City of God. Their judgements in matters of art—i.e. in the art of civic living (which is their especial art)—are not merely universal-human. They are not merely factually correct. They are 'guided'. In a word, the citizens are artistically, theologically, and philosophically—inspired.[59]

(*c*) The dialectician or philosopher. The philosopher who is approved in the Dialogues, has always two sides to his nature. He is (1) never a mere dialectician, a questioning mind, as such. His judgements always have (2) a non-logical side which is moral, deeply rooted in community feeling. This helps to keep his judgements humanly balanced. Persons elected to become members of the golden class which is given dialectical training, are, first and foremost, members of the silver class, in exceptionally good standing. Whatever their specifically intellectual gifts, they have 'taken the dye' of the approved community virtues. Severe and repeated tests have shown beyond the possibility of doubt, that they possess, and can be trusted, under all circumstances, to keep characters which are steadfast. Nothing likely to happen to a human being will ever make them cowardly, intemperate, impious, unfriendly, disloyal to the community, or unjust.[60]

This is essential. Otherwise, the study of philosophy might turn a man of intellectual capacity, with the potentialities of exceptionally good citizenship, into a mere 'intellectual'. He might become a one-sided questioner or critic of life: standing on the sidelines and jeering at all the informal, non-logical understandings which keep a man loyal to his community. If a young man without a firm balance-wheel throws himself wholeheartedly into the questioning attitude (characteristic of philosophers), he is in danger of educating himself out of these understandings. He may educate himself into a realm which is all questions and no answers. In such a realm, there is no place for good citizenship, or for any but narrowly intellectual standards.

Such a man is turning himself into a caricature of Socrates. He is arguing himself into a position of 'ignorance', by maintaining that he no longer understands or knows what his fellow-citizens all accept without question. Without the balance of a strongly knit character which accepts (even while questioning) the ethical basis of community understandings, such an intellectual becomes a man without a country. For civic purposes, he is useless. He is a pure sceptic, an animated zero.[61] A faith which inquires (as in the case of Socrates) is one thing. An inquirer without faith is something else. From a community standpoint—and this is true of Plato's quasi-ideal communities quite as much as of the historical Athens—such an inquirer is 'corrupt', and is in danger of corrupting others. If all other measures fail, he must be cut out of the community by a surgical operation.[62]

The dialectician or philosopher is not, however, himself competent to pass judgement on matters involving an experience of detail or of technique which he has not acquired. During part of his life, he has withdrawn into specialized, intellectual, highly abstract studies. These are designed to develop insights which will fit him for the position of administrator.[63] These disciplines will make him a good chairman for almost any committee of experts which may be set up to make recommendations on matters of community importance. He can act as chairman of a judging committee in such matters as agriculture, marketing, the religious calendar—or matters involving music, poetry, painting, etc. He will not, indeed, have the appreciation of detail possessed by the experts in such fields. But he will be able to take their concrete suggestions, and gradually weld them into a final recommendation. He will bring out their full positive value in relation to the community aspect of the idea of good. So made over, the suggestions of the experts will be fit to take their place in the system of community law (on which the philosopher-magistrate *is* an expert).[64]

In a word, the dialectician plays in the community the part which should (ideally) have been played in Athens by Socrates, 'the only true statesman of his time'. He is a master of method who can bring out the maximal value, for community living, of the factual experiences and political suggestions of his fellow-citizens. *They* bring him their problems, discussing these from the standpoint of their specialized experience. *He* enables them to make their best possible contribution to the regulations in accordance with which the life of the model city guides itself.[65]

In matters of art, it is the musical experts (for instance) who investigate and establish all details concerning the musical scales ('harmonies') and rhythmic patterns suited to confirm the citizen-artists in their life of artistic citizenship.[66] As we read in the *Republic*, we are to 'take Damon into our counsels'.[67] It is similar experts who nominate teachers and adjudicators for the community music festivals (in the *Laws*), and they sit in committee with the philosopher-magistrate, in deciding how far new forms of music are admissible. Are they truly expressive of the ideals immanent in model citizenship? If 'the same', they are admitted, whatever their source. If 'better', they are promptly adopted. It is only if 'inferior', that they are rejected. This is the way in which the philosopher-magistrate judges, in matters of art. He functions as a dialectical focus for the detailed judgements of the experts; and he elaborates these so as to bring out everything they contain which can be of positive use to the life of the model community.[68]

The magistrates (or philosopher-kings) are not, however, pure zeros, mere focal points around which the judgements of individual experts can crystallize. As select members of the 'silver' class, they have all been through the mill. Their judgements thus always represent the norms implicit in the community's way of living. They not only guide the empirical judgements of the experts toward a formulation which is intellectually consistent. They guide them toward a formulation which does full justice to the standards inherent in the community, the standards of a life which accepts and enjoys model citizenship.

Sometimes, apparently it is the opinion of the expert board that really settles the question under discussion.[69] At other times, apparently community feeling is more decisive. For instance: in poetic celebrations of great actions, the community is concerned that the composition of the verses shall be entrusted to veterans. This means, to men who have demonstrated their community spirit by taking part in the deeds which are being celebrated—even though a technical expert in journalism might find something to criticize in the *tournure* of their phrases.[70] But, whichever factor predominates, the point is that, in the final judgement which sets the seal of community approval upon the recommendation of the expert artists, *all* factors receive due consideration.

In a word, in the final judgement in matters of art, we find a balance between (1) the universal-human feelings of everyman, (2) the expert artists' recommendations in the field of their technical *expertise*, and (3) the philosopher-magistrate's trained insight into the requirements of life in a quasi-ideal community. No one individual is a final judge in matters of art. For finality: humanity, technique, experience, and insight are all requisite. These are found (in combination) only in the work of well-balanced, philosophically guided committees: whose judgement is representative, in the end, of the entire model city or ideal republic.[71]

NOTES

1. *Laws* 658a f., 665c f., 670a f., 809e f., 816d f.
2. *Ion* 535 f., *Rep.* 475cd, 476b, 590c f., 604c f., 607e f., *Theaet.* 151a. For further interpretation of the evidence on what Plato has to say of adolescence, cf. R. C. Lodge, *Plato's Theory of Education*, pp. 201–209.
3. *Rep.* 395d f., 397a f., 606c, *Laws* 655c f., 800d, 814c, 816d f., 935b f.
4. *Prtg.* 347c f., *Theaet.* 169d ff., 177d, 179bc.
5. *Laws* 658cd.
6. *Rep.* 514 f.
7. *Gorg.* 502b, *Rep.* 492b f., *Laws* 659a f., 817a f.
8. *Rep.* 328a.
9. *Lach.* 178, 179e, 181d, *Euthyd.* 271e f., 273c f., *Laws* 796b f., 813e, 833e f.
10. *Charm.* 163d, *Prtg.* 315a f., 337a, 340 f., *Crat.* 384b.
11. *Rep.* 372d f., 404c f.
12. *Rep.* 557b ff., *Theaet.* 172a f.
13. *Prtg.* 318a f., 327 f., *Gorg.* 452d f., *Rep.* 600c, *Theaet.* 178d f.
14. *Prtg.* 310e, 328b, *Meno* 91de, *Rep.* 492 f., *Theaet.* 161d.
15. *Rep.* 493a f., *Theaet.* 178d f.
16. *Prtg.* 322d f., 324b f., *Menex.* 235 ff., *Gorg.* 452d f., 454e f., 456a f., *Rep.* 493b f.
17. *Apol.* 34b ff., *Rep.* 338d f., 492a f. S. Alexander (*Beauty and . . other Forms of Value*), says (p. 176), 'The impartial tribunal [of aesthetic judges] is a conspiracy of the qualified as against the unqualified, whose judgement they reject as . . . unaesthetic.' Sometimes I [R.C.L.] suppose this might conceivably be the case. But for Plato, if the tribunal is *genuinely* qualified, and the other is *genuinely* unqualified, he is properly disqualified.
18. *Gorg.* 458e ff., 463a ff., *Rep.* 346a f.
19. *Rep.* 493c f., 605a f., *Theaet.* 166e f., *Laws* 658 f., 670b.
20. *Symp.* 201b, *Rep.* 493de.
21. *Rep.* 499e f., 601b, *Laws* 667b f., 802c.
22. *Prtg.* 319d f., *Meno* 92d f., *Rep.* 499e f., 501c f., *Tim.* 47de, *Theaet.* 166c–167d, *Laws* 628a, 950b. The chief difference between Plato and Protagoras, is that Socrates insists upon the necessity (1) of rigorous selection, (2) of careful education in

science and dialectic, so as to bring out insight into the principles at the back of the mind (*Rep.* 533–540).

23. *Prtg.* 317de, 335d ff., 348a f., 358, *Gorg.* 497a f., *Rep.* 336b, 338a, 339e f., 344d f., 449 ff., *Soph.* 218a.

24. *Gorg.* 506b, *Meno* 86e f., 98b ff., *Rep.* 612a ff., *Theaet.* 208e ff., *Parm.* 135d ff., *Phil.* 23b.

25. *Prtg.* 338b f., *Gorg.* 509b, cf. 448d f., 463b f., *Rep.* 354bc, 453c 6–7, 532d f., *Phil.* 16ab.

26. *Gorg.* 495ab, *Rep.* 474ab, *Soph.* 217c f.

27. *Prtg.* 329 ff., *Gorg.* 499c (cf. 495ab), *Rep.* 337a f., 338c d., 339a f., 344d f., 349a.

28. *Gorg.* 486d f., *Theaet.* 150c, 151e ff., 157cd, *Soph.* 217c ff.

29. *Euthyd.* 282c, *Theaet.* 185d f., *Soph.* 269d.

30. *Meno.* 84 f., *Theaet.* 201d ff., *Laws* 951e f., 961ab.

31. *Meno* 85c, *Pol.* 277d.

32. *Euthyd.* 282b f., 289c ff., *Meno* 85d, *Theaet.* 150d.

33. *Meno* 84bc, *Theaet.* 210c, *Soph.* 230b f.

34. *Symp.* 208c–212b, *Rep.* 506c ff., 532d f., 595e ff., *Phaedr.* 243e ff., 261 f., 276a f., *Phil.* 15c ff.

35. *Prtg.* 352ab, 355e–358a, *Gorg.* 457c f., *Rep.* 493a f.

36. *Gorg.* 501 ff., *Rep.* 475c ff., *Laws* 667c ff.

37. *Rep.* 400 ff., *Laws* 654 ff., 665b f.

38. *Laws* 810d f., 817a f.

39. *Meno* 97a–99e, *Theaet.* 200e ff. Alexander, *op. cit.*, p. 59, says, 'The poet does not know till he has said it, either what he wants to say or how he shall say it. Excitement caused by the subject bubbles over into words or the movements of the brush or chisel. When the artist has achieved his product, he knows from seeing it or hearing it what the purpose of his artistic effort was.' An example would (I suppose) be Goethe's (later) account of the Helena-episode being finally given a place in *Faust, Pt. II*, or Poe's (later) account of the way he wrote *The Raven*. But (as we all know) it often takes someone else, a later artist or critic, to tell us what the (unconscious) purpose was. It seems [R.C.L.] to be irrelevant to artistic creation, that the artist should at any time (before, during, or after) know clearly and correctly the purpose of his work. That is what Socrates, in the *Apology* (22a f.) seems to be telling us. I would compare also Kant's account of the Imagination, as a 'blind' faculty (*Kritik der reinen Vernunft*, A, 100 ff.). Cf. also Croce, *op. cit.*, p. 15, 'reflective consciousness . . . is not essential to [artistic genius]'.

40. This 'something more' is furnished by philosophic reflexion, as stimulated, e.g., by the Socratic elenchus. That is to say, it is members, not of the silver, but of the golden class, who develop insight into the 'idea' (*Rep.* 476 ff., 520 ff., 533 f.).

41. *Phaedr.* 286c f. So in modern times, we always treat with respect such statements as those of Matthew Arnold, that 'poetry is a criticism of life', or of Wordsworth, that 'poetry is emotion recollected in tranquillity', or of Keats, that 'A thing of beauty is a joy forever', although our philosophical authorities are only too well aware that, taken *au pied de la lettre*, such would-be definitions could easily be pulled to pieces by any Socratic questioner, ancient or modern. (Cf. e.g, Croce, *op. cit.*, pp. 13, 89, 90, 155; Alexander, *op. cit.*, pp. 50, 117, 177, 183–184, or the lectures on poetry (or art) by *any* authoritative professor of our time.)

42. *Rep.* 349d f., *Tim.* 68b f. (with Taylor's comment on 68a 4–5), *Laws* 659 f., 671a, 769a f.

43. *Rep.* 349e, 531ab. In modern times, Paganini, who tuned his violin into a professionally unacceptable key, in order to be able to perform a piece whose 'positions' would otherwise have been impossible, was regarded, by his expert colleagues, as (to that extent) a charlatan. (Cf. articles on Paganini and on Scordatura in Grove's *Dictionary of Music*.)

44. *Laws* 765a f.

45. *Apol.* 22c, *Rep.* 493d, 500d 2–3, *Phaedr.* 237ab, 244a f., *Laws* 668 ff.

46. *Ion* 535a f., e f., *Rep.* 345e f., *Phaedr.* 245a.

47. *Ion* 534b f., *Meno* 81a, *Symp.* 211a f., cf. 180a, *Rep.* 335c, 340de, 341c f., 346b f., *Laws* 653d f., 657a, 790c f., 829b f.

48. *Prtg.* 353a, *Rep.* 475c ff., 530e f., *Laws* 658 f., 665 ff., 746 f.

49. *Lach.* 183a f., *Menex.* 234c ff., *Rep.* 492b f., *Laws* 625d ff., 655d ff.

50. *Laws* 745e f., 801b f., 811b f., 817a f., 822e f. It is largely with reference to this kind of evidence that the modern reader sometimes thinks that freedom of judgement in Plato's ideal community or model city is dreadfully circumscribed, and claims that there is an element of 'fascism' about the philosopher's ideal constructions. For discussion of this interpretation, see R. C. Lodge, 'Plato and Freedom,' *Trnsct. Roy. Soc. of Canada*, Vol. III, Series III, June, 1949, Section Two, pp. 87–101. Such critics tend (I think) to forget that the situation in our own times is not so very different. While it is always possible for us, if we think a public building 'looks funny', or an Epstein statue or a Picasso painting is 'grotesque', or *L'après-midi d'un faune* is 'musically meaningless', to say so outright; which of those of us who profess to a degree of 'education' and desire our pronouncements to be taken seriously, does not first see what our authoritative reviewers have to say about such art-works, and then rather carefully re-phrase our first reactions, so as to make them agree, more or less, with what 'the best authorities' have decided? To which of us, as concertgoers, has not the *cliché*, 'Well, there's never anyone quite like Beethoven, is there?' been used as a very present help, when we have been pressed to commit ourselves?

51. *Lach.* 184d f. *Prtg.* 353a, *Meno* 97 ff., *Rep.* 429b f., *Tim.* 37c, *Phil.* 55d f., *Laws* 864a, 964c.

52. I have in mind here the attitude taken by the interlocutors in the *Phaedo* (78a), in relation to Socrates, as their acknowledged leader, or of Glaucon and Adeimantus in the *Republic* (357d, 367b f., 450d f., 506b f., 532d f.), again in relation to Socrates, as their acknowledged leader; or of Protarchus and his compeers in the *Philebus* (19d f.), again in relation to Socrates. This is paralleled by the attitude of Megillus and Cleinias in the *Laws* (969cd), in relation to the visiting professor from Athens, whom they desire to co-opt as their intellectual expert adviser.

For a modern parallel to the receptive attitude of Plato's citizens (who do not feel that their freedom of judgement is impaired by what is being done for them) we might consider the attitude of our present-day citizens toward the arrangements made for the radio broadcasting of music considered 'good'. There are broadcasting stations which almost specialize in this sort of thing. There are commercial stores which almost specialize in providing scores, records, and books of the most approved types. Such stations and stores are certainly helping to create and extend 'musical appreciation', the development of an 'opinion' in matters musical, that would be regarded as 'right'. There is no doubt that music-minded citizens who enjoy this sort of thing, do not feel that they are being unduly 'regimented'. They accept wholeheartedly the arrangements being made for them. Plato's citizens are merely, *mutato nomine*, our own selves—what we should nowadays call 'well-adjusted' men and women.

53. In modern times, we find a certain antithesis between the moral and the aesthetic sides of life. Some writers value morality above art. Others value art above morality. As an example of the first, cf. Hannah More's Epilogue to *The Search after Happiness* (1773),

> One virtuous sentiment, one generous deed,
> Affords more generous transport to the heart,
> Than genius, wit or science can impart;
> For these shall flourish, fearless of decay,
> When wit shall fail, and science fade away.

As examples of the second, we might refer to the modern tendency to be a little blind to Wagner's failings on the moral side, because of his undoubted excellence as an artist; or the position maintained by G. Bernard Shaw in *Love among the Artists*.

Kant tended to regard art as the handmaid of morality. Its function was (he insisted) to amplify and drive home, by appealing to the imagination to do its best to satisfy the demands of the practical reason (*Kritik der Urteilskraft*, I, 1, sect. 49—E. T. Bernard, pp. 197–202). Readers of Plato who focus their attention upon *Rep.* 395–398b, 400e–402c, 598e f., *Laws* 800 ff., and similar passages, rather easily suppose Plato's view to be somewhat like Hannah More's. But this (I think) is erroneous.

Plato's view really is that the life of the ideal community is itself an art, the highest kind of art, the true art. Writing verses, or chiselling chips off a block of marble, or applying paint to this or that surface (however skilfully in a technical sense), is a secondary occupation. It is hardly worth the effort, if a man has the ability to do something better, such as practising the art of ideal citizenship. Technical excellence in speaking or writing, is something which the freeborn citizen deems hardly worthy of his attention. One leaves that sort of excellence to inferior persons—professionals, foreigners, and slaves! (*Prtg.* 347c f., *Symp.* 176e, *Gorg.* 485a f., *Phaedr.* 275c–278d, *Laws* 810b, 812c f.).

54. *Symp.* 209a f., *Rep.* 395a f., *Laws* 653 ff., 803c f., 835d f.

55. *Ion* 534c ff.

56. *Apol.* 31cd, *Crat.* 421a 6 ff., 428c, *Meno.* 81a, 99b f., *Rep.* 496b, *Phaedr.* 234d, 242bc.

57. *Laws* 811c f.

58. *Rep.* 395bc, 433c, *Laws* 665c, cf. R. C. Lodge, 'Plato and Freedom', *Trnsct. Roy. Soc. of Canada*, 1949, Vol. XLIII, pp. 91–99.

59. *Rep.* 378d ff., 401b f., 411e f., 427bc, 443bc. *Laws* 653c ff., 811c f.

60. *Rep.* 412b ff., 414a f., 425a f., 429d f., 441d f., 484b ff., 490a f., 498e f., 502e f., 535–541, *Laws* 965 ff.

61. *Rep.* 487d, 489b f., 497d f., 537d ff.

62. *Apol.* 21a f., *Gorg.* 509a f., *Rep.* 497c, 538–539, *Soph.* 268a f., *Laws* 769c, 907d ff.

63. From twenty to fifty, those picked out for training as 'full' guardians, cease to live as the general citizens, the 'auxiliaries', live. They do, indeed, hold various positions of command; but for much of their life they are withdrawn into the

study (*Rep.* 412b f., 414ab, 415a f., 417a f., 458c, 537c–540b, cf. 517d, 519c f.). Similarly in the *Laws*. The 'junior co-opts' of the Nocturnal Council are withdrawn from the general civic life, and are set to study dialectic and law (*Laws* 951d f., 961bc, 964 f., 968d f.). (I am aware that the word *dialektike* does not occur in these passages. But, whatever the reason for the absence of the technical term, the co-opts are trained similarly to the candidates for leadership in the *Republic*.)

64. *Laws* 657a f., 659d f., 660a, 738b f., 764c f., 772a f., 799a, 801c f., 802a f., 809, 811b f., 812c f., 816bc, 817d, 828ab, 829c f., 848d f., 934, cf. *Prtg.* 319bc. So also the visiting professor from Athens (in the *Laws*) requires the co-operation of Megillus and Cleinias, with their concrete experience. Cf. also *Epist.* 322de.

This evidence, as interpreted here, is inconsistent with the interpretation of Plato's government as 'totalitarian'—e.g. in the *Journal of Education*, 1945, pp. 58, 164, 224. I am in agreement with Messrs. Lauwerys and Neurath, however, that a reader prepossessed in favour of 'fascism' or 'nazism', especially if he neglected this evidence to which I explicitly call attention, and emphasized certain passages from parts of the *Republic*, might think that Plato's writings indicated a sympathy with the chief tendencies of modern totalitarianism.

65. *Gorg.* 509a f., 521d, *Theaet.* 150b f. As a modern parallel to the function of Plato's higher judges as chairman of recommending committees, we might refer to the way in which modern governments frequently appoint an experienced judge as chairman of a commission intended to conduct an inquiry, or to make important recommendations for legislative consideration.

66. *Rep.* 401b f., cf. 395c ff., *Laws* 654e ff., 663b f., 722d f., 783a, 817b f.

67. *Rep.* 400b f.

68. *Laws* 764c f., 810d f., 817d.

69. *Laws* 657bc, 738b f., 764c f., 772a f., 799a, 828ab, etc.

70. *Laws* 660a, 801c ff., 810a, 829c f.

71. *Rep.* 398a, 607 f., *Laws* 811b f., 817b f. For Plato, the true art is (I think) always the art of living. That is, it is the life of ideal citizenship, so far as this is possible for beings who remain human.

P

CHAPTER ELEVEN

The Aesthetical Value-Judgement

So far, we have concluded that the final value-judgement in matters of art includes factors derived from (1) the non-logical background of universal-human feeling, (2) the technical *expertise* of persons regarded as competent artists, and (3) trained insight into the potentialities of life in a quasi-ideal community. These factors have to be held in balance, as indicated by judicious experience within a model city.

Ideally speaking, that is, there is one great art. This is not 'rhetoric' (as believed by the Sophists).[1] It is not 'mathematics' (as believed by the Pythagoreans). Nor is it abstract logic (as believed by the Eleatics).[2] Still less is it money-making, power-seeking, or the cult of pleasure (as the business man, the general, and the *viveur* are all-too-ready to suppose).[3] As Plato teaches, it is the 'royal' art of the statesman or philosopher-king; to which carpentry and sculpture, weaving and embroidery, trumpet-signalling and music, military drill and interpretative dancing, folk-language and literature, painting and the rest of the arts, all make their proper contributions.[4]

The master-art of statesmanship weaves all these activities into a progressively balanced way of living, which does full justice to each and all of them.[5] Each citizen does his 'own' work, the work for which, by natural inclination and by as much educational training as he can take, he is best fitted; and the web of community living, so fabricated by the diverse activities of all classes and individuals (young and old, men and women, rich and poor, bond and free), emerges as the final art-product.

Plato thinks of this, sometimes as the web of life, sometimes as a grand choric dance, sometimes as a great drama, in which chorus, protagonist, and deuteragonists perform unceasingly their proper rôles: something like an extended Platonic Dialogue in action.[6] To us moderns, the image of a great orchestra performing a community symphony, perhaps with a choral prelude and finale, is more familiar. But in any case, the picture is quite clear. Ideally speaking, art is the art of life, of life in the finest form of community activity which our minds can work out as possible for man. This is the general form and content of the aesthetical value-judgement.

Here, however, we come upon a difficulty. In spite of the aesthetical suggestiveness of such phrases as '*web* of life', 'choric *dancing*', 'community *drama*', and the many references to the place of the other arts that render life 'charming', is the final value-judgement (with which we are now dealing) specifically *aesthetical*? For instance, would not our formula, wtih a very few superficial changes of emphasis, turn out to be much the same as the Platonic formula of the *ethical* value-judgement? If we inquire, whose life is the shining exemplar of the *ethical* aspirations of humanity, shall we not be told that it is what we are here considering as the *aesthetical* ideal: namely, the life of the citizen or magistrate of the model city— or of the silver and golden classes in the *Republic*? Again, is it not this self-same life which assimilates itself to the life of the immortals, and becomes community participation in *the life of the gods*? Is it not also, beyond reasonable doubt, the life which realizes *the greatest possible happiness for man*?

We could obviously continue this line of questioning, almost indefinitely. To sum it all up: if we set ourselves to discover the Platonic formula for the 'highest human good', would it differ essentially and in principle, from our formulation of the *aesthetical* value-judgement? Should we not find ourselves concluding, at the end of a carefully documented investigation of the complete evidence, that the highest good is ideal living, so far as a man can participate in it? It is a way of living (that is to say), richly empirical, with its details so re-arranged that it constitutes an organic part of a single, harmonious, consistently systematic, totality of experience. It is a complete life, expressing adequately the functioning of all factors that go to make up 'the concupiscent element' as well as 'the spirited element' and 'the rational element'—all balanced under the guidance of the over-arching principle of 'the good'. By participating in such a life, the individual human being achieves cosmic, and more than cosmic significance, and at the same time realizes his own deepest happiness and well-being.[7]

We might even ask whether, in view of the metaphysical

significance of the 'idea of good', even the specifically *ethical* part of the formula does not become, in the end, a hypothesis which is transcended, or at least transmuted into something of deeper and more spiritual finality. To put it quite simply: do not all the apparently distinct interests of life (the interest in food, in sex, in money and power, in pleasure and artistic achievement, in association with one's fellows and with the ideal figures of the heroic and religious tradition of Hellas), one and all find their final direction and control in the all-embracing life of the model city? In fact, are not the philosopher-king, the philosopher-artist, the philosopher-businessman, the philosopher-lawyer, the philosopher-physician, the philosopher-mathematician, the philosopher-teacher, and the rest, all (in so far as they become imbued with the spirit of philosophy, with insight into the idea of good) beginning to talk the self-same language? Are they not tending to converge and coincide? Are they not becoming, academically and in principle, fused into identity?[8]

A careful examination of the evidence will indicate (I think) that each and every avenue of human experience, when pursued beyond a certain point, opens up, to the Platonist, vistas leading to the idea of good, the pot of fairy gold which awaits the intrepid traveller at the end of *every* rainbow. Is not this the 'unhypothetical first principle', the unconditioned absolute presupposed in all the arts and sciences? Is it not the principle of ideality, as such, to be reached (if at all) by questioning the assumptions, the specific presuppositions of the particular arts and sciences; using these as stepping-stones leading out into the Beyond? In so conjuring up the image of a single, ultimately all-embracing and all-transmuting, absolute experience, is not Plato formulating in philosophical terminology the aspiration embedded in the non-logical sources of Hellenic language; the language which welds together its ethical and aesthetical feelings in such words as *kalokagathia*, in order to express the unity of moral beauty and manly perfection?[10]

If, then, it is true that, ideally speaking, all specific ideals are so many concrete applications of one and the same ultimate principle of ideality; then the *final* judgement in aesthetics overlaps and merges with the final judgement in ethics and politics, in epistemology and metaphysics, in religion and aspiration; indeed, in all the arts and sciences. But, in that case, what becomes of the *proximate* judgements in matters of art? What happens to the specific judgements which restrict themselves to considerations of *balance*, *measure*, *symmetry*, and *charm*—considerations which are not necessarily prominent in judgements of economic, ethical, religious, or metaphysical significance and value?

To find the Platonic answer to this question, we have to come down from the ideal realm, and enter the world of actuality. It is only ideally that there is only 'one' value-judgement. In the world of actuality, value-judgements are 'many'. They are specifically distinct, however difficult it may prove to defend their distinctness, when faced with the questioning of a dialectician.[11] The situation is much the same as we find in connexion with the so-called 'virtues'. These too are either 'one' or 'many', according as you consider them from the standpoint of the ideal realm, or of the actual world. Courage, self-mastery, justice, friendship, piety, and the rest, seem, at first sight, very different from one another. From the standpoint of the average citizen (who is plainly a member of the actual world), or even of a Protagoras (who does little more than amplify the views of the average citizen), these virtues are obviously 'many', characteristically distinct.[12]

Courage, for instance, with man as with the other animals, rests upon the instinct of pugnacity. It is the tendency to react with violence, when faced with obstacles, whether physical or moral.[13] Even members of the informal academy which so easily gathers around Socrates, prove willing to assign to courage a distinctive anatomical basis in a particular segment of the nervous system.[14] Is it not clear, to all persons with any experience of actuality, that self-mastery or 'temperance', with its tendency, not to rush in (like courage), but to keep out of areas of disturbance, to avoid conflict and behave quietly and with restraint—is almost logically distinct from courage; almost its precise 'contrary'?[15] Justice, again, rests upon the herd-instinct, the tendency to associate (for protection and for other biosocial purposes) with one's fellows, living together behind the same city walls.[16] And wisdom rests upon the instinct of curiosity and the emotion of wonder.[17] Is it not entirely obvious that these virtues are 'many', specifically distinct; readily recognizable, both as what they are and as not what they are not?

And yet: when you submit yourself to the dialectician's questionings, when you develop insight into what is ideally involved, do you not find that (ideally speaking) each of these virtues which at first sight seemed so undeniably distinct, gradually overlaps with the rest, converges with them, merges, and in the end coincides, in a virtue which is 'one'? Is not the ideally just man (the citizen of the model city) courageous and self-controlled, friendly and religious, and also (if a member of the philosophically trained magistrate-class) wise? Is he not himself competent to explain to all serious inquirers the apparent riddle of the 'one' and the 'many'? Of course he is![18]

That is to say, the more you decide to abandon the ideal realm with its all-unifying principle, and to plunge into the actual world with its multiplicity, with differences magnified into distinctions, and distinctions intensified into divergences, and divergences multiplied in the direction of infinity; the more fragmentary and unreal does your resulting experience become.[19] You are leaving forever the realm of all-comprehensive wisdom, and are making your way through the warring Hellenisms toward the confusions of Barbarism, and indeed toward the characterlessness of animality. You are sinking toward the sub-human level, and eventually toward the utter disintegration of chaos: structureless, lawless, meaningless.[20] In a word, you are taking the pathway which leads away from health, both spiritual and physical, through a one-sided athleticism, toward various levels of disease, and ultimately toward dissolution and death.[21]

Apply this to art. Suppose you separate the practice of art from the life of citizenship. You specialize in art, art for art's sake. As you proceed along the line you have chosen, you specialize yet further. You withdraw from the community art of choric dancing. You devote yourself to the more special art of devising dance-steps, or to composing lyrics, as such, or instrumental music, as such. You select themes taken, not from ideal human living, but from the mathematic-mechanical possibilities of your instrument.[22] What is the result? Is it something that the group can sing around the camp-fire, as its members recondition themselves for the strenuous idealism of the next day? Is it something expressive of their historical background with its great heroes, or of their ideal destiny under divine guidance?[23] Of course not. Is it something less universally ideal, but still with concrete traditional significance for an actual community, something like the war-chants of Tyrtaeus, or the processional hymns to Apollo or Artemis? Again, of course not. Looked at by an unprejudiced intelligence, what is it but technique, speed, and dynamics; a cascade of mere notes, a 'meaningless rush of brutish sound'?[24] It is the same with the so-called Corybantian dancing. This is all frenzied excitement, but with no positive value for peace or war, or indeed for human beings engaged in any of the purposes of a wise community living. An art which draws away from life, is an art which is *in extremis*.[25]

We might compare this with what happens in the political and economic fields. The various types of civic constitution found in Hellas, if held in judicious balance, in relation to the principle of the ideal community, are all very well. Properly counterbalanced, a little of 'aristocracy', of 'oligarchy', of 'democracy', even an occasional touch of 'dictatorship', fit into their places in the general scheme.[26] But if you once divorce them from the spirit of the ideal republic, you find them arranging themselves into a series leading progressively downward, toward a social disintegration which is at the opposite pole from ideal community living.[27] Something of the same sort can be envisaged, if you concentrate upon the economic side of life, upon money-making pursued for its own sake, with no higher vision. In the end, 'plutocracy' also negates and defeats itself.[28]

In precisely the same way, if artists or art-critics once try to separate, from the spirit of model citizenship, the actual types of norm current in artistic circles in Hellas, they will find they are making a great mistake. 'Measure' or 'the mean', 'symmetry' or 'balance', 'purity', 'beauty' or 'charm', 'unity', and the like, are quite all right in their proper place. Their proper place is in the life of the model community. The inspiration immanent in ideal social living, and the informal understandings implicit in such living, provide such norms as 'measure', 'balance', and 'charm' with an ideal frame of reference. Given that background and outlook, they can safely be used in constructing and weaving the web of life.[29] But if you insist upon separating them, you will find yourself rendering them liable to a progressive deformation. They will tend, finally, toward an end which is at the opposite pole from the artistic end of a rich community living.[30] In the end, you will find that you are tending to negate yourself; not merely as a citizen, not merely as a human being, but as an artist—i.e. as a producer of works designed to charm by their unity, their symmetry and observance of the principle of the mean. Your work may obey all the technical rules of your trade; and may yet be flawless to a fault, frigidly regular, artistically still-born.[31]

Consider more in detail a few of these norms commonly regarded as highly acceptable to Plato himself. 'Unity', for instance, is frequently supposed to be an expression of the principle of ideality which is postulated as the technical source of all values.[32] It is unity that 'helps Socrates to speak and to think'. It is unity that raises those who learn to make a proper use of it, out of the multiplicity of sensory experience (with its unceasing ebb and flow of inconsistencies and contradictions) to the 'plateau of Truth', the realm of pure essences which can be apprehended by 'mind, the pilot of the soul'.[33]

As applied to art-works, this can be interpreted with two characteristic types of reference. You may refer (1) to the units, as such, i.e. to the individual elements which can be put together so as to constitute this or that concrete whole; or you may refer (2) to the whole, the larger unity which can be constituted out of such-and-such elements.

Let us look first at (1) the elements. Consider, e.g. the individual planks which can be used to construct a wagon, or the individual mud-bricks which can be used to construct a Greek house.[34] Or we might consider the individual letters of the alphabet, the S, O, C, R, etc., which can be used to build up (on their mechanical side) syllables or names, nouns or verbs.[35] Or we might look at something more abstract; at the lines, straight or curved, which can be used to construct a line-drawing; or at the colours, Red, Green, Blue, and the rest, which can be applied to a line-drawing so as to turn it (in Hellenic practice) into a painting.[36] Or we might consider the elementary rhythms, the trochees and dactyls out of which dances are made up; or the elementary tones which go to make up the musical scales, and can be applied to the dance-rhythms, so as to turn them into music—or applied to words, so as to turn them into songs.[37] We might even look at the more elementary geometrical figures, such as the triangles which can be used in constructing the tetrahedra, octahedra, icosahedra, etc., of Pythagorean physics.[38]

All such elements, considered as units possessed of an individuality, a regularity, a character, a meaning of their own, have (for the mind which can discriminate, i.e. can separate them out and apprehend them as intelligible units) a certain relatedness to something within the mind. In apprehending them, the mind comes alive. It exercises its proper function. In so doing, it experiences a characteristic 'pleasure', its own proper type of satisfaction. The elements thus apprehended as mind's objective correlates, are regarded as possessing 'charm' or 'beauty'. Since this quality (if it *is* a 'quality') is attributed to them, not in their relation to other elements, but merely as apprehended by mind, apprehended as individual elements, in themselves; their beauty or charm is said to be, not relative, but absolute.[39]

There is something, that is to say, about the straightness of an absolutely straight line, or about the curvedness of a good curve, which is distinctly pleasing to the discriminating mind. It is so definitely precisely what it is, an example of the principle of 'the same'.[40] So too with the triangularity of a regular triangle. Again, with the colours; there is something definitely satisfying about a White that is really white, about a Red that is really red, and so on. We speak of it as the 'purity' of the colour. And similarly with the 'purity' of pure tones in music. Such experiences (we say) are satisfying 'in themselves'. This is quite apart from some other kind of charm which may come to them in this or that relation.

The elements, that is to say, of an art-work have (a) this 'absolute' sort of beauty or charm. A young child or adolescent (for example) has a certain charm of his own, which belongs to him in respect of his youth. This is quite independent of whether (b) he is developing himself into a good citizen or a mischievous delinquent, a good husband and father, or a crusty bachelor.[41]

Let us now look at (2) the larger unity which can be regarded as constituted out of such elements. As Socrates never tires of pointing out, there is not one of these aesthetical elements which, when put into this or that wider context, does not seem to possess a different kind of value. This contextual value is not absolute. It is 'relative' to the particular context. Individual threads, for instance, can be put together (as warp and woof of a patterned weft) in such a way as to contribute to the beauty of the larger whole, the woven pattern of a drape or rug.[42] So also Purple may be regarded (when viewed absolutely) as 'the most inherently beautiful of the colours' known to the Greeks. But, in certain contexts, Purple will not seem aesthetically right. The Greeks applied paint to their marble statues; in order (doubtless) to enhance the human charm of human features and human costumes. It might be supposed that, where the eye is the most beautiful of these features, it should be painted Purple; so as to enhance its human beauty. But it is only the natural colour of the eye which, in such a context, would look 'right'. The Purple (however beautiful as Purple) would look 'wrong'.[43]

That is to say, the colour proper to a given context receives, from its place in this context (i.e. from its relation to the other human features—all properly coloured), an additional enhancement, a contextual rightness apprehended by the mind as entirely satisfying. If we are interested in the larger unity, in the painted statue as a whole, this sense of contextual propriety may quite overshadow the degree of absolute beauty which belongs to a given colour (apprehended by the mind) in its own right. In certain contexts, as Socrates says, there is no colour which may not appear (to our larger aesthetic judgement) 'ugly'. It is also true that (in its proper context) there is none which may not appear (to our larger aesthetic judgement) 'beautiful'. That is to say, the absolute beauty of an element may be enhanced by the further charm lent to it by its relation to the other features of its context.[44]

As Plato sees the matter, the ideal larger context for all aesthetical elements is provided (for human beings) by life in the model city. Here everyone has (1) his own, natural value and charm, and (2) the additional value and charm which come from occupying his proper place, and fulfilling his proper function, in the model city. The colours of his face and body (for instance) do not have to be put on externally, by the use of physical cosmetics. They are vital. They grow from the inside out. They represent the natural glow of health. They come as the natural consequences of participating in the health-giving life of the model city: with its regular gymnastics, its hygiene, its religious processions and community dances, its military drill and its outdoor sports.[45]

The enhancement of charm, which comes from participating in such an ideal context, thus takes precedence over the elementary or rudimentary charm which characterizes the elements in their own right. Thus, the alert, flexible, wiry strength of the militarily trained citizen, always ready, always at the top of his form, is superior to the over-specialized muscular development of the sleepy professional athlete, who has withdrawn from regular, community living, in order to devote himself to his one-sided, brutalizing regimen.[46] And the all-round healthiness of the good citizen is superior to the apparent health of the valetudinarian: who is forever stimulating excessive reactions of this or that part of his body, at the expense of the whole. Pills and potions may remove this or that symptom. But they may at the same time weaken the patient and postpone recovery.[47]

So also the normal expressiveness of the good citizen's life provides a guide in the art of living, superior to the technique of voice or pen exhibited by the foreign virtuoso, however highly trained. The professional (a man without a country) may indeed have specialized in stringing words together in accordance with a much advertised body of abstract rules. But it is never this professional Lavengro, but the citizen-amateur, the veteran who has himself participated in the heroic deeds he is describing, who alone can be trusted to express in his verses the true spirit of the model city. Without the spirit of the whole behind him, to vitalize his words and rhythms, these elements, in spite of their own original and inherent charm, are comparatively lifeless and dull.[48]

It is the unity of the wider context, the spirit of ideal community living, that pervades the life of its members, and guarantees the functional unity of each. In the ideal republic or model city, and nowhere else, the farmer is truly a community farmer, the carpenter or weaver a community carpenter or weaver, the teacher or magistrate a community teacher or magistrate. His detailed, day-to-day activities are inspired by the spirit of the whole. This strengthens him to do his 'own' work. Thus he finds himself, in devoting his life to the service of the ideal city which exists 'in heaven'.[49]

This enhances the various activities of his life: by providing for each the satisfying simplicity which comes from accepting a single over-arching identity of direction. This bestows upon them, in spite of their individual variety, a significant togetherness, a functional unity and ideal purposiveness which they would otherwise lack.[50] As Leibniz is to say in a later age, it is a way of combining the greatest possible individuality and variety with the greatest possible unity and order.[51]

Of the power of this wider context in the military sphere, the Hellenes were already well assured. If the unity of the higher command was broken, it was, as soon as feasible, restored. When the disciplined mercenaries of whom Xenophon writes, learned that their leaders had been treacherously slain by the orders of Tissaphernes: after a very short period of despondency, they elected new officers, under whose unifying leadership they cut their way through the numbers surrounding them, and carried through the long 'march of the ten thousand' to the sea.[52]

Plato deliberately extends this unity of purpose to the whole of community living. His plan—a precise, mathematically calculated application, to social living, of the divine plan for humanity—provides for everyone occupying the position of magistrate, citizen, metic, artisan, or slave, an ideally suitable rôle in the community drama. In playing this rôle, he is able to live out his own life, realizing his own natural (absolute) value, and at the same time to enjoy the further (relative) significance which comes to him from his association with the other members of the cast. The great drama moves forward along its divinely ordered path: a path leading (if all play their parts well) to the greatest possible realization of human, of cosmic, and of more than cosmic value.[53]

If the disciplined unity of an army (symbolized in the unity of the higher command) is once broken, the army ceases to exist. It becomes dissolved into its elements. In its place, we have a mere aggregate of individuals, each fighting for his own hand, and no one getting anywhere. The 'one' has become a 'many'. So, if the over-arching unity of the model city goes, community living gradually degenerates into a free-for-all; in which all higher values are progressively lost. The organized simplicity of the unifying plan disappears, and its place is gradually taken by progressive degrees of complexity, a divergent multiplicity which slips over toward chaos.[54]

The true aesthetical judgement, therefore, which takes precedence over all partial sensitivities, is the official verdict, in matters aesthetical, of the committee of community artists, acting under the chairmanship of the appropriate community executive. It is this which, in the last resort, is alone competent to represent the life of the model city, with its entire background and outlook. Humanly speaking, such a judgement is necessarily, in matters of art, final.[55]

The reference to 'simplicity' and 'complexity' in the Dialogues (in connexion with the norms of the aesthetical judgement) is susceptible to misunderstanding; and it must be confessed that opportunities for misunderstanding, at least at a first reading, are easily found. Plato clearly insists upon the importance, in all matters of art, of 'simplicity'. He shows an obvious distaste for any sort of 'complexity'. The misunderstanding takes the following form:

In the old days (it is thought) life was simpler and art was simpler. Representative Platonic *personae* dislike almost all 'modern' tendencies in art, and gladly hark back to the past, whenever possible. They deliberately prefer the elementary, the archaic, the almost naïvely simple idioms of the past.[56] This does not mean merely that they prefer geometrical diagrams (with their exact measurement) to the tasteful distortions of freehand drawing or modern sculpture.[57] They object to virtuosity and to multiplicity in any shape or form. A man should practise 'one' art; never two arts; and, quite certainly, never 'many'. A polymath like Hippias, with evidence of his virtuosity in many arts carried around on his person, is simply ridiculous: a figure of fun.[58] And the Hellenic admiration of the wizardry with which a Homer appears to be an authority in several fields, is utterly absurd.[59] Nature does not operate that way. It simply bestows, at best, upon one man, one art.[60]

The objection to complexity, plurality, and multiplicity, is carried further: into the field of human instruments. The flute, as an instrument of music, is to be rejected; because its vent-holes can be made to produce (according as your finger covers an entire hole or only a (varying) part of it), not one tone each, but a variety of tones. The modern new-fangled instrument which contains so many strings, that you can play *all* Hellenic scales upon it (instead of *one* only), is to be rejected, in favour of the traditional four-stringed lyre, each of whose strings (when properly tuned) responds with a single definite tone.[61]

The point of the misunderstanding is this: Plato is being supposed to prefer everywhere the simple, as such, to the complex, as such. This is understood as meaning that he prefers the number 'one' to the 'indefinite dyad', namely, to the indeterminate pluralism of all numbers higher than 'one'. He prefers (it is supposed) that a musical composition should be restricted to the potentialities of a single scale (and, further, that all Hellenic scales but two are to be excluded).[62] He prefers a line-drawing to a painting, and tends to regard 'embellishments' in any art as unnecessary excrescences, as external distortions which should, so far as possible, be stripped off, leaving only the barest essentials.[63]

So widespread is this misunderstanding, not only among casual readers and among practising artists, but among scholarly interpreters of the Dialogues, that it will be well to look somewhat closely at the evidence which renders this interpretation unacceptable. In the first place, the 'one man, one art' principle does NOT mean—what it is supposed by the interpreters to mean. It does NOT exclude a high degree of what would naturally be called 'complexity'. Look at the life of (a) a carpenter, (b) a musician or painter, (c) a citizen, and (d) a magistrate—all in the model city.

(a) Concerning the carpenter; all that the rule says is, that a man earning his professional living by the practice of this art, shall not be permitted to charge professional fees for practising a further art, such as weaving, or cobbling, or music-making. He specializes in carpentry. But this does NOT mean that he is forbidden to patch his own clothes, or to repair his own shoes, or to take a part in community singing, or to look after his health by attending to the securing of proper exercise, rest, and sleep, as well as of suitable food and drink. It does NOT say that he is not to look after the proper development of his family and apprentices (if any), that he is not to associate with his fellow-artisans in fixing professional *expertise* and of fees to be charged for expert services. It does NOT say that he is not to sit (if elected by competent authority) on an advisory committee, under the chairmanship of an appropriate magistrate, to play a part in community legislation on all matters directly affecting the art of carpentry.[64]

That is to say: the carpenter, as such, will be a practitioner of the following arts: (1) the art of working in wood, (2) the very different art of securing remuneration, at professional rates, for his work, (3) the art of mathematics, on its practical side (i.e. as concerned (a) with measuring and calculating the patterns used in his woodwork, and (b) with the cost of living, as he purchases, in the community market, not merely the materials and tools used in his trade, but also the day-to-day supplies of food, clothing, etc., required for himself and his household).[65] He will also be prepared (4) to train or educate his sons and apprentices in the practice of his profession; and (5) to learn to behave, in all matters involving his relations to his fellows, his employers and employees, the citizens and magistrates of his community, and indeed in respect of his residence-permit, as professional usage and the law shall direct. When we consider also (6) the extent to which he may find himself called directly into the community service on this or that advisory committee, we begin to realize that the life of a carpenter, participating (and properly participating) in a wide variety of activities in the model city, is at least considerably more 'complex' than appears at a first glance.[66]

(b) Consider now the musician. If under this term we include, not merely the virtuoso, but the composer, and consider the life open to him in the model city, we find this to be somewhat more complex than the life of the carpenter. Allowing for the technical differences between working in wood and composing music: the musician (like the carpenter) shares in (2) the art of securing professional remuneration for his work, (3) the art of mathematics (a) *more Pythagoreo* (in the model city), (b) in connexion with the cost of living. He is also prepared (4) to accept state appointment as a music-teacher, with such duties as adjudicator perhaps added; and, of course, (5) to obey all the rules of good behaviour in his profession and in the city.[67] He is also (6) liable to be called on for expert advice on legislative committees. But furthermore, his life on its technical side, tends to be more complex than the life of the carpenter. As a musical composer (1), he has to be technically expert over the entire range of 'music'. In the model city, this includes expertness in the fields of poetry and dancing (for choric dancing is not broken up, by excessive specialization, into three separate arts—one concerned only with words, a second only with the accompaniment, and a third only with the dance-movements); and there is a direct suggestion that a certain degree of research into the elements common to these three sides of the musician's art (i.e. an unusual degree of theoretical accomplishment), may be expected.[68]

(c) Or look at the citizen, the plain, ordinary, average citizen. In the model city, this man lives a very rich 'mixed' or balanced life. He earns his living by farming, i.e. supervising the production of food on his agricultural lot, and its distribution in the community market. He is also (normally) liable to the duties of military service, with very high standards of professional *expertise*.[69] He is responsible, at all times, for the proper cultivation of his lot, for the payment of community taxes, and for intelligent co-operation with his fellow-citizens and with the magistrates in nearly every phase of his living. As a boy, he is never left to himself. He is always following his leader; and when he is a man, things are much the same. It is his chief glory if he can obtain the prize for good conduct, i.e. for obedience to the spirit of the laws, which is the spirit of model citizenship.[70] He has to know enough of practical mathematics, of personal hygiene and of the arts, to fulfil all his duties; and he has to be prepared to take his part in electing officials and attending meetings where public business is transacted.

That is to say: the citizen + farmer + soldier +, like the musician, is expected to be competent in two or more arts. He has also sufficient practical acquaintance with a variety of minor arts, to fulfil adequately an enormous range of duties. Finally, he has to be especially alert at all times, ready to respond to any new emergency that may arise. His mornings, from dawn to noon, are occupied with his more serious work. His afternoons are free (if one can call it that) for such relaxations as military sports, choric singing, and group dancing—and, as he grows older and his muscles stiffen, telling moral stories to the young. His evenings appear to be spent in social life, i.e. in playing intellectual games, varied (as he grows older) by the Hellenic equivalent of checkers; until, at a very late hour, he is finally permitted to retire for a brief period of sleep. In other words, a rather full range of activities awaits his every available hour. The trivial round, the common task, will furnish him with full-time occupation.[71]

(d) Of the life of the magistrate in the model city, it is not necessary to add much. He may, indeed, be withdrawn (by the age of thirty or so) from the more routine duties of the citizen group. But *en* _revanche_, he is loaded down with responsibilities and duties of an arduous nature, which leave him no time at all to feel that he can sit back on his reputation and let the world go by. He 'toils' at his studies, and often has to work far into the night.[72] He has to be prepared to meet the most searching criticism; and there is no limit to the responsibilities that may be thrust upon him.[73]

In the _Republic_, it is true, philosopher-kings are given quasi-sabbatical leaves, and are permitted to enjoy an early retirement. But in the _Laws_, we hear nothing of this. On the contrary, the more conscientious a man has been in the performance of his duties, the more likely he is to be selected for the service (as he grows older) of travelling inspector of institutions, or minister of education—or at the least, of ambassador or priest. And while some of the priesthoods are not particularly onerous in their routine duties, a really good man is likely to be elected to one of the higher priesthoods. This involves accepting membership on the 'nocturnal council' (whose responsibilities are unlimited), or possibly on the small but ultra-responsible committee of revisers, whose functions include checking the qualifications and conduct-in-office of all other magistrates. These higher appointments are _ad vitam_, and we do not hear (in the _Laws_) of any vacations for such officials, or permitted retirements—unless we are to assume that, on reaching the age of eighty or thereabouts, _all_ officials are encouraged to accept _emeritus_ status.[74]

These examples are intended to point the moral and adorn the tale. In the model city, there are no drones or idlers (such as you would find, e.g. in Plato's Athens). Everyone has an occupation. This is suitable, interesting, and useful. While no one (with the possible exception of the magistrates) could reasonably regard himself as driven or overworked, or as nagged to the point of asking, 'What's the use?' and giving up; there is not much time that is really wasted. Even what Plato calls 'relaxation' is really about as stimulating as our modern practising for a concert, or exercising in a sports club, with due attention to the exacting standards of competitive public performance. Nothing is excessive. Much of the activity would be regarded as voluntary. But the dweller in the model city, like some model citizens today, keeps pretty well on his toes, all of the time. The art of life is a severe taskmistress.[75]

That is to say: 'simplicity' does NOT mean what a narrowly realistic interpretation of the 'division of labour' principle might lead us to suppose. It does NOT mean that the model city is run like the assembly line in a modern factory, with each worker doing, with exaggerated efficiency, the one thing he has been trained to do. Plato's interest is not in technical efficiency (which he would have regarded as demoralizing), but in human life as a whole;[76] and each citizen leads an especially rich, full, and well-balanced life. His life really represents the ideal of model city richness concentrated in the direction of carpentry or music, or farming or administration; but always permeated by the complete background and outlook of the city. The spearhead of his life is (doubtless) his specific occupation; in which he does the work that is 'his own'. But behind the spearhead is the long shaft of the spear. It is this which provides his life with its steadiness, its significance, and, in the end, its concentrated force. His specific function is never something narrowing, like hammering this particular nail, tuning this particular string, or planting wheat, this year, in place of oats. It is always a particular expression of the idea of the whole, of the ideal life for man; in fact, of the 'idea of good', the principle of ideality, as such.[77] This idea gives meaning and value to his varied activities, reducing them from what might otherwise (as in Athenian democracy) be a relatively unorganized multiplicity of competing interests, to a closely knit pattern.

That is to say: the 'simplicity' of the idea which unifies his life, provides room, in that life, for a *greater* 'complexity', i.e. variety of interests, than would be possible without organization. In a word, the model city is at the opposite pole from Plato's Athens. Athens is a city in which painters, poets, musicians, and other one-sided artists, withdraw from civic activities to practise their innumerable individual arts. Each lives a life which, except in respect of the specific art upon which he concentrates narrowly, is a little 'queer': impoverished, almost unhuman. The model city, on the contrary, is a city whose every citizen lives a life richly artistic in its every phase, and vitally human; although the citizen may never handle a mallet and chisel and may never leave behind him a collection of literary or pictorial 'doodlings'.[78]

In the second place, if we look at the arts themselves; the evidence shows that Plato does NOT enjoin a narrowing division of labour. He does NOT prefer line-drawings, as such, to paintings, or semi-illiterate verse to a finished poem.[79] On the contrary: every effort is made to correct the tendency (in Hellas) toward excessive specialization. Gymnastic and music (as Plato understands these terms) are not pursued separately. They are always integrated.[80] Again, the composition of lyrics, of musical accompaniments, and of appropriate

Q

dance-movements, is not to be pursued separately. In the model city, these are inter-implying parts of one and the same community art: completely integrated.[81] Education and business are not two 'banausic' techniques, to be forbidden to citizens, and abandoned to the care of a few cheap foreigners, imported for the purpose. They are carefully integrated into the life of the model city: permeated (as far as possible) with its spirit, as well as with factual obedience to its laws.[82] Such integration enriches the arts, and makes each (as far as possible) a concentrated expression of the life of the model city, with its entire background and its entire outlook. That is why a metic or a slave, if he has demonstrated his loyalty to the spirit of the city, receives rather special treatment.[83]

The norms of the aesthetic judgement, accordingly, are never matters of technique, as such. Technique is (of course) important in its place. But that place is elementary. Judgements which cannot penetrate beyond questions of technique, tend to be superficial.[84] In judging a picture, you can criticize (if you so desire) its lack of 'symmetry' or 'balance' or 'unity'. Why not? You can probably draw attention to 'distortions' here and 'peculiarities of colouring' there. Why paint eyes purple, or horses blue? But does such criticism cut very deep?[85]

In judging literary compositions, you can criticize (if you wish) obscurities in the expression, archaisms of thought or language. You can be severe about inconsistencies among the ideas, faults in the arrangement of topics, improprieties in the sentiments or imagery. True enough, you can.[86] Are there not innumerable possibilities of formal error? Are not the text-books of the professors full of such things—with really fearsome names attached to them? Yes, indeed. But again, is not this sort of criticism absurdly superficial? Does it ever go to the heart of an aesthetical question?[87]

With Plato, such technical norms, while prominent in the minds of certain practitioners and their professorial teachers and critics, are not taken seriously. Socrates even goes out of his way to suggest how technical handbooks might, in the future, be written. His essay emphasizes the value of clear definition and logical consecutiveness. It insists upon the fundamental importance of analytic psychology in the equipment of the would-be successful writer or public speaker: in addition to natural capacity and broad experience.[88] But even this outline sketch of a normative text-book is treated by Socrates with his accustomed irony; precisely as he is ironical about his one 'inspired' excursion into the field of 'scientific etymology'.[89] What he does take seriously is training in science and 'deep speculation', i.e. something like the 'higher 'education of the *Republic* and *Laws*. For these develop maturity of judgement along with depth of insight.[90]

In a word, technique is one thing. Maturity of insight and interpretation is something different; and it is this maturity of background and outlook that (as Plato views the situation) characterizes the truly aesthetical judgement. This judgement sums up in concentrated form the entire life of the model city. Its true norms are, accordingly, the norms of that life. They are (as the visiting professor from Athens never tires of pointing out) the laws of the city itself. Perhaps it would be truer to say, the 'spirit of the legislator', his insight into the ideal principle of community living.[91]

That is why, in coming to conclusions upon matters of art, we always (in the *Laws*) find convoked an official committee of artistic experts, operating under the chairmanship of a philosophy-trained community magistrate. The conclusions reached by such a committee have the finality of a considered verdict. This verdict is representative of the views of the entire model city. The ultimate standard or norm of the aesthetical judgement is thus: the ideal life for man. This guides all detailed judgements in the minor arts of painting, poetry, music, and the rest. It integrates their elementary or 'absolute' aesthetic values with its own life; and its principle permeates all judgements on artistic matters: whether these are made by the ordinary citizen, the citizen-magistrate, or (in the model city) the artistic technician.

The idea of good (which is the principle that guides life in the model city) permeates every phase of that life: whether lived by the citizen, the citizen-magistrate, the artist or artisan, the metic or the slave. The life they live is the good life, the ideal life for man. The living of this life is *the* human art, art *par excellence*. What such artists in living as the citizen, or as the artistic committee with its community magistrate, judge to be acceptable as 'art', is thus (from the standpoint of the model city) entirely sound.

The citizen's opinions in matters of his all-dominating art, are 'right' or 'true'. He differs from the citizen-magistrate only in not having enough educated insight to say *why* they are right or true. The magistrate can go further, and can show plainly *why* such-and-such examples of alleged 'art' are, or are not, acceptable.[92] Such matters as archaisms (for example), or embellishments, or distortions, are doubtless, in themselves (i.e. when considered in the elementary or 'absolute' sense) aesthetically good or aesthetically bad. But for the over-arching aesthetical judgement which takes account of wider, contextual values, the entire question is: *Are these* (archaisms, embellishments, distortions, or what not) *functional in the life of the model city?* If so functional, then (whatever their elementary or absolute value) they are aesthetically correct. If not so functional, then (however charming in themselves) they are to be rejected. This is the wider judgement. It decides with finality all aesthetical questions.[93]

NOTES

1. *Prtg.* 318e, *Gorg.* 448c, 451d, 452d f., 454b f., 456a f., 459c, 520a f., *Menex.* 235a f., *Pol.* 303e f.

2. *Rep.* 531e, 537d ff., *Parm.* 135bc, *Soph.* 241e ff.

3. *Gorg.* 451e f., 466b f., *Rep.* 402e f., 421c f., 520c f., 549b f., 553d ff., 560e f., 581c ff., 586a f., *Laws* 679b, 691c f., 705 f., 714b ff., 728a, 742e f., 831c f., 836a, 870a f., 875b f.

4. *Euthyd.* 291 f., *Symp.* 209 ff., *Pol.* 260c f., 276b f., 292e f., 296e f., 300c f., 305c f., 308c f., 310e f.

5. *Rep.* 424a f.

6. *Rep.* 411e f., *Pol.* 309b f., 311bc, *Laws* 653d f., 664a f., 669d f., 804d f., 811c f., 817a f.

7. The phrases of this paragraph are taken (with a little synthesizing) from R. C. Lodge, *Plato's Theory of Ethics*, pp. 173, 391–393, 476–477: which were written to summarize a rather lengthy and detailed investigation of the Platonic evidence.

8. Cf. *Laws* 964b f., 966d f.

9. *Rep.* 509a f., 510b ff., 533b f., cf. *Phaedr*, 247b ff.

10. The adjectives *kalos* (beautiful) and *agathos* (good) are not fused together into a single word, at least in Classical Greek (as far as the best authors are concerned). But they are very frequently used together, in almost inseparable union. The noun *kalogathia* (which does fuse the two concepts) might well be looked up in the Greek Lexicon.

11. I have in mind the questionings of Socrates (e.g. *Prtg.* 329c ff., cf. *Rep.* 537d f., *Laws* 964b f.). The indication is, that such questionings (perhaps as well as the questionings of Euthydemus and Dionysodorus) might lead to moral scepticism.

12. Cf. *Lach.* 195a, *Prtg.* 329d f., *Meno* 71d f., *Rep.* 493a f., etc.

13. *Prtg.* 350a f., *Lach.* 196e f., *Rep.* 375a f., *Laws* 633b f., 791b f., 963e.

14. *Tim.* 70a–d.

15. *Charm.* 159b, 160e, 161b, 163a, *Phdo.* 68c, *Phaedr.* 256ab, *Tim.* 72a, *Pol.* 306b ff., *Laws* 710a.

16. *Prtg.* 322ab, *Crito* 50c f., *Rep.* 351c f.

17. *Rep.* 475b f., *Theaet.* 155d.
18. *Laws* 963c ff.
19. *Rep.* 511c, *Phil.* 15b–18e.
20. *Rep.* 351a f., 422e f., Bks. VIII–IX, *Tim.* 30a, 41 f., 50e f., 52d f., 69b, 90 f.
21. *Rep.* 403d f., *Tim.* 81b ff.
22. *Rep.* 397bc, 398d, 531a f., *Laws* 669b f.
23. *Rep.* 372b, e, *Laws* 664b f.
24. *Laws* 669d f.
25. *Laws* 790d f., seems to ascribe a certain medicinal value to such dances. But see 796d 5–6, and esp. 815c f.
26. *Gorg.* 507e f., *Rep.* 589a f., *Pol.* 308d ff., *Laws* 693d, 694a, 701e.
27. *Rep.* 445c f., 449a, 543d ff., 580a f., 587b f., *Pol.* 291c ff., 301c f., *Laws* 712b f., 739c f.
28. *Rep.* 330a, 343de, 362b f., 421d, 521a f., 550e f., 552 ff., 562b, *Laws* 679c, 728e f., 741e, 742e f., 831c f.
29. *Symp.* 201c, 211e f., 218e, *Rep.* 399 ff., 425a, 444e, 500e f., *Pol.* 305d ff., *Laws* 661a f., 773a f., 858c f. For further discussion of the entire evidence, see R. C. Lodge, *Plato's Theory of Ethics* Cf. XIX ('The Mean . . .'), pp. 442–455.
30. *Lysis* 216d, *Symp.* 209a ff., *Rep.* 400e f., 544 ff., 587e f.
31. *Gorg.* 503d f., *Rep.* 602 f., *Phaedr.* 245ab, 249d f. (cf. 260e ff.), *Soph.* 228a f., *Phil.* 64d f., 66a, *Laws* 858d f.
32. Cf., e.g., A. Fouillée, *La philosophie de Platon* (Paris, 1869), pp. 44 ff., 456, 467–468; A. W. Benn, *The Greek Philosophers* (London, 1882), Vol. II, pp. 229, 234.
33. *Rep.* 523 ff., *Phaedr.* 247c, 248bc, 265d f.
34. *Theaet.* 207a f.
35. *Crat.* 423b ff., *Theaet.* 201e ff., *Soph.* 253a, *Phil.* 18.
36. *Crat.* 434a, *Tim.* 67a f., *Pol.* 277bc, *Laws* 934c 1.
37 *Crat.* 424d f., *Rep.* 399e ff., 522a, *Tim.* 47a f., *Phil.* 17b f., *Laws* 669d, 802d f.
38. *Tim.* 48b f., 53c ff.
39. *Phil.* 51b f., 53. Cf. F. C. Tilney, *op. cit.*, p. 21, 'Although we enjoy musical symphonies, we can also enjoy sounds for their own sakes in a comparative way. There are qualities of sounds and of colours too.' (We might compare also the song, 'Her gestures, motions and her smile, Her lips, her voice, my heart beguile'.)

Dewey (*Art as Experience*, pp. 119 ff.) states roundly that 'qualities of sense have aesthetic quality not in isolation, but in their connexions'. This could reasonably be read as a deliberate disagreement with what Plato says (*Phil.* 55). For Plato certainly seems to say that (whether as a matter of psychology, we directly experience pure colours and tones, or lines and triangles—in a complex context—or not), we do attribute a kind of aesthetical quality to visual, auditory, and intellectual experience, when this is regarded (by the logical analysis of the analytic psychologist) as a distinguishable aspect of the total experience. Plato maintains that we can and do (by analytic logic) separate out and distinguish the redness, greenness or blueness of a colour-experience, and the peculiar tonal quality of this or that note in a musical composition; and he adds that we can and do regard such 'pure' colours, tones, or figures, as having a peculiar aesthetical quality.

There is here a simple question of fact. I find myself (on the whole) in agreement with what Tilney says. I do (when listening to music, or when looking at pictures) find myself distinguishing between (1) the contextual beauty of sounds, and (2) their tonal beauty. It may be, that I should not experience this tonal beauty apart from the superb touch of a Schnabel and possibly not then, apart from his rendering of an inspiring concerto of Beethoven's. That is quite possible. But many listeners find themselves making this sort of distinction, and attributing aesthetical quality to 'qualities of sense'—just like Plato. Is not this a fact which should be readily verified, one way or the other?

In the same way, there are many pictures in which the colouring (as such) seems to be an essential factor in producing the total aesthetical effect (I do not understand Dewey to believe otherwise). Do we not, in fact, often find ourselves tending to distinguish the beauty of the colours (as such) from the contextual or compositional factor (cf. *Rep.* 420cd)? Does not this distinction play a recognizable part in comparisons of 'old masters' (1) before and (2) after an attempt has been made to 'restore' the original colouring? Do we not similarly, in comparing a colour-photograph with the actual scene reproduced, make this same distinction?

(On the other side, I confess that Croce seems to agree, on this point, with Dewey —although for reasons different from Dewey's.)

40. *Tim.* 35–37c.

41. *Charm.* 154b f., *Symp.* 217a, 218e f., *Phil.* 53a.

42. *Euthyd.* 281ab, de, *Rep.* 476a f., 479a f., *Pol.* 281a, 282c f., 284a, 285a, *Laws* 661a f.

43. *Rep.* 420cd. The actual colour used for painting the eye was Blue in Thrace (*glaukon*, i.e. sea-colour, a lightish blue, acc. to *Tim.* 68c). So Xenophanes, referred to by Clem., *Stromata* VII 22, p. 841 P (as quoted Ritter and Preller, sect. 100, n.b). In Hellas, the colour was *melan*, a very dark colour, with no admixture of White. This does not mean that Hellenic eyes were naturally Black; but merely that, in order to make the eyes of statues 'look' right, the painters applied *melan*; somewhat as sculptors, in order to make the proportions of their statues 'look' right (i.e. to the spectator) would distort the actual proportions (*Pol.* 277c).

44. How far the beauty of the larger whole (as apprehended in the aesthetical judgement) should (or should not) be analysed into the (enhanced) beauty of its individual constituents, and how far it is a 'new' thing, emerging from the constituents into a self-existent kind of beauty, the charm of the pattern (as such), is not really discussed in the Dialogues. The question, however, if not actually brought into focus, is at least indicated, *Theaet.* 201e–208c, and indeed elsewhere.

45. *Gorg.* 452ab, 465b, *Rep.* 412a f., 425a f., *Tim.* 87d f., *Phaedr.* 239cd. *Phil.* 25e f., *Laws* 673a f., 734s, 795e, etc.

46. *Rep.* 404a f., 411c f., *Laws* 796c f., 813b f., 830c f., 832d f., 942d f.

47. *Rep.* 405 ff., *Tim.* 88b f.

48. *Apol.* 24d f., *Phaedr.* 245a, 268e ff., *Laws* 829c f.

49. *Rep.* 370bc, 374a f., 394d f., 397d f., 592b, *Laws* 846d f.

50. *Rep.* 399e f., 401a f., *Laws* 659 ff., 800 ff., 814d ff., cf. R. C. Lodge, *Plato's Theory of Ethics*, Ch. IX.

51. *Monadologie*, sect. 58.

52. *Anabasis*, III i 46 ff., cf. Homer, *Iliad* II, 204.

53. *Rep.* 592, *Laws* 737b f., 745 ff., 902e ff.

54. *Rep.* 422d f., 462a ff., 546 ff., *Laws* 739b f.

55. *Laws* 656c f., 764d f., 801b–802c, 817a, cf. *Symp.* 209a–212a, *Rep.* 377c ff., 401a f.

56. *Laws* 656 f., 664b f., 699b f., 700d f., 797a ff. Cf. P.—M. Schuhl, *Platon et*

l'art de son temps, 1934, Ch. I and Appendix I. (This study is admirably exact, but its studied factuality does not [I think] altogether exclude the possibility of a somewhat different interpretation of the evidence.)

57. *Soph.* 253d f., cf. Schuhl, *op. cit.*, pp. 7–9.

58. *Hipp. Min.* 368 f.

59. *Menex.* 235ab, *Rep.* 595b, 596c, 598d f., 601b, 602d, 607c, e, *Phaedr.* 244a, 245a, *Soph.* 235a.

60. *Prtg.* 322c f., 324e f., *Rep.* 370a f., 374a f., 394d f., 397d f., etc., *Laws* 846 f.

61. *Rep.* 399c f.

62. The two referred to are the Dorian and the Phrygian (*Rep.* 398d f.). These are used (by a professional convention) in connexion with courage and temperance, respectively. But it is quite plain that the music used in connexion with the Symposia of the model city will have to be the 'harmonies' conventionally used in connexion with revelry; and that the music used in connexion with the mating-dances of the model city will be erotic rather than (let us say) processional in character; and it is not entirely certain that the 'wilder' music associated with Corybantic dancing, will be excluded from the model city—that is, if it is prescribed as a feature of (approved) medical treatment. Presumably also the music used in connexion with the exhibitions of comedy, whose observation is allowed to grave citizens in the model city, will not be either Dorian or Phrygian. The music of the model city will thus NOT be confined strictly to 'marching-chants and hymn-tunes' (*Laws* 671 f., 771e f., 772d, 790d f., 816c f., cf. *Rep.* 403a, 458d f., 459e f., 571b f.).

63. *Crat.* 414b f., 417d f., 421d, *Rep.* 397d, 399a f., 401d f., 611cd, *Soph..* 253a, *Phil.* 17bc, 55d f., *Laws* 802c f., 812d f.

64. *Laws* 846d f., cf. *Prtg.* 319b f., *Rep.* 397de. Cf. R. C. Lodge, *Plato's Theory of Education*, pp. 16–21, which discusses carpentry in its artisan context.

65. For 1, see *Rep.* 428c, 597b, d, *Soph.* 266c.

For 2, see *Rep.* 346a f.

For 3, see *Rep.* 522c f., 602c, *Pol.* 283d f., *Phil.* 55d ff., *Laws* 643c.

66. For 4, see *Rep.* 421e, 466e f., 537a, *Laws* 643b f.

For 5, see *Rep.* 349d f., 369d ff., 372e f., 377, 386 ff., 401, 455c f., *Laws* 801c f.

For 6, see *Prtg.* 319b f., compared with *Laws* 657a f., 659d f., 660a, 738b f., 764c f., 772a f., 799a, 801c f., 802a f., 809, 811b f., 812c f., 816bc, 817d, 828ab, 829c f., 848d f., 934. (This evidence is hardly [I think] consistent with the modern interpretation (e.g. *J. of Educ.*, 1945, pp. 58, 164, 224) of Plato's model city government as 'totalitarian'.)

67. *Rep.* 530d f., *Laws* 657ab, 764c f., 804c f., 810 ff., 835a.

68. *Crat.* 424c f., *Phil.* 17c f., *Laws* 669d f., cf. 657a f.

69. *Laws* 785b, 942 f. (cf. *Rep.* 374 ff., and *Laws* 743d f., 794d f., 813e f., 921e f.).

70. *Laws* 715c, 729d, 730e, 762d f., 822e f., 919e, 935c, 942a f., cf. 961a, 964b.

71. *Laws* 807c f., cf. 664d.

72. *Laws* 808c, 817e f., 951d f., 961a f., 966c, 968a f.

73. *Laws* 754c f., 945b ff., 952a f.

74. *Laws* 945b–948a. Seventy-five is the age set for retirement of certain of the higher magistrates (*Laws* 746c). Sixty is the age set for retirement of 'travelling inspectors' (*Laws* 951d). Sixty is the earliest possible retiring age for an ex-director of education (*Laws* 765d f., compared with 951d). It is conceivable, however, that ex-directors may be called upon to act as members of the nocturnal

council indefinitely. There is a suggestion that, while the director of education holds office primarily for five years (with a further five years as 'emeritus' on the nocturnal council), i.e. from fifty to fifty-five (or, as emeritus, to sixty), those 'released from office' (*hoi apēllagmenoi*, 951e), who would be fifty-six, or sixty-one, or sixty-six years of age (and so on), might still be expected to serve as councillors (in one capacity, if not in another); for they are certainly 'the best of the citizens'. In Plato's model city, there is no rest for the good! Like the idea of good, they work overtime.

75. *Rep.* 552a f., 554c f., 555e f., etc., *Laws* 807c f., 822e f., 900 e f., etc.

76. *Laws* 643d f., cf., *Rep.* 590c f., *Soph.* 229 f.

77. *Rep.* 395c f., 540a f., *Laws* 811c f., 817b f.

78. *Prtg.* 347c f., *Symp.* 209a, *Rep.* 397a f., 398a, 401b f., 424d f., 475c f., 586b f., 595 ff., 605a f., 607 f., *Phaedr.* 275d ff., *Laws* 664b ff., 800 ff., 834e ff., 857c f., etc.

79. *Ion* 530b, 534d f., *Prtg.* 339b, *Rep.* 391a, 595b f., 607a, c, *Phaedr.* 234e f., 264a f., *Theaet.* 152e f., *Laws* 658d f., 669d f., 776e f.

Painting adds colours to an otherwise bald and unconvincing outline drawing, or to a marble statue, and embellishes it, conferring upon it the semblance of life: by using pigments in nature which resemble the things imitated (*Crat.* 424d f., 434a, *Phaedr.* 275d, *Critias* 107b f., *Pol.* 277bc, *Laws* 769a f., 923c 1). As to the 'semi-illiterate verse', I think Plato regards the civic life of his model city as the finished poem, while journalistic virtuosity in verse-making would be the truly semi-illiterate verse (*Laws* 811b f., 817a f.).

80. *Rep.* 410b ff., *Tim.* 87e ff., *Pol.* 310d ff., *Phil.* 61b ff.

81. Namely, the art of choric dancing, expressing the community spirit in the three parallel forms of gesture (1, dance-movements, 2, song-movements, 3, rhythmic word-chants). See *Crat.* 422e ff., *Rep.* 398c ff., 401 f., *Laws* 654a, 657c f., 664b f., 669d f., 802b f.).

82. *Laws* 881d f.

83. *Laws* 850a f., 881c 2–3, 914a 6–8. Cf. 'Plato and Freedom', pp. 94–98.

84. *Phaedr.* 267e ff.

85. *Rep.* 420c f., *Soph.* 235e f., *Laws* 668d f. (For 'blue horses', I have in mind the well-known picture with this title, painted by Franz Marc [1887–1916]).

86. *Prtg.* 347c f., *Rep.* 377c ff., etc., *Phaedr.* 234e f., 264a f., 277e f., *Laws* 800b f. 810e f.

87. *Phaedr.* 266c f.

88. *Phaedr.* 269d ff.

89. *Phaedr.* 266bc (*ei men orthōs ē mē, theos oide*), 273e (*phasin hoi sophōteroi hēmōn*), 274a (*epicheironti kalon*), 274c f. (Socrates's story of Theuth), seems, while serious in doctrine, to exhibit an ironical tone. Commentators and modern interpreters generally take the doctrine very seriously, and omit all consideration of the irony. Also 277c (*kath'hoson pephuke . . .*). For the irony, cf. *Crat.* 396d f., 399a, 400a, 407e, 428c.

90. *Phaedr.* 269e f., *Symp.* 211e f., *Rep.* 535c f., 540a f., *Laws* 968c f.

91. *Symp.* 209 ff., *Phaedr.* 278ab, *Laws* 811, 817, 858c f., 957c f.

92. *Laws* 964b ff., cf. 885d ff., 909a f. For evidence of Plato's view of artists as being especially concerned with 'wisdom and virtue', i.e. the life of States regulated by law, cf. *Symp.* 209a ff.

93. *Laws* 811b f., 815c, 817b f.

Croce would not accept Plato's view that you can make of life itself (e.g. in the model city) an art. For Croce, there exists a sharp distinction between the economic and ethical (practical) life, on the one hand, and aesthetic experience, on the other (cf. e.g. Croce, *op. cit.*, p.50. 'We condemn as erroneous every theory which annexes the aesthetic activity to the practical. . . . The aesthetic fact is altogether completed in the expressive elaboration of impressions. When we have achieved the word within us . . . expression is born and complete; there is no need for anything else.' Cf. also pp. 51, 60, 112. Croce agrees that, if one wishes to *publish* his poem or *perform* his musical composition *publicly*, in a given city, he must expect to come to some sort of terms with the economic and ethical position maintained in that city; but this should not, and properly speaking does not, influence an artist's work, *qua* artistic (see esp. pp. 51-53, 59, 61).

In other words, for Croce, it is artistic, to *write* a Utopia. To try to *live* accordingly, is possible, but falls outside 'art'. For Plato, on the other hand, *to live as a citizen of Utopia is artistic*. To *write* a Utopia, however well you write, is a secondary and inferior activity, which *merely* '*imitates*'.

CHAPTER TWELVE

Sensation and Aesthetic Quality

I N the chapters which follow, I propose to bring together for interpretation certain points in Plato's treatment of aesthetics which seem to me not to be accepted by present-day authorities on aesthetics: perhaps because these points are not understood as (I think) Plato understands them. In each of these chapters I select for interpretation topics whose correct understanding throws (as I conceive) further light upon the theory of aesthetics sponsored in the Dialogues.

Do the simpler sense-data and the simpler intellectual patterns have aesthetic quality? Plato says, Yes. John Dewey (for instance) says, No. Is there something aesthetically charming about the whiteness of pure white, the redness of pure red, the purpleness of pure purple? That is to say, when these colours are considered merely as pure colours; entirely apart from questions involving the appropriate place and function of such colours in a wider context, whether pictorial or social? Plato says, Yes. Dewey says, No. Is there something aesthetically charming about a pure tone (such as E in alt., as sung by a Lily Pons, or as produced on a flute or a stringed instrument by a master: again, considered in itself, merely as a pure tone), quite apart from whether it forms the conclusion of a sequence in some musical composition? Plato says, Yes. Dewey says, No. Again, is there something aesthetically charming about the straightness of a straight line, about the curvedness of an ideally perfect circumference of a circle, about the regularity of an ideally perfect isosceles or equilateral triangle? Again, Plato says, Yes. Dewey says, No.

If Plato means what he says in the *Philebus*—and it is said by Socrates, without the slightest suggestion of hesitation, doubt, or ambiguity,[1] and if Dewey means what he says in *Art as Experience*— and it is said very firmly, as well as very clearly and definitely[2]—we are apparently faced by an *impasse*: a flat contradiction of authorities. Let us look into them, and let us make quite sure what each philosopher really means by what he says.

Let us inquire, first of all, what Plato means, what his position involves. It involves something more than a question of simple inspection, something to be settled by an introspective report, made by a trained observer: looking at colours or geometric figures, or listening to pure tones in some psychologist's laboratory. Plato is always reluctant to have us subordinate our reason to our ears or eyes.[3] We will begin, then, by looking into the account of sense-perception which we find in the Dialogues: an account which we have every reason to believe acceptable to Plato himself.[4]

Sensuous perception, as Plato understands it, is a complex process involving at least two chief factors. Of these, the one is physical, the other psychical. Assuming a physical continuum in a state of flux (the position of Ionian science, as expounded by Heraclitus): Let X and Y be two purely physical bodies. Let Z be the body of a living organism with a well-developed brain (and spinal cord), in which is located a centre of self-motion which animates the tissues of the body. This (brain or centre of self-motion) may be regarded as the seat of whatever consciousness the organism may come to possess (the position of Pythagorean science, as expounded by Timaeus); and let X, Y, and Z be in a state of physical interaction.

Motion of X (let us call it, s) affects both Y and Z. It stimulates (in both) 'vibrations', reactions of physical type. Let us call the Y-reactions, r_1 and the Z-reactions, r_2. With certain kinds or degrees of stimulation, s_1, the physical vibrations, r_1 and r_2 are generically indistinguishable. That is to say, the fact that Z is a living organism with a brain, makes no appreciable difference to r_2 (as compared, with r_1); and r_2 makes no ascertainable difference to Z, with its brain (as compared with Y, which has no brain). In a word, the brain (or centre of self-motion which animates the organism) is not affected one way or the other. r_2 is, and remains, precisely as physical as r_1; and if we *must* speak of a Z-consciousness in connexion with the physical process, r_2—we must call it *un*consciousness.[5]

On the other hand, with certain other kinds or degrees of stimulation, s_2, a living organism with a brain, behaves differently from an inanimate body. In both cases, physical vibrations (r_3 in Y and, r_4 in Z) result: much as before. But in the case of Y, nothing further develops. With Z, however, certain further processes, m, involving the brain with its centre of self-motion, make their appearance. In the living organism Z, there are now taking place two specifically distinct kinds of vibratory process. These are: (1) r_{4a}, r_{4b}, r_{4c} . . . , some of which (r_{4a}) do not affect the brain and its centre of self-motion at all. These remain precisely as external and physical as r_1, r_2, and r_3. Others of them, however (r_{4b}, r_{4c}) do somehow affect the brain, or (as Plato puts it) 'penetrate to the seat of consciousness within'.[6]

The second kind of vibratory process (2) consists of the new processes, m_{1a}, m_{1b}, m_{1c} . . . , which are initiated from within the brain, i.e. from the centre of self-motion which animates the bodily tissues of Z. Doubtless some of these m-processes (let us say, m_{1a}) do not connect with the r-processes at all, but remain in what Plato calls 'the intellectual place'. If so, we are not further concerned with them.[7] But certain of the m-processes may connect with certain of the r-processes: in such a way that (in a case symbolized by rm), we may experience consciously the sensation of whiteness. Our consciousness is 'filled with whiteness', and X is being experienced as 'a body which is white'.[8]

The mechanism by which this is effected, as explained in Pythagorean science, is somewhat obscure. The 'vehicle of the soul', centred in the brain, but extending, in its circumference, beyond the circumference of the brain, is pictured by Timaeus as a structure consisting of two revolving circles, one inside the other, touching at two points of their circumferences. The diagram makes one think of a modern gyroscope, but the Greek text does not suggest *axial* rotation.

The function of this structure, with its two revolutions, is to animate the bodily tissues by stabilizing their organic motions and keeping them true to pattern: so that each organic-tissue-motion fulfils its proper function in the life of the organism as a whole, and in the environment with which the organism is interactive.[9]

The body is made up of the elements of fire, water, earth, and air (diagrammed for us as geometrical solids [tetrahedra, icosahedra, cubes, and octahedra, respectively]), held together in accordance with a principle of proportion differing from one species to another.[10] What holds 'the triangles' together and maintains the balance, the specific proportion upon which the health and indeed the life of the organism depend, is the animating principle. As long as, in the organism's interactivity with the environment, the animating principle overcomes the environmental shocks, and maintains the appropriate functioning of the various bodily organs, life persists. When the control of the animating principle weakens, then disease, disintegration, and eventually death, all make their appearance.[11]

It is not the body, but the animating principle which (with the co-operation of bodily sense-organs interacting with changing motions in the environment) apprehends 'whiteness' or 'redness', a particular tonal quality, an olfactory quality, etc. It 'identifies' these, when they impinge upon that one of the two circles which Timaeus calls 'the circle of the same', whose epistemological function seems to be something like the function of the principle of identity in Aristotelian logic.[12]

It 'identifies' by apprehending the *eidos*, the 'form'. Imagine the animating principle conversing (as it were) with itself. 'What (it asks itself) have we here: in this *s*, this stimulus which is disturbing the regular motion-patterns of the organism I am trying to control, and is penetrating right to my own circle?' Using its own immanent categories (viz., similarity [identity], motion, unity, being, etc.) to guide its judgement: the animating principle answers its own question approximately thus: 'This *s* (it says) has tetrahedronal form. This means that it is a kind of fire or brightness. It is in a state of motion. It is flame-coloured, in fact, is an example of redness . . .'[13] The animating principle then proceeds to guide purposively the final reactions of its bodily organism, in accordance with what it conceives to be for the best, in the given situation.[14]

So far, the self-consciousnesss of the animating principle, in association with the immediate reactions of its bodily organism, as stimulated by a given *s*, is being considered cognitively: in its function of 'identifying' this or that (organically amplified) stimulus; catching (as it were) the bird of thought upon the wing, and fitting it into its appropriate pigeon-hole in the mind's cognitive system.[15] But the bodily reactions stimulated by a given *s*, are not necessarily passionless: something that the animating principle registers unemotionally and indifferently as *A* or *B* or *C* (as redness-as-such, as triangularity-as-such, as motion-as-such). On the contrary: bodily reactions can be highly impassioned. The body may be in a state identified by applying the concept of hunger. And this experience is felt (as well as identified) as an example of pain. Provide suitable food. Then, while the body's emptiness is being replenished, the animating principle feels, as well as registers, pleasure.[16] Similarly, when the bodily state is identified by applying the concept of fatigue (a state also experienced as painful), a suitable degree of rest, which reconditions the bodily tissues, is normally apprehended (i.e. enjoyed, as well as registered) as pleasurable.[17]

Among reactions thus identified as pleasurable, we can discriminate, and can select those which are further identified as aesthetical. These may be predominantly sensuous, or predominantly intellectual. Normally (for instance) we find ourselves attracted, strongly attracted, by the natural charm of a human being in the bloom of youth: a Lysis, a Charmides, perhaps an Alcibiades. The reactions of our body to such a stimulus are doubtless non-logical, instinctive, largely racial. In the case of a Charmides, they may be quite recognizably sexual.[18] But our animating principle can (and does normally) distinguish the charm that is aesthetical, from the pull of the appetites and emotions: from passionate *eros*, from the panic of fear, from paralysing horror, from unreasoning rage.[19]

The appetites and emotions have about them a roughness, a crudity, an impulsive violence, an impatience of control, which render those who are swept away by them, un-Hellenic, Barbaric, perhaps infra-human. They become wild, as beasts are wild, with a definite tendency away from orderly patterns of living, a tendency toward frenzied passion, toward utter chaos. They are at the opposite pole from those who possess the vision of the idea, and pursue the life of rational self-control.[20] Only people who let themselves go into their feelings, people who give way to the promptings of appetite, people who are vicious, ill-educated, devoid of insight—in a word, people who are definitely unsuited to the regular rhythms of life in the model city—take pleasure in such relaxed, hysterical, and indeed insensate activites.[21]

Persons of sound aesthetic judgement, on the other hand, are calmer and more self-controlled. They take pleasure in the patterned, well-balanced life of law and order. They move at all times with dignity and restraint. In all they think, say, and do, they guide themselves (as far as is humanly possible) by the vision of the idea. They may (it is true) be little more than puppets, pulled this way and that. But they 'hold fast to the golden cord of reason'.[22] Against the pull of the instincts and animal desires they set the power of the idea; and by organizing their habitual ways of acting, speaking, thinking, and feeling, in accordance with the 'preambles' of civic legislation, they find they can use 'the Muses' as auxiliaries in making of civic living the one great art, the veritable human drama.[23]

No doubt there are many levels of this aesthetical judgement. Not all are capable of philosophy, with its clear vision of the idea. Many can only appreciate what to them is 'ideal beauty', when they see it before them, embodied (as they think) in this or that concrete form. The sensuous, as such,[24] the play of imagery, as such, represents, for most people, as far as they can see their way.[25] Others, like the Pythagoreans, can appreciate the beauty of law, of order, of mathematical patterning.[26] It is only the philosophers who can penetrate to the rationale of the entire range of the beautiful, and can see, behind this or that empirical example, the authentic charm of the transcendental idea. When they have achieved this vision, they realize that the source of our feeling of beauty is everywhere some feeling (however dim and indistinct) of the principle of ideality. It is the philosophers who, once they have clearly beheld this vision, can use it to guide them in constructing patterns for living which will help their less gifted fellow-citizens to live, in their own ways and at their own levels, the 'mixed' or balanced life of civic idealism.[27]

In a word, it is some feeling for the idea of good which is the ultimate support of the aesthetic judgement, throughout the whole of its range. When we look at colours, it is their 'purity' which suggests to us the ideal which (in their way) they embody and suggest. Not every shade of white, of red, of purple, but 'pure' white, 'pure' red, 'pure' purple, i.e. the idea of white, the idea of red, the idea of purple —that is what gives us the feeling of beauty, of aesthetic charm, in colour experiences.[28] So also in the realm of tones. We all distinguish 'pure' tones, 'musical' tones, from mere noise. It is the 'purity' (approximate purity) of certain tones, that suggests to us the latent ideal; and it is only in so far as the tones we hear seem (in their purity) to embody and in some way express that latent ideal, that we experience them as 'charming'.[29]

So also with the more intellectual experiences. It is the approximation to ideal regularity, to quasi-ideal straightness, to quasi-ideal triangularity or circularity, that gives to the figures of geometry (both plane and solid) their characteristic and undeniable charm.[30] It is the approximation to ideal unity, ideal duality, ideal triplicity, etc., which gives to arithmetic, in addition to its utilitarian uses, its aesthetic value, its charm for the philosopher and would-be philosopher.[21] And from what source does philosophy itself receive its charm? Is it not from the dimly felt beauty, dignity, and power of reason on the one hand,[32] and, on the other, of the idea of good?[33] Is it not toward the development of reasoning power, and toward rational insight into the good, that the would-be philosopher is perpetually feeling his way?[34] Is it not of the good, that a Socrates (even before he has finally attained to the vision) is making use: in re-fashioning his life, and indeed the lives of all who are able and willing to respond to the charm of what moves him?[35]

Even in the commonplace instance of a young man like Glaucon, is it not because he attributes to this or that object of his (varying) youthful affections, a quasi-ideal beauty, both of form and of spirit: that he finds himself willing to accept (for the time being, and perhaps as stepping-stones) what are—factually regarded—very imperfect and empirical images of the ideal? Does he not accept them, not finally and in their own right, but in so far as they seem (although with only partial certainty) to present an answer to his quest: a quest, however, which ultimately is transcendental and eternal?[36]

Similarly of the systems of written law to be studied by candidates for administrative positions in the model city. It is not because the laws investigated have empirical actuality (i.e. have been tried out in this or that Hellenic community), that the candidate studies them and is impressed by their charm. It is because (as with the travelling inspector of institutions) the study of them helps him to appreciate and understand better the underlying ideal—the ideal more perfectly embodied in the institutions of the model city, the philosophers' model, that he feels drawn to them and regards them as beautiful.[37]

Let us now return to our starting-point. When Plato declares flatly and without circumlocution that we apprehend beauty, 'absolute' beauty, when we look at a pure white or pure red, when we listen to a pure tone, when we contemplate a perfectly straight line, a perfectly regular triangle or circle:[38] it is not the sensuous, or even the intellectual quality of such experiences that intrigues him— as it might intrigue a Glaucon or some member of the Pythagorean fraternity.[39]

It is not the colouredness of the experience, or its toned-ness, or even its patterned-ness, *as such*, that is (as Plato views the matter) the source of its 'charm'. It is not, in any way, its character *qua* empirical, *merely* empirical, that suggests to us the idea of beauty, of absolute beauty. From the empirical, as such, to the transcendental, as such, there is no possibility of constructing a bridge.[40] To know merely 'what we like', that gay, contrasting colours give us 'pleasure', that tones, dancing with precarious balance upon a meaningless rush of rhythm, 'excite' us, that imitation for imitation's sake (mere baseless mimicry of superficial phenomena devoid of ideal quality), awakens 'pleased recognition' in us—what is all this, but the child's pleasure in anything that attracts his attention, the empty nonsense of a puppet's motions, as he is drawn hither and yon by the pulls of chance? Ask the Pythagoreans, and they will tell you how worthless, how utterly meaningless, such experience is.[41]

What makes our experiences meaningful and worth while, is (according to Plato) always something more than empirical; something transcendental, ideal, absolute. It is the idea of beauty which enables those of us in whom insight into the ideal realm is developing (from its place in the back of our minds), to see some veritable shadow of beauty, some dim approximation, some actual participation, here and there around us; everywhere, indeed, where such participation really exists. And where does it exist? What is the evidence of genuine participation? Our eyes see colours, our ears hear sounds. Where there is 'purity' of colour or of tone, our minds apprehend, in this 'purity', the authentic sign of the ideal. Our eyes see lines and figures drawn on paper. Where there is 'regularity', our minds apprehend the ideal: rectilinearity, triangularity, circularity, the ideal principles, of which the lines and figures used by geometricians are a kind of half-way house between the empirical and the ideal.[42]

That is to say: where there is definiteness of character, simplicity or unity, there is evidence of ideality. Ones, twos and threes, suggest ideality. The indefiniteness of an undetermined 'plurality' does not. It suggests the characterless all-abroadness of chaos. A tetrahedron, octahedron, or cube (the mathematical forms—according to Pythagorean science—of fire, air, and earth, respectively) suggests law and order, ideal patterning. The nondescriptness of pre-cosmic matter (or of indeterminate space) which is not yet anything as definite as 'fire', 'air', or 'earth', does not. That is why something which is not mere indeterminate colour, but is a definite whiteness, a definite redness, and so on (or why something which is not mere patternedness, but a definite straightness, triangularity, or circularity) suggests beauty, absolute beauty. Such experiences exhibit determinate character. They participate directly in ideal quality.[43]

Let us now pass to consider what Dewey means by his statement that elementary *sensa*, when considered in isolation, i.e. apart from a wider context of experience, do *not* possess aesthetic quality.

Aesthetic quality, according to John Dewey, is a resultant which emerges only when a number of conditions are realized. In Aristotelian terminology, it is a conclusion which goes beyond the evidence of its premises, taken singly, but arises from their synthesis or

R

fusion.[44] Not one of its elements, taken in isolation from the rest, possesses aesthetic quality.[45] No shade of 'red', for instance, however 'pure' (supposing that it could be separated—a psychological impossibility[46]—from other experiences, sensuous, emotional, and volitional, and from the objective world[47]), possesses aesthetic quality in its own right. The more you abstract 'red' from all connexions of context, the more it approximates to sterile meaninglessness.[48]

Actually, red is beautiful in our eyes, primarily, when it is apprehended as an integral part of a wider experience: e.g. as the red of this sunset, coming to us as the culmination of a day of labour, largely successful. The 'red' is then expressive of the peacefulness of rest after toil. It glorifies our whole day, dramatizes the human venture, and lends religious significance, a sense of fulfilment through communion, through union with others in origin and destiny, to human life.[49]

In a secondary sense, if we come to think of pure reds, pure whites, pure purples, and the rest of our *sensa* as somehow beautiful; we should realize that it is always in virtue of their wider fringe of associations that *sensa* come to be credited with this attribute. It is the 'organic reverberations' of countless sunsets (and other consummatory experiences) enjoyed in the past, which lend to a perceived 'red' or 'purple' its (secondary) aesthetic halo.[50]

To suppose, then, that the elementary *sensa*, as isolated, are beautiful in their own right, and that the beauty of a sunset can be regarded as a 'synthetic' whole, an aggregate constructed of elements all possessing aesthetic quality *per se*, is to commit the traditional fallacy of *hysteron-proteron*, placing the cart before the horse.[51]

So also with lines and angles, and indeed with the regular figures of plane and solid geometry. It is from our wider experiences that lines (of whatever sort) derive what we sometimes think of as their 'immediate' aesthetic qualities. In fact, it is easy to realize that they seem to have analogous moral qualities. That is how we come to think of lines as 'wavering' or 'majestic', as 'upright' or 'crooked', as 'earthbound' or 'aspiring', as 'intimate' or 'coldly aloof', as 'enticing' or 'repellent'. They carry with them (as Dewey puts it) the properties of objects and situations from which we have abstracted them.

If we are passionately devoted to the study of geometry, and are conscious that its applications enable us to solve theoretical problems, as well as to design patterns of interest and usefulness in daily life: all kinds of feelings associated with a sense of superiority, and of intellectual brotherhood, will soon become an apparently integral part of our experience of the straight lines, the right angles, and the wonderful curves with which we operate. That is why the ancient Pythagoreans came to have an almost religious feeling for their pet right-angled triangle.[52]

In a word, the apparently 'immediate' aesthetic and moral qualities of 'straight' and 'square', as of curves that are 'dangerous', are all derived, by association, from objective situations much more complex than anything abstractly linear.[53] They are almost precisely analogous to the apparently 'immediately' perceived non-visual qualities of 'wetness', 'slipperiness', or 'coldness' of the blues and greens, whites and yellows, used in painting a seascape or a picture of winter ice.[54]

Let us proceed to compare the position thus indicated, with what Plato says. Plato, as far as concerns the aesthetic values which become attached to colours, tones, and lines, from the wider contexts in which they are experienced (e.g. in the context of life in the model city), says much the same as Dewey. Plato's model citizens live a very full life. Their capacities and interests as human beings, are all stimulated and integrated. In the model city, art is not a thing apart: to be sought chiefly in museums, concert-halls, and picture-galleries. Every phase of the citizen's life is graceful, harmonious, and balanced. It is throughout aesthetically attractive. It has the colours of health, and the dignity and serenity which come from a satisfying adjustment to a well-selected environment, and from a consciousness of togetherness in a great community drama directed by a Leader in whom all have unswerving confidence: God.[55]

In a life of such overall richness and charm, the dawns and sunsets are suffused with a glow which can only be indicated, suggested, and symbolized by the red and yellow pigments of a technician's painting-palette. It is the glow of hope, of faith, of love of the community. Such reds and yellows, transfigured by the imagination, are not experienced apart from the life of model citizenship. That life enhances, and permeates with its values, the tones and harmonies of the ritual chants, the rhythms of the processional marches, the dances and exercises of the sports grounds, the lines and figures of the students' mathematics, the talk and general behaviour of all who dedicate themselves to their beloved community.[56]

So far, there is nothing (I think) about which Plato and Dewey would quarrel, or (even remotely) tend to disagree. Equate, in principle, the life of an idealized Athens-plus-Sparta-plus-Corinth (or

Cnossus), with the life of an idealized American democracy (Middle-West style)—and why not?—and while there are (of course) certain differences in matters of detail between an ancient shadow-play and modern television, or between the congregation in an ancient temple of Apollo and the congregation in a modern religious centre (pragmatist style): would it not prove perfectly feasible to translate most of the 'preambles' of Plato's institutions into the terminology of John Dewey, and most of the glorification of 'communion' and 'participation' thought to characterize Dewey's (idealized) democracy into the language of the *Republic* and *Laws*? Would not Dewey feel about as much at home in the model city as Socrates would in an idealized version of Chicago or New York?[57] Both philosophers feel shocked at the crudity, the superficiality, and the blindness of the so-called 'democracies' of their own time. Both call for a radical revulsion from the 'mad scramble for pleasure and power' which characterizes (as both insist) the mass of their contemporary fellow-citizens.[58] Both philosophers believe that only when 'philosophers are kings', i.e. when humanity is re-educated to the point of participating in the fundamental values of experience, as revealed to 'the eye of the mind', will there be a possibility of surcease from human ills.[59]

So far, there is no serious difference in principle between the ancient and the modern philosopher. Let us now look a little more closely at what Plato means by his 'pure' colours and tones, and by his 'ideally' straight lines. Plato has no thought, and no vestige of a thought, of trying to 'isolate' the experience of 'red' or of 'Middle C' or of a 'right angle', and of studying it 'absolutely by itself'—whatever that might mean. Such a problem might conceivably intrigue an experimental psychologist, physiologist, or physicist. It might seem worth trying, to find out how close you could get to a 'direct' experience of a so-called 'simple idea of sensation'. You might have a bit cut out of one of your sensory nerves, and spend years in studying your reactions as the severed ends gradually grew together again. You might play tricks with the rods and cones of your retinal apparatus, or with the apparatus involved in hearing. You might try to cut out the effect of memory images, and even of the imagination. Why not? No doubt there is plenty of good clean fun to be got out of such attempts.

But nothing of that sort means much to Plato. Even the Pythagorean science of Plato's time does not seem to think it could be done, at least with colours;[60] and the Heraclitean scientists, whose views on this point were presumably accepted by Plato, definitely regard sensation as, in principle, complex. It results from a number of factors, some external, and some internal to the organism. So far also, then, there is no serious difference between the ancient and the modern philosopher.[61]

In a word, Plato understands (1) that our experiences, all complex, are recognizably, at this point or that, enhanced, aesthetically enriched, by our participation in wider social and biosocial wholes. The red of a sunset, while doubtless aesthetically satisfying even to a Spartan warrior, is more satisfying to a cultured Athenian—and still more so to a member of the model city. The richer the life, the more it enriches, by a sort of irradiation, all its elements. But Plato also thinks (2) that, while you can never, by any device, eliminate this contextual enhancement, there is something about the red, as such, actually as 'red', that is aesthetically satisfying: to a Socrates, no less than to a Cleinias, a Megillus, or a travelling professor from Athens.[62]

So also music is doubtless exhilarating as a way of participating in community feeling. But its tones, simply as tones, as Middle C or E in alt., have (Plato thinks) a beauty or charm of their own. As a philosopher, you may learn to disapprove of this or that kind of poetry, music, painting, or dancing. But as a human being, you still fall under the spell of the artist whose work you have learnt to condemn. His wizardry somehow brings out the 'absolute' charm, which belongs to the rhythms, the tones, or the colours, in their own right.[63] It is apparently this 'absolute' attribute of the sense-qualities that is called in question by the statements in Dewey's authoritative book. Let us try to understand more precisely what is meant.

As to the factuality of the experience to which Plato refers, it is not too difficult and remote for us at the present day. Any concert-goer can distinguish the tones produced by a beginner (or by a relatively unmusical performer), from the tones produced, on the selfsame instrument, by a great artist. This is altogether obvious in the case of the violin. But it is also verifiable in the case of the piano. The artist's 'touch' brings out tonal qualities which must, surely, be 'there' —or how could he bring them out?—and as to their beauty or charm, there seems to be no doubt. When a Heifetz is playing the violin, or a Schnabel is playing a piano concerto of Beethoven's— quite apart from the broader and deeper beauties which are due to the inspiration of the composer, there is a magical quality about the tones, as such. We (like Plato) would naturally call it, their 'purity'. It is so wonderful that, on listening to a Schnabel record (e.g. of the

'Emperor' Concerto), we find ourselves asking if, perhaps, he is playing on a very special kind of instrument, something altogether finer than the usual concert piano. So too a Madame Novaës playing (before our eyes) a theme by Glück, makes us wonder how she manages to produce, from what we plainly see to be a piano, these entirely amazing tones.

Similarly with colours. We all know that if we look at a lake-scene through brown or green glasses, the outlines of the rocks and trees stand out more definitely. The colours, the greens and blues, become brighter and purer than colours normally seen by the naked eye. They are like the colours brought out by a colour-photograph of the same scene; or like the colours reflected in a medium like the film of a soap-bubble. Or we may try to see 'black', by looking, first, at ordinary black paper, and then comparing it with the laboratory 'Hering black' of a prepared surface which absorbs more of the light-rays, and then with the black of a piece of thick black velvet (which is even more light-absorbent), and finally with the black of a 'Dunkel-tonne', i.e. a box lined with black velvet, which is supposed to be about as far as one can go in absorbing light-rays. Each new experience makes the former 'black' look, by comparison, greyish, even medium-greyish; and it is not difficult to imagine the curve of deeper and deeper 'blacks' continued beyond the Dunkel-tonne 'black' to a black even more 'pure'. Such ultra-pure 'colours' (if we may—like the Greeks—think of 'black' as a colour), when compared with the less 'pure' shades of the same hue, seem to us to possess a 'beauty' or aesthetic charm; and this appears to be quite independent of the beauty which might be conferred by a social or biosocial context.

So much for the factuality of the experience of 'purity' in the case of tones and colours. How does Plato 'explain' the aesthetic charm involved? Consider a Pythagorean scientist, experimenting with his monochord. He is looking for analogies between (1) the sound-vibrations he can produce on his instrument and (2) mathematical patternings, ratios which he can express in a definite numerical formula.[64] It is immediately obvious, that he can produce an indefinite number of such vibrations; and that, if he abstracts from the way in which the 'sounds' so produced affect, or do not affect, the musical artist's ear, any one of them is as susceptible of scientific investigation, as any other. Mathematically speaking, a Pythagorean, if he was willing to disregard the preferences of the musical ear, could construct n mathematically precise scales: basing the units (notes) of these scales on *any* intervals, large or small, that he might (arbitrarily) select. Such scales would doubtless correspond to progressions of vibrations that could be produced on his monochord, and (to that extent) verified.

However, as is well known, the Pythagorean scientist, like other scientists of Plato's time, does not proceed in this lordly way. He is looking for analogies between (1) mathematical patterns and (2) phenomena, not merely perceptible by the senses, but regarded as significant for the life-purposes of human beings. The arts are all relative to the desires and interests of men, as men interact with their environment; and this affects the art of music.[65] Musicians can doubtless hear a very large number of sounds, such as the experimenter can produce on his monochord. But only a few, actually a very few, of these stand out as suitable for the purposes of the music of a given time and place. Practising musicians have a feeling, both for their pitch, and for their tonal quality; and they use that feeling to guide their empirical efforts at tuning their tetrachords rightly.

What is this rightness? It is something that the trained musical ear can listen for, and can recognize, when it hears it. This is not arbitrary. It is something which technical musicians agree among themselves to accept, as in the order of nature. If you tried to be individual, and insisted upon being arbitrary: tuning the strings of your tetrachord a little more tensely or laxly than your fellow-artists, you would be considered, not more, but less, of a musician. In a word, a musician just has to accept certain definite, distinct tones as 'given', as sense-data. These are what they are. After they have been standardized by the rules of the musicians' guild, they have to be taken as final.[66]

These, then, are the data which the Pythagorean scientist accepts. For these he tries to find mathematical analogies. He has no difficulty in counting, reducing to a numerical formula, the vibrations of his monochord (which produce the standardized tones). He proceeds to look for wider mathematical patterns which shall be analogous to the relations recognized by musicians as subsisting between certain notes of their accepted scales. He discovers the mathematical formula for the concords of the octave, of the fourth, and of the fifth (apparently, not of the third). He can also work out the numerical relations of the other tones of the Hellenic scales, and can look around him, in *rerum natura*, for further analogies.

The Pythagorean, Timaeus, develops (with mathematical detail) an analogy between a Greek musical scale, and the intervals of the heavenly bodies investigated in Pythagorean astronomy. The 'notes' of the celestial scale (if you can call them that) are not verifiable; for they are not audible to human ears. Nevertheless, the fact that the numerical intervals between them correspond somewhat precisely to the intervals between the notes of the human scale, suggests interesting possibilities. These are speculative, since they cannot be verified. But at any rate, there seems to be a parallelism here between the patterns of a series of human sense-data, and the patterns of the great world; and it is easy to suggest that a human music, consciously based upon cosmic standards, might have even greater significance for human beings, than harmonies and sequences resting on human feeling (i.e. on 'pleasure') alone.[67]

Pythagoreanism is a way of life; and it is characteristic of Pythagoreans to urge that human beings should (wherever possible) 'imitate' the patterned rhythms of the cosmos, and should achieve thereby a kind of satisfaction which is at least aesthetic.[68] Practising musicians will doubtless still continue to meet and agree upon the rules of their craft. They will still take pleasure (both as individuals and as members of their guild) in producing and in recognizing the tones, scales, and other patterns characteristic of their way of life. But they will also enjoy a deeper feeling of satisfaction from their faith that Pythagorean music is not superficial play, but 'imitates' and to some extent reproduces the tones and patterns of the great world around them. Their art is based upon something of cosmic significance.[69]

Beyond this, members of the Pythagorean brotherhood do not go. In spite of their mathematical techniques, and the speculative possibilities opened up by the discovery of such analogies, they keep pretty close to the facts of sensory experience. Anything that seems likely to lead beyond the sense-data themselves, and beyond the social experience which standardizes the rules for the successful practice of their arts, is left a little vague and undeveloped. No doubt, there is something 'there'. But it is prudent for human beings to stick to their techniques, and to leave the ultimate background—to itself.[70] Mythology, religion, and poetry are (after all) not science. It is better, on the whole, for the members of the brotherhood to trust to their sense of fraternity. A mystical feeling of loyalty to their way of life as a brotherhood, assisted by acceptance of the *'ipse dixits'* of their leader, Pythagoras, will suffice to occupy the background. As to their outlook as individuals, they will do well to converge upon the solution of individual problems as these arise. They can apply scientific method to the problems of health and disease, of birth and growth, of senescence and death; in a word, to the problems which are of concern to biosocial humanity.[71]

So far also, there is not much about which Pythagorean thought (as reflected in the Dialogues of Plato) and pragmatic thought (as reflected in the writings of John Dewey) would have occasion to quarrel. Dewey too has no doubt that there is a certain 'parallelism' between human value-patternings and the patterns of the great world. And Dewey too is a little vague, doubtless deliberately so, about speculations which seem to lead away from science, into the field of the mythological, the poetical, and the religious. Dewey too is quite sure about the wisdom of trusting to our sense of human fraternity, or (as he likes to express it) 'democracy'. And Dewey too is entirely convinced that, with an almost mystical acceptance of this sense of the value of (idealized) 'democracy' as a background, there should go a forward-looking concentration upon the individual and group solution of biosocial problems, as these arise, by the application of scientific method.

But at this point, we have to register the beginnings of a divergence between the ancient thinkers and the modern. Where the Pythagoreans are content (for the most part) to accept and contemplate, and to derive from such contemplative acceptance a broad aesthetic satisfaction; there is no evidence of this sort of attitude about modern pragmatism. There may be a broad satisfaction which can be called aesthetic. But it is aesthetic in a different way. It is aesthetic in both cases, in so far as the broad, total experience of integration is concerned. But where the ancients are willing to contemplate and accept, the modern seems determined to act. He reconsiders, rejects, and experiments, in order to find more satisfying ways of interacting with nature; and this modern attitude does not fit in with anything which we find in the ancient world.[73]

The Pythagorean imitates and conforms. The modern thinker also conforms—but chiefly to the impulses, the biosocial impulses, which he regards as fundamental in his own nature. Science has armed him with weapons which enable him to meet the environment upon more nearly equal terms. His attitude is indeed shot through with a sense of objectivity.[74] But he does not propose to yield priority (with 'natural piety' or anything of the sort) to the patterns, however powerful, found existing in an external and conceivably hostile nature. For him, the patterns implicit in human nature come first. It is human needs, the human life-cycle, and human satisfactions

which, in the eventual resolution of their conflict with the environment, come to occupy, in his integrated and broadly aesthetic
experience, the dominant place.[75]

Here, then, is the beginning of one line of divergence. As to the
other, that is, as to whether reds and purples, Middle Cs and isosceles
triangles, have a beauty of their own, a charm which is independent
of the penumbra which comes to them from their life-context, the
difference is not yet as great as might (at a first glance) appear. In
virtue of the 'parallelism' between human patterns and some of the
patterns of the great world (a parallelism as acceptable to Dewey as to
the Pythagoreans), it could be claimed that the aesthetic satisfaction
taken in pure or vivid, sharply characterized, tones and colours—is
primarily a function of their cosmic, rather than of their biosocial,
significance. What enriches our perceptual experience, and raises it
to the aesthetic level, is nature: nature shining through and enhancing, glorifying our human experience with its more powerful
and more perfect illumination.[76] Nature's tones and rhythms come
through in our best music, and nature's laws achieve formulation in
our geometry and arithmetic, and so bestow significance on our
science no less than on our arts. It is all empirical, is readily verified,
and induces (in ancient and modern philosophers alike) contemplative acceptance of man's place in the scheme of things.[77] The only
difference is between the ancient tendency to conform, and the
modern tendency to experiment and (where possible) to control.

Plato, however, goes further. He is not satisfied with the empiricism characteristic of the Pythagoreans, and with their readiness to
concentrate upon the solution of problems which are biosocial and
relate to a possible verification in sensory experience. He expects his
academically trained students to speculate boldly; to interest themselves in problems which transcend any sort of empirical, sensuous
verification.[78]

There is a highly intriguing analogy between (1) the patterns of
visual experience (with its vivid colours), and (2) the patterns of
auditory experience (with its vivid tones). To an inquirer who is not
afraid to be an intellectual, this analogy is most suggestive. At times,
Socrates (in his youth) is inclined to think that the Pythagoreans are
right. It may be (he says) that these sensuous distinctions are to be
accepted as merely empirical, 'such as the senses reveal them to us'.[79]
Tonal intervals have, indeed, their law. This can doubtless be formulated in mathematical terms. But it is perhaps going too far, to
speak of the 'colours' of music. It is audacious, to look for a kind of

colour-scale, with precise intervals showing where red leaves off and yellow begins, where yellow leaves off and green begins, where green leaves off and blue begins. It is too bold, to formulate precise mathematical rules for constructing colour-mixtures such as purple or orange. There does not seem to be any definite way of tackling this sort of problem experimentally. Perhaps it is wiser to let the speculative suggestion drop, and leave the whole matter where it belongs: in hands more than human.[80] So Timaeus; and Socrates, as a mere listener to the great scientist, is inclined to agree with him. Even in his maturity, Socrates does not disagree about the colour-scale possibility. At least, laboratory experimentation does not seem promising in this field.[81]

But in the *Republic*, where Socrates definitely withdraws from empiricism and expresses a convinced enthusiasm for transcendental investigations resting upon pure logic or dialectic, the non-empirical solution of purely speculative problems is made a regular part of the higher education offered to all members of the 'golden' class, the future philosopher-kings and philosopher-queens.[82] In the *Philebus*, the latest Dialogue published in Plato's lifetime, the tonal qualities are added unhesitatingly to the lines and figures of mathematics; and the visual qualities, the pure colours, are added, with equal lack of hesitation, to the tonal qualities. All alike are regarded as participating in ideal quality.

The vivid red or purple we see with our eyes, the vivid tones we hear with our ears, are like the lines and figures used by geometers. They are a kind of half-way house between the (impure) sensory experience on the one hand, and the ideal experience attributed to pure reason, on the other. The geometer reasons, not about the triangle he sees, drawn before him; but about the ideal or quasi-ideal figures he conceives in his rational imagination. So the artist paints, not with pigments prepared for his use, the empirical mixtures of earth and water, but with the ideally vivid colours conceived in his artistic imagination.

So too the musician composes with his mind set, not upon the empirically strained chords of his everlastingly unsatisfactory tetra-chord, or the almost fiendishly unsatisfactory vent-holes of his empirical flute, but upon the ideal tones of a transcendental realm (lying beyond the physically cosmic realm itself) conceived by his artistic imagination. The 'purity' of the tones he hears, suggests to his mind the ideal tonal quality of an ultra-cosmic scale, with its utterly perfect notes. This is the realm which opens itself to the artistic imagination, no less than to the purely rational imagination of the trained philosopher. It is the ultra-transcendental charm of the ideal realm, which guides him in his life as an artist. This is true of the genuinely inspired painter or poet, of the genuinely inspired musician or statesman, and of those who, whether as citizens or as magistrates, play their part in the inspired drama of the model city.[83]

The aesthetic halo which we apprehend in the presence of a beautiful youth or maiden, in the presence of a noble action, in the presence of a beautiful system of laws or a beautifully reasoned theorem, hovers before our senses whenever, in our simplest experiences, we sense the 'purity' of a colour or tone, the strictness of a straight line or circle. Once we have really apprehended the transcendental principle of ideality, of ideal beauty, we become able to see, even in our simplest experiences, the authentic mark of the ideal.[84] We do not (like the Pythagoreans) merely 'imitate', merely copy actual, physical models which seem finer than our human faculties can, of themselves, produce. We participate directly, through our artistic intuition, in the ideals which transcend, not merely human senses, but also the verifiable facts of the cosmic world. It is as so living, that we become practitioners of the 'science' which can apprehend, as Plato says, 'beauty as such'.[85]

The truly artistic life is not (as Plato sees it) a *vita contemplativa*. It is not a life withdrawn from activity and concentrated upon perception[86] or reflexion.[87] It is the life which realizes in practice the ideals which it apprehends. The citizens of the model city are themselves the *personae* of a drama which is, precisely, ideal community living. They live artistically. They project themselves into their rôles. They make, each of them, an individual contribution to the integrated life of the whole. The general citizens, indeed, are living in a kind of dream-*aura*. They are all dreaming parts of one and the same dream. But their life is not a mere dream, like the life of those who are blindly impelled by the impersonal forces of pleasure (as such), or wealth or power (as such). It is a dream which has a sense of guidance toward a final, ideal vision. This vision they are capable of apprehending (for the most part) only through art. They are helped by the music, the architecture, the marches and rituals which are an ever-present feature of their life.[88]

In their life of dramatic community action, they have a sense of its rationale, of the idea of good toward which, and under whose guidance, they are working. They understand that, so far as the vision can be grasped clearly and distinctly, and can be reasoned about in conceptual terms, their leaders (the members of the golden class who have been selected and educated for that especial purpose) are penetrating as far as human beings can be expected to penetrate.[89] But it is not merely in the pauses between activities, the pauses for reconditioning and reflexion, that they are conscious of this. There *are* such pauses; but the pauses are pulsations in the onward movement; and it is in the forward movement of the whole community that human living is genuinely aesthetic.[90]

It is at this point, where transcendentalism definitely comes in, that a writer like John Dewey diverges finally and unmistakably from a writer like Plato. Both have the sense of a community dream: a dream in which fellow-citizens seek to live up to the community ideal. But Dewey's dream is, and remains, deliberately empirical; while Plato's dream is, and remains, deliberately transcendental. Dewey believes that Plato (and others of his way of thinking) go too far, that they really lose themselves in the mists of the higher idealism. Plato believes that men like Dewey (such as the humanists led by Protagoras and Gorgias, and to a slight extent the Pythagorean fraternity) do not go far enough, that they fail (for that reason) to attain to the highest possible human enlightenment.

This divergence, then, we recognize. How does it affect our question as to whether the elementary *sensa*, the reds and purples, the Middle Cs, and the straight lines and geometric figures, have or have not aesthetic quality? For Plato and the citizens of his model city, *every* human experience, so far as integrated into ideal community living, participates in the higher ideals. Sunsets in the model city are brighter than elsewhere. Music in the model city is more wonderful, more truly enjoyable, than the music of other communities, communities not permeated by the higher idealism. Geometry pursued by the selected candidates for the highest possible development of insight for the service of the ideal community, is more meaningful than the content of a compulsory school course in elementary mathematics. Every detail of such experiences, so far as it leads upwards toward the ideal vision, every pure colour, tone, or line, participates in ideal beauty. It is precisely in so far as it does so, that it is itself magically charming. That is the constant view of the mature Socrates and his associates.[91]

How would it be with persons who (unlike Socrates and his disciples) have not yet opened their minds to the ideal vision, or have closed them to anything 'transcendental'? Is red or purple (as such) always and under all circumstances possessed of a unique magic, an absolute charm, when viewed by a young Cleinias or Charmides, or by an intellectual of the humanist stamp symbolized by Protagoras or Gorgias? Are the numbers, the ones, twos, and threes of arithmetic, are the lines and figures of geometry, always magical, charming, beautiful, to the schoolboy, if his interest is perhaps in school sports rather than in study; or to the practical man of affairs who has outgrown his school enthusiasms?[92]

The answer is, No. All such persons, and this includes highly cultivated concertgoers and the habitués of art-galleries too, regard the alleged charm or beauty of *any* part of our experience as a function of *all* the factors which enter into the situation. In one situation, purple is 'the most beautiful of the colours'. In another, it would be quite out of place. For such persons, aesthetic quality is (as with John Dewey and so many others) *always* a matter of the context.[93] No aspect of experience possesses aesthetic quality in its own right, but only in association with other aspects in the wider context. For such persons, red, however characteristically incarnadined, however intense the 'purity' of its hue, is devoid of 'absolute' or transcendental value. There remains for it only the empirical consecration, which the emotionally guided selection of an empirical artist's hand can bestow.

In a word, it is only for a transcendentalist that the tones, colours, and lines of our experience have an 'absolute' aesthetic value. For all others, they have necessarily only the contextual values which belong to an experience which is through and through empirical.[94]

NOTES

1. *Phil.* 51c f., 52e f.

2. *Art as Experience* (New York, Minton Balch, 1934), p. 120, 'Qualities of sense have esthetic quality—not in isolation but in their connections; as interacting, not as simple and separate entities.' So also B. Croce (*Aesthetic as Science of Expression* . . .), p. 163, refers to Plato's view of 'colours and sounds as possessing beauty in themselves' with complete disagreement.

3. *Rep.* 531ab, *Theaet.* 184b f. Dewey (*op. cit.*, pp. 120–121) refers to 'laboratory conditions', to prove that colours are never directly experienced in isolation. I [R.C.L.] suppose he means, as Green, for instance, if observed under special conditions of apparatus which make the visual field terminate in a sharp edge (which produces a contrast-effect) has, Dewey says, 'a bluish edge'.

I do not understand Plato to maintain anywhere that his position, at any point, rests upon faith in the possibility of 'experiencing directly' a single *sensum* in complete 'isolation' from other *sensa*, from relations, and from the observer's own total organic, and indeed total intellectual response.

I suppose that 'pure' white or 'pure' purple is (for Plato) a kind of *eidos*, an ideal conceived in the mind, which guides the pictorial artist, as he keeps on painting in, painting out, and painting over, until he at last approximates to his ideal. The artist never quite realizes this ideal, because the empirical pigments are never entirely satisfactory (*Crat.* 434a, *Rep.* 420c, 484d, 501bc, *Tim.* 41d, *Laws* 769a f.). Similarly, empirical musicians keep on tensing and relaxing the strings of their instruments, until they approximate to producing an ideally satisfying tone (*Rep.* 349d f., 531b, cf. *Laws* 657ab). I take it, the 'ideally satisfying' tone or colour would be approximately what was pronounced—officially—satisfactory, in the judgement of 'the wisest and best', i.e. a committee of artistic experts working under the chairmanship of a guardian or philosopher-king.

On the question of simple inspection, perhaps I should refer to the statement of F. C. Tilney, *The Lure of the Fine Arts*, London, 1931. He writes (p. 21), 'Although we enjoy musical symphonies, we can also enjoy sounds for their own sakes in a comparative way. There are qualities of sounds and of colours too. . . .'

4. Aristotle, *Metaph.* 987a 32–35 is, surely, authoritative on this point. If anyone ever could speak with knowledge, it would be Aristotle. For a modern (who was not there, and thus is hardly in a position to speak with dogmatic certainty) to venture to challenge Aristotle on this point is (I take it) the height of absurdity.

5. *Tim.* 64bc, *Theaet.* 191e, *Phil.* 34a. The symbols (used in the interests of clearness) are not Platonic. I use *s* for the stimulus, *r* for the reaction, and *m* for mental. As some slight justification for being thus technical in connexion with Pythagorean science, may I refer to *Tim.* 53c?

6. *Phaedr.* 245d f., *Tim.* 43c, 64b, 67a, *Phil.* 33d f., *Laws* 894d f.

7. *Theaet.* 184b ff., cf. *Phdo.* 79a f.

8. *Theaet.* 153d f., 156d f., cf. 184c f. Cf. also *Tim.* 45b f., *Phil.* 34a.

9. *Tim.* 34b ff., 42cd. A. E. Taylor's erudite *Commentary* throws considerable light upon a number of the admitted obscurities—as to whose interpretation there were serious differences of opinion even in antiquity. There is a tendency among scholars today, to regard *any* interpretation (except, possibly that of the individual scholar who is writing) as inevitably 'amateurish'.

10. *Tim.* 53b ff., with Taylor's *Commentary*.

11. *Tim.* 43b f., 81 ff., 87c ff.

12. *Tim.* 37a f.

13. *Tim.* 31b, 58c, 67a, cf. *Crat.* 409b. For the 'conversation of the soul with itself', see *Theaet.* 185c ff., 189e f. Cf. also *Rep.* 523 f., 602c f., *Tim.* 34b, *Phil.* 38c f., and *Phdo.* 94c f.

14. *Tim.* 37a f., 47a f. (E.g. a modern motorist, recognizing a signal light as RED, shifts his foot to the brake and brings his car to a stop.)

15. *Theaet.* 197c ff.

16. *Rep.* 585a f., *Phil.* 31e f., 35a f.

17. *Rep.* 404a, 535b 5–7, *Tim.* 88de, *Phil.* 42cd, *Laws* 646c.

18. *Charm.* 154 f., *Lysis* 204b f., 207a, *Symp.* 217 f., *Phaedr.* 253e f.

19. *Ion* 535b f., *Lach.* 196d f., *Gorg.* 503d f., *Symp.* 209b f., 212a, 218e, *Rep.* 400d f., 403a f., 444de, 458d, 484d, 501b, *Phaedr.* 250d f., 253c ff., *Soph.* 227e f., *Phil.* 64d f., 66a.

20. *Ion* 534a, *Charm.* 155cd, *Rep.* 402e f., 430e, 571c f., *Laws*, 790d, 815c.

21. *Laws* 655c f., 659e f., 798d f.
22. *Laws* 644d f., 795d, 803c f., 814d f., 816a.
23. *Laws* 643e f., 653d f., 671a f., 722 f., 802a f., 811b f., 817a f.
24. *Rep.* 475c f., cf. *Symp.* 210a, 211b d.
25. *Gorg.* 465c, *Rep.* 476a–c, 515a f., 517e, 520c 5, 8, *Phaedr.* 252d, 276a 9–10, *Soph.* 236a, 264a f.
26. *Symp.* 210d 4–6, 211c 6, *Rep.* 510b–511a, 528cd, *Phil.* 51c, cf. *Laws* 747a f.
27. *Symp.* 212a f., *Rep.* 500d f., 540a f., *Pol.* 310d f., *Phil.* 27c f., 61b ff. (See further, n. 35 *infra*.)
28. *Lysis* 216c, *Symp.* 215 f., 211e, *Rep.* 452de, 520de, *Phil.* 51a f., 52d f., 59c f.
I draw particular attention to this evidence, in view of the statement in F. C. Tilney (*op. cit.*, p. 22), 'The philosophers of antiquity made no provision for Colour in their theories of Beauty, possibly because they did not know Colour as we know it. They saw rainbows, but their eyes appear to have seen less in them than do modern ones. . . .'
To the statements in the text, and the evidence referred to in this note, I should perhaps add that the Greeks regarded paintings as coloured drawings. That is to say, the design was first sketched in as a drawing, and the colours were added afterwards as embellishments. Painters are represented (by Plato) as being very fastidious about this colouring. They are said to keep on painting in, painting out, and re-painting, without ever attaining to final satisfaction. It is suggested that they might make arrangements for subsequent generations of painters to keep up the good work of re-touching the colours! See esp. *Laws* 769a f., and *Pol.* 277bc (where it is said that the colouring bestows vitality and clearness upon the outline drawing), and *Laws* 934c 1.
29. *Phdo.* 100c, *Phaedr.* 250d f., 254b, cf. *Laws* 669e.
30. *Rep.* 523 ff., 528cd, *Phil.* 51b f.
31. *Rep.* 522e f., 524e f., 525d.
32. *Rep.* 499d, 508e f., 527d f., 532ab. (I would not like to suggest that Jowett's translation of *aute he mousa* (499d) as 'the Muse *of Philosophy*' [italics mine] is untrue to the spirit of the passage. But it does add words not in the original, and words that might be considered important and helpful to my interpretation.)
33. *Rep.* 505b, e f., 517c 1–2, 518c, 534b f.
34. *Rep.* 500b f., 505a, 511b–d, 517b, 531a f., 532e f.
35. *Rep.* 500a f., 505 f., 506c f., 508e f., 540a f., cf. *Phdo.* 78a, 99d f., *Theaet.* 150d f., 161ab.
John Wild, *Plato's Theory of Man* Cambridge, Mass., 1946, Harvard University Press), points out (pp. 72–73) that 'This goal may be achieved . . . only to a limited degree . . . Here and there, dialectic succeeds in laying bare certain formal structures so that we may go . . . both upward (hypothetically) . . . and downward (from genus to species) . . . The final portion of philosophy is the construction of . . . grounded opinions (speculation).'
Like most readers, I regard Wild's book, not only as erudite and well documented, but also as showing insight, genuine insight, into the problems discussed; and it may be that his interpretation (which sticks very close to the text) is correct.
But I must also point out that most interpreters venture to go a little further. They think that in *Rep.* 532 and 540 (for instance) the possibility of a complete insight into the idea of good is envisaged, perhaps postulated. It should then be possible to construct a system of pure or formal science (like the dialectical parts

of the *Sophistes* and *Politicus*, and somewhat like the scientific parts of the *Timaeus*), but without descending to anything more directly empirical than establishing the interrelation of abstract ideas (*Rep.* 511bc).

If so, the further application of the idea of good, and of the abstract system of scientific ideas dependent upon this, to human living, has to make use of sentiments, images, and biosocial feelings natural to man: which are not (and cannot be made) completely rational. We find this exemplified in *Laws* 947 (and indeed *passim*), as well as indicated in the *Republic* (e.g. in the myth of Er, but also elsewhere).

36. *Rep.* 498e f., 529a f., 533a f.

37. *Symp.* 210cd, *Rep.* 498d f., 500c f., *Laws* 811, 817, 951 f.

38. *Rep.* 500b f., 525d, 528cd, *Phil.* 51b f., 53a f.

39. *Rep.* 529a f., 530e f.

40. *Rep.* 529bc, d 5, 530bc, 531a f., 532a f.

41. *Phdo*, 64d ff., *Gorg.* 493 f., 500d f., *Rep.* 395c f., 397a f., 475c f., 476b f., 479a f., *Tim.* 47d f., *Laws* 644c f., 655d, 657e f., 667c f., 669e, 700d f. Cf. Aristot., *Poet.* 1448b 5–20, *Metaph.* 987b 9–14.

42. *Symp.* 211d f., *Rep.* 476 f., 479e, 484cd, 486d, 510d, f., 517bc, *Tim.* 53a f., *Phaedr.* 248d f., 250 (cf. *Meno.* 81b ff.), *Theaet.* 185c f., *Phil.* 52e f. Cf. Aristot. *Met.* 987b 14 f.

43. *Rep.* 523d, 524d f., 526a, 527b, 529d f., 531e, 532c, *Tim.* 30a f., 49b–52d, 53c f. Cf. Aristot. *Met.* 987b 20 f., 988a 10–13.

44. *Art as Experience*, pp. 37, 107, 267, 330. For Aristotle, see *De Anima*, 430a 26 ff., with G. Rodier's notes, esp. on 430a 28–31.

In the account of the text I do not attempt to reproduce every turn of every phrase in the writings of John Dewey which deal with the subject of Art (cf. Dewey, *op. cit.*, pp. 108, 117). I simply try to keep in the central current of his thought, and express, in what terms I can, his meaning, in so far as it seems to relate to Plato's Theory of Art—with especial reference to the question whether elementary *sensa* and relations have aesthetic quality.

In a word, this is a book on Plato, rather than on Dewey; and I think I can reasonably be forgiven for my sins of omission, if I consider, in the present context, only those parts of Dewey's work which have a bearing upon the interpretation of *Philebus* 51–53. My references here draw attention, at each cardinal point, to the chief passages which I have had directly before me, and whose meaning I have tried to condense without falsification.

45. *Ibid.*, pp. 12, 119–120, 326.

46. *Ibid.*, pp. 120–121 refers (rather casually) to an experiment 'under laboratory conditions'. If you look at a 'simple' colour (like pure red), you observe that it is 'complex', at least 'to the extent of having a bluish edge'.

A more detailed report would make clear that the 'edge' (which, if you are looking at a brightly illuminated colour, will sometimes be reddish, sometimes greenish, and sometimes bluish) is largely, if not entirely, a function of the apparatus you are using. If the coloured surface you are observing terminates in a sharp edge, you get a contrast effect. If you are looking at R, the edge will look green; if at G, the edge will look red; if at B, the edge will—given medium lighting—look yellow, and vice versa. With bright lighting, the edge—with whatever colour you start—will change, in the order R, G, B, R, G, B. . . . The edge-colour will creep inward over the face of the original coloured surface: until, as it reaches toward the centre, you will observe that the edge has now changed to the next colour in the series, and so on. Similarly, if you look at a fixation-point on a large piece of white paper in bright sunlight (without any sharp edge anywhere), you will observe all the 'primary' colours spread (in small amounts, almost like a mosaic, except that there are no sharp edges) over the surface.

In other words, Dewey is entirely correct in maintaining that, as a matter of psychological experience under laboratory conditions, we do not seem able to narrow down a single isolated 'red' or 'white' (cf. also Dewey, pp. 203, 219).

But that is not all that needs to be said. Dewey is apparently disagreeing with some authority who has maintained that we can and do observe, as a matter of psychological fact, a 'simple' colour (such as 'red') 'in isolation'. I am myself ignorant in such matters. I do not know of any authority who maintains anything of the sort. Locke's description (in the *Essay*—for refs. and their interpretation *vide* R. C. Lodge, *The Meaning and Function of Simple Modes*. . . . University of Minnesota Press, 1918, Ch. V) shows that he supposes our actual experience to be, at all times, highly complex. It is not by psychological observation, but by logical analysis, that we separate out the notion of a simple idea such as 'red' (Locke names the simple idea as 'scarlet').

Aristotle even describes (in the text of the *Parva Naturalia* that has come down to us, not quite accurately) the 'flight of colours'—to which Dewey's account, perhaps indirectly, refers. Kant is perfectly clear that, while we can and do make logical distinctions, sensation is, as a matter of psychological fact, shot through with intellectual elements. In the case of Plato, I am unable to find any text which states or implies that he supposed we could apprehend 'red' *in isolation from* other, sensory, emotional, volitional, and social experiences—except by a logician's distinction.

In other words, as far as the complexity of direct experience is concerned, when viewed as a matter of psychological observation, apart from the logician's distinctions, there is no difference (and, as far as I can see, no occasion for difference) between the view upon which Dewey insists, and the views held by other thinkers, including Plato.

47. *Ibid.*, pp. 146–147, 203, 276 ff., 306, 308.

48. *Ibid.*, pp. 89, 194–195, cf. 231, 233, 306.

49. *Ibid.*, pp. 18, 77, 79, 81, 129, 139, 160, 193, 201, 215, 229, 263–264, 270–271, 327, cf. 329. Is not this 'religious' quality (pp. 270 f.), this sense of communion with others, found wherever men get together? That is to say, is it not found in sport-life, in club-life, in church-life, in social life generally, as well as in get-togethers in which the enhancement of experience by *art* is predominant?

50. *Ibid.*, pp. 18, 122–123, 128, 157, 162, 169, 218–219, 249, 265 (cf. *Experience and Nature*, p. 303, cited in *Art as Experience*, p. 272).

51. *Ibid.*, pp. 12, 294.

52. Plato, *Rep.* 526d–528d, *Tim.* 53c–54b, cf. Burnet, *Early Greek Philosophy*, 2nd edit., sect. 48. For Dewey, see *Art as Experience*, p. 280. (I refer to the Pythagoreans here, to indicate that Dewey's view has behind it a long and honourable tradition.)

53. *Art as Experience*, pp. 19, 89, 99. Cf. Aristot., *Metaph.* 986a 22–986b 2.

54. *Ibid.*, p. 123. I cannot bring myself to believe (in the light of the evidence referred to in preceding notes) that Dewey means us to take quite literally what he writes about sounds on pp. 237–239. He is there comparing what is heard (as

a medium of expression) with what is seen. In this context, he regards sounds as 'agitating directly, as a commotion of the organism' (we might compare Plato, *Rep.* 401d f., *Tim.* 47c–e)—whereas the appeal of what is *seen* is 'indirect'. He further distinguishes words from 'raw sounds' (from which, he says, words 'have been formed by the art of communication'). Exclamation and interjection, indeed, 'retain their native aspect as sounds'; but literature (using words 'charged with meanings absorbed through immemorial time') operates with 'loaded dice'. Music, as distinct from literature, operates with sounds 'not subjected to transforming art', i.e. with sounds 'as such', or 'raw' sounds.

With this context as a background, he writes that sounds 'have the power of *direct* expression. A sound is *itself* threatening, whining, soothing, depressing, fierce, tender, soporific, *in its own quality*' (italics mine).

Any intelligent reader, trained in logic, would feel this to be hardly consistent with the flat statement (p. 120 and context) that *no* sense qualities have aesthetic quality, *except in their connexions*. I do not think the later passages (pp. 237–239) are intended to supersede this earlier statement. Dewey does not (as I understand him) mean that a tone such as Middle C or E in alt., has aesthetic quality *in itself*, *in isolation from* other aspects of a highly complex experience of an organism interacting with its environment. He is still opposed to the view, popularly ascribed to Plato (in the *Philebus* passage), that 'pure' tones (if understood as *isolated* tones) do have aesthetic quality.

Incidentally, apart from this particular context (pp. 237–239) I cannot bring myself to believe that Dewey would care to maintain what he writes about the 'raw' sounds with which music is alleged to operate. Do we not all know that the tones used by musicians are NOT 'raw'? They have position on scales, and it is a matter of common knowledge that scales are conventional, and have a long history, particularly in relation to their musical expressiveness (cf. Plato, *Rep.* 398b ff.). I do not suppose for a moment (from the general tenor of *Art as Experience*) that Dewey would care to challenge the summary in Grove's *Dictionary of Music* (New York, 1914, Vol. IV, p. 534), 'Scale is an intimate fusion of melody and harmony. The music of any period tends to fall into certain accepted melodic figures . . . related to a central tonic note. These constitute a convention, which alters as time goes on, and . . . has a history.'

Nor do I suppose that Dewey does not perfectly understand that the sounds produced by musicians with their flutes, trumpets, violins, drums, and grand pianos, are far from 'raw'. Each has a timbre due to the characteristic overtones produced by this or that musical instrument. It is also perfectly obvious that Haydn, Mozart, Beethoven, and the rest, write in particular musical idioms. In a word, precisely like literary artists, they operate with what Dewey calls 'loaded dice'. Musical tones, like words, are, precisely, 'charged with meanings absorbed through immemorial time'.

In fact, on due reconsideration of his own book (esp. pp. 240, 265–266, 270, 315, 326, 332–335), Dewey would, surely, himself desire to write that music (like speech) 'is informed with the temperament and the ways of viewing and interpreting life that are characteristic of the culture of a continuing social group'. Hence the usual distinction between music that sounds 'Chinese', 'Russian', or 'French'.

55. For Plato, *Rep.* 401 f., 475b ff., 598d ff., *Laws* 644d f., 654 ff., 659d ff., 810 ff., 817a f., 903b ff.

For Dewey, *Art. as E.*, pp. 5–8, 272 f.

56. For Plato, *Laws* 665c, 801c f., 803d f., 811b f., 814d ff., 819b ff., 829d.
For Dewey, *A. as E.*, pp. 194 f., 273 ff.

57. Readers of *Phdo.* 64 ff., may feel inclined to doubt this. I have in mind *Crito* 51 f., *Rep.* 419 ff., cf. 587d f., *Phaedr.* 230c f. It is plain that the citizens in the *Laws* are expected to love their model city. At least, there is a waiting-list for vacancies for full citizenships, and metics are represented as desiring to be admitted to residence, and indeed to extended residence. (For the waiting-list, see *Laws* 856a, 877d, 923 f. For metics, see *Laws* 850b f., 920bc.)
For Dewey, *A. as E.*, pp. 19, 22–23. Dewey admires the social side of Plato's philosophy, and criticizes it chiefly for not being social enough, i.e. as not providing a larger choice of careers for citizens (*Democracy and Education*, pp. 201–205, chapter, 'Philosophy' in *Whither Mankind?* (ed., Chas. Beard), pp. 330–331).

58. For Plato, *Phdo.* 64c f., *Gorg.* 491d–509b, 521d, *Rep.* 558d ff., 584e ff.
For Dewey, 'Philosophy' in *Whither Mankind?*, pp. 328–329.

59. For Plato, *Rep.* 473c f., 540ab. The *Republic* and *Laws* are nowadays (as to some extent in ancient times too) understood to be treatises on this kind of re-education.
For Dewey, cf. *Democracy and Education*, chaps. vii, xxiii, cf. also in *Whither Mankind?* pp. 328 f., 331.

60. For Plato, *Tim.* 68b, d.
For Dewey, *A. as E.*, p. 157 (for the function of pure colours in modern painting) —as opposed to Plato's time, when a painting was usually a coloured drawing (*Pol.* 277b).

61. For Plato, *Theaet.* 184b ff.
For Dewey, *A. as E.*, pp. 218, 221, 233, 246, 255–256, 264, 268, 272, 293.

62. For Plato, *Phil.* 51 ff.
For Dewey, *A. as E.*, pp. 122 f., 194 f., 215, 315, 326–327.

63. For Plato, *Prtg.* 339–348a, *Menex.* 235a, *Symp.* 187ab, *Rep.* 401d f., 595b, 596c, 598d, 601b, 602d, 607c, *Tim.* 47c, 67a f., *Theaet.* 206ab, *Phil.* 55e f., *Laws* 669d.
For Dewey, *A. as E.*, pp. 157, 237–239.

64. For Plato, *Rep.* 522c, 531a f., *Phil.* 17b f., cf. Aristot. *Metaph.* 925b 32 ff.
For Dewey, *A. as E.*, pp. 146–147, 150–151, 158–159, 185.

65. For Plato, *Rep.* 533b f.
For Dewey, *A. as E.*, pp. 5–6, 12, 15, 19, 22, 81, 116, 147–148, 221, 230, 233, 246, 255–256, 261–264.

66. For Plato, *Rep.* 349de, *Tim.* 43b f., *Theaet.* 156c f., 184b, de, 206ab, *Parm.* 130d 2–3, *Phil.* 55e f., *Laws* 655a f., 657a 80b 3, 799ab, 800a, 802b f.
For Dewey, *A. as E.*, pp. 237–239, cf. 22, 25, 62, 158–159, 162, 183.

67. For Plato. *Tim.* 25–26, 47a f. (with Taylor's *Commentary*), *Laws* 655cd, 700de.
For Dewey, *A as E.*, pp. 87, 146–148, 151, 158–159, 185.

68. For Plato, *Tim.* 47d.
Dewey (*A. as E.*, pp. 152 and context, and p. 170) points out that 'sensitivity to natural rhythm' is not a 'conventional' or merely external imitation in the sense of mimicry; but substitutes (so far as it is 'artistic') 'personal perception' for a formally correct reproduction of details.

69. For Plato, *Tim.* 47c f., *Laws* 657ab, etc.
For Dewey, *A. as E.*, pp. 150, 195.

70. For Plato, *Rep.* 531bc.

For Dewey, see *A Common Faith* (1944), and cf. John L. Childs, *Education and the Philosophy of Experimentalism* (1931), pp. 61, 83, 115, 135, 227. As a rule, Dewey shrinks from anything in any way 'absolute'. His book on religious experience was only written recently in his life (1944), and is very small, especially on the positive side. (The writings of E. S. Ames are widely regarded as dealing with the religious implications of pragmatism.)

71. For Plato, *Tim.* 53c f., 81b ff.

For Dewey, see 'The Need for a Recovery of Philosophy' in *Creative Intelligence* (1917), esp. pp. 65 ff.

72. For Plato, *Rep.* 526b, 527c. *Phil.* 55d f., *Laws* 747a f.

For Dewey, *A. as E.*, pp. 194–195, 215.

73. The Pythagoreans are said to be satisfied to 'imitate', without really 'participating' in such a way as to derive anything more than aesthetical satisfaction (see Aristot. *Met.* 987b 10–14).

74. For Plato, *Phaed.*, 265e, *Pol.* 287b, *Laws* 700, 709a f.

For Dewey, *A. as E.*, pp. 15, 19, 162, 164.

75. For Plato, *Rep.* 544d (cf. 458d), *Laws* 739c f.

For Dewey, *A. as E.*, pp. 15, 19, 22–23, 58–62, 158–159, 168–169, 185, 195, 221–222, 228, 231, 233, 246, 250, 255, 261, 270–271, 287, 326.

76. For Plato, *Laws*. 709a f.

For Dewey, *A. as E.*, pp. 14, 24, 25, 48–49, 77, 79, 87, 146–148, 243, 269, 291. Dewey's 'naturalism' includes human wants, capacities, and activities, as opposed to a 'realistic' naturalism which regards 'nature' as exclusive of *human* nature.

77. For Plato, *Rep.* 529 f.

For Dewey, *A. as E.*, pp. 212–221, 228–230, 246, 252–257. This brings out Dewey's view that man's interactivity with nature involves a great deal of activity on man's part. Activity, however, is not the entire story. It is only one of the factors in aesthetic experience (pp. 274–275).

78. For Plato, *Rep.* 524e f., 526d f., 530a f., 531a f.

For Dewey, *A. as E.*, pp. 189, 194–195, 242–244, 248, 268, 322, 348.

79. For Plato, *Crat.* 424c f., *Rep.* 523 f., *Theaet.* 202 ff., *Parm.* 130c f., *Soph.* 253a f., *Phil.* 17b f.

Dewey (*A. as E.*, pp. 209, 237–242) sees contrasts rather than close parallelism. For accepting the revelations of the senses cf. *ibid.*, pp. 22, 70, 74, 87, 106, 120, 124, 179, 201, 203, 218–219, 237–239, 255.

80. For Plato, *Tim.* 47, 68b f., *Laws* 655a. For Socrates, and the wisdom of not pursuing scientific inquiries too far, cf. *Phdo.* 99d f., 100b f., *Parm.* 130b f., 135c f.. In Dewey's way of thinking, these patterns derive from the 'reality' in which not only the physical environment, but human interactivity is a factor (*A. as E.*, pp. 19, 22, 87, 146–148, 151, 158–159, 185, 221, 231, etc.).

81. A. E. Taylor, in his *Commentary on the Timaeus* (esp. pp. 479, 487), in commenting on *Tim.* 67c 2–68d 7, shows that the theory being expounded is characteristically Empedoclean. Taylor sees (implied) more of a 'colour-scale' (p. 489, comment on *Tim.* 682 4–5, d 4–7) than does Timaeus himself—who expresses rather complete scepticism.

82. For Plato, *Rep.* 526a, 527b, 530b, 531c f.

. For Dewey's account (surprisingly sympathetic) of the artist's tendency toward some sort of transcendentalism, see *A. as E.*, pp. 195, 267–268, 275, 280.

83. For Plato, *Rep.* 395bc, 401 f., 484cd., 500e f., 540, 592ab, *Tim.* 22c, *Pol.* 308c–311c, *Laws* 682a, 811b f., 817a f. (Cf. also *Lysus* 213e f., *Ion* 531c, *Meno* 99e f.).
For Dewey, *A. as E.*, pp. 62–63, 272 f., 287.

84. For Plato, *Symp.* 210–212a.
For Dewey, *A. as E.*, pp. 185, 273–275, 290.

85. For Plato, *Symp.* 210de, 211e f., *Rep.* 500e ff., 510c f., 529d ff. Cf. Aristot. *Met.* 987b 10–14. (Jowett translates 'beauty *everywhere*' [italics mine], which goes a little beyond what Plato actually writes in the *Symposium* passage (*toioude*). Jowett's extension of the connotation of Plato's words, is doubtless allowable in terms of the technical logic of Jowett's time; but it is doubtful whether a careful student would care to make use of such an extension today.)

86. For Plato, *Rep.* 475c ff., 522a f.
For Dewey, *A. as E.*, pp. 17–19, 48–54. While stressing the importance of conscious design in human work (as opposed to the nest-building constructions of animals), Dewey emphasizes his view that human art is largely subconscious and 'inspired'. That is to say, art is not (like the life of Plato's model citizens) the result of deliberate planning—if we confine our attention to the general citizens (silver class), as opposed to the philosophy-trained magistrates (golden class) with their committees of expert advisers (see Dewey, *op. cit.*, pp. 62–63, 70, 73–74, 77). There is actually a somewhat similar suggestion in Plato (*Phaedr.* 245a).

87. For Plato, *Rep.* 519c f., *Phaedr.* 245a.
Dewey stresses the relation of artistic 'work' and perception (*A. as E.*, pp. 37, 44, 46, 48–49, 60, 194–195, 233, 237, 239, 253–256, 263–265), but guards against the popular association of 'passivity' with contemplation and reflexion.

88. For Plato, *Rep.* 505 f., 519e f., *Pol.* 277b f., *Laws* 817a f.
For Dewey, *A. as E.*, pp. 275–276, 281.

89. For Plato, *Rep.* 533a, 534e, 540a f., *Laws* 964b f., 967d f.
In Dewey's way of thinking, community leaders should function like orchestral conductors: bringing out what their associates have to offer, and being regarded by these associates with respect (see *Reconstruction in Philosophy*, 1920, p. 203).

90. For Plato, *Rep.* 498 f., 540b, *Laws* 807d f., 817b f.
For Dewey, *A. as E.*, pp. 19, 22–23, 144–145, 155–156.
Croce (*Aesthetic as Science of Expression and General Linguistic* [tr. Ainslee], 2nd edit., London, Macmillan, 1922) would disagree with Plato's position here. Croce draws a very sharp distinction between 'aesthetics' and 'practical life', i.e. 'economic and ethical activity'. From this standpoint, Plato, as an artist, has *completed* his artistic work, when he has *written* the *Laws*. By writing, he has 'given suitable form and linguistic expression to his impressions' of civic living. If Plato (unreasonable fellow!) now insists upon going further—upon *trying to live* (whether in Athens, in Syracuse, or in some imaginary model city) in the spirit of the regulations of the *Republic* or *Laws* (as Plato undoubtedly thinks should be done, cf. *Rep.* 592—comment by R.C.L.), Plato is, to that extent, passing out of art into practical living. In trying to be more than a writer, he is ceasing to be an artist.

In a word, according to Croce, it is not possible for a writer (like Plato) to put his art into his life. He can only put it into a book.

We have here a very serious difference of opinion between Croce and Plato. Many artists have undoubtedly attempted to do precisely what Croce, with his sharp distinction between art and life, thinks cannot be done. At least we know of many who, besides Plato, have tried to put their art into their lives, rather than merely into their books or pictures. They have gone on record as saying so, with every appearance of conviction.

I think myself that an administrator's art (whether in conducting an orchestra, or directing an opera or a play, or in marshalling military forces, or in acting as the chief executive of a university, a business firm (like Chester Barnard), or a family) is concerned with life: with practical, economic, political, or ethical living; directly and essentially. Why not? Does not an administrator put his art into his life? Many of them think and say that that is precisely what they do. With an artist of this stamp (e.g. Plato's philosopher-king, *Rep.* 540a), is not this primary?

If in later years a Francis Bacon, a Chester Barnard, or a Thucydides, writes some kind of autobiography, does not the written life (as compared with the life as lived) often seem a secondary affair? Would Croce seriously maintain that it becomes *more* artistic when it is 'contemplated', or 'recollected in tranquillity'? Readers of *Boswell in Holland* (1952) for instance, find James Boswell directing his own life; and very artistically too, as he learns to express himself, to 'be a man'. His struggles to realize his 'plan' are (surely) at least as artistic as the written plan itself!

At any rate, Boswell would certainly not have regarded his efforts at artistic self-expression as *completed* by writing his journal. He would not feel that he had worked them out of his system, by putting them down on paper. He wanted, not merely to imagine himself as a 'great man', or to write about himself as a 'great man', advertising himself as a 'great man'. He did all these things, it is true. But he wanted more. He wanted to turn himself, in actuality, into a great man; and his writing was undertaken as a means to that end, not as an end in itself.

It may be true that (in the end) Boswell succeeded only in turning himself into the kind of great man whose greatness consists in his biographical artistry, his journalistic virtuosity. But that is something else. So too Plato (as we know) wanted to create, to call into being in the space-time world, some Platonopolis, some actual image of the ideal city of his dreams: an image that should enjoy full economic and political actuality. That this ambition was frustrated, and that to find himself *nur noch Lehrer* was, according to his biographer (Wilamowitz), painful to him. He certainly regarded the creating of literature, even of master-pieces like the Platonic Dialogues, as of *secondary* importance (*Phaedr.* 277e f.).

All we can do, then, is to register the serious difference of opinion which separates Croce, on this point, from Plato. Are we to say, 'Poor Plato!' or 'Poor Croce!'?

91. *Laws* 658e ff., 665c f. It has sometimes been thought that participation in the higher idealism (at least for the slaves, the workers, and the general citizens) is not really aesthetically satisfying, but is—a little dull and boring. But it is to the point to compare, e.g. Frank D. Ashburn's picture of the life of schoolboys at Groton (*Peabody of Groton*, McCann, New York, 1944), somewhat as Nettleship in his *Lectures on the Republic of Plato* illustrates by reference to the English Public Schools. In such schools, the control over the personnel strongly resembles the control over citizens exercised in the model city. But the aesthetic appeal of the well-ordered life, with the bells of its chapel, and the authorized songs and dis-ciplined sports, seems beyond doubt; and it is to be supposed that, where the planning is well done, and where there is always a great man in charge (like 'the Rector' at Groton, or the head of a quasi-Platonic Academy in the model city), the life is itself a fine art, experienced and enjoyed as such.

Dewey thinks (*A. as E.*, p. 31) that 'the elevation of the ideal beyond immediate sense, has acted to impoverish and degrade all things of direct experience. ' But this (while it might conceivably be true of *some* 'transcendental idealists') does not seem to be true of Plato—as least, if we take seriously the evidence of such passages as *Rep.* 401 f., 529c f., cf. *Phaedr.* 230b.

92. For Plato, *Rep.* 411c f., 498a.

For Dewey, *A. as E.*, pp. 18, 122–123, 128, 157, 162, 169, 176, 180, 195, 218–219, 249, 265.

93. For Plato, *Rep.* 349d f., 420c f., 495c ff.

For Dewey, *A. as E.*, pp. 95–96, 120.

94. Present-day American readers, who may be inclined to think (from the statements so frequently made by members of Dewey's school of thinking) that it is characteristic of Americans to be 'empirical' rather than 'transcendental' in their ways of looking at things—can learn something by reading a book like Joseph L. Blau's *Men and Movements in American Philosophy* (New York, 1952, Prentice-Hall), esp. chaps. 3, 4, and 6.

CHAPTER THIRTEEN

Freedom and Artists in the Model City

To the modern reader, it is painfully evident that for what is commonly supposed to be art, that is to say, for painting and poetry, music and dancing, architecture and sculpture, as such, Plato has no exaggerated respect.[1] He finds Homer (doubtless the greatest of poets) attractive.[2] But it is only a Homer bowdlerized and rather completely rewritten to order, whose poems can safely be put into the hands of trusting youth in the model city.[3] Persons commonly regarded as artists (that is to say, painters, poets, musicians, *et hoc genus omne*) are, as we all know, quite irresponsible people. They have absolutely no restraint, no judgement, no *reverentia virginibus puerisque*.[4] They cannot possibly, in a well-ordered community, be permitted to compose at their own sweet will, and especially cannot be permitted to publish the results without let or hindrance.[5] The community executive will have to be stern and ruthless. He will have to put them in their proper place, and see that they stay there.

Plato knows (just as well as we do) that too many regulations ring the knell of art for art's sake.[7] But the passing of such art, he is prepared to face with complete equanimity. Art-galleries, concert-halls, and the rest, are not (he insists) needed in a well-ordered community. We are really better off without them. The only kind of art for which there is a place, is the art that is functional in the institutions of the model city; the art which fosters community courage, self-control, justice, and the other virtues of good citizenship.[9] The community which pays the piper has the duty, as well as the right, to set the standards and call the tune. All this is elementary, and no Hellene for a moment thinks otherwise.[12]

Hellenic artists, in a word, are technicians: engaged by the community to perform services considered desirable by the community.

Architects are engaged to design and supervise the erection of community buildings: temples, court-houses, palaces.[11] Painters are engaged to keep the interior *décor* of such buildings in appropriate repair: retouching the eyes and draperies of the statues and wall-coverings.[12] Poets are engaged to re-phrase the traditional prayers and praises offered to the community gods and heroes.[13] Musicians are engaged to supply suitable accompaniments to hymns, to marches and other dance-movements, whether ceremonial or military, considered desirable in the community.[14]

That is to say, the business of the Hellenic artist is to amplify the community *ethos*; of Sparta (if you like), or of Athens, or of any other empirical city with its traditional background and destiny; or (if you permit) of a more ideal, more 'model' city, like that of the Magnetes in the *Laws*.[15] The artist's function is to give appropriate expression to this *ethos*: to modernize it, to keep it in fashion, to provide just enough variation and novelty to preserve its effectiveness and charm.[16]

But one thing should be perfectly clear from the outset. Technicians are never to be mistaken for great educational authorities, great leaders, community statesmen. They are community servants: precisely on the level of carpenters, weavers, and potters. Great statesmen are very rare; and it is the great statesman, the practitioner of the 'royal' art, who is the true leader. He is the true educator, the veritable artist. He is the creator, protector, and guide of the community and its life.[17]

So Plato, we feel. So Aristotle, we find.[18] And so, we are a little surprised to discover, are some of our most characteristically modern philosophers as well. Take John Locke, a common-sense realist, if there ever was one; the authentic voice of British experience, muddling through toward success in our difficult modern world. What our world needs (he sees so clearly) is leaders, administrators, executives; men of sound judgement in practical affairs.[19] If you find your son (he says) developing a taste for poetry, an itch for making music, a passion for the life of an artist; nip it in the bud. Turn his mind, his heart, and his soul toward worthier objectives. Make a man of him: a truly useful member of the governing class. Leave the arts to the class where they belong, the class indicated by the term, *Graeculus esuriens*![20]

Or take Kant, the idealist, the philosopher of transcendental feeling, the prophet of the imagination straining to furnish sensuous and emotional expression for the dictates of pure reason (no less!), when this becomes, of itself, practical. The artist's function (as Kant and his followers see it) is ancillary. His to amplify, to render attractive and empirically effective the voice (if you please) of Duty; to suggest that a halo hovers over the drill-sergeant's categorical imperatives; to sweeten the necessary doctrine of service to the all-powerful modern State—military service, civil service, educational service, social service. Ours not to reason why. Ours but to do until we die; while humanity, through our self-conditioned (autonomous) efforts, gradually works its way, in an ever more closely knit political and industrial community (a league of nations, save the mark!), along the line of its manifest destiny.[21]

And we ourselves? Do not we, for the most part, believe (a little hopelessly) that life is real, earnest, and—inevitable? Do not we, for the most part, feel that 'entertainment' or 'escape' art provides, at best, temporary alleviation? Can it give us more than a resting-place, a favourable pause (as the psychologists express it), an evening out, a moral holiday, before we take our final plunge into the self-denying drabness of the trivial round, the common task? And is not the suggestion of romantic glamour which, for a moment, flickers before the eyes of our workers, really an *ignis fatuus* which leads all who follow into a bog, until they are as much *adscripti glebae* as any medieval serf ? The victims play, regardless of their doom. So our poets and dramatists assure us; and as to the other function of modern art, is it not a childishly obvious reinforcement of the imperatives of necessity? Do your best, your very best, and do it every day! Little boys, and little girls, that is the wisest way. Play up, play up, and play the game—such as it is!

Yes, in the modern world, the thought of 'obligation' hangs heavily upon us. It has taken, in ethical theory, the place (so we are told) of the more positive 'highest good' of the Greeks. The more you look around you, nowadays, that is, the more (surely) you find yourself thinking of the other 'social' animals: the busy bee, the industrious ant, and (why not?) the termite, with every last individual working, willy-nilly, for the group.[22] Is it not all just a little gloomy, even when you meet with it in a noble word-artist like Joseph Addison, or a well-meaning writer like Aldous Huxley? Is there anyone who fails to see Schopenhauer, with his pessimistic philosophy of withdrawal, waiting just around the corner?[23]

In fact, is not this the old-fashioned acquiescence in the universal compulsoriness of law which we find in ancient Stoicism, whether of emperor or of slave—associated with a detachment of spirit, a withdrawal of the will from the course of events, a refusal (as the Christian authority says) to yield an 'inner consent to the world, the flesh, and the Devil':[24] Does not all this make acceptance of something like Plato's theory of the function of ordinary art (as a pill-sweetener which reinforces the directives of nature,[25] or as superficial entertainment in which we seek to forget the pressure of events[26]) practically unanimous?

In such a world, how can we speak of anyone as being 'free'—free, that is, to choose his own life, his own ideals, and his own techniques? And is not this particularly true of the artist: who, at best, finds himself compelled to create as the all-powerful community bids him?

Let us look more closely at the Platonic text. Let us discover for ourselves what it is that Plato teaches; first, about freedom in the model city, and then, about the degree of freedom which awaits the artist, the poet or sculptor, the musician or architect, the public speaker or public dancer.

During the first three years of a child's life in the model city (as indeed elsewhere), he gradually becomes a family baby. This means that he is cared for by mother and nurse, and gradually learns to take on the rhythms of family living. Parents and nurses do for him everything that he is unable, as yet, to do for himself. They see that he is properly bathed and dressed, exercised, fed, and rested; all in accordance with the best medical opinion as to the correct treatment of growing infants.[27]

At first, the principle which animates his body has very little power of control over the body's movements. He is hungry or sleepy. Perhaps the digestive processes are not working well. Perhaps his limbs are unduly restricted. For this reason or that, he has little upsets. He is uncomfortable, not really master of the situation, not himself. He soon discovers that he requires attention. If he is taken up into a parent's or a nurse's arms and rocked gently back and forth, this rhythmical shaking tends to assist the body to go through its rhythmical processes properly. Everything is under control. Pleasure is felt. Telemachus is himself again.[28]

A baby very soon learns that, in order to secure attention (leading to pleasurable self-feeling), all he has to do, is to cry and make a fuss. Someone is sure to come. Plato points out that, if improperly indulged by parents and nurses, a baby easily develops, during this three-year period, a number of highly undesirable social habits; habits which will be a nuisance, not only to others, but to himself, when he shall have outgrown the family-baby stage. Plato insists, therefore, that the baby shall be indulged 'neither too much, nor too little', but in accordance with 'the principle of the mean', avoiding any sort of extreme. In this way, he will be acquiring balance, the beginnings of what later will be the civic virtues of courage, self-control, and the like.[29]

The point is, that, even at this very early period of his life, the baby has a principle of self-initiated motion: the animating principle (*psyche*) which can be influenced (by wise care) so as to develop, not 'self-will', but a more desirable form of 'self-control'. This principle is essentially 'spontaneous'. It is free to develop this way or that. It can develop a balance, a 'natural bent' (e.g. in the direction of courage rather than of cowardice), which may be of great assistance to it, and indeed to the model city, later on. The point is, that the baby's *psyche* (i.e. animating principle) is essentially spontaneous, self-determined, growing from within outwards. It is amenable, as it interacts with the motion-tendencies of its own body and of the external world, to influences which may have, for it, a value directly educative.[30]

During the next three years, the family baby (in the model city, as elsewhere) gradually becomes a neighbourhood child. Precisely as, in our own time, in our parks and community playgrounds, we see pre-school youngsters gathering, under the aegis of this or that mother, attendant, or playground authority; they play together, day after day, in accordance with the immemorial practice of the younger members of the human tribe. Precisely so in the community playgrounds, set aside for the purpose in the temple precincts of the twelve districts of Plato's model city. Here the nurses bring their charges, morning after morning; and each playground is under the control of a matron empowered to see that no unauthorized person interferes with the children and their play.[31]

And their play? Children's play is both natural and spontaneous. 'From three to six years . . . children have certain forms of playing which are natural (*paidiai autophyes*). These they practically discover for themselves (*autoi aneuriskousi*), when they are brought together.' They run, skip, and jump. They play ball. They play with dolls. Some of them play a kind of 'prisoner's base'.[32] Such games have a wonderful value in educating for future citizenship. There is a pretty direct relation between playing according to rules, and living (later) according to laws.

In these particular games, the local children are gradually taking on the rhythms of neighbourhood living. They are learning, not merely to develop themselves as individuals. They are learning to play together, to give as well as to take; in a word, to develop social balance. Here also there is place for a wise supervision. A little suitable punishment (where necessary) will discourage excessive self-will, and will encourage the development of socially desirable habits. Such punishment is designed, not to disgrace the children, but to give more positive community direction to their growing spirit as free citizens of a free community. In the *Laws* as in the *Republic*, guardians are always 'artificers of freedom'.[33] The social habits thus acquired are courage, self-control, friendship, and the beginnings of social justice. For the playground matron represents, not merely the authority, but the entire spirit of the model community, with its full and free life (under law) for all.[34]

At seven (or thereabouts) comes the next stage of education. The sexes are separated. The boys are taken to a boys' school, the girls to a girls' school. Here they learn to become schoolboys and schoolgirls. Instead of the matron, there are masters for the boys, and mistresses for the girls. The sense of discipline is a little more marked, and the direction of the games is more definitely professional. But the curriculum (if it can be called anything so formal-sounding) is still largely playful. It is all quite natural for growing boys and girls. We should nowadays class such school-activities as extra-curricular, and as properly belonging in sports-schools, or in the junior departments of athletic clubs.

The boys like to throw things. They are taught to throw straight, and eventually to hurl light javelins, patterned after the javelins actually used in military combat. The boys like to run and race, and play soldiers. They are taught to march in formation, and to use the quick-step, like actual soldiers. They are taught to race competitively, along a prescribed course, carrying arms suited to their size and strength. Boys like to play with bows and arrows. They are taught how to do this with military precision. So too they are given spear-drill. Boys like to ride. They are taught equitation, as like strict military equitation as possible. Every month, the community has one or more field-days, in which those who can, compete in quasi-military sports. The school training prepares the boys for these, and their natural desire to excel in such competitive sports, and to win prizes, encomia, and the approbation of the community, receives here full scope.[35]

In the *Republic*, it is further urged that the children should be taken as spectators (mounted on swift horses, and under the direction of experienced veteran-officers), to look on at actual combat, in which they will see their parents fighting against the enemy. Their officers act as tutors, explaining the wherefores of each evolution, and (if danger comes too close) know when to beat a retreat. In this way, the natural aggressive impulses, and the natural desire to help their parents and the community, tend to develop into the civic virtue of disciplined courage. The children are thus prepared for the serious conflicts of adult life in Hellas.[36] In the *Laws*, the children similarly look on, during the military field-sports, at the *mêlée* of the adults; in which real weapons are used, and deaths, as well as serious wounds, are to be expected.[37]

The girls in their schools, from the age of seven to the age of ten, learn much the same things as the boys are learning; and they too compete in the monthly sports-meets. But while it is entirely natural for them to wish to do most of the things the boys do, the difference in their muscular strength, and the general tendency of girls to be quieter, more graceful, and a little more dignified, than the boys, is taken into consideration. Girls compete only against girls, never against boys; and the physical tasks in which they compete, are deliberately made less exhausting than the tasks set before the boys.[38]

In both cases, while the degree of community discipline is more in evidence than at the playground stage of education, the activities of growing boys and girls are based upon the inner urge of spontaneity seeking its own level, upon the natural bent. This impulse is merely given a socially desirable direction; a direction which will provide social satisfaction for the children, as well as prove (it is hoped) eventually of assistance when they come to live the life of adults in the model community. Throughout, the elders look on, and enjoy vicariously the youngsters' health, zest, and growing community spirit. It is all one big family, as the young become, not merely schoolboys and schoolgirls, as such, but members of the community, being gradually, *via* the family, the playground, the schools, and the field-sports, integrated into the full life of the community.[39]

From ten to thirteen, schoolchildren take up the study of 'letters'. This term includes spelling, reading and writing, and involves intimate acquaintance with selected masterpieces of the traditional literature. The spelling is acquired by appealing, throughout, to natural interest, and by encouraging the children to solve, for themselves, problems which are well within their capacity. They learn, first, to spell, read, and write their own names, letter by letter, and syllable by syllable. They then learn to spell, read, and write the names of their comrades and friends. They are encouraged particularly to notice identical syllables and letters in the different names. For instance, that THE is identical in the names THEAETETUS and THEODORUS. They proceed always from what they already know, as they seek to extend their mastery of the art of spelling to the new names. It is all learned much as they have already learned to acquire mastery over physical movements: to throw straight, to run in formation, and the like. That is to say, it is learned as a kind of game. The teacher shows them how to succeed in doing what they are trying to do; and they try until they succeed.[40]

The writing, that is to say, the correct formation of the standard letters of the Hellenic alphabet, is learned, not by a pure freehand effort, but with the assistance of patterns. Hellenic students write by making grooves with a stylus in the wax of a writing-tablet. They are provided with stylus and tablet; and the teacher makes for each child, letter by letter, and syllable by syllable, the grooves which show the correct form of the letters which spell out the child's own name; and then, other names and words.

The child learns, by putting the point of his stylus in the grooves made for him by the teacher. By following the grooves, he feels for himself what it is like, to form correctly the letters of his name. He then tries to make similar movements freehand. By alternating, trying the patterned groove and then trying again to make a similar groove for himself, eventually he learns to make, for himself, letters which are not too hopelessly unlike the teacher's patterns. Plato is particularly careful to point out that minute perfection is not to be insisted upon, in the case of a child who is to be a freeman. Success which is to be the child's own success, comes from within; and it will probably come, like mastery in throwing straight, gradually.[41]

Reading, for a Greek child, is never silent reading. The child reads aloud, learning by heart, and acting out dramatically, what he is reading. He throws his whole self into what he is doing; and that is why both form and content of what he reads, are educationally of great importance. What he reads has to appeal to his own interests. It has, at the same time, to have some positive relation to the background and outlook of his own community. That is why the authorized 'reader' of a Hellenic school (not unlike the authorized 'readers' of our own schools) consists of simplified versions of the sayings and doings of local worthies, with appropriately patriotic sentiments. As the child 'speaks pieces', he is projecting himself imaginatively into the actions, the feelings, and sentiments, to which he is giving dramatic expression.[42]

In a word, the child is now becoming, far more consciously, a member of his community. He is taking on, in the gradually forming patterns of self-expression, the traditional background and outlook of his group. A child in the Athenian schools, acting out a patriotic chorus from the *Persae*, or declaiming one of the great speeches of Pericles, is teaching himself to become an Athenian citizen: a lover and defender of democratic freedom. A child going through the system current in Sparta, as he acts out the heroic poems of Tyrtaeus, is learning to project himself into, and assimilate himself to, the disciplined comradeship of the Spartan citizen. In Plato's model city, while some regard is always paid to local traditions, it is member-ship in a more completely rounded, more nearly ideal community, that is being acquired. That is why the literature studied and acted out has to be revised, rewritten in the spirit of idealism.[43]

From thirteen to sixteen, the boys and girls who are growing up spontaneously into the beginnings of citizenship in the model community, are given a short course in the fundamentals of Greek music. Boys and girls take naturally to singing and dancing, and to playing on simple instruments. They are taught to develop their powers of tonal, rhythmic, and harmonious self-expression along lines that will enable them to follow with enjoyment the socially approved patterns.[44]

Plato is aware that the range of musical capacity varies con-siderably; and this short course is not designed to develop specialists, or to be too severe in its standards, for boys and girls whose achieve-ment comes (perhaps) a little slowly—i.e. for those whose sense of pitch is not very accurate, or whose feeling for harmony is a little unreliable, or whose appreciation of the niceties of rhythmic balance in the more advanced compositions is retarded; in a word, for those who (for whatever reason) seem to have a distaste for good music— whether 'classical' or 'modern' in type. It is simply a course in what might be called 'basic' music.[45] Its purpose is to prepare young people to take their part, gladly and willingly, in the chants of the regular temple services, in the monthly community festivals, and doubtless also in the more informal entertainments where nothing more artistically ambitious than 'harmless pleasure' is in view.[46]

Good taste and a feeling for teamwork and orderliness are the natural concomitants of such musical education; and the action-songs, especially the choric action-songs, are of great community

T

value. They are enjoyed, not only by the immediate participants, but by the parents and well-wishers who look on and listen. The onlookers enter vicariously into the youthful zest and competitive vitality of the various choruses and soloists who are dedicating themselves, perhaps even more thoroughly than they themselves at the time realize, to a life lived in the spirit of the community.[47]

At about seventeen, the formal education of the prospective citizens comes to an end, as far as the scholastic institutions are concerned. It is followed by military life (of one sort or another) for most of the boys, by domestic life for most of the girls, and by close attention to the laws of the community, for all. Here, as in the earlier education, some consideration is given to natural interest and capacity. It is expected that most of the boys will take kindly to camping, and to military duties calculated to be of obvious benefit to the community. It is expected that they will devise a number of rules for their own self-government.[48] It is expected that some of the girls will continue to take part in vigorous field-sports, and will not object to competitive racing on foot for a few years.[49] And it is obvious that both sexes will take a healthy natural interest in the activities connected with courtship and matrimony.

All this is spontaneous and natural; and the educative oversight provided by the authorities will merely give to this natural bent a direction which makes its development useful to the young people in their capacity as junior members of the community.[50] In fact, it should be plain that the entire life of the citizens from birth to death follows these general lines: building the community way of doing things upon the natural interests and capacities of its individual members. How, indeed, could things be otherwise?[51]

The function of 'education' (throughout) is to develop, not robots conditioned to respond with an external and mechanical inevitableness to the rules and laws of the approved behaviour-patterns, whether military, civic, or merely social. It develops, rather, self-controlled, self-directed young citizens: expressing themselves spontaneously and naturally in their chosen careers in the model community.[52] Where each follows his natural bent, the bent natural to him, not only as a member of this or that age or sex group, but as an individual, he does what Plato calls 'his own' work. That is to say, his contribution to the life of the community is his own original contribution.

And it is essential to the community that this should be so; that each, in serving the whole, should contribute something different from his fellows, something growing from the depths of his own individuality. Only thus can the life of the community be suitably enriched, and be (itself) the expression of freedom.[53] There is about individuality a vitality, a certain non-logical charm; which no book of rules, however rationally consistent, can create or can do without. The excellences of life evade logical definition, as anyone who talks with Socrates soon finds out. But that does not make them less significant, less excellent.[54]

We are now in a position to apply this to art. Suppose you are a high-ranking official in the model city, and you find that what the community needs is a funeral oration, a new poem, or a new choric dance, to celebrate a new occasion—or it may be some kind of academic exercise to pick out the most promising of the young musicians who are growing up. What do you do? You cannot just give an order: telling a subordinate, *any* subordinate, to produce an appropriate oration, poem, musical composition, or what not; or appointing an approved citizen, just *any* approved citizen, to hold an examination and pick out the winners for you. You will have to look around for experts in this or that field. You will need people who really have it in them, to judge excellence in a work of art, or to create original compositions of high artistic value.

That is to say, you will have to fall back on men of natural capacity and strong personal interest in music (or whatever the art with which you are concerned). You will need men whose individual capacities and interests have been taken into account in their education. You may be as powerful as you please. You may be as full of community feeling and understanding as anyone could desire. You may have won the prize of virtue in the model city. But this does not make you, honoured sir, competent to compose poetry or music, to paint pictures, or to design public buildings, or even to teach growing children. For such things, you have to call upon the artists and artisans. You summon the specialists who, in virtue of their natural gifts and spontaneous interest in expressing themselves in music, poetry, painting, or architecture, or possibly in teaching, have thrown themselves wholeheartedly into these arts. In a word, you send for men who have made of themselves competent creators and critics; experts in their own individual fields.[55]

To put it simply: you call a committee of 'those who take an interest in such things'. You ask for their expert advice. You stimulate them to put their trained talents at the service of the community. You offer whatever incentives appeal to such men. You pay them a salary or a fee. You provide living-quarters. You grant them community recognition. You give them authority in their own fields of *expertise*. You encourage them to draw up the rules under which men of their craft will operate. You use your power (such as it is) to make the recommendations on which you and they come to an agreement, official. You stamp their recommendations with the seal of community approval. And you are particularly careful, at all times, to leave to each and every artist a zone of indetermination within which he is both permitted and encouraged to use his own judgement. You let him contribute something extra, something individual, something unanticipated and original in matters of detail. Artists are like that. Only if you encourage them to follow their own ideas and use their own trained taste in their own ways, will they be able, as well as willing, to do their artistic best for the community. In a word, if the community expects them to co-operate, the community must co-operate with them. It must respect their individuality and freedom, and must support them in the exercise of their own artistic spontaneity.[56]

All this is for Plato, himself a writer, and a highly original writer, elementary and obvious. He says this, but he hardly bothers to bring it into focus and make it central; because (with him) it is never, even remotely, in doubt. He is himself busied in the creation of a new art: the art of philosophical dialogue. Each of his Dialogues differs from its predecessors in *tournure* as well as in technique. You never know beforehand, quite what he is going to say, and certainly not, how he is going to say it. Probably he does not himself know. He just 'follows the argument, whithersoever it leads'. And he expects, and allows for, novelty and progress, doubtless in himself as an artistic writer, and certainly in others; quite certainly, in the members of his model city.[57]

Writing, as he does, with his attention sharply focused upon the problems of administration, it is the capacities, the interests, and the insight of the administrators upon which he is particularly insistent. It is the administrators who, when their education has finally fitted them for their function, practise the 'royal art' without further let or hindrance. The qualified artist acts always for the benefit of the community, and is always (in his own field of *expertise*) a little above and beyond the uninspired questioning of lesser men.[58] Free themselves, administrators are artists in the highest sense. They are 'artificers of freedom' to the community as a whole. They ensure freedom to the rest of the golden class, to the silver class, to the classes of copper and iron; yes, and (in so far as such a thing is possible in the model city) to the slaves as well.[59]

Modern readers, observing this concentration upon the governing class, and the comparative neglect of the other classes, are rather easily inclined to think that only the 'guardians' or magistrates are really free. They readily allow themselves to be persuaded that the artists, artisans, and slaves (so far as slavery is really an accepted institution in Plato's utopias) give what might be called 'command performances'.[60] Influenced by the emphasis in our own time upon 'statism', they are inclined to see in the *Republic* and *Laws* something of the unlovely attitude nowadays denounced as 'totalitarianism'.[61]

This, while natural in modern times, is hardly, perhaps, in accordance with an unprejudiced reading of the entire *Dialogues*. Plato, while centring his attention upon the administrative artists called 'philosophers', uses (as anyone can see) the physicians, poets, musicians, and other artists incidentally: to illustrate the points he is making about his practitioners of 'the royal art'. That is because, as Plato sees the matter, *all* artists (as such), whatever the field of their *expertise*, are, within that field, free to use their own well-developed judgement, and are, further, each within his own field, 'artificers of freedom' to others also.

It is primarily by artistic appeals to the imagination, that human beings are raised to the level of self-determination, and to self-direction in accordance with the ideals envisaged by their growing insight.[62] That is to say, sincere and competent practitioners of *any* art, achieve (within that art) the liberation of the talents which are natural and spontaneous within them. And further: they stimulate to similar self-liberation, all who are capable of appreciating the artistic vision and its call. The model city of the *Laws*, taken by and large, is essentially a set of administrative arrangements which make it possible for very large numbers of individuals with very varying backgrounds and outlooks, to achieve, in the freedom of community life, the ability to practise together their own arts, and to enjoy the fruits of their fellow-citizens' arts.[63]

NOTES

1. *Gorg.* 501d f., *Rep.* 475c f., 479, 533b f., 595 ff., *Phaedr.* 275c f., 277e f., *Phil.* 55e f., *Laws* 667c ff., 811, 817.

2. *Ion* 530b, *Symp.* 209d, *Rep.* 383a, 391a, 595b, 598d f., 607a f., *Theaet.* 152e, 194e, *Laws* 776e.

3. *Rep.* 377d f., 389d f., 390d, 401a f., *Laws* 802a f.

4. *Rep.* 383c, 394c f., 600e f., 605a f., *Laws* 656cd, 801c, 829de.

5. *Rep.* 387a, d f., 388c f., 391e f., 595, 605c f., *Laws* 669b f.

6. *Rep.* 607e f., *Laws* 800 ff., 817d f., 829c f.

7. *Pol.* 294, 295b f., 297a f., 299e. For the general rules accepted by Plato, see *Phaedr.* 271d f., cf. 270b f.

8. *Rep.* 372e f., 475c ff., 595 ff., *Laws* 811, 817a f.

9. *Gorg.* 503a f., *Symp.* 211c f., *Rep.* 402b f., 499e f., *Laws* 660a f., 662a, 823b f.

10. *Euthyd.* 291b, *Pol.* 305d, *Laws* 663e f. Cf. Aristot. *Nic. Eth.* 1094a 26–1094b 11. Croce, *op. cit.*, pp. 111, 116–117 similarly recognizes the right of the 'economic and practical life' to control external publication of art-works.

11. *Rep.* 401b, *Critias* 115c f., *Pol.* 259e f., 280cd.

12. *Crat.* 424d f., *Rep.* 420cd. *Critias* 107b f., *Pol.* 277bc, *Laws* 769a f.

13. *Rep.* 377b ff., 391c f., *Laws* 802b f.

14. *Rep.* 398d ff., *Laws* 656c f., 658e f., 661b f., 800 ff., 814d f.

15. *Laws* 625d ff., 629d ff., 658d ff.

16. *Laws* 660 ff., 664 ff., 798b ff., 802a f. Cf. Tilney, *op. cit.*, pp. 207, 215, as to the absence of mechanical reproduction in Hellenic art. 'There are no facsimiles, only variations on a common theme.'

17. *Euthyd.* 291 f., *Gorg.* 521d, *Rep.* 428d, 540d, 546d f., *Pol.* 293a, 297bc, 299d, *Laws* 643d f.

18. Aristot. *Pol.* 1326a 35–1326b 25. Cf. Homer, *Il.* 2, 204.

19. Locke, *Some Thoughts Concerning Education*, 4th edit., London, 1699, sects. 174, cf. 170, 197, 203.

20. Locke, *identid.* Cf. Ben Jonson, *Every Man in his Humour*, Act I, Sc. I, lines 17–24, 76 (possibly influenced by Th. Kyd, *The Spanish Tragedy*, ad init.). For Plato, cf. *Gorg.* 484d–485d, 487cd.

21. For Kant, I have in mind, not merely his specifically ethical treatises, but his *Kritik der Urteilskraft*, and his essay *Zum ewig. Frieden*. For the later idealistic development, I would refer specifically to Wundt's *Ethics* (E.T., 1908), esp. Vol. I, pp. 264–267, Vol. II, p. 120, Vol. III, pp. 70, 80, 83, 139–144, 155–158, 210, 271–275.

22. This is the thesis, e.g., of André Siegfried's book, *England's Crisis* (tr. Hemming, New York, Harcourt, 1931).

23. For Addison, see *Spectator*, No. 159. For Huxley, see *Brave New World*. For Schopenhauer, see *The World as Will and Idea*, Bk. IV, sects. 57, 58, 68.

24. I have in mind, e.g., Marcus Aurelius, *Meditations* IV 19, VI 34–36, X 6, XI 15, etc.; Epictetus, *Encheiridion*, V, VIII, XXXI (Higginson, II 218, 219, 229), etc.; St. Augustine, *The City of God*, Bk. XIV, ch. vi, Bk. XIX, ch. iv; cf. Abélard, *Ethics or Know Thyself*, chs. ii, iii, x–xiii (reprinted in B. Rand, *Classical Moral Philosophers*, pp. 179, 181, 182, 187, 189, etc.).

25. *Laws* 709a–d, cf. *Gorg.* 456a f.
26. *Gorg.* 521d ff., *Pol.* 288cd, *Laws* 658 ff., 667c ff., 673a.
27. *Rep.* 373c, 460c f., *Laws* 789d f., 791e f.
28. *Tim.* 64e f., 81a f., 83e, 88b f., *Phil.* 31d f., *Laws* 790c f. For the value of rhythm, cf. *Tim.* 47de.
29. *Rep.* 619a, *Laws* 691c, 792a f. Cf. R. C. Lodge, *Plato's Theory of Ethics*, cf. xix.
30. *Phaedr.* 245c f., *Tim.* 90c f., *Phil.* 30a f., *Laws* 790e–793, 894e ff.
31. *Laws* 793d f.
32. *Rep.* 536e, *Laws* 643c, 794a (cf. *Euthyd.* 277b, *Phdo.* 110b, *Theaet.* 146a, 181a, etc.).

I do not understand Plato as meaning that infants actually originate *ex nihilo* the entire detail of their spontaneous ways of playing. They are at all times very much influenced by their social environment, i.e. by what they see older children, their parents, and other persons, doing. That is why carpenters' children pick up (naturally, first in play and later in serious imitation) the ways of behaving which are characteristic of carpenters; while potters' children pick up the behaviour of potters. Children in the model city pick up naturally the beginnings of the social habits which are characteristic of model citizens. Their running, throwing, and jumping, have a slightly military twist. Their playing with dolls has a domestic background and outlook. Their 'prisoner's base' is even more definitely of a military character.

33. *Rep.* 397bc, 425a, *Laws* 718c f., 720e ff., 793e f. Cf. R. C. Lodge, *Plato's Theory of Education*, pp. 220 ff., cf. also *Trnsct. Roy. Soc. of Canada*, Vol. XLIII, Series III (1949), pp. 87–101.
34. *Rep.* 386 ff., 389d ff., 401 ff. Life in the model city of the *Laws* is definitely based upon 'the natural bent' and 'natural inclinations' of the young citizens, guided by artistic influences (choral singing) in the direction accepted (as most desirable) by the 'eldest and best'.
35. *Laws* 794c ff., 813d ff., 829a ff., 942, cf. *Rep.* 537a.
36. *Rep.* 466e f.
37. *Laws* 829 ff.
38. *Laws* 785b, 829b, 833c f., 834d, cf. *Rep.* 456a, 457ab, 466d.
39. *Laws* 643c f., 657d, 796c f., 830d f., cf. *Rep.* 425a, 537a.
40. *Charm.* 161d, *Rep.* 402ab, *Theaet.* 203a f., 206ab, 207c f., *Pol.* 277e f., *Laws* 810c f., 811d f. Cf. also Tilney, *op. cit.*, as in note 16, *supra*.
41. *Prtg.* 326cd, *Gorg.* 485a f., *Laws* 810b.
42. *Prtg.* 326a, *Rep.* 386 ff., 395c f., 401a f., *Phaedr.* 228a f., *Laws* 665c, 802a f., 810e f. Cf. Kenneth J. Freeman, *Schools of Hellas* (1908) p. 97.
43. *Rep.* 377 ff., *Laws* 629 ff., 800 ff., 817d, cf. 903b f.
44. *Laws* 809e f.
45. *Laws* 657a f., 658e f., 659d f., 668 ff., 802c f., 810a f., 812c f., cf. *Rep.* 397d. Cf. Erich Frank, *Plato u.d.s–g.Pythagoreer*, pp. 161–167.
46. *Laws* 653c f., 657b f., 659d f., 764c f., 811e f., 828a f., 834e f.
47. *Laws* 664 f., 814d ff., cf. 657d.
48. *Laws* 760b ff., 813d f., cf. *Rep.* 416c f.
49. *Laws* 829, 833c, 834d.
50. *Rep.* 458d f., 468bc, *Laws* 721bc, 772d f., 774a, 776ab, 783d f., 929a f.
51. *Rep.* 374 f., 423d, 443c f., 444d, 456a f., 484c f., 540d, 544de, *Tim.* 17cd.

Phaedr. 265e, *Pol.* 287bc, *Laws* 643c 7, d 2, 765a 5 f., 772d, 794a 2, 979a f., 961b 2–3, etc.

What Plato teaches is not (I think) different in spirit from what is taught at the present day by John Dewey, as to the importance of basing the educational curriculum upon the natural action-tendencies of children. Dewey formulates the schoolboy's natural interests as 'the interest in conversation or communication; in inquiry, or finding out things; in making things, or construction; and in artistic expression' (*The School and Society*, revised edition, 1916, University of Chicago Press, p. 45).

52. *Laws* 643d f., cf. *Rep.* 299 f., 405ab.

53. *Rep.* 345c ff., 369b ff., 374b 7–8, e 3–6, 375 f., 395b f., 397d f., 406e f., 409c f., 412ab, 415a f., 576e f., etc. I feel there is kinship of intellectual pattern between Plato's thinking here, and his thinking in *Phil.* 16b ff. (which is also attributed to 'Socrates').

54. Aristotle apparently writes as though Socrates was actually trying to find definitions of the various virtues recognized as important in Hellenic thought (*Met.* 1078b 18–32). If so, it should be obvious to any reader of the Socratic Dialogues, that his efforts tended to result (in spite of *Rep.* 367b, d, 612) in failure (cf. *Meno* 71a f.). P. Friedländer (*Platon I*, Berlin & Leipzig, 1928) maintains (p. 5) that to interpret Aristotle's remarks as historical in intent, is a misunderstanding. His own view is that, while Socrates does seek 'the just', 'the courageous', 'the temperate', and 'the wise' (more seriously than other thinkers, who pursue only 'shadows') by the use of words, he also incorporates these virtues in his own living and dying, as forms visible to the eye of the soul (*ibid.*, pp. 15–16). I would be understood as having also in mind, Wilamowitz, *Platon*, 2nd edit. (Berlin, 1920), esp. pp. 106 ff.

55. *Prtg.* 319bc, *Rep.* 333, 374 f., 429b f., 433d, 434a–c, 467d, 537a–d, *Tim.* 17cd, 18b 7, *Pol.* 259e f., *Laws* 657a f., 659d f., 738b f., 764c f., 799a, 802a f., 811b f., 817d, 828ab, 829a f., 846d f., 920b f., cf. 926. It was regularly expected of the Athenian dramatists, that they would exhibit originality in their handling of the incidents, in the national legends which formed the themes of their plays. For the modern view, we might compare Croce, *op. cit.*, p. 136. He emphasizes the essential non-repetitiveness of the artistic impulse toward expression.

56. *Pol.* 294 f., *Phil.* 55e f., *Laws* 770b, 772a f., 802bc, 191d f., 920d f., 934bc, cf. *Epist.* 322de.

57. For discussion of the evidence, see R.C. Lodge, 'Plato and Progress' (*Philos. Review*, 1946), esp. pp. 659–667. This is not a 'zone of indetermination' in matters of incidental detail (law being necessarily too general to cover all individual cases). Innovation, while discouraged in the case of children and others regarded as *in statu pupillari*, is expected in the case of experts (men like Damon) and qualified adults (e.g., in committees of artistic experts functioning under a trained community executive).

58. *Rep.* 342, *Pol.* 293a f., 295d f., 300cd, 305c f., 308d ff.

59. For discussion of the evidence, see R. C. Lodge, 'Plato and Freedom' (*Trnsctns. Roy. Soc. of Canada*, Vol. XLIII (1949)), esp. pp. 90–99.

60. Doubt has been expressed recently, as to whether slaves (*douloi*), although obviously present in the model city of the *Laws*, (although deliberately not used by young men on military service, *Laws* 763a), are ever even mentioned in connexion with the ideal city of the *Republic*. Such passages as *Rep.* 567e, 569a, 578e,

refer (as has been pointed out) not to the ideal city, but to the 'tyrant's city'. Such passages as *Rep.* 469c, 471a, merely say, there shall be no *Hellenic* slaves in the ideal city. They do not raise the question of possibly *Barbarian* slaves.

However, I find one passage which does refer to *douloi* in connexion with the ideal city. In enumerating the types of person in the ideal community who 'do their own work', *Rep.* 433d 2 includes *douloi* as well as *eleutheroi* (freemen) in the list.

There does, then, exist this one reference to *douloi*. But there are plenty of references to *oiketai*, in the sense of 'domestic servants' (nurses and other menials); although doubtless the nurses who look after the 'silver' and 'golden' babies are *demosioi, public* slaves—because the golden class does not have *private* household life. Liddell and Scott's references indicate that *oiketai* are more truly slaves than are *douloi;* for *douloi* may be freedmen (still owing a certain meed of service) whereas *oiketai* are in a state of non-manumission.

I myself suppose that, in connexion with the silver and golden classes, there are *oiketai*, a non-enfranchised class of workers; in the *Republic* much as in the *Laws*. But it may well be that in the *Republic* these menials are all community servants, and do not 'belong' to individuals, as such. In the *Laws*, there are community menials, who keep the streets and temples clean, etc.; but, as there are private families, these private families undoubtedly possess private *oiketai*. The words *oiketes* and *doulos* are sometimes distinguished, sometimes used interchangeably by Hellenic writers.

For the freedom of the 'guardian', which rests upon insight into the 'form', see John Wild, *Plato's Theory of Man* (1946), p. 146; and for the control of artists, see p. 62.

61. E.g., Chr. M. Wieland, *Aristipp* (in *Werke*, ed. Pröhle, Berlin, 1882–1887, Vols. IV, V); R. H. S. Crossman, *Plato Today* (London, 1937), Warner Fite, *The Platonic Legend* (New York, 1934), and (more recently) the discussion centring around the papers of Messrs. Neurath and Lauwerys in the *Journal of Education*, 1944–45. These views are widely held at the present day.

62. For the evidence of this function of the 'imagination' see R. C. Lodge, *Plato's Theory of Education*, 1947, pp. 122–136.

63. *Laws* 846d ff., 920b ff., cf. *Rep.* 369b ff., 462 ff.

One sense of 'freedom' in relation to the work of artists, a sense quite frequent in modern works on aesthetics, is not (I think) in Plato at all. It is thought (nowadays) that artistic creation is uphill work, that the artist labours with his problem (perhaps, after all, this is indicated in Socrates's account of his *maieutike*, in the *Theaetetus?*) is held in its grip, until eventually he solves it: by painting his picture, completing his symphony or poem or novel. He has then (we feel) 'worked it out of his system', has *'freed himself* from its Protean clutch', and has turned it into an *'überwundener Standpunkt'*. (Cf., e.g. Croce, *op. cit.*, p. 21, 'By elaborating his impressions, man frees himself from them. By objectifying them, he removes them from him and makes himself their superior. The liberating and purifying function of art is another aspect . . . of its character as activity. Activity is the deliverer, because it drives away passivity.'

I do not find in Plato's Dialogues anything which I feel to be akin to this. On the contrary, Plato (if I understand him correctly) feels that the philosopher-king (for instance) achieves freedom, not by writing a book or painting a picture or composing a tone-poem, or anything of the sort; but by living the life of a citizen-magistrate in the ideal republic or model city.

The 'freedom' of which he is an artificer, both for himself and for his fellow-citizens, is the ability to live the ideal life for man (i.e. as a member of the civic drama-cast) in the model community. You do not 'free yourself' from this. You do not cast it aside as an *überwundener Standpunkt* (cf. Croce, p. 96). On the contrary, you achieve freedom by learning to live a full human life as a member of such a community. As compared with the 'freedom' you thus achieve, the ordinary artist, who is apparently satisfied to write a book or paint a picture, has hardly begun to live, or to conceive in what true 'freedom' consists.

Croce, who elsewhere and in general seems to have a conception of the artist's life as the activity of 'spiritual self-expression' in relative independence of the mechanical side of physical art-works (*op. cit.*, pp. 51, 60 f., 96, 97, 104 ff., 116 f., 123, 125, etc.) does not really, in the end, soar above the physical art-work. Expression (with Croce) is not really expression, until it 'synthesizes' the various physical elements (the pigments brushed on to the canvas, the tones produced by the violin-strings, etc.). If you try to separate the expression as a plan or dream in the mind of the artist before he tackles the concrete manipular problem of getting it all down in his poem or on his canvas, you find (according to Croce) that you cannot do it. Expression demands the space-time medium, as well as the artist's imagination.

CHAPTER FOURTEEN

The Function of Knowledge in Art

ONE of the fundamental difficulties in the tissue of Plato's thinking centres around his conception of human knowledge. What is the nature, what is the function, and what are the limitations of such knowledge? The difficulty affects Plato's ethics, his politics, his physics, and his aesthetics.[1] The difficulty comes to a head (as most readers soon discover) in the case of the *persona*, Socrates. Socrates is universally supposed to teach that 'virtue is knowledge' (as indeed is believed by all contemporary teachers of practical wisdom, the so-called 'sophists').[2] Socrates deliberately spends much of his life criticizing the poets and artists, the statesmen and generals, and all other would-be leaders in Athens. He experiences no difficulty in showing that every human being, from a young man on the threshold of life[3] to a successful man of the world[4] or a great teacher,[5] falls into inconsistencies, the moment you put his alleged wisdom to the question. Not one of these actual, would-be leaders of mankind has knowledge! And yet it is (surely) quite clear that, ideally speaking, he *should* have knowledge. To set oneself up as a leader of humanity, a guide to the good life, without *knowing*, clearly, distinctly, and objectively, in what the 'good for humanity' consists—what presumption, what almost incredible folly![6] It is the artist's business (if he is to know his business) to have a firm and clear grasp of such things. If he has not—and the evidence indicates that he usually has not—what sort of an artist *is* he?[7]

Most artists are what Plato calls 'empirics', experimentalists. Like most of us, they have a vague feeling for value in general, and (more specifically) for what seems to have value in their own particular fields.[8] They depend upon experience (such as it is). A painter (in Hellas) draws an outline sketch of this or that object—which (for one reason or another) attracts him to try his hand at reproducing its appearance. He then daubs in a number of colours, trying what happens with this or that combination of pigments, painting in, painting out, painting in again; never entirely satisfied. He does not know quite what *would* satisfy him; but he keeps on trying. If (after a while) the result looks pretty good to him, and pretty good to his brother-artists; and if his public (which commissions and pays for his paintings) likes it well enough to purchase it and hang it: in the end, he (though still reluctantly) lets it go. Then he turns his hand to something else.[9]

It is all very empirical. It is very much a matter of trial and error. When he has once let it get away from his control, it is quite unable to maintain itself against criticism: whether over-valuing, or disparaging. If he has painted a 'Shoemaker at his Last', or a 'Hellenic Galley Sweeping into Harbour', he knows that every cobbler or sailor who looks at his picture (while not pretending to *expertise* in the technique of painting) will see all sorts of mistakes in matters of factual detail. It is really safer to stick to mythological subjects, like the 'Battle of the Gods and Titans': where the beings depicted are entirely imaginary, and any resemblance to persons and events factual and known is purely coincidental![10]

The same sort of thing happens in poetry. Homer has a wonderful time, telling what Athene and Here said and did on Olympus, what time Zeus was off week-ending somewhere; or how Heracles, after his labours, was elevated to a place among the gods, only his 'shade' remaining in Hades. And the way Homer appears to know the special names used by the gods for what mere mortals call this and that— simply marvellous! There is not much of an empirical check upon this kind of fine writing![11]

But when it comes to Homer's saying that the Achaeans, though camping on the shores of the Hellespont for ten long years, were not allowed to eat fish, but only roast meat; or telling how their medical advisers permitted them, when dangerously wounded, to partake of highly inflammatory food and drink; or describing in detail how Odysseus constructed a ship to carry him over the wine-dark sea in rough weather;—well, this sort of thing falls within human experience. The poet's friends will have to be prepared to expect criticism accordingly![12]

In a word, artists depend upon what experience they have, and doubtless make the most of it. But their experience tends to be fragmentary, pieced out with a good deal of guesswork and wishful thinking. In fact, most human experience is like this; and it would be quite a mistake, to regard anything so empirical as furnishing a sound basis for genuine knowledge.[13]

In some of the arts, the workers guide their efforts by measurement. They even try to approximate to the more exact patterns of arithmetic and geometry. So far as it goes, this is a step in the direction of true knowledge.[14] But just how far does this really take them? After all, are not the arts, one and all, relative to human wants and to the community's idea (such as this is) of what it really wants and needs? Very few actual artists, in *any* field, go much beyond this. They are fairly well satisfied to give their paymasters about what their paymasters think they want. But is praising the Athenians (when among the Athenians), that is to say, is simple flattery, a safe guide to sound, objective knowledge? Obviously, not.[15]

Just what is this 'knowledge', which artists should have, but apparently do not? Will Socrates kindly tell us? Socrates has devoted his life to such questions. He, if anyone, will know the answers. It is precisely here that we come upon what is always so exasperating about Socrates. He is quite sure that no one else knows the answers. But he is also sure that he himself does not know, either.[16]

If pressed, he admits that he has an idea. In fact, everyone has a sort of idea of what he wants, toward which he is obscurely working. You might call it, 'the good'. But the idea is deplorably vague and confused. It remains obstinately in the background of our thinking. If we try to bring it out into the foreground, and make it focal; well, it is a sort of *x*. You can regard it as the unknown ground, perhaps a rational ground, of knowing and being. You might say it is the *ratio cognoscentis*, the *ratio cognoscendi*, and the *ratio essendi*—why not? That is all (doubtless) true, so far as it goes.[17]

But after you have surveyed the intelligible realm of ideas from end to end (if you ever do succeed in this), you will still find yourself thinking of 'the good' as the *ultimate* principle of ideality, a ground that itself transcends human knowing (and indeed transcends being, as human creatures understand being). Is the principle of essentiality, itself an essence? Ah, well; even if you suggest that God knows it in its utter finality, are you not left with the hopeless conclusion that there is (unfortunately) a gap between God's knowledge and yours?[18] Even if you suppose that divine inspiration might conceivably help a man across that gap; would what the man glimpsed in that experience really be *knowledge, human knowledge*?[19]

In a word, Socrates recognizes (1) a best, i.e. an ideally best, and (2) a second-best. As to the ideally best, it can perhaps be formulated as a postulate, as an aim to be worked towards, not with any hope of immediate achievement. It is remote. Such a regulative ideal is more than a Socrates, more than a single generation of students, however competent and however eager, even if their leader is a Plato, can hope to formulate in words that human beings can understand. It is what is known as 'Plato's secret': which cannot be told, and should not be told, if it should one day become more clearly and distinctly known.[20] To work toward this, requires a new science, the science of dialectic; and heaven knows how many generations of the future history of philosophy![21]

What is the second-best? Well, it is about what you might expect from the actualities of the human knowledge-situation. In a number of areas of human experience, patient observation has discovered what might be called traces or indications of behaviour-patterns. This is empirical. But continued co-operative observation and co-ordination would doubtless lead to something further. It would be a mistake to anticipate a very rapid increase of such knowledge within a few generations. But tentative generalizations of considerable practical value can gradually (no doubt) be achieved.

An example is the field of social psychology and sociology. Perhaps history might be included. The resulting 'social science' is not (it must be admitted) very scientific. It is not usually accepted as coming up to a high standard of 'knowledge'. But it is useful. Progressively so, as Protagoras and his fellow-students and practitioners of the art of government have discovered—to their undoubted advantage.[22]

Similarly in such fields as agriculture and medicine. Continued co-operative observation and experimentation have helped gradually to build up a fairly respectable nexus of empirical generalizations which can be used, pretty effectively; although such generalizations boast little more than an approximation to objective knowledge. Practising farmers and doctors find such generalizations indispensable.[23]

So also observations, long continued and carefully co-ordinated, have enabled empirical astronomers to discover a few patterns in the positions and motions of the celestial bodies; and such patterns have been found quite useful, e.g. by ships' captains, for their navigational purposes.[24] All such 'natural science' is also far from being ideally satisfactory as 'knowledge'. But, fragmentary as it is, and mixed up with subjective factors such as wishful thinking, it certainly has its uses.[25]

The Pythagorean brothers have gone somewhat further. In fact, they have taken an immense stride forward. By abstracting the patterns indicated by observation, and comparing them with the far more regular patterns discovered by arithmeticians and geometricians, the Pythagoreans have made a good many rather exciting kinds of discovery. There appear to be analogies between the behaviour-patterns observed in different fields of experience; and analogies drawn from mathematical figures have proved (to some extent) empirically verifiable in more than one experiential area.[26]

For instance: given certain hypothetical assumptions, you can make mathematical deductions. For quite a number of these, you will find physical analogies in the behaviour-patterns of actual phenomena. Some of these have, it is true, no demonstrable practical use. But to an intellectual, this is all rather fun; and *some* of it, no doubt, will have practical applications.[27] Thus, a good Pythagorean of Plato's time can apparently construct a working model which will reproduce (on a small scale) the movements of the chief heavenly bodies;[28] and he can work out the interrelations of geometrical *analoga* of earth, water, fire, and air, in ways which seem (to the mathematically trained intelligence) to explain certain of the physical transformations observable in nature. For instance, he can explain the transformation of water into ice by the subtraction of heat, or into vapour by the application of fire.[29] And deductions similar in principle have an obvious importance for the phenomena of health and disease. In fact, this becomes the standard method of explanation adopted by Aristotle, Galen, and medical science for many, many centuries.[30]

A wide range of interesting and useful investigation for those who dedicate their lives to the pursuit of knowledge, thus opens itself to the inquiring mind. And this is (on the whole) about as far as inquirers of the Pythagorean type are willing to go. They catalogue the behaviour-patterns observed in nature; and they seek for these a more exact, mathematical formulation. Their guiding assumption is, that 'things are numbers'. For the most part, they confine themselves to investigation of the properties of mathematical patterns which appear to have some verifiable relation to the behaviour of empirical phenomena. For them, such investigations constitute 'science'. Anything less, and indeed anything which tries to be more, simply is not 'knowledge'.[31]

Socrates, however, goes further, much further; even though what he suggests still falls within the field of his 'second-best'. It proves

possible, he thinks, after a great deal of experience in the mathematically developed arts and sciences, to carry abstract thinking
beyond the point where the Pythagoreans stop. The Pythagoreans
are 'friends of ideas'. But they do not carry their friendly interest in
abstract, conceptual thinking, nearly as far as, e.g. the Eleatics. It
proves possible to abstract concepts, not merely from their ordinary
setting in sensuous and practical experience, but from the technical,
mathematical formulation given them by the Pythagoreans.

Thus, you can define a concept in relation to other concepts. You
can classify and divide concepts, arranging them in systems which
follow the patterns indicated as in nature or even beyond observed
nature. You can reason from analogy; applying the systematic order
found within one area to another area of conceptual thought.[32] You
can investigate the abstract presuppositions of the more exact
sciences; pushing your inquiry into their assumptions until you
discover (hypothetically) upon what yet more general and abstract
assumptions these, in turn, depend. Eventually you find something
like what a later age will call 'categories': ideas so comprehensive in
scope as to extend over, not one, but most (if not all) of the sciences.
These are not given to us in sensory experience. They are not visual
in quality, or tactile or auditory. They are something more universal.
The mind seems to discover them by pure, non-sensuous reflexion;
by asking questions of itself, by conversing with itself, rather than
with an external *datum*.[33] Inquirers who devote themselves to this
new kind of knowledge, Socrates and his followers call 'dialecticians'.

The chief dialecticians of Socrates's time are found in the Eleatic
school. Parmenides and Zeno are highest in repute. For abstract,
non-sensuous reasoning, they are without peers. They are 'friends of
ideas' in a higher sense than the Pythagoreans. But, as anyone who
reads the well-known passages from Zeno's controversial book can
see (and as some readers of Parmenides's book really think, whatever
they say), this sort of thing looks like clever logic-chopping. It is a
queer kind of game, played with rules far too strict for the counters
used.

If you use empirical concepts, that is to say, imperfect concepts,
second-best concepts derived from a few sensory experiences and
not entirely purified, not raised to a strictly conceptual level; it is
easy for a competent dialectician to bring out the imperfections, to
show the inconsistencies lurking beneath the surface of your thought.
Thus, Socrates has no difficulty whatever in bringing out the inconsistencies implicit in the too-empirical concepts of a Laches, a

Charmides, or a Polemarchus. He can do it even with debaters of some repute as intellectuals, such as Gorgias, Protagoras, or Thrasymachus.[34] Zeno says flatly, that if the Pythagoreans make fun of Parmenides's reasoning, he can apply his dialectical method to show that they are themselves living in houses of glass. It is all good clean fun for intellectuals.[35]

Similarly, Parmenides has no great difficulty in showing Socrates (who had, as a young man, fancied that *his* 'ideas' were superior to these empirical weaknesses), that the Socratic position also is merely human, after all. It is a kind of 'second-best' which is absurdly vulnerable, itself riddled with contradictions.[36] In fact, it looks as though dialectic is useful, chiefly, either for the confusion of a pretentious opponent, or, possibly, for inducing complete scepticism as to the powers of the human intellect.[37]

You might, just conceivably, suggest a third alternative. It does not, indeed, get you anywhere; and you might regard it as a useless pastime, indeed, as simple nonsense. But it might have, for a serious would-be artist in the realm of thought, the kind of value which technical finger-exercises have for the serious would-be artist in the realm of music. It provides a useful, indeed indispensable training in dexterity.[38]

Socrates (and this is the point) makes claim to just this kind of dexterity. When it comes to technique in abstract reasoning, he regards himself (as others regard him) as a leader.[39] But the position is so obviously 'second-best', that Socrates finds it unsatisfactory. He is prepared to criticize any and every position set before him by others. He is adequately equipped to bring out clearly any and all inconsistencies it may contain. But, while this technique helps him to reveal weaknesses, it does not give him positive truth. To show that no one else thinks with technical consistency, i.e. that no one else is in possession of satisfactorily formulated 'knowledge', is all very well, as far as it goes. But to know that he is himself in the very same position (if you push him into a corner), i.e. that he too is not in possession of satisfactorily formulated 'knowledge', is only a first or second step toward knowledge. It is still, obviously and admittedly, second-best.[40]

Socrates would very much like to go further. He would like to achieve (perhaps with the co-operative assistance of others), however gradually, something a little more like ideal knowledge. He is looking for something more consistent, more unified, and at the same time more factual, than the position in which, after Eleatic self-criticism, he finds himself, along with the rest of the seekers after 'knowledge'.

What he suggests is the systematic, co-operative research which we find exemplified in the history of philosophy, from the time of Socrates himself down to and including the present day, and indeed many days in the future. The way is long and arduous. The pot of gold will not finally be unearthed until the end of the rainbow has been reached. Socrates suggests the continued pursuit of science by the scientists, and the continued practice of the arts by the artists. Their work provides the indispensable groundwork, without which no higher discoveries can be made. He suggests, further, the continued exploration, by dialecticians, of the conceptual and categorial presuppositions of the sciences and arts, particularly of the more exact sciences and arts.[41]

He distinguishes for us two lines along which we can look for gradual improvement as we search for 'knowledge'. There is (1) the 'way up', the inquiry into presuppositions. For instance, in the mathematical sciences, instead of asking (as the mathematicians do) what you can deduce from a group of postulates and definitions (such as odd and even, acute-, obtuse-, and right-angles, triangles, rectangles, squares, circles, and the like) which you just assume without question; instead of this (the usual procedure of mathematicians), you put their postulates and defined terms themselves to the question. You ask, upon what further presuppositions these *data* depend.

By co-ordinating the mathematical sciences, treating them as a group dependent upon common principles, you will tend to find that you can simplify their assumptions. You can reduce them to a fairly small group of inter-implying concepts;[42] and you can relate these to a still smaller group of higher principles, the 'categories'. These (formulated at first somewhat like this: Equality and Inequality, Similarity and Dissimilarity, Identity and Difference, Permanence and Change, Rest and Motion, Unity and Multiplicity, Whole and Parts, Being and Non-being, and the like) can similarly be reduced to a much smaller number.[43]

It is quite obvious that you can introduce a greater degree of simplicity into any such list, if you arrange your terms in two parallel columns. You can link together (in one column), Equality, Similarity, Identity, Permanence, Rest, Unity, Wholeness, and Being; and you can link together (in your second column), Inequality, Dissimilarity, Difference, Change, Motion, Multiplicity,

Part, and Non-being. Something like this is worked out by one of Plato's immediate successors in the conduct of the Academy;[44] and it is easy to see how you could simplify yet further. You might succeed in reducing each of your two columns to a single principle. This would give you, e.g. (*a*) Identity and (*b*) Difference (usually translated 'Sameness and Otherness' in Plato's own account of the Pythagorean world-view);[45] or perhaps you would prefer terms like (*a*) Order and (*b*) Variety (as you find them in the thought of a Leibniz).[46]

If you desired to simplify yet further, you might try to reduce all such categories to a single highest principle. This would conclude your dialectical research in the 'upward' direction. You would end with something like Plato's principle of ideality and value. He calls it 'the good' or 'the idea of good'. If you favoured Aristotle (as many do), you would find yourself saying that all Greek philosophy (from its beginning in Thales and Anaximander to its favoured formulation in Aristotle and his successors) is seeking for the ultimate 'substance' which underlies all phenomena of change or motion. 'Substance', or possibly 'ultimate reality' would be your highest principle. If you took the more subjective line favoured by thinkers of another school, you would formulate the final principle as a 'principle of pre-established harmony'. You would say that it 'combined the greatest conceivable Variety with the greatest conceivable Order' (Leibniz); or you might prefer the 'synthetic unity of an ideal self-consciousness' (Kant). There would be nothing to prevent you, if you so desired, from naming your highest principle, 'The Absolute Experience', or, more simply, 'The Absolute', or (even more simply) 'God'.[47]

The fact that opinions differ, as to how such an ultimate principle should be formulated, is a sufficient indication that the task of philosophers in following the 'upward' path to its final termination is not yet (1952) completed. Socrates has no idea whatever that he himself, or any member of his own generation or century, is likely to complete this quest. As he sees it, the quest extends indefinitely into the future. The 'second-best' use of such a principle (not yet quite adequately formulated), is as a heuristic principle, or as what Kant later is to call a 'regulative' principle. It urges knowledge-seekers to simplify and clarify their presuppositions, in relation to whatever bodies of experience are relatively organized as sciences and arts. As such a principle, the 'idea of good' (however you formulate it) assists toward the gradual integration of what (in our still 'second-best' condition) represents our approximation to 'knowledge'. Progressive integration is, in fact, the best we can expect, humanly speaking.[48]

Let us now consider (2) the 'way down'. Ideally speaking (if, that is to say, we had somehow achieved 'the best', and our insight into the unhypothetical first principle was complete), we should be able to turn around and apply our principle of ideality to the highest categories which we had reached in our 'upward' path. We should be in a position to integrate, re-organize, and re-formulate in a final way, our recent abstractions (still containing some slightly empirical material) labelled 'idea of good', 'ultimate substance', 'pre-established harmony', 'ideal self-consciousness', 'absolute experience', and the like. Having squeezed out of these (as it were) the last residue of unintelligibility, or mere factuality accepted as such, we could then use the quintessential rational resultant as a standard, by which to integrate, re-organize, and re-formulate in a way which would also be final, such categories as identity and difference, order and variety, unity and multiplicity, permanence and change, etc.[49]

We should then be in a position to take a second step 'downwards'. We could integrate and re-organize the more general and abstract assumptions of, e.g. the mathematical sciences. Realizing their inter-implications, we could simplify them, reducing their factual multiplicity to intelligible unity. We should find that we could understand the regularity of closed figures (such as the right-angled triangle of the Pythagoreans), in terms of our re-formulated principle of order, or unity, or however it would be named. Our partly-integrated tissues of inter-implying propositions (constituting the body of arithmetic, plane geometry, etc.) would thus, in the end, become completely-integrated, reorganized into a final deductive system, based upon these higher principles. The system would become intelligible throughout: completely apprehensible by the human mind. There would remain no obscure and partial proofs, no alternative proofs of varying degrees of cogency. The inter-implication of the parts would be complete. The insight derived from our grasp of the higher principles would permeate the entire structural system of mathematics: down to the very last detailed universal-proposition, and the very last standardized and adequately defined concept.[50]

That is what we should do, if we had achieved insight into 'the best'. But we have not achieved such insight. We are not likely to do so, within measurable time. What, then, is the second-best 'way down'? It is like the ideal just sketched. But it operates with imperfectly formulated higher principles. As, in our 'upward' path, we gradually achieved re-formulations of our higher principles, we now turn around and, using these improved (but still imperfect) formulations, we reorganize and re-formulate what comes under them.

That is to say, we gradually purify, clarify, and re-integrate the various partly-integrated bodies of experience which constitute what the Pythagorean type of mind calls the sciences, or 'knowledge'. Working both upwards and downwards, or rather, alternating the direction of our work, we gradually improve our empirical approximations to knowledge: clarifying, simplifying, and integrating, with ever-increasing scope and insight, e.g. the mathematical sciences. Something like Descartes's integration of geometry and algebra in 'analytic geometry', illustrates what Plato has in mind; or something like the way in which schoolchildren now learn to solve many a problem in arithmetic, geometry, and algebra, by using 'graphs'. In the history of science and philosophy, we are doing this sort of thing all the time: proceeding empirically, in both the upward and the downward direction.[51]

How about the function of knowledge (thus understood) in relation to art? Let us consider the art of administration. The administrator who has been trained in the more exact sciences and arts, and has improved his knowledge so as to have worked his way fairly well up to the 'second-best' level, operates approximately as follows: He first insists upon being given a free hand. The social situation which he is to organize, must be purified of prior empirical commitments, so as to give him a clean sheet.[52] He will then construct an outline of a social-political system calculated to provide (under the conditions of his own century) opportunities for the maximal development of civic potentialities.

This outline he will proceed to fill in very gradually; looking now toward the best available conceptions of justice, self-control, and the other civic virtues, and now at the available human material. Thus he will 'mingle and temper the various elements of life into the image of a man'. This 'man' he will conceive according to the most perfect pattern that an artist can construct—for a being who is to remain (of course) merely human. So we find it stated in the *Republic*.[53]

In the *Politicus*, the practitioner of the 'royal' art of administration is depicted as gradually, very gradually, weaving together into a single balanced pattern the various dispositions of men thought of as possible material for good citizenship. Throughout, the administrator is guided by the best available knowledge, both of philosophical principle and of psychological and sociological science.[54] It is the same in the *Laws*. Here the administrator, given a fairly clean sheet, first outlines his picture. He then fills in most of the structural pattern. Decisions about individual cases, he leaves (of course) to the appropriate officials at each level. What the administrative artist constructs, is a kind of organizer's blueprint. It contains places for all the priestships, magistracies, citizenships, artisanships, and assistantships that would be needed (according to Hellenic ideas) to carry on the life of a model city of 5,040 civic families.[55]

The administrative artist is well aware that the *personae* of his utopian drama are (as yet) the merest puppets: conceptual counters, not creatures of flesh and blood. He knows that the knowledge by which he orders his inter-implying system of concepts (knowledge of dialectic, of law, and of social statistics—quite as much as knowledge derived from general psychology and sociology) is far from adequate. It will not apply satisfactorily to individuals.[56] But then, an administrator does not believe that flesh-and-blood human individuals are really much more than puppets. At best, they cling to the golden cord of reason, and try to live rational self-directed lives. But (if you view them with philosophic detachment and objective insight) are they not really rather second-best material: puppets indeed, drawn this way and that by motives which are non-logical and faintly absurd; puppets with whom the High Gods play the best game they can?[57]

In a word, the administrator, convinced that his art requires an infinity of time for its perfection, keeps on at his task of re-organization. He looks, now toward the ideal, and now toward the actual. He regards all laws and human institutions as second-best devices: requiring perpetually to be unmade and remade by someone like the original artist—according as his knowledge (both of philosophical principle and of the social sciences) gradually, throughout the long centuries ahead of the race, improves. At times, conscious of the enormous gap between the ideal of which he dreams, and the very limited actual materials which are all he has with which to operate, he is disposed, perhaps, to give up and retire into his dream.[58] But then again, recognizing that he is himself human, and that 'a sad necessity is laid upon him', he admits that the only live option for a man of goodwill and trained insight is to follow the path which leads forwards. He returns, therefore, to his unending task of seeking and applying to his art, the further resources which come only from increase of knowledge.[59]

Let us examine a second example of art, the art so eagerly sought after and practised at Athens: the art of rhetoric, of persuasive public speaking. As practised by the great orators of the immediate past (Pericles and his fellow orator-statesmen), this art obviously made use, a kind of inspirational use, of the stimulus that comes from association with scientists and 'high speculation'.[60] But as written up in the text-books of the professors, there is very little about this art that deserves the name of 'knowledge'. There is very little insight into principle, and very little knowledge of analytic psychology and factual sociology. There is little more than a pretentious formalism and a fearsome terminology applied to the barest elements of the art; together with technical training in preparing and uttering tissues of emotive commonplaces on both sides of this or that debatable topic.[61]

Indeed, when it comes to factual knowledge, one of the very greatest professors apparently prides himself upon his lack of qualifications.[62] To speak persuasively and convince a political assembly—or, for the matter of that, a group of jurors in a court of law—to vote in accordance with reason and justice: you do not need (it seems) to know very much about the facts of the case, or even about reason and justice (beyond the barest essentials). If you are a Protagoras, you let fly with a salvo of words. You stir up all sorts of pleasant and patriotic imagery; and you leave your audience confused and flattered into voting as 'great men'. They do not quite know how the trick has been worked—doubtless with psychological mirrors.[63] If you are a Gorgias, you make play with a tissue of brilliant antitheses. Apparently, you consider fully both sides of the question under discussion; and you leave, in the mental and moral systems of your audience, only one acceptable conclusion; together with a strong feeling that justice and reason are being observed, grasped, and followed by all.[64]

This is the art so highly in repute at Athens in Socrates's time. Socrates admits its immense practical influence in dealing with untutored crowds of his fellow-citizens. But he is amazed at the lack of knowledge on the part of its professors, whether teachers or practitioners. Apparently, a good speaker feels himself competent to speak on *any* subject of general interest; whether he knows anything definite about it, or not. Frequently, indeed, he will speak extempore —and not unimpressively, at that. A great poet like Homer seems (to many of his audience) to possess an almost universal wisdom—although the inherent absurdity of this, as soon as Socrates raises the question, is undeniable.[65] You even find a professional reciter like Ion, sincerely convinced that the inspiration of Homer's style makes him (Ion) an expert in military science: competent to command great armies on the field of battle![66]

As opposed to this, not merely all-too-empirical, but utterly superficial, conception of the art of rhetoric, Socrates outlines the minimal requirements which have been accepted as canonical in all subsequent works on oratory, down to, and including, the handbooks of our own day. First, there must be a natural gift for public speaking. For this there can be no substitute. But this involves far more than a feeling for mere words and phrases. It takes a great man, to make a great speech. And the great man must be sincere, inspired, carried along by faith in the cause for which he speaks.[67] In the second place, he must have a good deal of knowledge, both theoretical and practical. If oratory is 'the art of enchanting the soul', the orator simply *must* know something of psychology. He must know, at least, that human beings fall into various types; and that men of 'type A' can only be enchanted by word-patterns, sentiments, and gestures of 'type A'. The abstrusities of which Pericles made such brilliant use in speaking before the cultured Athenians, would surely have been wasted upon an audience of pure-blood Spartans. Much as the ancient equivalent of 'basic English' would have been wasted upon a group of ultra-sophisticates.[68] That is to say, the orator must know the chief differences of human types, both in theory and in practice; and he must know how to adapt his message to whatever type he sees before him.

It is also necessary for him (as we say nowadays of barristers) to have read his brief through before coming into court, and to have acquainted himself with factual knowledge on the subject with which his speech is to deal. Generalities, however brilliant, will not be enough. In a word, his attention will alternate, from the effect he is trying to produce, to the audience, with whose co-operation he is trying to produce this effect. He brings the two into ever closer interpenetration. Thus, in the Dialogues, we see Socrates always carefully considering the interests, the capacities, and the knowledge of his interlocutors; with whose co-operation he is endeavouring to bring out the meaning and value of this or that theory.[69]

Finally, the speaker requires (it is true) to possess something of the technique of words, of definition and classification, and doubtless of the elementary distinctions found in the professors' handbooks. But technique is the least important of the necessary requirements.[70]

All these requirements, upon which Socrates insists, are, however, merely 'second-best'. The most important of all is, philosophic insight, the 'wisdom' of which the philosopher is perpetually in quest, but which he never quite reaches. The best a mere mortal puppet can do, is to mingle all the gifts that he and others have, so that they work together to bring closer to realization in the biosocial environment of man, the model city, of which Plato indicates for us the outlines.

All other human arts, the art of the painter, of the poet, of the musician, and of the embroiderer, weaver, potter, and carpenter, are similarly to be improved. That is to say, it is as brought into vital relation to the kind of knowledge available in the model city (the knowledge residing in committees of artists of specific type operating under the chairmanship of one of the philosophy-trained executives), that these arts reach their highest (though still 'second-best') development. They become functional in the life of the model city; and the institutions depicted by Plato are plainly intended to enable the artists employed in the service of the model city, to become permeated with the spirit of its life. Its 'idea' penetrates into the subject-matter upon which they operate; into the techniques with whose aid they give it form; and especially and at all times into the spirit with which they work. That is why only veterans compose the official encomia of military prowess. That is why the experts appointed to teaching positions, must first show that they have imbibed and have thoroughly understood the principles of the model city.[71]

One thing further remains to be understood. Readers of the *Dialogues* frequently feel that Plato's ideals are too utterly transcendental, altogether out of this world. In fact, with the *Phaedo* as well as the *Republic* in mind, they feel that this transcendentalism is what is especially characteristic of Plato's way of thinking.[72] While a glance at the evidence upon which they insist shows how easy it is, to come to this conclusion: I do not believe that this 'otherworldliness' is deliberately intended by Plato himself.

Thus, while it is definitely stated that the ideal republic 'exists in idea only', and its pattern is 'laid up in heaven', and 'there is nothing like it on earth', and so forth; it is also stated (in the selfsame context) that men of goodwill can, while living here below, 'live after the manner of that city'. That is to say, they can order the details of their concrete living in accordance with the indications of the ideal pattern. This they could hardly do, if the pattern were too remote from the interests and capacities inherent in humanity. Plato is quite well aware that it will not do, to set the ideal too high.[74]

His 'second-best' pattern accordingly calls for a way of living which is human, and well balanced on all sides. It provides for each side of human nature (from the primitive, none too enlightened side concerned with eating, drinking, and sexual experience,[75] to the side concerned with comradeship, self-mastery, and good citizenship,[76] to the side concerned with art, religion, and natural science,[77] and finally to the side concerned with the yet higher intellectual life possible for the wholehearted seeker after wisdom), its due share of self-realization.[78]

This does not mean (as egalitarians suppose) that each side of our nature has an inherent right, as compared with the other sides, to *equality* of self-realization. It does not mean that a man of goodwill (e.g. a member of the silver class) lives a life alternating between hedonism and asceticism, between idleness and overwork, between high art and buffoonery; that he is so many-sided as to have lost his unity and become (as it were) chaotic. On the contrary, he lives a life organized on principles, not egalitarian, but hierarchical. His natural appetites, his economic interests, his pursuit of health, of friendship, beauty, power, and knowledge, are integrated, regulated harmoniously under the supreme direction of wisdom. His life is the outcome of (as it were) a sound political constitution, guided by rational statesmanship.[79]

Even so (it may be said) all this is very general. But Plato goes a good deal further into the realm of the specific. The life depicted in his Dialogues is not intended (e.g.) for savages or for barbarians. It is designed for inhabitants of a small city-state, Hellenic style. It is intended, primarily, for a fourth-century (B.C.) group of self-governing Greek freemen; with tendencies toward Spartan discipline, on the one hand, and Athenian culture, on the other.[80] In the background, strongly influencing the foreground, are the poets, prose-writers, orators, teachers, generals, and other leading figures of Hellenic history; and behind all that Plato says, we have to remember what is ever present to his mind: the non-logical hopes, fears, and superstitions which (in the long period from pre-Homeric and perhaps pre-Egyptian times to the time of Plato himself) have gradually brought into existence and operation the folk-attitudes and folk-beliefs, the folk-languages, folk-arts, and folk-institutions, upon which he counts, and upon which his philosophizing deliberately builds.[81]

In a word, the life of the model city is not intended to be 'universal', although modern authorities sometimes say so. It is a kind of locus or curve, based upon points taken here and there in the traditional past of Hellas, and projecting indefinitely toward the future; a future envisaged by Plato as growing organically out of all that is most civilizing and most rational in the way of life actually achieved by his people, the Hellenes.[82] But Plato does not attempt to sum up to infinity the progression indicated by his curve. On the contrary, he arranges, so far as he can, for the leadership, at all times, of a philosopher of insight, who shall be competent to guide aright the life which will have to meet new and changing conditions which lie beyond his own purview. He leaves to others yet unborn, the execution of measures calculated to solve, for the best, the as yet unenvisaged problems which are sure to arise.[83]

In that life, the activities of individuals are definitely specific. Each member of the model community practises one art, and one art only. Philosophical insight does not somehow wash out the differences between one art or occupation, and another. On the contrary, it helps each to become more definitely, more specifically, itself; and to make to the life of the whole, the characteristic contribution which this artist, and this artist alone, can best make. Community fellowship, and an enlightened faith in co-operation, do not lead to confusion, or to interchangeability of the various artists. On the contrary, they provide a background against which each musician, each painter, each poet, each carpenter, weaver, and potter, can do his best work; devoting himself wholeheartedly to the realization of his own 'idea'.[84]

It is in this way that knowledge assists the artist to be a better artist in his own specific field. The co-operative direction of appropriate committees (each highly specific) assists the individual artist to 'know himself'. It releases his specific powers for concentration upon their specific technical operations. As his mallet and chisel release the beauty slumbering in stone, or his plectrum sets free the great hymn of peace quivering in the strings of his lyre, he rejoices to be playing a part, along with his fellow-artists, in a great drama in which he (like the rest) can be, ever more fully, his own self. It is still, no doubt, a world which is 'second-best'. For human beings are not yet as gods; and the best they can do, still leaves something to be desired.[85] But the knowledge placed at his disposition in the model city, enables him to feel, with every fibre of his being, that things are moving in the right direction; and that, in that onward movement his own artistic activity is significant and helpful.[86]

NOTES

1. Thus: in the ethics, there is a great difference between the ethics of (1) the golden class (who guide their own lives, as well as the lives of all other members of the community, by reference to the idea of good (*Rep.* 504d f., 540a f.)) and (2) the silver class. The ordinary citizens of the silver class live a life directed, not so much by insight into principle, as by artistic conditioning. They do not reach the philosophical level of excellence, but merely exhibit the 'civic virtues'. They live at the level of 'habit' (*Rep.* 518e, 619d).

The same sort of distinction, between the ethics of the philosophy-trained magistrates, on the one hand, and the ordinary citizens, with their 'civic virtues', on the other, is found in the *Laws* (965 f., 968a).

As to politics, we have the major distinction between (1) the ideal republic, whose idea is in heaven, and (2) the model city, a second-best community, capable (Plato thinks) of existing on earth (*Rep.* 592, *Laws* 739).

As to physics, we have (1) the ideal pattern conceived by the demiurge (*Tim.* 27e f.) and (2) its 'copy', the world of 'becoming', i.e. the actual cosmos constructed by the demiurge out of imperfect material, always slightly tending toward chaos (*Tim.* 30a, 41d ff., 48 ff., 69b f.).

As to aesthetics, we have the distinction between (1) the ideal art of the creative demiurge (*Tim.* 28a 8, 29a 3, 6, cf. *Soph.* 266a f.), with which we might compare the art of the philosopher-artist, who constructs the institutions of the ideal republic, and is an 'artificer of freedom' (*Rep.* 395bc, 500e ff., cf. *Symp.* 211e f.)—and (2) the second-best art of the artists and artisans in the model city, who are well-trained and docile, as well as naturally gifted, but receive their insight at second-hand, *via* the supervision of appropriate committees of experts, each committee being under the chairmanship of a philosophy-trained executive (cf. *Laws* 656d f., 659d f., 660a, 746c f., 772a f., 799a, 801c f., 802a f., 811b f., 812c f., 816b f., 817d, 829c f.).

2. Cf. U. v. Wilamowitz-Moellendorff, *Platon*, 2nd edit., Vol. I, pp. 107–109.

3. E.g., *Lysis* 222d f., *Charm.* 162b f., *Prtg.* 311b f., *Euthyd.* 278e f., 291 f., *Rep.* 232 ff., *Theaet.* 146 ff.

4. *Gorg.* 495 ff., *Meno* 80a f.

5. *Prtg.* 333a f., 360d f., *Gorg.* 460e f., *Rep.* 350c f.

6. *Apol.* 21b f., (cf. *Alc. I.* 118 ff.), *Gorg.* 515 f., 521d f.

7. *Apol.* 22a f., *Gorg.* 501b ff., *Rep.* 602a f.

8. *Symp.* 206a, *Rep.* 422c, 467a, 505e f., *Laws* 889c, 957b 2, 968b 8 (*re* outline sketch, see *Laws* 934c 1). Cf. also John Wild, *Plato's Theory of Man* (Cambridge, Mass., 1946), pp. 52–53 (n. 31), and 58.

9. *Rep.* 601a f., *Pol.* 277bc, *Soph.* 235e f., *Laws* 769ab.

10. *Rep.* 598c, 601a f., *Phaedr.* 275d f., *Critias* 107.

11. *Crat.* 391d f., 396d ff., *Critias* 107a f.

12. *Ion* 537 f., *Rep.* 404c, 405e f., 596c f., 600 f. Homer's account of the art of ship-building (in reference to Odysseus) is taken very seriously in *Ency. Brit.*, article Boat, Vol. 3, p. 761, second column.

13. *Rep.* 529 ff., cf. *Gorg.* 448c, 463, 501a f.

14. *Prtg.* 356c f., *Rep.* 602d f., *Pol.* 283d ff., *Phil.* 17d f., 55d ff.

15. *Gorg.* 464b f., 501d ff., *Menex.* 235, *Rep.* 492 f., 533b f., *Soph.* 222e.

16. *Rep.* 506b f., cf. *Gorg.* 509ab, 521d.

17. *Rep.* 505e ff.

18. *Rep.* 472b f., 506d f., 508e f., 517bc, 533a, 540ab, *Parm.* 133b f., *Soph.* 265 ff.

19. *Rep.* 508e f., 517c f., 532e f., 534e, *Tim.* 29c f., 48b f., 51e, 53cd. Cf. A. Lafontaine, *Le plaisir d'après Platon* (Paris, 1902), pp. 159–160. Cf. also Erich Frank, *Plato u.d.s–g. Pythagoreer*, pp. 108–109, 117 n., 272, 295 n.

20. *Phdo.* 78a, 97b, 99c f., *Rep.* 506e f., 509a f., 533a f., *Phaedr.* 276b f., *Laws* 968d f., *Epist.*341b f. Cf. P. Friedländer, *Plato I*, pp. 68–97, and R. C. Lodge, *The Great Thinkers* (London, 1949), pp. 25–29.

21. *Phdo.* 77e f., 101d, *Rep.* 497c f., 533c f., *Tim.* 37e f., *Phil.* 57e–58d, *Laws* 769e f., 811d f., 817a f., 858a f., 957d.

22. *Prtg.* 328bc, *Crat.* 391c, *Rep.* 493a f., *Theaet.* 161d, *Laws* 747c f., 858b f.

23. *Symp.* 186 ff., *Rep.* 408d f., 533b, *Phil.* 55e f., *Laws* 720d f., 743d, 889a f., 949e.

24. *Rep.* 527d, *Tim.* 47a f.

25. *Phdo.* 96 ff., *Rep.* 533c f., *Tim.* 81b ff., cf. 59cd.

26. *Crat.* 424b f., *Rep.* 531bc, 534a, *Tim.* 53c ff., *Soph.* 253a, *Phil.* 17 f.

27. *Tim.* 27bc, 59cd, *Rep.* 528cd.

28. *Tim.* 40c f.

29. *Tim.* 58a–60a.

30. *Tim.* 81 ff. The doctrine of the 'four temperaments', the fiery (choleric), the earthy (phlegmatic), the airy (sanguine), and the watery (melancholic), has persisted almost down to our own time. The use of mustard (or a hot bath) to cure a patient suffering from a chill (by warming him), and to regard health as the adjustment of a balance of opposites (the hot vs. the cold, the moist vs. the dry)— such things have not yet entirely vanished from among us.

31. *Rep.* 531b f., *Phil.* 16b–17e. Cf. Aristot. *Met.* 985b 22–986a 12.

32. *Rep.* 531e–534e (cf. 335b f., 340c ff., 535 ff., 507b ff.), *Phaedr,* 265d f., 270d f., 277bc, *Parm.* 135c ff., *Soph.* 218b f., 251 ff., *Pol.* 262c f., 285a f., 287bc.

For reasoning from analogy (whose use is widespread in the Dialogues), cf. e.g. *Charm* 165c ff., *Hipp. Min.* 373b f., *Gorg.* 465b f., *Phdo.* 70d ff., *Rep.* 341 f., 375 f., 459, etc.

33. *Phdo.* 101d, *Rep.* 511bc, 531d ff., 540a, *Theaet.* 185c f., *Parm.* 136 ff., *Soph.* 243d ff., cf. John Wild, *op. cit.*, p. 72.

34. *Gorg.* 482c ff., *Rep.* 350cd, 358b, *Parm.* 128e ff., *Theaet.* 151bc. etc.

35. *Parm.* 128c f., cf. 135cd. The confusion shown by Protagoras has been attributed (e.g. by Bonitz, *Platonische Studien*, esp. the studies of *Protagoras* and the *Theaetetus*) to the dialectical superiority of Socrates (*Prtg.* 336b f., *Theaet.* 166 ff., cf. *Phil.* 16b f.). Many interpreters have felt much the same about the confusion of Thrasymachus in *Rep. I* (cf. *Rep.* 350cd, 357a, 358b, 367c).

36. *Parm.* 130b ff.

37. *Phdo.* 90b f., *Rep.* 537d ff.

38. *Parm.* 135d f.

39. *Lach.* 187e f., *Prtg.* 336c, 361d, *Gorg.* 472 f., 509a f., *Phdo.* 77e f., 88d ff., *Rep.* 364b f., 367b, d, 474ab, 487b f., 497d f., 504b f., 506b f., 531d ff., 595 ff., 608b f., etc., *Theaet.* 169a–c, *Phil.* 16 ff.

40. *Lach.* 200e f., *Charm.* 169 ff., *Euthyd.* 291a f., *Meno.* 71a f., *Phdo.* 99c f., *Rep.* 506b ff., 533a, *Theaet.* 150c, 161a f.

41. *Phdo.* 77d ff., 101d f., *Rep.* 503e f., 511, 525b f., 526d f., 531c ff., 539c f., *Theaet.* 185 f., *Phil.* 55d ff., 61de.

42. *Phdo.* 101d, *Rep.* 510b–511c, 531d, 532cd, 533b f., 540a.

43. *Phdo.* 74b ff., *Theaet.* 185c f.

44. Many authorities (like Erich Frank) think this is Speusippus. For the technique, see Aristot. *Met.* 986a 22 ff.

45. *Tim.* 36c ff., *Theaet.* 158e, 186a, *Parm.* 139 f., *Soph.* 254e f.

46. See *Monadologie*, sect. 58.

47. Any student who has taken a course in 'History of Philosophy' is able to identify the names of well-known thinkers to whom it is usual to attach these labels ('the good', 'substance', and 'God'). But a student who has penetrated further into the thought of metaphysicians who still regard themselves as at the 'second-best' level of knowledge, is aware that Hellenic thinking is far more fluid than the sharp academic distinctions of these labels suppose.

There is no difficulty (for instance) in finding in Plato's Dialogues, passages which seem to imply that Plato could well have accepted, as a reasonable formula for the 'unhypothetical first principle', such a term as *Being* or *Substance* ('what *is*'). Cf. e.g. *Tim.* 51e f., *Phaedr.* 247c f., *Phdo.* 78d, *Rep.* 585c f., *Soph.* 247d ff. We might compare also, *Rep.* 485b, 486c, 490b, 500c, 501d, 521cd, 537d. For a modern interpretation, see John Wild's 'realistic' interpretation of Plato's thought.

There are other passages which indicate that the concept of *Mind* would have seemed to Plato a reasonably acceptable term, e.g. *Phdo.* 97c f., *Soph.* 249a, *Phil.* 28c, 30c f., cf. 22d, *Laws* 895c f., 897d f., 961c. It could also be maintained, quite plausibly, that the term *God* would not have aroused in Plato any fundamental objections; on the basis of such passages as *Rep.* 597b f., *Soph.* 265b f., *Laws* 903b ff. For modern interpretations, see Wilamowitz, *op. cit.*, pp. 421 ff., and R. C. Lodge, *Plato's Theory of Ethics*, Ch. XI and pp. 465–466.

As further evidence of this fluidity, I would draw attention to the very large number of different-appearing candidates for the position of 'Highest Human Good'—i.e., highest from a 'second-best' standpoint—discussed in the Dialogues. According to the depth of insight by which these terms are interpreted, any one of them can be taken as a reasonable 'second-best' formulation of the highest good. That is to say, for the philosopher, all such terms (understood by non-philosophers with varying degrees of insight which tend to leave non-philosophers 'fighting over shadows') ultimately tend to converge and coincide. Cf. R.C.L., *op. cit.*, esp. Part III, where this is shown in some detail.

At present, I would like to add to the list, that the 'second-best' highest good (for man) might well be formulated, in accordance with *Laws* 739b f., 807b f., 817b f., as 'The life of the model city.'

48. *Rep.* 521d–534e, cf. 473a, 508d f., 517bc. Cf. Wild, *op. cit.*, pp. 72–73.

49. *Rep.* 511a f., *Theaet.* 185c f., *Soph.* 247d ff., etc.

50. *Rep.* 511b, *Phil.* 16c ff.

51. Cf. *Rep.* 529 ff.

52. *Rep.* 501a, 540e f., cf. *Laws* 702bc, 708a f., 736–737b.

53. *Rep.* 501b f., 540a f.

54. *Pol.* 305d ff. In the *Politicus* and *Laws*, Plato's factual knowledge seems to have improved from what we find in the *Republic*. In the *Republic*, the courageous mate with the courageous only, with the idea of improving the breed (*Rep.* 459 f., 48c f.). In the later Dialogues, the courageous are encouraged to mate with the more timid, with the idea of ensuring the unity of the group, by bringing about an approximation to the general average (*Pol.* 310 f., *Laws* 773, cf. 929e f.).

55. *Laws* 737b ff., 751 ff., 759 ff., 764ff., 778a, 803a f., 813a f., etc. Cf. R. C. Lodge, *Plato's Theory of Education*, Appendix I ('Numbers in the Model City.'), pp. 284–286.

56. *Laws* 645d, 770a f., 772a f., 773b f., 835d ff., etc.

57. *Laws* 644d f., 803b. Cf. Leibniz's thought of himself as 'the great reconciler', competent to adjust inferior monads to one another indefinitely. His conception of God is almost as of a puppet-master.

58. *Rep.* 472b f., 508e f., 517bc, 592ab, *Parm.* 133b f., *Pol.* 294a f., *Laws* 969b.

59. *Rep.* 412ab, 473a, 497b f., 500d, *Theaet.* 176a, *Pol.* 299e ff., *Laws* 769b f., 969a f.

60. *Gorg.* 455d f., 515 f., *Phaedr.* 269e f.

61. *Phaedr.* 266d ff.

62. *Prtg.* 318d f., *Gorg.* 456a f., 459 f., *Phaedr.* 272d f.

63. *Prtg.* 320c–329a, 334 ff., *Menex*, 234c f., *Rep.* 344d, 493a f. By 'psychological mirrors' I mean the trick of praising the Athenians to their faces (*Menex.* 235d, cf. *Gorg.* 463 ff. It comes out (322d, 324c) in the 'Apologue' of Protagoras).

64. *Gorg.* 452c ff.

65. *Gorg.* 459, *Rep.* 596c f., 598de, *Phaedr.* 237c, *Phil.* 48e f., *Laws* 701a, 727a 7–8, 732a, 863c 5–6. For *ex tempore* speaking, cf. Demosth. *Olynthiac I* (Reiske, *Orat. Attici*, 9.7).

66. *Ion* 540c f.

67. *Gorg.* 495a, 500c, 517ab, *Rep.* 349a, 536b, *Phaedr.* 242e f., 245a, 246de, 247c f., 269d f. (I have in mind also the phrase from Longinus (?) *De Sublimitate*, *Hypsos megalophrosunes apechema*, 'Elevation is the echo of a great soul'.)

68. *Prtg.* 342b f., *Phaedr.* 260e, 269e ff, 273c f., 277 f.

69. *Prtg.* 340 f., 352 f., *Euthyd.* 275a f., 277d–282e, 288b f., 291d f., *Meno.* 75d f., 84a f., *Rep.* 336d ff., 368 f., 474ab, 506b ff., 533a, etc., *Theaet.* 144e ff., 150c f., 151d f., 154c ff., 162d f., 185c f., etc. This method is used also in the 'dialectical' Dialogues: in which the visiting professor from Elea selects, e.g. Theaetetus, to act as his respondent (*Soph.* 217c f., *Pol.* 257c f., 258cd. etc.).

70. *Phaedr.* 260de, 265d–272c, 277 e.f.

71. *Laws* 811c f., 817a f., 829c f.

72. Cf. Adam, edition of Plato's *Republic*, Vol. II, pp. 169–170.

73. *Rep.* 590–592b, cf. 540a f.

74. *Parm.* 134, *Laws* 739.

75. *Phaedr.* 251e–256d, *Rep.* 461bc, 559, 571b–572b, *Laws* 667b, 671–674, 780–785, 835 ff.

76. *Rep.* 403bc, 430d ff., *Phaedr.* 265ab, *Laws* 837b f. Cf. R. C. Lodge, *Plato's Theory of Education*, pp. 126–128, where further evidence is interpreted.

77. *Rep.* 427bc, *Laws* 774de, 828ab, 865d, 871c f., 873d, 958d f., etc. Cf. R.C.L.,

op. cit., pp. 134–136, 150–181. In general, *every* institution in the model city is conceived to be under the guidance and protection of some god.

78. *Laws* 951e f., 961a f., 964 ff. In general, the higher magistrates (those eligible to the Nocturnal Council) have received much the same education as the higher guardians of the *Republic*.

79. *Rep.* 561, 586 ff., 589d f., *Laws* 964 ff. Cf. Wild, *op. cit.*, p. 78.

80. *Rep.* 422d f., 470e, *Laws* 737b f., 740b f., 771, 810e f., 817a f.

81. This is illustrated by, e.g., *Prtg.* 325 ff., 389d, *Menex.* 234b f., *Gorg.* 492e f., *Crat.* 391d ff., 425 f., 432e ff., *Rep.* 376d f., 382d, 386 ff., 395b f., 405d ff., 424e f., 427bc, 458d f., 492, 522a f., 603c f., *Theaet.* 176, *Pol.* 271 ff., *Laws* 643a f., 653c f., 656c ff., 663d ff., 678 ff., 738b f., 781e f., 793a f., 796b f., 800a f., 802d f.

Cf. also J. Adam, notes to *Rep.* 382d, 414b, and J. A. Stewart, *The Myths of Plato*, pp. 20–51, cf. pp. 451–456, and R.C.L., *op. cit.*, Ch. VIII, esp. pp. 150–178.

82. The 'modern authority' whom I have particularly in mind is A. E. Taylor. See esp. *Ency. Brit.* (19th. edit.) Articles, PLATO and SOCRATES (Vol. 18, pp. 53–54. and Vol. 20, pp. 919–920).

83. *Phdo.* 77e f., *Rep.* 412ab, 497c, *Laws* 769b ff., 969a f.

84. *Rep.* 370a f., 374a f., 394e f., 397e, *Laws* 846d f. (It might be felt that the union of executive and contemplative functions in one and the same person, involves a certain degree of duality; whether we are thinking of the 'philosopher-kings' of the *Republic*, or of the dialectically trained magistrates of the *Laws*. The philosopher-artist, the philosopher-physician, and the philosopher-lawyer also seem somewhat dualistic. But for Plato, philosophical insight seems to *unify* (e.g. the virtues), rather than to introduce or confirm analytic divergences. It does not (with Plato) multiply *entia praeter necessitatem*.)

85. *Tim.* 41d f., *Soph.* 265 f., *Laws* 803e f.

86. *Laws* 817a f. Cf. Wild, *op. cit.*, p. 76, esp. 'The *primary* task of virtue is to achieve actual insight (*sophia*) so far as possible. On this all other virtue depends. . . . (The work (*ergon*) of virtue is "life itself" (*Rep.* 353d) "according to its real nature" (*Rep.* 443c), whereas art is "rational action flowing out into the external world" (*ibid.*).' (I ask one question: Does not life itself 'flow out into the external world'?)

Bibliography

ADAM (JAMES).—*The Republic of Plato*, edited with critical notes . . . Cambridge University Press, 1905.

ALEXANDER (SAMUEL).—*Beauty and the other Forms of Value*. London, Macmillan, 1933.

ARISTOTELES.—*De Caelo, Ethica Nicomacheia, Metaphysica, Parva Naturalia, Poetica, Politica, Problemata*. Berlin Edition, 1831–70.

ASHBURN (FRANK D.).—*Peabody of Groton*. New York, McCann, 1944.

BECHER (WALTER).—*Platon und Fichte: die königliche Erziehungskunst*. Jena, Fischer, 1937.

BENN (ALFRED WILLIAM).—*The Greek Philosophers*. London, 1882. 2nd. edit., New York, Dutton, 1914.

BURNET (JOHN).—*Early Greek Philosophy*, 2nd edit., London, Black, 1908.

BURNET (JOHN).—*Platonis Opera* recognovit, brevique adnotatione critica instruxit, Oxford, Clarendon Press, 1899–1912.

BUTCHER (S. H.).—*Aristotle's Theory of Poetry and Fine Art*. . . . London and New York, Macmillan, 1895.

CAMPBELL (LEWIS).—*The Sophistes and Politicus of Plato*, with . . . notes. Oxford, Clarendon Press, 1867.

CHILDS (JOHN L.).—*Education and the Philosophy of Experimentalism*. New York, Appleton-Century, 1931.

COLLINGWOOD (R. G.).—*The Principles of Art*. Oxford, Clarendon Press, 1938.

CROCE (BENEDETTO).—*Aesthetic as Science of Expression and General Linguistic*, tr. Ainslee, 2nd edit.,London, Macmillan, 1922.

CROSSMAN (RICHARD H. S.).—*Plato Today*. London, Allen and Unwin, 1937.

DEWEY (JOHN).—*A Common Faith*. London, Oxford University Press, 1934.

DEWEY (JOHN).—*Art as Experience*. New York, Minton, Balch, 1934.

DEWEY (JOHN).—*Creative Intelligence*. New York, Holt, 1917.

DEWEY (JOHN).—*Democracy and Education*. New York, Macmillan, 1916.

DEWEY (JOHN).—Philosophy, in *Whither Mankind?* (ed. Beard). New York, Longmans, 1930.

Encyclopaedia Britannica.—14th edition. London and New York, 1929.

ENGLAND (EDWIN B.).—*The Laws of Plato*. Text, . . . Notes. University of Manchester Press, 1921.

FITE (WARNER).—*The Platonic Legend*. New York, Scribner, 1934.

FOUILLÉE (ALFRED).—*La philosophie de Platon*: exposition, histoire, et critique de la théorie des idées. Paris, Alcan, 1869.

FRANK (ERICH).—*Plato und die sogenannten Pythagoreer*: ein Kapitel aus der Geschichte des griechischen Geistes. Halle, 1923.

FRANK (SOLOMON).—Education of Women According to Plato; in Lodge, *Plato's Theory of Education* (*q.v.*).

FREEMAN (KENNETH D.).—*Schools of Hellas.* London, Macmillan, 1908.

FRIEDLÄNDER (PAUL).—*Platon I.* Berlin and Leipzig, de Gruyter, 1928.

GROVE (SIR GEORGE).—*Dictionary of Music and Musicians,* 3rd. edit., (ed. Colles). New York, Macmillan, 1948.

HENRI (ROBERT).—*The Art Spirit* (Notes, compiled by Margery Ryerson). Philadelphia and London, Lippincott, 1923, 1930.

JOWETT (BENJAMIN).—*The Dialogues of Plato,* translated. . . . 3rd edit., Oxford, Clarendon Press, 1892.

KANT (IMMANUEL).—*Critik of Judgment* (tr. Bernard). London and New York, Macmillan, 1892.

KRAEMER (S.).—*Orpheus in Paris* (tr. David and Mosbacher). New York, Knopf, 1938.

LAFONTAINE (ALBERT).—*Le plaisir d'après Platon et Aristote:* étude psychologique, métaphysique, et morale. Paris, Alcan, 1902.

LAUWERYS (J. A.) and NEURATH (OTTO).—Nazi Textbooks and the Future, I and II; and Plato's 'Republic' and German Education. In *Journal of Education,* London, 1944–45.

LOCKE (JOHN).—*Some Thoughts Concerning Education,* 4th edit., London, 1699.

LODGE (RUPERT C.).—Plato and Freedom, in *Transactions of Royal Society of Canada,* Vol. XLIII, 1949.

LODGE (RUPERT C.).—Plato and Progress, in *Philosophical Review,* Vol. LV, 1946.

LODGE (RUPERT C.).—Plato's Secret, in *Dalhousie Review,* Vol. XVI, 1936.

LODGE (RUPERT C.).—*Plato's Theory of Education.* London, Kegan Paul, 1947.

LODGE (RUPERT C.).—*Plato's Theory of Ethics:* the moral criterion and the highest good. London, Kegan Paul; New York, Harcourt, Brace, 1928.

LODGE (RUPERT C.).—*The Great Thinkers.* London, Routledge and Kegan Paul, 1949; Boston, Beacon Press, 1951.

LODGE (RUPERT C.).—What Socrates Knows, in *Transactions of Royal Society of Canada,* Vol. XLV, 1951.

MEYER (HANS).—*Geschichte der alten Philosophie.* München, Kösel und Pustet, 1925.

MORE (PAUL ELMER).—*Platonism.* Princeton University Press, 1917.

NAHM (MILTON C.).—*Aesthetic Experience and its Presuppositions.* New York and London, Harper, 1946.

NATORP (PAUL).—*Platos Ideenlehre:* eine Einführung in den Idealismus. Leipzig, Dürr, 1903.

NETTLESHIP (RICHARD LEWIS).—*Lectures on Plato's 'Republic'* (ed. Benson). London and New York, Macmillan, 1901.

NEURATH (OTTO).—See LAUWERYS (J. A.).

PLATONIS.—*Opera.* See BURNET (JOHN).

RITTER AND PRELLER.—*Historia Philosophiae Graecae,* 8th edit., Gotha, Perthes, 1898.

RODIER (GEORGES).—*Aristote, Traité de l'âme:* traduit et annoté. Paris, Leroux, 1900.

SCHILLER (FERDINAND C. S.).—*Plato or Protagoras?* Oxford, Blackwell, 1908.

SCHOEN (MAX).—*The Enjoyment of the Fine Arts.* New York, Philosophical Library, 1944.

SCHUHL (PIERRE-MAXIME).—*Platon et l'art de son temps.* (Arts plastiques). Paris, Alcan, 1934.

SIEGFRIED (ANDRÉ).—*England's Crisis* (tr. Hemming). New York, Bruce, 1931.

STEWART (J. A.).—*The Myths of Plato.* London and New York, 1905.

TAYLOR (ALFRED EDWARD).—*Plato: the man and his work.* New York, Lincoln MacVeagh, 1927.

TAYLOR (ALFRED EDWARD).—*A Commentary on Plato's Timaeus.* Oxford, Clarendon Press, 1928.

TILNEY (F. C.).—*The Lure of the Fine Arts.* London, Chapman and Hall, 1931.

TOVEY (DONALD).—Beethoven, in *Ency. Brit.* (*q.v.*).

WIGGAM (A. E.).—*Exploring Your Mind with the Psychologists* (interview with Dr. Catharine Cox Miles). New York, Bobbs-Merrill, 1928.

WILAMOWITZ-MOELLENDORFF (ULRICH VON).—*Platon,* 2nd edit., Berlin, Weidmann, 1920.

WILD (JOHN).—*Plato's Theory of Man:* an introduction to the realistic philosophy of culture. Cambridge, Mann., Harvard University Press, 1946.

WOOLDRIDGE (H. E.).—*Oxford History of Music,* Vol. I. Oxford, Clarendon Press, 1901.

WUNDT (WILHELM MAX).—*Ethics,* E.t. London and New York, Macmillan, 1908.

x*

Index of Names

Index of Subjects

The
International Library

OF

PSYCHOLOGY, PHILOSOPHY
AND SCIENTIFIC METHOD

Edited by

C. K. OGDEN, M.A.
Magdalene College, Cambridge

The International Library, of which over one hundred and thirty volumes have now been published, is both in quality and quantity a unique achievement in this department of publishing. Its purpose is to give expression, in a convenient form and at a moderate price, to the remarkable developments which have recently occurred in Psychology and its allied sciences. The older philosophers were preoccupied by metaphysical interests which for the most part have ceased to attract the younger investigators, and their forbidding terminology too often acted as a deterrent for the general reader. The attempt to deal in clear language with current tendencies whether in England and America or on the Continent has met with a very encouraging reception, and not only have accepted authorities been invited to explain the newer theories, but it has been found possible to include a number of original contributions of high merit.

Published by

ROUTLEDGE & KEGAN PAUL LTD
BROADWAY HOUSE: 68-74 CARTER LANE, LONDON, E.C.4.

1953

PHILOSOPHY AND PSYCHOLOGY

INTERNATIONAL LIBRARY OF PSYCHOLOGY, PHILOSOPHY AND SCIENTIFIC METHOD

A. PSYCHOLOGY

GENERAL AND DESCRIPTIVE

The Mind and its Place in Nature. By C. D. Broad, Litt.D. £1 10s.

Thought and the Brain. By Prof. Henri Piéron. Translated by C. K. Ogden, M.A. 17s. 6d.

The Nature of Laughter. By J. C. Gregory. 15s.

The Psychology of Philosophers. By Alexander Herzberg, Ph.D. 15s.

The Mind and its Body: the Foundations of Psychology. By Charles Fox. 15s.

The Gestalt Theory and the Problem of Configuration. By Bruno Petermann. Illustrated. £1 1s.

Invention and the Unconscious. By J. M. Montmasson. Preface by Dr. H. Stafford Hatfield. £1 1s.

Neural Basis of Thought. By G. G. Campion and Sir G. Elliot Smith, F.R.S. 12s. 6d.

Principles of Gestalt Psychology. By Prof. K. Koffka. £1 17s. 6d.

EMOTION

Integrative Psychology: a Study of Unit Response. By William M. Marston, C. Daly King, and E. H. Marston. £1 8s.

Emotion and Insanity. By Dr. S. Thalbitzer. Preface by Prof. H. Höffding. 10s. 6d.

The Measurement of Emotion. By W. Whately Smith, M.A. With Introduction by William Brown, M.D., D.Sc. 12s. 6d.

The Laws of Feeling. By F. Paulhan. Translated by C. K. Ogden, M.A. 15s.

2

The Psychology of Consciousness. By C. Daly King. Introduction by Prof. W. M. Marston. 17s. 6d.

Pleasure and Instinct: a Study in the Psychology of Human Action. By A. H. B. Allen. 17s. 6d.

PERSONALITY

Personality. By R. G. Gordon, M.D., D.Sc. £1 1s.

The Neurotic Personality. By R. G. Gordon, M.D., D.Sc. 15s.

The Psychology of Character: with a Survey of Personality in General. By Dr. A. A. Roback. *Revised Edition.* £2 2s.

Problems of Personality: a Volume of Essays in honour of Morton Prince. Edited by Dr. A. A. Roback. £1 4s.

Constitution-Types in Delinquency: Practical Applications and Bio-physiological Foundations of Kretschmer's Types. By W. A. Willemse. With 32 plates and 19 diagrams. 17s. 6d.

Conscious Orientation. Studies of Personality Types in Relation to Neurosis and Psychosis by Dr. J. H. Van der Hoop. £1 1s.

ANALYSIS

The Practice and Theory of Individual Psychology. By Dr. Alfred Adler £1 1s.

Psychological Types. By C. G. Jung, M.D., LL.D. Translated with a Foreword by H. Godwin Baynes, M.B. £1 10s.

Contributions to Analytical Psychology. By C. G. Jung, M.D., LL.D. Translated by H. Godwin Baynes, M.B. £1 5s.

Character and the Unconscious: a Critical Exposition of the Psychology of Freud and Jung. By J. H. van der Hoop. 17s. 6d.

Problems in Psychopathology. By T. W. Mitchell, M.D. 12s. 6d.

The Development of the Sexual Impulses. By R. E. Money-Kyrle. 17s. 6d.

SOUND AND COLOUR

The Psychology of a Musical Prodigy. By Prof. G. Revesz (Amsterdam). With a portrait and many musical illustrations. 14s.

Colour-Blindness: with a Comparison of different Methods of Testing Colour-Blindness. By Mary Collins, M.A., Ph.D. Introduction by Dr. James Drever. 16s.

3

Colour and Colour Theories. By Christine Ladd-Franklin. With nine coloured plates. 17s. 6d.

LANGUAGE AND SYMBOLISM

The Symbolic Process, and Its Integration in Children. By J. F. Markey, Ph.D. 14s.

The Meaning of Meaning: a Study of the Influence of Language upon Thought and of the Science of Symbolism. By C. K. Ogden, M.A. and I. A. Richards, M.A. Supplementary Essays by B. Malinowski, Ph.D., D.Sc., and F. G. Crookshank, M.D. £1 5s.

Principles of Literary Criticism. By I. A. Richards, Lecturer at Magdalene College, Cambridge. £1 1s.

Speech Disorders. By S. M. Stinchfield. With eight plates. £1 1s.

The Spirit of Language in Civilization. By K. Vossler. 17s. 6d.

CHILD PSYCHOLOGY, EDUCATION, ETC.

The Growth of the Mind: an Introduction to Child Psychology. By Prof. K. Koffka. Translated by Prof. R. M. Ogden. £1 10s.

The Language and Thought of the Child. By Prof. Jean Piaget. Preface by Prof. E. Claparéde. £1 1s.

The Child's Conception of Physical Causality. By Prof. Jean Piaget. £1 1s.

The Child's Conception of the World. By Prof. Jean Piaget. £1 3s.

The Child's Conception of Number. By Prof. Jean Piaget. £1 5s.

Judgment and Reasoning in the Child. By Prof. Jean Piaget. 18s.

The Moral Judgment of the Child. By Prof. Jean Piaget. £1 1s.

Educational Psychology: its Problems and Methods. By Charles Fox, M.A. *Revised Edition* £1 3s.

The Mental Development of the Child. By Karl Bühler. 12s. 6d.

The Psychology of Intelligence and Will. By H. G. Wyatt. 17s. 6d.

Infant Speech: A Study of the Beginnings of Language. By M. M. Lewis. *New Edition.* £1 8s.

The Psychology of Intelligence. By Prof. Jean Piaget. 16s.

The Origin of Intelligence in the Child. By Prof. Jean Piaget. *In preparation.*

The Nature of Learning, in its Relation to the Living System. By G. Humphrey, M.A., Ph.D. 17s. 6d.

The Mentality of Apes, with an Appendix on the Psychology of Chimpanzees. By Prof. W. Koehler. With nine plates and nineteen figures. £1 1s.

The Social Life of Monkeys and Apes. By S. Zuckerman. With 24 plates. £1 1s.

The Psychology of Animals, in Relation to Human Psychology. By Prof. F. Alverdes. 14s.

The Social Insects: Their Origin and Evolution. By Professor William Morton Wheeler. With 48 plates. £1 4s.

Theoretical Biology. By J. von Uexküll. £1 4s.

Biological Principles. By J. H. Woodger, B.Sc. £1 10s.

Biological Memory. By Prof. Eugenio Rignano. Translated, with an Introduction, by Prof. E. W. MacBride, F.R.S. 16s.

ANTHROPOLOGY, SOCIOLOGY, RELIGION, ETC.

Psychology and Ethnology. By W. H. R. Rivers, M.D., F.R.S. Preface by Sir G. Elliot Smith, F.R.S. £1 1s.

Political Pluralism: A Study in Modern Political Theory. By Kung Chuan Hsiao. 15s.

The Individual and the Community: a Historical Analysis of the Motivating Factors of Social Conduct. By Wen Kwei Liao, M.A., Ph.D. £1 1s.

Crime and Custom in Savage Society. By Prof. B. Malinowski. With six plates. 16s.

Sex and Repression in Savage Society. By Prof. B. Malinowski. 18s.

Religious Conversion. By Prof. Sante de Sanctis. 17s. 6d.

The Theory of Legislation. By Jeremy Bentham. Edited, with an Introduction and Notes, by C. K. Ogden, M.A. £1 8s.

B. PHILOSOPHY

Philosophical Studies. By Prof. G. E. Moore, Litt.D., Editor of *Mind.* £1 5s.

The Philosophy of " As If ": a System of the Theoretical, Practical, and Religious Fictions of Mankind. By H. Vaihinger. Translated by C. K. Ogden. £1 8s.

Five Types of Ethical Theory. By C. D. Broad, Litt.D. £1 5s.

Speculations: Essays on Humanism and the Philosophy of Art. By T. E. Hulme. Edited by Herbert Read. With a frontispiece and Foreword by Jacob Epstein. 15s.

The Metaphysical Foundations of Modern Physical Science, with special reference to Man's Relation to Nature. By Edwin A. Burtt, Ph.D. £1 5s.

Possibility. By Scott Buchanan. 12s. 6d.

The Nature of Life. By Prof. E. Rignano. 12s. 6d.

Bentham's Theory of Fictions. Edited with an Introduction and Notes by C. K. Ogden. With three plates. £1 1s.

Ideology and Utopia: an Introduction to the Sociology of Knowledge. By Karl Mannheim. £1 8s.

Charles Peirce's Empiricism. By Justus Büchler, Ph.D. 17s. 6d.

The Philosophy of Peirce. Selected Writings. Edited by Justus Büchler, Ph.D. £1 8s.

Ethics and the History of Philosophy: Selected Essays. By C. D. Broad, Litt.D., Professor of Moral Philosophy, Cambridge University. £1 1s.

Sense-Perception and Matter : A Critical Analysis of C. D. Broad's Theory of Perception. By Martin E. Lean. £1 1s.

What is Value? An Essay in Philosophical Analysis. By Everett W. Hall, Professor of Philosophy in the State University of Iowa. £1 5s.

Religion, Philosophy and Psychical Research: Selected Essays. By C. D. Broad, Litt.D. £1 5s.

LOGIC

Tractatus Logico-Philosophicus. By L. Wittgenstein. German text, with an English Translation en regard, and an Introduction by Bertrand Russell, F.R.S. 17s. 6d.

Foundations of Geometry and Induction. By Jean Nicod. With an Introduction by Bertrand Russell, F.R.S. £1.

The Foundations of Mathematics, and other Logical Essays. By F. P. Ramsey, M.A. Edited by R. B. Braithwaite. Preface by G. E. Moore. £1 1s.

The Nature of Mathematics: a Critical Survey. By Max Black. 17s. 6d.

Logical Syntax of Language. By Prof. Rudolf Carnap. £1 10s.

An Examination of Logical Positivism. By Dr. Julius Weinberg. £1 5s.

The Conditions of Knowing: An Essay Towards a Theory of Knowledge. By Angus Sinclair, O.B.E., M.A., F.R.S.E., Lecturer in Philosophy, Edinburgh University. £1 1s.

A Treatise on Induction and Probability. By G. H. von Wright, Professor of Philosophy, Cambridge University. £1 10s.

Bertrand Russell's Construction of the External World. By Charles A. Fritz, Junr. £1 3s.

C. SCIENTIFIC METHOD

METHODOLOGY

Scientific Thought: a Philosophical Analysis of some of its Fundamental Concepts in the light of Recent Physical Developments. By C. D. Broad, Litt.D. £1 10s.

Dynamic Social Research. By John T. Hader and Eduard C. Lindeman. 15s.

The Sciences of Man in the Making: an Orientation Book. By E. A. Kirkpatrick. £1 1s.

The Doctrine of Signatures. A Defence of Theory in Medicine. By Scott Buchanan. 12s. 6d.

The Limits of Science: Outline of Logic and of the Methodology of the Exact Sciences. By Prof. Leon Chwistek. Introduction and Appendix by H. C. Brodie. £1 10s.

HISTORY, ETC.

An Historical Introduction to Modern Psychology. By Gardner Murphy, Ph.D. With a Supplement by H. Kluver, Ph.D. £1 10s.

The History of Materialism and Criticism of its Present Importance. By F. A. Lange. With an Introduction by Bertrand Russell. £1 10s.

Philosophy of the Unconscious. By E. von Hartmann. £1 8s.

Outlines of the History of Greek Philosophy. By E. Zeller. New edition, re-written by Dr. Wilhelm Nestle and translated by L. R. Palmer. £1 1s.

Psyche: the Cult of Souls and the Belief in Immortality among the Greeks. By Erwin Rohde. £1 12s.

Plato's Theory of Ethics: The Moral Criterion and the Highest Good. By R. C. Lodge. £1 10s.

Plato's Theory of Education. By R. C. Lodge, Professor of Logic and the History of Philosophy in the University of Manitoba. £1 1s.

Plato's Theory of Art. By R. C. Lodge, M.A.(Oxon), F.R.S.(Canada). £1 5s.

Plato's Theory of Knowledge. The Theaetetus and the Sophist of Plato. Translated, with a Running Commentary, by Prof. F. M. Cornford. £1 5s.

Plato's Cosmology: The Timaeus of Plato. Translated, with a Running Commentary, by Prof. F. M. Cornford. £1 8s.

Plato and Parmenides. Parmenides' " Way of Truth " and Plato's " Parmenides ". Translated with an Introduction and Running Commentary, by Prof. F. M. Cornford. £1 1s.

All prices are net.

HEADLEY BROTHERS LTD
109 Kingsway London WC2
and Ashford Kent